THERE ARE NO ACCIDENTS

The Deadly Rise of Injury and Disaster—Who Profits and Who Pays the Price

JESSIE SINGER

SIMON & SCHUSTER

New York London Toronto Sydney New Delhi

Simon & Schuster
1230 Avenue of the Americas
New York, NY 10020

First Simon & Schuster hardcover edition February 2022

SIMON & SCHUSTER and colophon are
registered trademarks of Simon & Schuster, Inc.

For information about special discounts for bulk purchases,
please contact Simon & Schuster Special Sales at 1-866-506-1949
or business@simonandschuster.com.

The Simon & Schuster Speakers Bureau can bring authors to
your live event. For more information or to book an event,
contact the Simon & Schuster Speakers Bureau at 1-866-248-3049
or visit our website at www.simonspeakers.com.

Interior design by Kyle Kabel

Manufactured in the United States of America

1   3   5   7   9   10   8   6   4   2

Library of Congress Cataloging-in-Publication Data has been applied for.

ISBN 978-1-9821-2966-8
ISBN 978-1-9821-2969-9 (ebook)

With *love and rage*
in memory of
ERIC JAMES NG
(1984–2006)

Tell yourself it was an accident
Isolated incident, part of the job
Yeah, well, tell that to the families
Kids without daddies
Tell it to God

—Steve Earle
Coal Country

Contents

THERE ARE
NO
ACCIDENTS

Introduction

Not an Accident

This is a book about how we die in the United States. In particular, it is about the significant subset of those deaths we ignore—the *accidents*. More people die by accident today than at any time in American history. The accidental death toll in the United States is now over 173,000 people a year, or the equivalent of more than one fully loaded Boeing 747-400 falling out of the sky, killing everyone onboard, every day. Americans die by accident more than by stroke, Alzheimer's disease, diabetes, pneumonia, kidney failure, suicide, septicemia, liver disease, hypertension, Parkinson's disease, or terrorism. Yet despite the death toll, there is no fun run for accidental death research or public memorial for the accidental dead. What we call accidents—the traffic crashes, the house fires, the falls and drownings—rarely register as a point of public concern. Why are accidents so common? Why are accidents killing us more than ever? Why don't we talk about it? And what can we do to stem the rising tide of death and life-altering injury? This book seeks answers to those questions.

We can start with that 747. One of the many reasons accidents fail to register as a cost to society is that they rarely involve a fully loaded 747. Most of the time, when we die by accident, we die in ones and twos. These deaths do not make the nightly news. Rather, accidents are quick and lonely deaths, not reported beyond the police blotter, if at all. To die by accident is to fall down, or get run down, to drink the wrong thing or stand in the wrong place. More than a synonym for a traffic crash or a surprise pregnancy, "accident" is a euphemism for "nothing to see here."

One person dies by accident every three minutes or so in the United States, the deaths appearing unrelated and not particularly worthy of note. But if we take a closer look at *who* dies by accident in America, we must take note. Black people die in accidental fires at more than twice the rate of white people. Indigenous people are nearly three times as likely as white people to be accidentally killed by a driver while crossing the street. People in West Virginia die by accident at twice the rate of people over the state line in Virginia, and across the board, the states with the highest rates of accidental death are also the poorest. This book is about that, too—why some people die by accident and others do not.

Let's start with the simplest question: What is an accident? We can define it by what it's not: not a disease like cancer, not an act of God like the weather, not an act of intention like murder. But while true, this answer is too simple to encompass the complex phenomena of accidents. "Accident" can be an excuse, an explanation, a mea culpa, or a crime. An accident can generate a legal or emotional response or none at all. If you make a mistake and want forgiveness, you can say: *It was an accident*. But also, if you wish to forgive someone for a mistake they made, you can tell them: *It was an accident*. An accident could mean someone wet the bed, or cheated on their spouse, or got knocked up. It is a checkbox on a death certificate and also what happened when BP blew up a deep-water drilling platform and dumped more than 134 million gallons of crude oil into the Gulf of Mexico. The *Bulletin of the Atomic Scientists* has set their doomsday clock at 100 seconds to midnight—one reason is global warming; another is the risk of an accidental nuclear launch. And my best friend died by accident, at least according to the guy who killed him.

That is how I came to write this book.

When I was sixteen, I fell in love with a young man named Eric Ng. He was intense and kind. He was very handsome and very funny. We both had moms from Queens, a habit of sneaking out of the suburbs to go to punk shows on the weekends, and the righteous indignation of young activists. We made quick high school sweethearts and instant best friends.

In time I moved to New York City, and then he did, too. He became a math teacher and I a journalist. At twenty-three, my only life plan was that he would remain my constant.

Then, on December 1, 2006, Eric rode his bike into Manhattan but never rode home. A year later, I sat at the sentencing hearing of the man who had killed him, the wood-walled courtroom divided into victim and perpetrator like a wedding no one wants to attend. Before a judge sentenced the man who killed Eric to jail for driving under the influence and vehicular manslaughter, the man said he was sorry.

"Words cannot express how truly sorry I am," he told the court, "for this accident that happened."

It blares in my ear now—*this accident that happened*—the absence of accountability, the disembodied telling, as if the killer had nothing to do with the killing. But that day in court, I did not question it. I watched the children of the man who killed my best friend nod goodbye to their father and felt certain that Eric would not have wanted this—a man going to prison, more lives ruined, and so little done to prevent this from happening again.

To the epidemiologists who count the ways everyone dies in America, the term of art is "unintentional injuries." Accidents, by their count, are when a person suffers physical trauma by external force and without intention. In *The Injury Fact Book*, Second Edition, there is a list of the twenty most common ways to die by accident in America in 1988:

Motor vehicle crashes—traffic
Falls
Poisoning by solids/liquids
Fires and burns
Drowning
Aspiration—nonfood
Aspiration—food
Firearm
Machinery
Aircraft
Suffocation
Poisoning by gas/vapor
Excessive cold
Struck by falling object
Electric current
Pedestrian—train
Excessive heat
Pedestrian—nontraffic
Collision with object/person
Exposure, neglect

Epidemiologist Susan P. Baker, a pioneer in the study of accident prevention, compiled *The Injury Fact Book*. The book was a first-of-its-kind compendium and analysis of accidental death and injury in the United States, an important practical reference for people in the field of public health before the internet allowed access to the records of the Centers for Disease Control and Prevention (CDC). Inside, the three times Baker uses the word "accident," she keeps it in scare quotes—once to let the reader know that when she writes "unintentional injury," she means what you might call an accident, once to note that the idea of "accident proneness" has been thoroughly debunked, and a third time in a footnote:

*The word "accident" erroneously implies that injuries occur by chance
and cannot be foreseen or prevented. In much scientific work, the descrip-
tor "accident" is gradually being replaced by more appropriate terms,
such as "unintentional injury," descriptions of the injuries (e.g., "fractured tibia"), or specification of the injury-producing event, such as a
motor vehicle crash.*

Baker published that volume in 1992, and she would be proven
right—today, it is uncommon to find the word in the literature of the
profession, at least when the subject is physical injury. The National
Highway Traffic Safety Administration banned the word from government publications in 1997, and the *British Medical Journal* banned it from
its pages in 2001. The New York City Police Department said they would
officially stop using the word in 2013. At a meeting of the American Copy
Editors Society in 2016, an editor of the *AP Stylebook* (a grammatical
bellwether for most of the nation's newspapers) announced that editors
should avoid "accident" in cases of possible negligence because it "can
be read as exonerating the person responsible."

And Baker was not alone in her opposition. In 1961, the American
psychologist J. J. Gibson put a fine point on it—the word "accident," he
wrote, seemed to refer to a makeshift concept, a hodgepodge of implications legal, medical, and statistical:

*Two of its meanings are incompatible. Defined as a harmful encounter
with the environment, a danger not averted, an accident is a psychological phenomenon, subject to prediction and control. But defined as an
unpredictable event, it is by definition uncontrollable. The two meanings
are hopelessly entangled in common usage.*

To call something an accident means, at once, that you know it is a
risk and that it is out of your control. You would sound ridiculous, but it
would not be improper to cite both meanings in a sentence, saying, for

example, that you accidentally got into a car accident. Around 40,000 people will die in car accidents in the United States in 2022, and I can predict this because it happens every year. But we would consider each of those accidents an unpredictable event.

The physician William Haddon, the first administrator of the National Highway Traffic Safety Administration, called the idea that accidents were random and unpredictable, "the last folklore subscribed to by rational men." He considered it superstitious hooey to call something an accident—a holdover from an era when much of science was inexplicable and mysterious. In his Washington, DC, office he kept a swear jar—anyone who excused a traffic crash as an accident had to forfeit a dime.

But this word-shaming by public health officials has not had much effect in the world at large. Everywhere else, *accident* remains in common use. In the archives of the *New York Times*, the number of appearances of the phrase "it was an accident" rises from 1853 to 2009; Google Trends tracks a similar increase in the use of the word "accident" between 2004 and 2021. Despite the opposition of officials like Baker and Haddon, the word has relentless staying power.

And so do, it turns out, actual accidents. It is surprisingly likely that one will kill you.

One in twenty-four people in the United States will die by accident. And among wealthy nations, the problem is distinctly American. You are significantly more likely to die by accident in the United States than in Australia, Austria, Canada, Denmark, France, Germany, Italy, Japan, the Netherlands, Norway, Portugal, Spain, Sweden, Switzerland, or the U.K. And the gap is significant—in 2008, the rate of accidental death in the United States was more than 40 percent higher than Norway, the next-most-dangerous wealthy nation, and nearly 160 percent higher than the Netherlands, the safest wealthy nation. That year, you were three times more likely to accidentally drown in the United States than in the U.K., more than three times more likely to die in a traffic accident here than in Japan, four times more likely to die of accidental poisoning here than in Canada, and nine times more likely to die in an accidental fire here than in Switzerland.

Yet the U.S. government offers more money for research into the prevention of disease than it does for research into the prevention of accidents. In 2006, of the $11.9 billion in grants issued by the National Institutes of Health (NIH) to fund research into the twenty-nine most common ways to die, injury ranked second to last in amount appropriated, relative to the "burden of illness"—number of people killed and years of life lost. Only depression was more chronically underfunded. AIDS, diabetes, perinatal conditions, breast cancer, dementia, alcohol abuse, dental and oral disorders, cirrhosis, ischemic heart disease, and schizophrenia all received more funding in dollars *and* relative to the likelihood that any of these will kill you. In fact, as accidents began to rise as a cause of death in the early 1990s, funding for research fell. Between 1996 and 2006, as the rate of accidental death rose, NIH funding for injury-related death research fell by $578 million. This began to shift in 2016 when, after two decades of a growing opioid epidemic, the government passed the first comprehensive laws addressing the problem of accidental overdose, including funding for research. Still, in 2019, injury research received less than half the funding offered to study HIV, AIDS, dementia, or Alzheimer's—all of which killed fewer people and resulted in fewer years of life lost.

Accidental fatalities and injuries cost us $1.09 trillion in 2019. That is the burden of lost wages and medical expenses, the damage of crashed cars and burnt homes, and the cost of insurance payouts and rising premiums. While dying of disease takes time, and thus costs money, accidents come with the destruction of property, the poisoning of land, the loss of work and income. When survived, accidents also come with the cost of lifelong injury—a loss of quality of life measured at $4.5 trillion a year. Accidents add up to $2,800 per U.S. citizen, per year, in direct costs—out-of-pocket expenses, higher taxes, and more paid-for goods and services. And we pay for it, as individuals and as a nation. Overcrowded U.S. hospitals carry the burden, and municipalities endlessly repairing roadside barriers, expanding the capacity of their fire departments, and buying oil booms to have on hand in case of a spill. The cost of accidents can be counted in taxes paid and wages lost. And because American taxpayers, rather than corporations, carry most of these costs, letting accidents happen is perfectly profitable for corporate America, even when those accidents happen in unsafe American cars or in uninspected American workplaces.

In 1986, Baker counted 95,277 deaths by accident. Thirty years later, in 2016, the number had grown to 161,374. That year marked a dark milestone. Accidental death had become the third most likely way to die in America. From 1992 to 2019, the number of annual accidental deaths grew by more than 106 percent, more than three times faster than the population. The rate of accidental death was 55 percent higher in 2019 than it was in 1992. For people age one to age forty-four, it is the single most common cause of death—killing around four times as many people in that population as cancer or heart disease. If you die "before your time," it will most likely be because of an accident, and today, people in the United States die by accident at higher numbers than ever before. An accident injures ninety-two people every minute of the year and kills twenty every hour.

These numbers and most of the other accidental death statistics in this book come from the National Vital Statistics System of the Centers for Disease Control and Prevention, where epidemiologists track and analyze millions of death certificates a year. Doctors, medical examiners, and coroners produce death certificates, each filling out a cause-of-death section, where they include their opinion concerning "(a) the disease or injury that initiated the train of morbid events leading directly to death, or (b) the circumstances of the accident or violence that produced the fatal injury." In this book, we will largely leave aside the diseases and violence and concentrate on the accidents and injuries. It is these that added up to 173,000 accidental deaths (or what the CDC would call "unintentional injuries") in 2019, the latest year for which data was available.

Despite this wealth of information, spectacular gaps remain, which left me with places I could not take this book. For instance, medical examiners disagree on the classification of accidental shootings—with some arguing that if *someone* pulls a trigger, then the death should be classified as a homicide, not an accident, even if it is unintentional, even if the person pulling the trigger is a toddler. This would limit the number of accidental shooting deaths recorded to those that occur when someone drops a gun or it misfires—but again, there is disagreement on this, so the accidental shooting counts we have are likely a mix of accidental trigger pulls and misfires. That is a small gap—the Centers for Disease Control and Prevention recorded just under 13,000 accidental shooting deaths between 1999 and 2019—and even if the number were actually twice as high, it would be a relative drop in the bucket compared to the nearly 2.7 million accidental deaths in that time.

Other data gaps, however, are massive.

In 2016, medical researchers at Johns Hopkins University published a paper calling on the CDC to revise their coding system, which, they said, fails to record as many as 250,000 fatal medical errors a year. This is a significant enough death toll to bump accidental injury out of the top three causes of death in the United States and replace it with medical accidents alone. Medical examiners use a document issued by the World Health Organization called the *International Statistical Classification of Diseases and Related Health Problems* (now in its tenth revision and known colloquially as the ICD-10) to code and classify all deaths in the United States. This document simply does not have a code for some mistakes—if you die because your file was missing when a nurse came to assess your condition, or because your doctor misdiagnosed you, or because your anesthesiologist was new on the job.

"We have an under-reporting and an under-appreciation of the magnitude of the problem of medical errors," Martin Makary, a Johns Hopkins Hospital surgeon and one of the study authors, tells me. These mistakes run the gamut: errors of omission, diagnostic errors, communication errors, system errors, and even, simply, bad outcomes for patients whom doctors forgot or who otherwise got lost in the system.

But the result of not measuring these accidents is that they are never addressed. "Funding priorities in the United States are informed by our national health statistics," according to Makary. "Medical errors have been excluded from the national errors, so we have not had the funding that is deserved."

In the paper, Makary offers this real-world example: A young woman felt ill, and a hospital admitted her for extensive tests. At least one test was unnecessary—a pericardiocentesis, where a needle is used to remove fluid from a sac near the heart. The hospital discharged her, but she returned days later, hemorrhaging and in cardiac arrest. While an autopsy found that the pericardiocentesis needle also pierced her liver, resulting in her death, there is no code for conducting an unnecessary high-risk test and causing accidental injury, or accidentally grazing an organ during pericardiocentesis. Doctors coded the cause of death as cardiovascular—not an accident.

Accidents as we know them began to rise in number long before such details were being recorded: with the Industrial Revolution, when workers left behind skilled craftsmanship—on the loom or in the field or at the forge—and stood shoulder to shoulder in assembly lines. As the number of factories grew, so did the economy, and the number of people killed in work accidents, too. In time, some of those factories began to mass-produce automobiles. Then so many died from traffic accidents that cities built monuments to the dead and organized children to march in memoriam.

In those early decades of the twentieth century, accidental death rode high. But in time, lifesaving inventions, along with the shared prosperity brought about by widespread union power, public construction, and social welfare, helped prevent accidents. The rate of accidental death in the United States generally declined during the years 1944–1992. Since then, the rate of accidental death has grown by more than half, even while the overall U.S. fatality rate has generally declined.

It shouldn't be this way. In 1971, the government approved the sale of naloxone, a drug that can reverse an accidental opioid overdose. The U.S. government first required carmakers to install seat belts in every American car in 1974. In 1995, the U.S. Occupational Safety and Health Administration (OSHA) began requiring construction workers to wear safety harnesses. Airbag regulations began in 1998. These are examples of the wealth of harm-reducing innovations that should mean fewer people die from accidents at large, and in traffic accidents, work-fall accidents, and poisoning accidents especially. Yet traffic fatalities skyrocketed in 2020, falls are the leading cause of workers' deaths in the construction industry, and the Centers for Disease Control and Prevention tallies the death toll of the opioid epidemic at over 840,000 people since 1999, nearly every one classified as an unintentional injury by drug poisoning.

These are the cold, hard facts of accidents in America. But when you look closer, you see that there is nothing cut-and-dried in any one accidental death. The statistical story misses a lot. I found this out the hard way. When I decided to write this book, in the name of diligence, I did something I did not want to do: I sent a Freedom of Information Act request to the City of New York for the records of my best friend's death. They arrived in a thick manila envelope a few months later. For weeks, I let it sit unopened. At the time, I did not know what I was afraid to find inside—I was right, though, to be afraid.

Inside the manila envelope, I learned that my best friend died on the sidewalk of massive internal injury. I learned that the driver who killed him first told the police that he was not intoxicated, and later said that he'd had two vodka cranberry drinks. Newspapers would later report that he registered at twice the legal limit in a blood-alcohol test. I learned that the driver said that he was going 25 miles per hour but that the distance Eric's body flew from the point of impact meant that he was driving at least 60 miles per hour. Eric was twenty-two when emergency medical technicians moved his body to the Bellevue Hospital morgue. His killer was twenty-seven and was driving a gray 2000 BMW 528i on the sidewalk.

The police accident report included a diagram. In life, Eric had big muscles and olive skin and a tattoo on his bicep of a cityscape overrun by giant sunflowers, but in the diagram, he was just a stick figure near a drawing of a car and drawings of two bicycle wheels in two separate locations. Far away from the stick figure was a marking for a book bag and another I assumed to be his shoe, Chuck Taylors always, one of which, the report noted, the impact forced off his foot. The police included measurements, marking the distance these items had been thrown when the car hit his body.

There was a deposition transcript in the envelope, too, where the man who killed Eric told prosecutors what he remembered after the crash. He talked about the way Eric had died, described the noises and the movements. He guessed how far away he stood—a few feet—when he watched Eric's life end.

In time, the man said, a policewoman approached.

"She asked me what happened," the man recalled. "I said I got into an accident. My car hit this person."

"My car hit this person," he said, as though he wasn't even there.

I did not know any of this when I set out to write this book. The story of Eric's death that I knew was of an accident—a quick death—because when we talk about accidents, we do not talk about suffering. This was willful ignorance on my part. What happened to Eric was hard to look at, so I looked away. I did not want to think about the suffering. In this way, I understood the man who killed him. Neither of us wanted to look closer. A quick death, like an accident, is a comforting story for the rest of us—a distraction for the survivors, the killers and the grievers alike.

My closer look left me wrecked. It also helped me understand something about accidents that I had not before. It matters who tells the story of an accident. Eric did not live to tell the story of his death, so I never heard how he passed out of this world alone on the cold asphalt. Instead, the man who killed Eric told the story, at least at first—that was a story of a car hitting a person, an accident story, told by a man who had the momentary power of being the survivor. When that man went to prison, the prosecutors who put him there took over the telling—then, the story of Eric's death was the story of a bad person driving a car, a crime story. In accidents, power, in all its forms, be it a fast car or a plea deal, decides which story we hear. Across the United States, and across history, I found this as a common marker of accidents. The people who tell the story are always the powerful ones, and the powerful ones are rarely the victims.

In this way, surviving a mistake in America is a marker of privilege. On his bicycle, Eric lacked protection and could only travel as quickly as his legs could carry him. Up against a fast car, he would lose every time. His death was a contest of power in its most tangible form. But accidents are the predictable result of unequal power in every form—physical and systemic. Across the United States, all the places where a person is most likely to die by accident are poor. America's safest corners are all wealthy. White people and Black people die by accident at unequal rates, especially in those accidents where access to power can decide the outcome—the power to demand that your workplace is safe, the power to fireproof your home, the power to drive instead of walk. Accidents are not flukes or freak mishaps—whether or not you die by accident is just a measure of your power, or lack of it.

A Note on the Word "Accident" and Other Ways This Book Will Work

In my life outside these pages, I do not use the word "accident"—I haven't for years because, as the title says, there are no accidents. Writing this book, I found myself at a recurring semantic crossroads as to how to handle the current and historical uses of the word. This could easily be a book of ten thousand scare quotes—*but is it really an "accident"*? I asked myself the question again and again.

But, in the end, I left in every "accident"—and without the scare quotes—because I think you need to decide for yourself. I left the word on these pages so you could see when it starts to sound funny or disturbing to you, too.

Over the pages that follow, we will travel from turn-of-the-century New York City to modern-day West Virginia, and from the factory floor to the nuclear plant, in search of what we really mean when we say the word "accident." This book follows the structure of an accident: First we examine the preconditions of accidents, then the deaths and injuries, and finally the blame, punishment, and missed opportunities for prevention that come after. The first half of the book also examines, somewhat chronologically, the historic rises and falls of accidents in America, and the shifts in understanding of accidents over time. The second half of the book focuses on the modern accident epidemic. Throughout, we'll learn from the pioneers and professionals who have advanced our understanding of accidents.

This book is about the deceptively simple story told after an accident—that a person made a mistake and there is nothing more to see. And this book is about what we can learn—about ourselves and our society—when we seek out the real and complicated story. By doing just that, seeking the intricate story of power, vulnerability, and suffering behind any simple-looking accident, we can find ways to save tens of thousands of lives every year. We conclude with these solutions to the accident problem—how we can overcome the psychological crutch of victim-blaming, how we can repair the race- and income-based vulnerabilities that skew our accidental death rates, how we can revive the systems of accountability that give accidents a real cost for those who can, and fail to, prevent them, and how we can reimagine our streets, our homes, our hospitals, our workplaces, and our world at large, to put human life above efficiency, profit, or power.

Chapter One

Error

To understand accidents, we need to understand error—not just why we make mistakes, but how powerful people can use our mistakes against us. This book begins with error because questions of error almost always follow an accident—what a person, usually the person hurt, did wrong: Why was he driving so fast? Was she drunk at the time of the accident? Did they not know that the stove was on? Who wasn't paying attention?

Inherent in these questions is a presumption—that accidents are caused by accident-prone people, or people making bad decisions, or people we think did things the wrong way. This is true. People make mistakes, and human error is a part of almost every accident. The following pages are full of errors and bad decisions. The following pages are also full of errors that are inevitable, predictable, and unavoidable, and people making mistakes that you or I would have made, just as they did, because there was no other choice.

Before we can move forward, we need to be extra-clear about what we mean. A *human error* is a mistake. And a *dangerous condition* is an environment.

To slip is a human error. Water left on the floor is a dangerous condition. To exceed the speed limit is a human error. A road designed to encourage you to exceed the speed limit is a dangerous condition. To run an oil tanker aground on a reef is a human error. Requiring a twelve-hour shift for the pilot of an oil tanker is a dangerous condition.

For the past two hundred years, a debate over which of these factors matters more has defined our understanding of accidents. One side says that human error causes accidents, and that to prevent accidents, we must fix people. The other says that accidents happen under dangerous conditions, and that to prevent accidents, we must fix the environment. If you owned the wet floor, designed the road, or employed the captain of the oil tanker, you might say that accidents are a matter of human error. In this book, I will argue that we can trace all human error back to conditions that are—sometimes obscurely, sometimes obscenely—dangerous, and that we can almost always predict and prevent the deaths and injuries that follow our mistakes. I will argue that mistakes are inevitable, that people are not perfectible, and that the only answer to the accident problem starts with setting aside blame for human error. Accidents happen when errors occur under dangerous conditions, but you can create conditions that anticipate errors and make those mistakes less of a life-or-death equation.

Or you can focus all your energy on errors, and let the same accidents happen again and again.

Sidney Dekker, airplane pilot, director of the Safety Science Innovation Lab in Brisbane, Australia, and professor of aerospace engineering at Delft University of Technology in the Netherlands, describes the two sides of this debate as the "Bad Apple Theory" and the "New View"— the old theory that a few bad apples cause accidents or the new view that if people are making mistakes and getting hurt, it indicates that conditions are unsafe.

Applied to work accidents, for example, the Bad Apple Theory would tell us that a factory is inherently a safe place, and that accident-prone people and their mistakes make it unsafe. When accidents happen, by this logic, they are the fault of a few bad apples, and employers can make the workplace safe by removing the bad apples. After an accident, Bad

Apple Theory solutions could include firing, retraining, automation, issuing punishments, or creating new rules.

The New View says that the factory is not *inherently* safe and that instead, if people are getting hurt when they make mistakes, the factory is *definitely* unsafe. Subscribers to the New View believe that employers can make the workplace safer by fixing the dangerous conditions that *could* hurt someone *if and when* they make a mistake. After an accident, New View solutions could include changing procedures or factory designs to anticipate mistakes—slowing down the assembly line, or providing cushions for falls, guards for sharp objects, and protective garments for fragile human parts.

For subscribers to the Bad Apple Theory, the purpose of investigating an accident is to assign blame to whoever made a mistake. Once whoever is in charge assigns blame and hands out punishment, they can consider the accident solved. For subscribers to the New View, the purpose of investigating an accident is to identify the dangerous conditions that caused people to get hurt when someone made a mistake. Once the dangerous conditions are identified, they can be changed—to prevent the accident from occurring again or to reduce the likelihood of death or injury when another person inevitably makes the same mistake. Whichever theory wins the day decides what happens next—and this matters a lot. After an accident, do you fire the injured worker or do you fix the floorboard? Do you punish the driver or redesign the road? In the answers to these questions, we can find the ability to predict whether or not the same accident will happen again.

A great deal of power resides with whoever decides the answers to these questions. Who tells the story, and the story they tell, is the secret to the accident. Is it a story of a bad worker, or of a wet floor? A reckless driver, or a car that can easily accelerate to dangerous speeds? In America's workplaces and on America's roads we see a clear picture that what matters most in accidents is whose answers get heard.

We are going to jump back and forth in U.S. history, moving between the two most significant increases in accidental deaths prior to the present one: fatal worker accidents in the Industrial Revolution and fatal car accidents in the first fifty or so years after the invention of the automobile. We will see how automakers and industrialists used error as a pawn in accidents. In these two moments, we can track how the powerful profiteers of each era weaponized the simple fact that people make mistakes in an effort to distract, persuade, and manipulate.

To start, we will look at the traffic accident. In 1908, the year that Ford introduced the Model T, traffic accidents killed 751 Americans. By 1935, fatal traffic accidents had grown 50 times over—37,000 Americans dead and 105,000 permanently disabled that year alone. But when these accidents killed pedestrians, people used to refer to them by a far less innocuous term—to be killed by a car was car *murder*—until automakers changed how we understand the mistakes that people make on the road.

We can track that change in how the witnesses to accidents used to react.

Crying Car Murder

On a Thursday in the spring of 1931, a twenty-three-year-old man named Joseph Weitz worked into the early evening, driving a truck for the H. & S. Trucking Company. Weitz rumbled through an increasingly marvelous New York City. The first air-conditioned passenger train had made its inaugural run from New York to Washington, DC, just one week earlier. Earlier that month, President Herbert Hoover pressed a button in the White House to turn on the lights in the newly opened Empire State Building, the tallest building in the world.

Among these marvels was the automobile, which after years as a rich man's plaything was now accessible, affordable, and everywhere. Ten years earlier, there had been less than half as many cars and trucks registered in America. From 1921 to 1931, drivers registered more than a million new vehicles every year.

Weitz was rolling across Manhattan, on East Sixty-Seventh Street, when he heard screams rising above the din of the city. He pulled the truck to a stop in the middle of the street and climbed down from the cab.

He saw a crowd huddled at a spot his truck had just passed. A boy lay in the middle of the road. The boy did not move. The crowd grew.

After some time, a patrolman named Burnett arrived from the police station down the block. He asked a few questions about the owner of the truck, and then he placed Weitz under arrest for the killing of six-year-old Irwin Ouser. It didn't take long for the crowd to realize that the accident now had a culprit. The crowd circled Weitz and Patrolman Burnett, pushing and screaming. No one paid any attention to the police officer as he ordered everyone to calm down.

Patrolman Burnett pulled Weitz from the mob, walking away from the dead boy lying in the street and back toward the truck. The crowd followed, grabbing at the driver. Burnett realized that he was losing control. He pushed Weitz back into the cab of the truck and drew his pistol on the crowd.

I will shoot anyone who touches the prisoner, he shouted.

The crowd had Patrolman Burnett pushed back against the truck by the time reinforcements arrived. One officer transported Weitz to the Sixty-Seventh Street police station. Another bore the bad news out to Israel and Adelaide, Irwin Ouser's parents, who both fainted when informed of their son's death.

The first-ever reported fatal traffic accident in America had occurred thirty-two years before this one, across town, when a real estate developer named Henry Bliss exited a streetcar at Central Park West and Seventy-Fourth Street and the driver of an electric taxicab struck him. There was no mob reported then. Something happened between that first traffic accident in 1899 and the 1920s, when news stories like Irwin Ouser's began to appear regularly.

The headlines of those 1920s news stories describe uncontrollable crowds incensed at drivers after everyday accidents, seeking blood for blood:

CROWD MOBS DRIVER AS TRUCK KILLS BOY;
Policeman, With Revolver and Nightstick,
Protects Man Till Help Arrives

CROWD MOBS CHAUFFEUR;
Men and Women Beat Operator of
Truck Which Crushes Lad to Death

MOTOR TRUCKS KILL 2 BOYS AND WOMAN;
Driver and Helper Flee From Crowd of 500
When Lad Is Hit in Seventh Street
POLICEMAN RESCUES ONE;
Points Pistol at Mob and Takes Fugitive to Safety

Sometimes the crowds grew massive. Sometimes the mob succeeded. But the plot was the same: a driver killed one or more pedestrians by accident, and then a violent mob of pedestrians attempted to kill a driver. Stories like these, which are all from the span of a few years, began appearing around 1920 before petering off a few years after Irwin Ouser's death.

Today, it is extraordinarily rare to hear of a riot incited over a traffic accident. A sober driver involved in a fatal car accident today is no more considered a murderer than a child who finds some poison under the sink is considered to have a death wish. But in the era of Irwin Ouser and Joseph Weitz, the fatal traffic accident was understood as a horrific crime. The historian Peter Norton, a professor of history and technology at the University of Virginia, first identified this trend in his book *Fighting Traffic: The Dawn of the Motor Age in the American City*. In fact, he found, the idea of car murder was widespread enough that in the 1920s, the City Club of New York, a reform-minded gentlemen's club, began to publish a map of child traffic accidents every year. They called the project the municipal murder map.

"Each black dot on the map marks a spot where a little New York boy or girl was killed by a street vehicle," the 1926 version read. "There are 200 of these child murder spots. And this is only Manhattan."

In the beginning, the story of car accidents was a story about murder. The storytellers were driven by the way the car changed the hierarchy of transportation. At the time, the walking people of America were at risk as they had never been before. Before cars, save for taking care when strolling closely behind a horse, no one told you how or when to walk. With the arrival of the automobile, and the traffic signals and traffic laws that would follow, pedestrians were not just downgraded and instructed, but killed in the streets in skyrocketing numbers. It is no wonder that those people, newly demoted and highly at risk, cried murder.

But just as the Ouser mob eventually moved on, the idea of car murder shifted, too. Evidence of this can be found in a later incarnation of the municipal murder map. While the City Club of New York abandoned their project in 1930, a year before Irwin Ouser died on East Sixty-Seventh Street, in 1971, someone other than a member of the City Club of New York would take up a remarkably similar project.

William Bunge relocated the map to Detroit, but the message was the same. He named one edition *Where Commuters Run Over Black Children on the Pointes-Downtown Track*. He titled another *Children's Automobile "Accidents" in Detroit*. Like the City Club cartographers, Bunge minced no words about his purpose. Every time he writes "accident," he uses those scare quotes:

> Going to school forces children to cross dangerous streets. In front of schools as many as five or six "accidents" occur like clockwork each year. If you can predict an event, why call it an "accident"? If you can point to a corner and say "next year five more kids will be hit here," it is the geography of the streets, the inner-city gridiron pattern left over from horse-and-buggy days, not negligent mothers, that is causing the deaths and injuries. If the streets were cul-de-sacs, as in the suburbs, these "accidents" would all but cease.

But unlike the City Club cartographers, William Bunge was not a member of his city's elite. Rather, he was a so-called radical geographer. You could find his name, snugly between Stokely Carmichael and H. Rap Brown, on the blacklist of political activists barred by the House Un-American Activities Committee from speaking on college campuses.

It is no coincidence that this project—mapping traffic fatalities to highlight the dangers of the automobile—left the purview of urban elites and eventually became the work of political radicals. When car accidents first rose, both the mobs crying murder and the City Club of New York crafting the municipal murder map were a problem for automakers, as both cast them as weapons dealers. To overcome this, automakers and their financially interested allies crafted a campaign that relocated that blame to human error. That's how questioning "car murder" as anything more than an accident became a politically radical act. It took a concentrated campaign by carmakers to erase their role in the car accident—one that continues today—so that everyone would stop demonizing cars and start buying them. Automakers and sellers, car parts manufacturers, and oil companies fought against restrictions dictating how cars were built, redirecting car-related ire toward the way that people walked or drove. With concerted campaigns about a few bad apples, these interest groups shifted a conversation about the shocking impact of powerful cars on pedestrian-dense city streets into a conversation about crazy drivers and pedestrians who just don't walk right.

Inventing the Jaywalker

One of the most effective tools employed in service of the human error side of the accident debate is setting up a bogeyman to blame. In *Fighting Traffic*, Norton traces a prime example of this rhetorical tactic in the invention of the word "jaywalker." He spent years searching the early records of what today we would call the automobile lobby—automakers, driving enthusiasts, oil companies, tire and car parts manufacturers, and car dealers, organized into auto clubs and associations—and found that the popularization of the jaywalker as a bogeyman can be traced directly to those desperate to find someone else to blame for the rise of traffic accidents.

Before the 1920s, the term "jaywalker" was an uncommon insult, a twin to an insult you have likely never heard: *jay-driver*. These disses were a call-and-response between a pedestrian and a driver. Each accused the other of being a sort of transportation hillbilly, a "jay" who does not know how to operate on city streets. And for a while, "jaywalker" was a genuine insult. When a New York City police commissioner used it in 1915, it was a serious enough offense that the *New York Times* wrote an editorial calling the language "truly shocking" and "highly opprobrious."

It is no coincidence that we lost one of these insults to time, while the other entered the lexicon. The automobile lobby marketed, pushed, and popularized the idea of "jaywalking" both as an insult and as law. Today, every state in the nation prohibits jaywalking, and all of them stipulate that if a car strikes a jaywalker, the pedestrian is at fault. It was part of an intensive campaign to shift the blame in traffic accidents from the dangerous conditions created by cars to human error. The auto lobby, previously in the business of advocating for paved roads and lower taxes and fees for drivers, was transformed by the outrage around traffic accidents, forced to concern itself with safety as a way to defend the automobile. That transformation began in Cincinnati, Ohio, where Norton uncovered the auto lobby's first attempt to shift the conversation around traffic safety in the effort to beat a ballot initiative.

In 1923, the people of Cincinnati decided that they wanted speed governors—devices that make it impossible for a car to go faster than a certain speed—on all vehicles owned by Cincinnati residents. Speed governors were a popular solution proposed as car accidents rose, with the cars' critics arguing that nothing should be going so fast on city streets. Some 42,000 people signed a petition to get a speed-governor law on the ballot. If passed, the law would have required drivers in the city to equip their cars with a speed governor set at 25 miles per hour.

(This is not a random number. The likelihood of pedestrian death in a traffic accident multiplies at speeds above 20 miles per hour because that is the maximum speed that our bodies can withstand on impact. Struck by a car going 23 mph, about 10 percent of people die. When the car is going 32 mph, 25 percent die. At 42 mph, 50 percent do not survive. At 50 mph, 75 percent of pedestrians struck will die and at 58 mph, 90 percent will.)

An immeasurable number of people would be alive today if it were not for what the nascent automobile lobby did next. Carmakers knew that fast and powerful cars were an important selling point. This is one reason that today cars' speedometers go as high as 160 mph, even if your car cannot actually go much faster than 100 mph. To distract from the cold, hard fact that speed kills, the automobile lobby shifted the blame from fast cars to human error.

The Cincinnati Automobile Dealers Association raised $10,000 to fight the speed-governor proposal. The National Automobile Chamber of Commerce sent representatives to the city to help local car salesmen rally votes against the proposal. On the day of the vote, the automobile lobby sent 400 workers to the polls to talk citizens into voting against the speed governors. And, Norton explains, it worked. Despite 42,000 people petitioning to get the law on the ballot, only 14,000 people actually voted for it. The speed governor lost, 6–1.

To exceed the speed limit is a mistake, a human error. The fact that cars can go so fast is a dangerous condition. And because the auto lobby was so successful in reframing the car-murder narrative, when we talk about speeding, we almost always talk about *speeders* as the problem, not how fast those cars can go.

In the Cincinnati speed-governor fight, the automobile lobby honed their chief tactic. To distract from the public outcry about how fast cars could go, they instead talked about individual recklessness or a few "bad apple" drivers spoiling the whole road. The gun lobby would copy this strategy decades later with the slogan: *Guns don't kill people. People kill people.*

But in short order, the automobile lobby would need more bogeymen, as protests against the destructiveness of cars were spreading around the nation. St. Louis, Baltimore, and Pittsburgh built monuments to children killed by cars. The protest movement made conspicuous what they called "white star mothers"—women who had a child killed by a driver, honored for their preventable and tragic loss. This is where the jaywalker steps in.

The auto lobby devised two counterpoints to the memorials and protests: education and enforcement—laws that governed who was allowed in the street and lessons to indoctrinate the public to these new rules. While some of the financial benefactors of car sales pushed municipalities to pass local traffic ordinances restricting pedestrians' access to the street, the American Automobile Association in particular focused on education, launching and funding a national traffic safety campaign in schools. Street crossing lessons became part of the curriculum, and those lessons reinforced the idea that now cars go first and pedestrians wait. Inherent in this education was the message that if a person did not wait and a driver killed them in the street, their death was caused not by the car's speed but by jaywalking—the pedestrian's error. The goal was to teach the next generation that the roads are for automobiles, not people. And since cars were new, and pedestrians had long ruled city streets, someone had to invent the idea that a person could walk improperly—the auto lobby did just that.

The automobile lobby also found new ways to inject human error into the car-accident conversation. Norton found that local driving clubs, like the Chicago Motor Club, began to place items in newspapers to ensure that "jaywalker" appeared in the press. In Los Angeles, the Automobile Club of Southern California even paid to paint the city's first crosswalks, producing and posting signs that read JAY WALKING PROHIBITED BY ORDER—POLICE DEPARTMENT—even though the term "jaywalker" didn't appear in the local traffic code. In New York City, the Automobile Club of America laid the problem out this way in one 1923 pamphlet: "Pedestrians often appear stupid or careless, and lots of them are."

The efforts were more than local. In early 1924, the National Automobile Chamber of Commerce created their own accident statistic news service, offered to newspapers for free, with the explicit goal of shifting public understanding of who was to blame for traffic accidents. What the news service offered were not neutral numbers—instead, each was a little human error story. Included, in each instance, was the person who was to blame. And the finger was almost always pointed at the reckless driver or the reckless pedestrian—erasing the inherent danger of the automobile from the equation. With the advent of the jaywalker, blame for the pedestrian especially rose. A few months after the news service began national distribution, even local officials noticed the shift in blame. In New York, in late 1924, the traffic court magistrate noted, "It is now the fashion to ascribe from 70 to 90 percent of all accidents to jaywalking."

Walter Chrysler himself even helped. In 1927, the president of the Chrysler Motor Car Company wrote an article for *The Outlook* titled "The Only Cure for Auto Accidents." It began:

> *There is nothing which distresses me more than to read in the newspapers about the death of a child in an automobile accident. I am a manufacturer of automobiles, and I have every appreciation of the contribution that the motor car has made to the happiness of the people of America. But I also have an appreciation of the fact that some practical way must be found to check the increase in the number of deaths and injuries resulting from automobile accidents.*

Chrysler's "only cure" was education for the bad apples. He wrote of the need to teach children not to play in the streets, chase after balls, or hitch rides behind vehicles on their roller skates and scooters, and of the need to train police officers to enforce these lessons. The catastrophic rise in deaths and injuries from automobile accidents, he wrote, was a problem of errors made by wild pedestrians, pedestrians in the rain obstructing their vision with umbrellas, and pedestrians crossing the street while reading books.

In time, automakers would invent other scapegoats to follow the jaywalker—most prominently "the nut behind the wheel"—a 1920s creation we will meet at the end of this chapter. There is no shortage of these human error bogeymen in the history of accidents: the accident-prone worker, the risk-taker, the addict, the criminal. Today, the nut behind the wheel and the jaywalker may catch less ridicule, but the road-rager, the drunk driver, and the distracted pedestrian have stepped into the bogeyman role.

Traffic accidents kill about as many people today as they did when the word "jaywalker" achieved wide currency, though by all appearances we care less. In place of mobs and murder maps, newscasters report traffic accidents as matter-of-factly as they do the weather—*bring an umbrella and leave a little extra time for a pileup on Highway 101*. We can credit this to the ways that automakers have modernized their jaywalker campaigns for the twenty-first century. During a recent rise in the number of pedestrians killed in traffic accidents, starting in 2009 and reaching a thirty-year high in 2019, the distracted pedestrian attracted particular interest. When the fatality rate began to climb, Ford Motor Company tried to introduce a new portmanteau into the lexicon—*petextrian*, a person who texts while walking. That one didn't catch on, but the idea of the "distracted pedestrian" stuck. So appealing was this idea that a survey of transportation officials in 2018 and 2019 found that a third believed that distracted walking was a serious safety issue. Those road planners and engineers estimated that 40 percent of pedestrians killed died because of distracted walking. (In reality, it is estimated to be the cause of 0.2 percent of pedestrian fatalities.) This same wrongheadedness drove legislators in New York City to pass a law to force the city's department of transportation to study the depth of the distracted pedestrian problem. The agency abided by the law and conducted a study. They found no evidence of any such problem.

The distracted pedestrian is a new version of an old trick—redirecting focus from a dangerous condition to an individual mistake. Automakers first learned it from a campaign waged during an earlier rise in accidental deaths—those in the workplace. At the tail end of the Industrial Revolution, captains of industry, newly responsible for the cost of workers' deaths and injuries, insisted that such fatalities were just accidents. In America's industrial mines and factories, those in control of working conditions popularized the idea that when workers got hurt, human error was to blame.

The Myth of the Accident-Prone Worker

The so-called careless worker appeared in industrial workplaces, coal mines, and rail yards a few decades before the jaywalker, but a similar story preceded the caricature. As a wide range of new industrial technologies appeared, from electricity in coal mines to the spread of the railroad, life got especially dangerous for workers—in 1900, at least one in every fifty workers in the United States was killed, or disabled for at least four weeks, in a work accident. As unions organized against increasingly unsafe conditions in the workplace, owners pushed a different narrative, that there was another simple reason people died at work: workers were accident-prone.

The idea that certain workers were more likely to have accidents than others—people who would eventually be branded "accident-prone workers"—ramped up after 1911, when a few states passed the nation's first workers' compensation laws. These laws brought about a massive shift in financial liability for workers and employers alike. Before this, when an accident happened at work, it was near impossible for a worker or the surviving family to get money from an employer. Workers were left unemployed, unable to work, and shouldering their own medical bills. In the case of a fatal accident, families often had to figure out how to manage the cost of living after losing their breadwinner. The only option a worker and their family had was to show, in court, that an employer had knowingly exposed the worker to deadly risk. Workers almost always lost these cases, if they could even afford the lawyer necessary to try to win. Otherwise, the death was understood as an accident, and the employer didn't have to pay.

Workers' compensation laws changed that arrangement, so "it was an accident" was no longer sufficient defense. Employers had to compensate workers injured on their watch. For the first time, accidents born out of a sped-up assembly line or an unventilated coal mine would affect profits. Accidents suddenly had a price. This cost inspired the owners of America's largest corporations to launch the first industrial safety campaigns—and those campaigns focused on changing workers' behavior by teaching them not to make mistakes.

Wisconsin was the first state to pass a workers' compensation law, in 1911. The following year, industrialists from all over the Midwest gathered in Wisconsin for what they called the First Cooperative Safety Congress—a meeting of corporate power to discuss worker safety. As more states followed Wisconsin's lead, the Congress went nationwide under the name National Council for Industrial Safety—a centralized organization to control and finance information about worker safety and accidents on the job. Suddenly safety education was everywhere in America's workplaces, a cottage industry of cures, pep talks, and the repeated message that, when accidents happened, it was mistakes made by clumsy, irresponsible, or drunk workers that were to blame.

One common place to find this argument was on posters tacked up in the rail yard or factory—something for workers to read while they ate their lunch or punched the clock. These were designed and sold by the National Council for Industrial Safety. The posters offered obvious, often infantilizing advice: what is and is not a ladder; how to pick up boxes; what a clean workstation looks like; what good shoes look like; the wrong way to pull a monkey wrench; when a rock is too big to pick up; how to tuck your pants into your socks—all focused on the role of workers' errors in accidents. By 1930, the posters were so popular among business owners that the council was adding forty-seven new ones every month, advertised in a catalog that ran over ninety pages long. In all, they created over seven thousand posters in less than twenty years.

On these posters, "Otto Nobetter" appeared frequently. If the jaywalker has an ancestral line, it begins here, with a cartoon worker who never gets it right. Otto walks across a breaking board. Otto picks up something interesting on the shop floor: a scalding hot metal rod. He *ought to know better*—get it?

Around this time, corporate interests also seized on new theories in applied psychology that suggested certain people were accident-prone. According to the theories, this was a trait that some people had—not learned but inherent. The psychologists, often hired by corporations, proposed that workplace accidents only happened because some workers were accident-prone. The National Council for Industrial Safety was printing all those posters for these unlucky, uncoordinated few.

Attempts to define and measure accident-proneness in workers appeared in some of the most important annals of academia. One study correlated a low accident rate among pilots with strong religious values. Another proposed that professional drivers who had more accidents than others were "mentally subnormal." Among coal miners who had more accidents, the psychologists found guilt complexes, problems with authority, a psychosexual need to court danger. A staff psychologist at the Process Engineering Corporation attempted to prove that workers who had more accidents also lacked "socially desirable personality dispositions." Another psychologist spent a few months driving and socializing with a group of taxi drivers. Among the taxi drivers with the highest rates of accidents on the job, he also noted a wealth of undesirable traits: high divorce rates; limited interests outside drinking, sports, and gambling; and childhoods marked by strict parents, alcoholic fathers, juvenile delinquency, school truancy, and gang membership.

Notably, for all these attempts to psychologize mistakes, none ever definitively proved that accident-proneness exists. Zero statistically valid cases were published. Not one experiment produced an affirmative result for an accident-proneness test.

It was not until the 1940s that researchers at last began to question the concept of accident-proneness. Critiques of the idea appear intermittently in the historical record amid countless attempts to demonstrate that accident proneness exists. As one research review put it, the body of work attempting to prove accident-proneness contained "a considerable amount of careless reporting, illogical reasoning, and a lack of familiarity with the statistical theory." To the authors, it was beyond explanation that the concept carried on: "For so many researchers to persist in pursuing the construct of accident-proneness, as it relates to personality, without any reliable results being found, is remarkable."

Making the case that accident-prone workers cause accidents was such an effectively distracting tool that it persisted for decades despite a lack of scientific proof. And even today, despite its spuriousness, the belief remains widespread. For one, it is hard to debunk such a vague notion. For another, it doesn't matter if anyone debunked accident-proneness or not. The point is not finding truth but creating ambiguity—the vague conclusion that if an accident happens, there must be *something* wrong with the person who had it.

Why Workers Don't Follow the Rules

One of the most common and effective ways to suggest that human error causes accidents is by making rules against mistakes. The workplace safety manual best exemplifies this process: *do not run, safety first, watch your hands.* In the Industrial Revolution and today, you can find these rules posted on the walls of factories where production lines run fast, machines are sharp, and you can be fired if you don't keep up. When a worker is killed or injured, the owner can point to these rules as proof that the accident was the result not of dangerous conditions but of a disobedient person.

In industrial work across the country, labor journalist Christopher Leonard has found that managers often point to these safety manuals after an accident. Accidents happen largely because owners change the production process, he says—speeding up the assembly line, for example—but the safety manual does not change. The rules become harder to follow when the pace of the operation is accelerated, and thus the work becomes more dangerous. Leonard tells me a story from his book, *Kochland: The Secret History of Koch Industries and Corporate Power in America*, about how conditions changed at Georgia Pacific paper mills after 2005, when Koch Industries bought the company.

Koch Industries paid $21 billion for Georgia-Pacific. To recoup their investment, Koch had to boost profit. This required increasing production. The company did both, and accidents followed. By 2017, the number of accidental deaths and injuries, the rate of accidents per employee, and the number of hours lost to accidental injury all rose. Four employees died on the job in a single spring and summer. That year, nine employees suffered accidental dismemberment.

When Leonard was reporting on Georgia-Pacific, many higher-ups at Koch Industries told him how much the company valued safety there—so much so that the company would print fifty-page manuals of safety protocol, explaining how workers could avoid making mistakes that lead to accidents. But at the same time, the company was making significant cuts to the workforce and laying off workers—in particular, union workers. Union rules stipulated that a worker could only operate the machine assigned to their job title, the one that someone had trained them on. If the person on the machine next to you left or got fired or their job title was eliminated, you couldn't just switch to their machine. This made production slower but people safer. When Koch Industries took over, they largely eliminated those rules. Managers asked workers to hop from job to job and machine to machine, learning each as they worked. This was riskier and much more profitable.

Again and again, Leonard found stories of Georgia-Pacific workers killed in accidents when they tried to improvise and fix a machine on the fly. Those workers were technically violating a rule, but in reality, they were just trying to keep up with the pace of the work.

I tell Leonard about the early industrial psychologists who spent so much effort trying to prove the existence of the accident-prone worker. "It was the case in the early 1900s," he says, "and it is the case today."

At Georgia-Pacific, starting in 2012, accidents rose dramatically year-over-year. Executives convened to address the problem. Leonard narrates for me what the executives in that meeting concluded: "Well, I guess the workers aren't embracing our policies fully enough. We've got to get to their hearts and their minds. We've got to just make them obey these rules."

The explanation from executives was that the rising accident rate was a human error problem caused by workers disobeying the rules. But what was really going on at Georgia-Pacific was that working conditions had changed.

"They were pushing people to work harder and fewer people to do more work. But they could not address that issue. It was not open to debate that you could accept a lower profit margin, slow things down, introduce inefficiencies into the system," Leonard says.

If the only job of executives is to maximize profits, then without a countervailing force to keep workers safe, accidents happen. This tension between safety and production defines the industrial workplace, where the pressure and desire to make money manifests in accidents. The slaughterhouse or meat processing plant—a slippery job using sharp implements to create a low-cost product—exemplifies this tension.

"The slaughterhouse today is much better sanitized, and we know a lot more about how to control cutting blades and spinning machinery, so you do not see the high level of horrific injuries you saw back in the early 1900s, but that doesn't mean it is safe. It is still one of the most dangerous jobs in America," Leonard points out. "The primary incentive for anybody who owns a slaughterhouse is to pump as many animals through that facility as you can in a week, because you have just invested a lot of money in the factory, the machinery, and in hiring workers. The way you recoup that investment is by slaughtering as many animals as possible and selling as much as possible."

Leonard describes sitting in the office of a manager at a Tyson Foods slaughterhouse in Missouri. The manager's computer went to sleep, and his custom screen saver came up. The mantra bouncing around his screen? RUN DEBONE FULL SPEED.

"What that means is run the debone line as fast as you can. Now, the debone line is an area where you've got employees sitting, sometimes shoulder to shoulder, holding incredibly sharp knives, cutting apart carcasses of chickens to cut them into the various products, like boneless chicken breasts or wings," he says. "What you have when you are running these lines really fast—it does not just increase the chance that somebody is going to get tired at the end of an eight-hour shift and accidentally cut their hand open, which happens frequently, but it means that you are seeing these systemic chronic injuries, like joint pain and carpal tunnel syndrome and tendinitis. The pressure to keep production really high hurts workers, and if the workers do not have a labor union to negotiate for a line slowdown or more safe conditions, you see what we see today, which is just rampant injury."

If you work in a chicken plant, your safety manual will explain the best ways to debone chicken to avoid an accident. However, those rules do not change depending on whether or not your boss runs the debone line at full speed. Where the primary incentive of a person who owns a slaughterhouse is to process as many animals as possible, for a person who works in a slaughterhouse, there are two different incentives: not getting hurt and not getting fired.

"When you put people in a dangerous environment, if you are not careful, they are going to get injured. But they never expect to get injured, and they never plan to get injured, so you can say that it was this unintentional thing and the circumstances are always going to be unique to the situation," Leonard explains. "The word 'accident' implies it was this totally unexpected surprise, but it really very rarely is in the workplace, because if this was a dangerous environment and if you increase pressure on people and reduce their training, they are going to get hurt."

The predictable, preventable accident seems unique after the fact, even though it is not uncommon. But in the aftermath, that seeming uniqueness prevails in a story of individual mistakes. Rules and safety manuals institutionalize human error as the cause of accidents. This explanation is also boosted by less formal sources, such as the rumor, the whisper campaign, and the racist stereotype.

Low-down Dirty Chicken Thief

On September 3, 1991, the Imperial Food Products factory—a chicken processing plant in Hamlet, North Carolina—caught fire when hydraulic fluid leaking from a hose sparked a gas-powered chicken fryer. It was a one-story building located in the Black half of town. There was little ventilation, a faulty sprinkler system, and floors slick with flammable fat. Twenty-five workers, the majority female and Black, died in the Hamlet fire. Most of the dead suffocated behind locked doors. Others burned to death.

One image from the charred building encapsulates the dangerous irony of accidents in America. It is a photo of a door inside the factory that bore a sign—FIRE EXIT—DO NOT BLOCK—and the padlock that bolted that door. It is the safety rule, warning of the potential for human error, and the unavoidable dangerous condition all in one. An insurance assessor later declared that "not a single door in the plant met the criteria of a fire exit." The plant operated for eleven years without an OSHA inspection. At the time, there were fewer than sixty OSHA inspectors for the whole state of North Carolina. After the fire, OSHA found 150 safety violations in the one-story building.

Bryant Simon, a professor of history at Temple University, spent years investigating the fire and its prehistory. In *The Hamlet Fire: A Tragic Story of Cheap Food, Cheap Government, and Cheap Lives*, he traces the history of the Imperial Foods chicken processing plant backward through the owners dodging OSHA inspections in the North, moving the factory to the South to avoid regulation, and choosing to locate it in a Black neighborhood because that meant they could hire workers who would have less power to protest dangerous conditions. Simon calls this process a social autopsy, a way of figuring out a true cause of death. He discovered that the cause of the death toll in Hamlet was not a random accident but a predictable one, born not of a worker's error but of underlying conditions—and not just the physically dangerous conditions of the workplace, controlled by the owners, but also the social conditions those owners were using to their advantage. This could be seen, in part, in how much the workers' identities affected how people described the accident after the fact.

Simon tells me about his first trip to Hamlet, twenty years after the fire, when he sat down with three local journalists who had covered the story at the time. All were older white men.

"They all insisted to me that the fire was an accident, and that it was caused by the owners of the plant, and that they were greedy, and if they were not greedy, nothing would have happened," Simon says. But this simple story eliminates the history and politics that brought those workers to labor under those conditions. "Those people did not just end up in that plant that day. Historical forces brought a particular kind of person to that plant, and the fact that no one cared about them didn't just begin that day."

Instead, Simon says, "what we call accidents are in some ways manufactured vulnerabilities."

The journalists Simon met in North Carolina, who insisted that the cause of the fire was the owners' greed, erased the way that race and class made the victims vulnerable. Those workers were vulnerable to taking any work they could get, being passed over for an OSHA inspection, and working under dangerous conditions—and they were vulnerable to being blamed for an accident. Another, more informal story cast the fire's victims in an even deeper shadow. This tale, which Simon repeatedly heard in rumors from local officials, implicated the victims in their deaths. The story was that the owners of Imperial Foods locked the doors to the plant because the workers were stealing chickens.

It is almost the same story as the one told in the aftermath of the Triangle Shirtwaist Factory fire eighty years before, when a ten-story building packed with scrap fabric burst into flames. There was little ventilation, and there were no sprinkler systems, too few exits, and flammable rags piled throughout. Of the 146 workers who died, mostly women, some suffocated behind locked doors. Many jumped from the building. Others burned to death.

With both fires, the official story described an owner's greed. But in both instances, another story passed as a rumor in the aftermath. It went like this: the owners locked the doors because the workers were thieves. In New York in 1911, they allegedly stole fabric. Floor managers searched bags and purses at the end of the workday and kept doors locked to ensure nobody could leave the factory without being searched. In Hamlet, the twenty-five victims died because the owners locked the doors to prevent the alleged theft of chicken.

In Hamlet, Simon heard the rumor from the fire insurance researcher, the fire chief, even the chief prosecutor, and workers who survived the fire reported it to the Associated Press. Whether or not this story is true is less important than what it justifies.

"This narrative that circulates below the surface persists, linking the locking of the doors to theft," Simon points out. He says that if the theft was a justification important enough that he was hearing it twenty years after the fire, imagine the weight it held when the fire first burned.

But the aftermath of the Hamlet fire differs in one crucial respect from its predecessor. The Triangle fire prompted nationwide labor reforms, including the passage of workers' compensation laws and requirements to change dangerous conditions in the workplace—requiring fire exits and alarms, sprinkler systems, and unlocked doors. In comparison, the Hamlet fire produced little outrage and few reforms.

"There is not an ideological transformation in the wake of this. It is just seen as a tragedy, and tragedy works a little bit like accident. If it is seen as a tragedy, then I do not have to rethink my basic perceptions of the world," Simon explains.

That big ideological switch did not happen after Hamlet, Simon theorizes, because the people who died were mostly Black women. The lawyer who represented the owners of Imperial Foods recounted to Simon his meeting with the district attorney prosecuting the case against his clients. That prosecutor explained that stealing chicken was just "what these people do." The victims, the prosecutor said, "were just a bunch of low-down Black folks anyway." The difference between what happened in response to the death of workers who stole chickens and the workers who stole fabric was that the former were Black.

On the fire's first anniversary, officials from Hamlet, white people, organized one memorial. On the other side of town, in a Black church, leaders in the Black community organized another. At the white memorial, they prayed for God to deliver the town and for the tragedy to pass. "They're not callous about it, but they want to see it as a way to bury the past and move on. Implicitly, there is a notion that you can do that, which suggested this was an anomaly," Simon says. "But for African Americans who are literally living near the plant that is still up with the yellow police tape around it, they understand that there is something much bigger going on here, and it is about their worth in this place."

In the Black church, on the other side of town, the prayers are not about an anomaly but an injury to their community, and not for it to pass but for political will to change it. Jesse Jackson is there, and he uses the Hamlet story to call for a renewed agenda of workplace safety, a revived labor movement, and a stronger social safety net.

It is the difference between saying this is a tragic anomaly and this is a tragic inevitability. If it was just an accident, if the dead are just chicken thieves or the factory owners are just greedy, it is far easier to ignore the conditions that drove the owners of that factory to set up shop in that place, far easier to mourn and move on.

Chalking this accident up to error was helped, too, by the fact that hardly anyone saw it. Imperial Foods was a small uninspected factory in a rural town, not a multistory building in New York City. And in accidents, this matters. The more people who see an accident, the more difficult it is to distract from how it happened. It is harder to hide dangerous conditions when everyone is watching, which is why, by the time millions of Americans owned a car, it was a lot more difficult for automakers to pretend that accidents only happened because of a few bad apples. They still pulled it off, but this time, instead of a covert campaign to villainize the pedestrian, the refusal to sacrifice profits to prevent accidents played out in plain sight.

Robert McNamara's Big Mistake

The accident-prone worker, the jaywalker, and the chicken thief are clever and malicious exaggerations of normal human mistakes. They attract attention by hyperbole and distract from dangerous conditions that would require the sacrifice of profits to correct. There is one more caricature to add to the cast: the nut behind the wheel.

This figure appeared as engineers discovered ways to make cars safer, and automakers knew those safety features would not come cheap. You don't hear the phrase "the nut behind the wheel" much anymore, but for decades, it stood as the de facto answer to the question of traffic accidents. This poem was published in the *Plain Dealer* in Cleveland in 1930:

> *Of all the auto parts*
> *That cause the accidents, we feel*
> *That what's to blame for most of them*
> *Is the nut behind the wheel.*

Blaming the nut behind the wheel was a favorite ploy of the National Council for Industrial Safety, the clearinghouse that printed safety posters for mine shafts and factory walls. It changed its name to the National Safety Council when it branched out into shaming human error in car accidents, too. As a cartoon driver in a fedora put it, on one of those posters, published in 1938, "It takes 1,500 nuts to hold an automobile together but only one to scatter it over the landscape."

In the 1950s, this trope drove Ralph Nader to start asking questions. He was in college and often hitchhiked up and down the East Coast.

Accidents were a regular roadside feature, and he noticed that the way that vehicles crumpled in a crash was not survivable—no matter the nature of the accident. Still, it was all blamed on the nut behind the wheel. But Nader suspected the vehicle itself was more at fault.

Those questions would ultimately lead to Nader's seminal book, *Unsafe at Any Speed: The Designed-In Dangers of the American Automobile*. The book laid out in unflinching terms the point that automakers knew how to make cars that prevented people from being hurt in accidents but did little to act on that knowledge. The nut-behind-the-wheel trope, Nader wrote, let automakers off the hook for making unsafe cars.

> *For decades the conventional explanation preferred by the traffic safety establishment and insinuated into laws, with the backing of the auto industry and its allies, was that most accidents are caused by wayward drivers who ipso facto cause most injuries and deaths. With the repetition of publicity themes about the "nut behind the wheel," industry and its captive safety councils bombarded public consciousness into believing that bad drivers were the cause and good drivers were the solution. Not only was their approach unscientific regarding drivers, but it conveniently drew attention away from the already available or easily realizable innovations that could be incorporated into vehicle and highway design to minimize the likelihood of a crash and to reduce the severity of injuries if a crash should occur.*

The "nut behind the wheel" was effective despite a mound of evidence that cars could be made safer by using seat belts, padded dashboards, and other innovations. According to Nader, the label even triumphed over efforts from inside the industry itself to make cars safer. He tells this story in an updated edition of his book, published a decade after the first.

In 1955, Robert McNamara, then an executive at Ford Motor Company, approved plans for a new ad campaign. He knew that his cars could not compete with the fresh-every-year aesthetics of the Chevrolet on the sales floor, so rather than compete, he offered a different product.

For the first time, Ford sold safety. The ad campaign touted a "Lifeguard package"—where drivers could pay extra for additional safety features built into the car.

Ford's Lifeguard package offered a seat belt, a recessed steering wheel less likely to impale the driver in a head-on accident, door latches that would not spring open and throw passengers onto the highway after an accident, a padded dashboard, and sun visors. He sent out bimonthly brochures to dealerships with real Ford and Chevy accident photos, complete with instructions to display the carnage side by side in showroom windows, where the Fords were always less worse for wear. The message was clear: when you got into an accident in a 1956 Ford, your injuries would be less severe than if you had been in a 1955 Ford or any car made by the competition. Human error does not matter, the marketing said, accidents happen, and Ford cars can keep you safer.

The car market in 1955 was not so different from the market as it is today—safety was less of a selling point than swift acceleration and good looks. Before Ford's campaign, whether or not you would survive an accident was rarely mentioned as a selling point for automobiles.

"At GM, cars were promoted as dreamboats in order to sell more cars," Nader wrote. "Ford was taking the romance out of cars, injecting collisions and casualties and other unpleasantness into the motorist's decision about which car to purchase."

This was a real threat to GM: McNamara was a rising star at Ford, and he seemed to genuinely care about safety. If he were allowed to continue, he could force his competitors to replace sexy cars with cars built and sold on sound engineering. So, halfway through the sales year, General Motors executives told their Ford executive friends—such as Ford's chairman of the board, who used to be GM's chief financial officer, and Ford's head of manufacturing, who used to be GM's head of manufacturing—to make McNamara kill the campaign.

"GM said stop and Ford literally screeched to a halt, with the aforementioned ex-GM Ford executives getting McNamara to switch gears to an advertising campaign that emphasized styling and performance rather than safety," wrote Nader. "McNamara came down with the flu and went to Florida for a long vacation; his career hung by a thread."

McNamara was forced to abandon the Lifeguard package halfway through the year. Ford told their ad agency to create a new campaign, free of safety messaging, at considerable expense. When McNamara returned from Florida, he fell in line, and the story that both GM and Ford told was that safety just doesn't sell. As the GM slogan went, "Ford sold safety while Chevy sold cars."

But that was not true. Between the first and second editions of his book, Nader dug up what he called a "little noticed press release" from 1956, which laid out how, because two of the safety features offered in the Lifeguard package were optional, it was possible to measure demand, and demand for the safety features was greater than any other optional feature Ford had ever offered. When Ford offered optional tinted glass in 1952, only 6 percent of customers ordered it. But in 1956, 43 percent of all Fords were ordered with safety padding, and one in seven Ford buyers requested seat belts. Even automatic transmission, a wildly popular feature, was only ordered by 23 percent of customers when Ford introduced it in 1951. People ordered so many seat belts that their supplier ran out; from 50 belts and buckles a month, Ford suddenly needed 1,000 a day. Ford estimated that the company would have sold 200,000 fewer cars that year without the safety campaign—a sales record—even with the company dropping it halfway through the year. When safety was a commodity, people bought it.

But all this was buried, evidence of cowardice among automobile executives who instead insisted that safety could not sell and that safety would not matter with a nut behind the wheel. If those executives had been brave, Nader writes, it might have spurred a market-driven leap forward in auto safety. Instead, ten years passed. Nader wrote a book, a surprise bestseller, laying out how carmakers failed to introduce improvements to their vehicles that they knew would reduce deaths and injuries. This included delaying the introduction of seat belts to avoid spending money, and retaining deadly design features, such as sharp and protruding instrument panels and steering columns that could not collapse, because they produced a better-looking car. Then, in 1966, Congress invited Nader to testify at a hearing on the federal government's potential role in traffic safety.

"A civilized society should want to protect even the nut behind the wheel from paying the ultimate penalty for a moment's carelessness, not to mention protecting the innocent people who get in his way," he told the committee. "These and other similar handy mottos are part of a self-serving ideology—there is no better word for it—of traffic safety strongly developed and perpetuated by the automobile industry in order to divert the public's gaze from the role of vehicle design."

Nader's work led to the first regulation of that industry, the creation of a federal department of transportation, and the regulatory wing that would eventually become the National Highway Traffic Safety Administration, which would mandate seat belts in all cars and the eventual introduction of airbags and antilock brakes, among a wealth of other safety requirements that put the onus for managing dangerous conditions on automakers.

But automakers did not go down without a fight. Around the time Nader's book came out, a decade after GM quashed McNamara's good idea, lobbyists succeeded in removing criminal penalties from motor vehicle safety laws, so no one could prosecute automakers for building unsafe cars. When federal officials proposed new safety standards for the 1968 models, Henry Ford II himself threatened to shut down his entire company. The safety proposals were "unreasonable, arbitrary, and technically unfeasible," he insisted. But those safety proposals included many protective devices that drivers already had the option to purchase, however briefly, with the Lifeguard package.

"We'll have to close down," Ford told reporters.

It could lead to "real trouble for this country," he threatened.

As with McNamara's Lifeguard package, when automakers finally acquiesced to safety, it came as an optional feature. It would take decades-long political fights to make seat belts and airbags mandatory, but in automakers' first offerings, a customer could pay extra for an airbag or a seat belt, so the rich were safe, and the rest died by accident. To see the absurd cruelty of this practice, it might help to imagine the corollary on an airplane: If you are seated in first class, you will find a life vest under your seat, which you should use in case of a water landing. Life vests are available to purchase in coach for an additional fee.

And this practice continues today. While driverless cars are a ways off, the RAND Corporation estimates that currently available autonomous technologies, such as emergency braking, adaptive cruise control, blind spot detection, alcohol sensor interlocks, and lane control, are so effective that an annual 17,000 people would survive accidents that today kill them, were every vehicle in the U.S. equipped.

These technologies are not mandated of automakers by regulation but are offered to the wealthy at a cost—so, if you can afford it, you can pay more to change the dangerous conditions inside your car and thus survive an accident. Otherwise you might die because you did not hit the brakes in time, in which case, the story of your accidental death will be that you should not have been driving like such a nut.

Chapter Two

Conditions

I almost died by accident when I was seven, playing Mother May I? near the edge of a cliff and then falling off the cliff—a true, dumb story. My mother said: *Take three ballerina steps forward.* And I asked: *Mother may I?* And then I did what she said, hands over head twirling, right over the low metal guardrail.

I dropped straight down ten or twelve feet onto wet pebbles right at the cliff's edge. As far as I remember, I blacked out on the way down, with a dim recollection of my mother screaming for my father as I fell. My next memory is of being cradled in my father's lap, in the back seat of our old Honda, his hand holding the wound on the back of my head, and my outfit—pink-and-white-striped culottes and a matching tank top with bows down the back—covered in blood. At the hospital, I received fourteen stitches for a minor head wound and a medical glove blown up, tied off, and decorated to look like a turkey.

My parents got some unnerving information. Had I landed two feet farther out from the cliff's edge, I would have struck a wooden walkway. Another two or three feet out from that, and I would have struck shallow water. Had I hit either of those less forgiving surfaces or weighed five pounds more than I did, I may have been brain-dead or just plain dead.

Hearing this story, you might have questions: How could we be so reckless? What was my mother thinking? Why did I not play somewhere else? These are questions of human error and personal responsibility. Psychologists call your desire to ask these questions—and especially to ask these questions about *other people's* accidents—the fundamental attribution error. There is significant evidence that the vast majority of people tend to see their own accidents as a product of the environment they were in at the time, and other people's accidents as a problem of human error and personal responsibility, even in the face of evidence to the contrary.

Now, should I have been playing Mother May I? next to a seaside cliff? Of course not. Should I have been better at ballerina twirls? Probably. You could call these errors, absolutely. Does noting these errors affect the dangerous conditions? Nope.

This book is almost exclusively focused on the built environment—our roads, homes, and workplaces—as this is where most accidents happen and where accidents are most preventable. But accidents also happen in natural environments—consider the rock climber who loses their grip, the hiker who gets lost and dehydrated, the surfer or skier who takes on a wave or hill beyond their skill level. I will largely leave these accidents aside, as they are both comparatively uncommon and significantly more complicated to prevent—the natural world is, in itself, out of our control, a dangerous condition. My cliffside with a scant guardrail is somewhere in between these two—an augmented natural environment, in this case augmented poorly.

However, no matter the environment, you can always find errors; like I said, I shouldn't have been doing ballerina twirls next to a cliff. You can find a person like me in most accidents—a person who made a mistake, who made a bad decision, or who somehow erred. Errors are present everywhere in this book, and if you are like most people, you are going to have the urge to steer toward these errors—asking questions of personal responsibility and noting the poor judgment you see in other people's behavior along the way. I warn you now: I will steer you away from this line of inquiry again and again.

This is not because I believe that poor judgment is absent from accidents or that personal responsibility has never saved a life. Rather, I will steer you away because this line of inquiry—blaming human error—is at best an inconsequential and largely ineffective answer to the accident problem. At worst, it actually sets the stage for the same accident to happen again. Of course I should not have been playing by the cliff, but talking about that will do nothing to prevent the next person from tumbling over. Fixing the guardrail will.

It may be poor judgment to ride a bike on an icy street, but in countries with far longer and more frigid winters than those in the United States, people bike year-round and are killed at a lower rate, because those countries have modified the built environment to prevent accidents. When a hiker gets lost or a climber falls, it is because they ceded their limited control in an environment largely out of their control. But outside the natural world, everything that causes accidents is in our control. Outside the hiker and the rock climber, we live in a built world, and for the rest of us, accidents are not about personal responsibility, they are about power.

From the Industrial Revolution onward, powerful corporate interests insisted that fallible people were the source of all accidents. This chapter is about the ones who proved them wrong. A better guardrail, for example, could have prevented my cliff fall entirely, but not my imperfect twirling. The severity of my injuries was not relative to my mistake but to what I collided with—by chance, I fell in the least sharp, hard place. Today we know that by controlling what we collide with and what collides with us, we can control whether we live or die.

Conscious Decoupling

Railroads were the site of one of the first nationwide data collection efforts on the accidental death of workers. After the federal government formed the Interstate Commerce Commission in 1887, it began to count casualties. One thing became quickly apparent: railroad work was exceedingly dangerous and the most dangerous job on the railroad was coupling cars. At the time, railroad workers used two chain links and a pin to connect train cars, and needed to stand between the moving cars in the train yard to join or separate them. For a decade in the late 1870s and early 1880s, close to 40 percent of all people injured or killed in rail-yard accidents came just from this act of connecting and disconnecting trains. Early statisticians counted 11,000 workers killed in coupling accidents in 1892 alone. Based on the newness of collecting accidental death data, the actual number is likely significantly higher. As a point of comparison, in 2019, around 5,000 workers died on the job—that's the total of every worker killed in every job across the United States.

These numbers were some of the first statistics collected on work-related accidents. When the death toll began to appear in newspapers, it shocked the public and members of Congress. Railroad worker unions had been pushing for safer working conditions for years, but it was these first counts of the official death toll that finally moved officials to act. Hearings began on railroad safety, and in 1893, Congress passed the Safety Appliance Act, requiring railroad companies to use automatic couplers—which allowed workers to connect or disconnect two railcars without standing between them—and air brakes on all trains.

Considering the power of railroads in America at the time, it may be surprising that the Safety Appliance Act ever got passed. Protests from powerful railroad magnates could have stopped the law in its tracks—as Henry Ford II did when seat belt regulations were first proposed. Or, as an editor at *Harper's* put it, "As long as brakes cost more than train-men, we may expect the present sacrificial method of car coupling to be continued."

Instead, this was a rare instance of profit margins and technology intersecting to enhance safety. Railroad officials did not acquiesce to the requirement for automatic couplers alone, but automatic couplers and another new invention that appeared right around the same time—the air brake.

The more cargo a train could move, the more money railroad

companies could make in a single run. The air brake allowed for even longer trains carrying even more cargo; air brakes had significantly more power to slow and stop a much heavier train. Railroad companies endorsed the legal requirement for automatic couplers because they put less slack between train cars, and with less slack, those longer, heavier trains stopped by air brakes were more stable. By the chance of concurrent innovations, the safer train was the more profitable train.

Before the Safety Appliance Act, the standard argument was that workers died by coupling and uncoupling cars because they were careless, drunk, or dumb. Changing working conditions disproved the argument. With the mandate for automatic couplers, the number of railroad work accidents fell dramatically. Between 1890 and 1909, coupling accidents fell by half. By 1902, just 2,000 died, down from 11,000—only 4 percent of railroad accidents came from car coupling, down from nearly 40 percent twenty years before.

Still, the automatic coupler only changed the perception of one type of accident, for one type of worker, in one industry—and that was only with a uniquely profit-driven argument for its requirement.

It would take a journalist and sociologist named Crystal Eastman to show America how prevalent and how alike accidents were across all industries—and what it would take to prevent them all. Her story begins in Pittsburgh mining country.

Crystal Eastman Counts the Dead

When work accidents in America first began to rise, evidence of their toll was anecdotal. And without hard data, only the best anecdotes stuck. These were stories of catastrophe, explosion, three hundred killed at once—not one miner who got electrocuted but an entire mine full of men that spectacularly exploded.

Mine explosions and fifty-car train derailments made headlines but hardly accounted for the majority of work-related deaths. Most workers died one at a time—while coupling cars or suffocating in a coal-mine cave-in. It was these accidents that added up. Crystal Eastman was the first person to back up this point with data. Between the summer of 1906 and the summer of 1907, she cataloged how workers died over the course of a year in Pittsburgh, Pennsylvania, and effectively debunked an idea that corporations had been pushing for decades—that careless workers caused work accidents. It was the first-ever sociological investigation into the accidental deaths of American laborers.

Eastman, then a twenty-five-year-old New Yorker, the daughter of two Protestant ministers, was standing in the morgue in Pittsburgh when she overheard a conversation between the coroner's deputy and a newspaper reporter. Their discussion—or the part of it that she could hear—was relevant to her investigation into how workers died in accidents, so she wrote it down:

REPORTER: - - - - - - - - - ?
CORONER'S DEPUTY: No, we haven't got anything for you today,
    Jim.—Well, hold on.—There's a man killed by a fall of slate out at
    Thom's Run. You don't want that, do you?
REPORTER: - - - - - - -.
CORONER'S DEPUTY: That's what I thought. No, there ain't anything
    else. So long.

The reporter finds nothing of interest because the morgue has no news of disasters or explosions, just another lone accidental death.

From the coroner, Eastman obtained the reports of workers' deaths in Allegheny County from July 1, 1906, to June 30, 1907. Of some 250,000 wage earners, 526 were killed in industrial accidents in the county that year. She also collected three months' worth of hospital records for the 509 injured in work accidents over three months of that year, 76 of which were life altering—an amputated hand, arm, or leg, a missing eye, a broken back. (She limited her count of injuries to three months because far too many occurred every day to record the total for a year.)

Eastman hired the photographer Lewis Hine, who would shoot

portraits of the dismembered and blinded workers and the orphaned families, along with an Italian investigator and a "Slavic" one. Some 1 million immigrants were arriving in the United States every year, and she needed investigators who spoke the languages that the population of the county spoke. (The Slavic investigator was also, helpfully, an engineer.) The four set out to find the full story behind those 526 deaths and 509 injuries. Eastman toured steel mills, railroad yards, and mines. She tracked down the injured and recorded their stories. She questioned workers who had seen others die, and sat down with the orphans and widows.

Allegheny County, which included the so-called Pittsburgh "Steel District," was meant to be a microcosmic sample. Eastman's idea was to look hard and thoroughly at this one county to understand better why so many Americans were dying in work accidents across the country. Her project began in a moment when no one was in charge of the work accident problem or had any sense of its scope. While mining and railroads had some government oversight, no one was talking about or looking at accidents as a whole. She wanted to understand how men and women died at work and what happened to families those workers left behind. The project was immense, and its effects still define how we talk about work accidents today.

"There is no bright side to this situation. By industrial accidents, Allegheny County loses more than 500 workmen every year of whom nearly half are American born,* 70 per cent are workmen of skill and training, and 60 per cent have not yet reached the prime of their working life. Youth, skill, strength,—in a word, human power,—is what we are

---

* Eastman writes, "Pittsburgh people generally have the idea that it is the foreign laborers, not Americans, who are killed and injured in such numbers every year," and thus not something to care about. She never expands on this anti-immigrant sentiment beyond what she does here, emphasizing U.S.-born work accident fatality rates to persuade her reader as to the severity of the problem. The corporations she would blame for the dangerous conditions that workers labored under used this same argument to dismiss these fatalities as accidents, arguing that workers were killed because they could not read English warning signs.

losing," she wrote, in the first chapter of *The Pittsburgh Survey.* "Is this loss a waste? This is a question which Pittsburgh and every industrial district must answer. If it is merely an inevitable loss in the course of industry, then it is something to grieve over and forget. If it is largely, or half, or partly unnecessary,—a waste of youth and skill and strength,— then it is something to fight about and not forget."

In December 1907, a few months after Eastman left Pittsburgh, the Monongah coal mine exploded not far away, in West Virginia. Of the 367 men and boys recorded as having gone to work that day, only 5 survived. For weeks the nation spoke of the accident with curiosity and awe, following in the newspapers the "gruesome details, street corner arguments about responsibility, schemes of relief for widows and orphans," as Eastman put it. It was still fresh news by the time she published her Pittsburgh findings. The attraction to the sensational, she thought, was part of the problem.

"Such catastrophes rouse the attention of the public by their magnitude," she wrote. "But suppose one man shoveling coal in some small 'room' far within a mine suddenly lies buried under a ton or two of slate—this causes no comment in a mining community. The sound of such stories is dulled to the ears of the public by monotonous repetition. Indeed, few of these common mining accidents reach the newspapers."

Massive disasters made for weeks of front-page headlines, but their sensation took up space that distracted from the true nature of the problem—which was that most workers who died did not die a hundred at once but by monotonous repetitions written off as accidents. The deaths of one year of Pittsburgh work accidents reiterated the point. Men died at work in ones and twos, day after day. Eastman wanted people to pay attention to these accidents that lacked the scale to spark the zeitgeist. What of the deaths that disappear? she asked.

"Most of the men in the community whose opinions count, have made up their minds about this accident question from what they have heard employers, superintendents, and casualty managers say. In other words, they believe that '95 percent of the accidents are due to the carelessness of the men.' Those emphatic, reiterated assertions, those tales of recklessness often repeated, have grown into a solid inert mass of opinion among business and professional men in the community, a heap of unreasoned conviction," she wrote.

Eastman's investigation proved those tales and assertions—that human error was the cause of accidents—to be wholly untrue. Workers did not bring about their own deaths but instead died at work under dangerous conditions, where they were forced to perform at a reckless pace, paid to work harder and move faster than was safe, without guard or net or railing. Of all the accidents Eastman tracked, she found the largest percentage could be attributed "solely to employers or those who represent them in positions of authority." In short, she wrote, to prevent accidents "the will of the employer is pre-eminently important." As she cataloged what caused the casualties she investigated, she documented, too, the "chief preventable conditions from which work accidents result." Failing to create a safe workplace was number one; requiring long hours on the job was number two; three was work made to happen at too great a speed. It was the first time anyone had ever demonstrated that the conditions faced by workers—and not their personal failings—were the cause of accidents at work.

Eastman's math was unassailable. But the true legacy of her Pittsburgh survey was less quantitative. In this moment, before workers' compensation laws were in place, Eastman created a new concern for the American worker by telling the story of accidents from the perspective of the victim's family—and with Hine's photos, painting a picture of what accidents cost. She explained the economic disaster left behind following nonfatal accidents: of the men who lost an eye by accident on the job, more than half were compensated $50 or less; half of the men who had been wholly and permanently disabled were paid nothing; $0 was offered to most of the men who lost fingers (two or more) or who lost an arm. She found that, to the families of more than half the married workers killed in a work accident, employers paid $100 or less, and of those, the employers paid 48 percent nothing at all. Even the $100 would cover only funeral expenses, nothing more. She drew attention to the mothers, who by Eastman's count bore the most tremendous burden of work accidents. When their breadwinner died, these sudden widows had no income and often many children, and soon after a work accident killed their spouses, they would lose their company housing, be forced to sell their furniture, and then have to figure out how not to starve in a world where all well-paying work was for men. The story would be the same for husbands too crippled to labor anymore—except, of course, in that case the injured would require the ongoing cost of care.

Eastman was a New Yorker, and in New York, a hub of American industry, the state legislature followed *The Pittsburgh Survey* with interest. Looking to replicate Eastman's model on a larger scale, they established a commission to recommend reforms and made her its secretary. The commission came back with much data and one major proposal: workers should no longer need to sue their employer to receive compensation for a work accident. Instead, the commission recommended, there should be a system of guaranteed recompense based on the scale of injury and the potential income lost. After a work accident, employers would be responsible for the wreckage left behind—medical bills, the economic livelihood of a family. It would mean that for employers, accidents would finally have a cost.

In 1910, the reforms took effect in New York. But the South Buffalo Railway Company, which was newly required to compensate employees for accidents on the job and also being sued by one of those employees for said compensation, appealed to the courts, claiming that workers' compensation was unconstitutional under the state constitution. On March 24, 1911, the New York Court of Appeals ruled in favor of the company, overturning the commission's reforms. The very next day, an accidental fire erupted inside the Triangle Shirtwaist Factory in Manhattan. Women jumped to their deaths in the middle of the nation's most populous city. For days, the unidentified charred bodies lay in public view. The Triangle fire was not just an accident of magnitude; it was an enormous accident watched firsthand in real time by America's elite and one whose aftermath played out at length in every American newspaper. Two months later, in Wisconsin, legislators would successfully pass the nation's first workers' compensation law, and nine other states would follow that year. New York State amended its constitution to again pass a workers' compensation law in 1913. Forty-two of forty-eight states would have the law by 1920. In 1925, the five holdouts were all southern states. Mississippi came last, in 1948.

By the end of the First World War, in most of the United States, when a worker had an accident, employers were legally required to provide compensation for medical care and lost work. For employers, this was a massive shift in their economic calculus. Work accidents once cost only as much as replacing a worker. Now the only way for an employer to reduce costs was to reduce accidents. The decline in work accidents was dramatic. Over the next two decades, deaths per hour worked would fall by two-thirds. At U.S. Steel, in the first decade of the 1900s, one in four workers suffered significant injuries every year. By the late 1930s, that number was one in three hundred.

Elsewhere, the accident story was not so rosy. On America's roads, no one had done what Crystal Eastman did for workers, debunking the idea that the careless caused accidents and assigning a cost to dangerous conditions. While the accidental deaths and injuries of workers generally declined from 1920 onward (with a 1960s exception that we will investigate later in this chapter), accidental death in general rose—driven by huge numbers of deaths of car drivers, passengers, and pedestrians. It didn't help that those car accidents occurred almost always in ones and twos—no mass disaster to push the government to act. Even if there had been mass road disasters to spur outrage, laws like workers' compensation did not translate. No one was accountable for the roads or the cars—so there was no way to make accidents more costly for anyone but their victims.

Forty years after Eastman published *The Pittsburgh Survey*, another cataloger of accidental death and injury would start to change all that.

Hugh DeHaven Falls Out of the Sky

In the fall of 1917, while thousands of American men were shipped overseas to join World War I, Hugh DeHaven, an American from Brooklyn, joined the Canadian Royal Flying Corps. (The U.S. Army declined to enlist him because his eyesight was poor, but Canada did not mind.) He traveled to Texas to learn to fly.

In a training session, DeHaven's plane collided with a second plane. Both planes fell five hundred feet. DeHaven's seat belt ripped open his abdomen and he ruptured his liver, pancreas, and gallbladder. The other pilot died. While he lay for six months in a hospital bed, waiting for his split organs to heal, the visitors to his bedside spoke of his miracle: *Man survives five-hundred-foot fall!* DeHaven was not so sure how miraculous his survival was. He replayed the day over and over in his head. Was it an accident? Was it fate? An act of God? Dumb luck?

On the other hand, maybe there was no such thing as accidents or luck. Out of the hospital, DeHaven examined the wreckage. He realized it was the sharp latch on his seat belt that caused his injuries and that his survival was thanks to being strapped to a cockpit that stood intact through the fall—the other plane's had disintegrated. His survival, he realized, meant that the human body, properly packaged, could withstand extreme deceleration. DeHaven spent the remainder of his tour on ambulance duty, picking up bodies after car accidents and airplane accidents. He found patterns among the injured and dead, not unlike the ones he discovered in his own survival. The people who crashed while nestled in a safe space were more likely to survive.

After the war, DeHaven took up two new hobbies. He collected newspaper clippings about other miracles—"Girl Falls 10 Stories, Lives and Tells of It," and so on—and he dropped eggs on his kitchen floor. Did you fling eggs across your high school physics classroom? You were copying his experiment. His thinking was that eggs were shipped all around the country. Millions of these fragile things rode trains and trucks, moved from boxes to shelves to carts, and largely remained intact. He wanted to know why a carton of eggs could survive an impact but a human head could not, so he climbed up on his countertop and started to drop his breakfast.

First, he dropped the eggs on a thick pad of foam rubber, then on a thinner pad, then on an even thinner pad. He eventually figured out that an egg would survive a hundred-foot fall if it landed on a three-inch-thick piece of rubber. The ten-foot fall from his kitchen counter required far less cushioning. It was not the fall that cracked the egg—it was the floor. The idea was a simple answer to the human error–dangerous conditions debate: Control how the egg hits the floor, and *it doesn't matter* if you accidentally drop it. It was all about packaging. A car could be a package. So could a plane, and an elevator, and a miner's helmet. A skull is a package for a brain.

From his newspaper clippings, DeHaven got the math to back up this observation. For each miraculous story of survival, he would debunk the miracle. He calculated the force of gravity of whoever fell out of a window, an airplane, or a hot-air balloon based on the distance they plummeted, the relative give of the surface where they crashed, and their weight. Among those miracles was Louis Zito, of Iselin, New Jersey, who slipped and fell 150 feet off a smokestack on Staten Island and went back to work two days later. Walter Cronkite interviewed Zito standing in the shadow of that fifteen-story-tall smokestack, as part of a CBS special on DeHaven's crash injury research laboratory at Cornell. In a bomber jacket, with a strong chin and a combed-back mop of hair, Zito looks like any unscathed young man of his era. The interview goes like this:

CRONKITE: *How does it feel to fall from that height?*
ZITO: *Well, I realized that there is nothing I could have done at the time. There was nothing to grab for or hold on to, so I figured my time was about up. I closed my eyes. I didn't want to see the ground come up.*
CRONKITE: *Do you feel that living through an experience like that was a miracle or how would you describe it?*
ZITO: *I think it was just plain luck.*

It was, of course, not luck. DeHaven determined that Zito hit the ground at around 60 miles per hour. The secret to his survival was that he fell not on solid concrete but rubble that absorbed and redistributed the energy of his velocity. (Remember when I fell off a cliff? Same thing. The difference between life and death was the give of the surfaces we hit.)

DeHaven found a woman who fell out a sixth-floor window and landed in a well-packed garden plot. She sat up on her elbow uninjured and mused to the building superintendent who ran over after her fall, "Six stories and not hurt." DeHaven found a woman who fell from the eighth floor and landed on a fence, which she partially broke, before falling to the ground. She walked herself to the hospital. Another woman fell from a tenth-story window and landed in freshly hoed soil. She fractured a rib and a wrist and then tried to get up, but no one would let her.

In the journal *War Medicine*, DeHaven published his findings. He also pointed out that impact, in plane accidents, is a two-step process. When his plane crashed, he remained strapped to the cockpit, but the other pilot suffered two sets of injuries, first from the plane crashing to the ground, second from his body crashing into the plane. This second impact, DeHaven determined, was the real killer—and the environment of that impact, which he called the "second collision," was much more significant to injury than cause or velocity. He calculated that the human body could withstand massive deceleration—two hundred times the force of gravity. The plane crashing into the ground did not injure DeHaven, because he was wearing a lap belt. It was the secondary impact, when his organs mashed against the belt's latch, that left him hurt.

DeHaven discovered that he survived a great fall because a lap belt strapped him down to an intact falling object. His "miracle" subjects survived because the places they landed gave way—absorbing some of the impact of the fall. He proved that you could protect a person inside a falling machine if you packaged them properly. Because of DeHaven's findings, the Air Force began to build airplanes not just to fly well but to crash well, too.

Two world wars later, DeHaven witnessed a gruesome car crash that pushed his research further. Just as he had ruptured his organs on a seat belt latch, the driver in the crash nearly died when a dashboard knob pierced his head. Fascinated by what seemed like clear causality, DeHaven began to apply his findings about falling airplanes to moving cars. He found like-minded officials at the Indiana State Police and convinced the force to take him in for a year, sharing photos of traffic accidents and coroners' reports like Crystal Eastman before him. By the end of 1953, DeHaven had compiled a list of the most dangerous parts in any automobile. The killers were pointed knobs, dashboards without padding, steering columns that could not collapse on impact—and the lack of seat belts to prevent people from smashing into all of that. His list was proof that accidents were in our control, regardless of the nut behind the wheel. All that mattered was how automakers built the cars.

DeHaven designed the three-point seat belt—the first one that held driver and passengers across the lap and chest—and received a patent for it. He invited automakers to a conference to present his findings. He detailed how they could build an instrument panel without sharp edges and showed them how to create a steering column that collapsed on impact.

DeHaven's conference took place in 1953, but it was not until 1967, under the public pressure that Ralph Nader wielded, that automakers implemented the collapsible steering column. Over half a million people died in traffic accidents in the years between. Scientists making their most conservative estimates say that over eighty thousand people have since survived traffic accidents explicitly because of a collapsible steering column. What happened in the fourteen-year gap was not an accident. If you died impaled on a steering column after 1953, when DeHaven laid it all on the table, but before 1967, when carmakers were forced to finally do something about it, you died because it was cheaper and easier to let you die than to help you live.

The accident-prone worker is a myth and the nut behind the wheel a clever distraction from the true cause of accidental death and injury— and we miss a wealth of information that could prevent accidents when we pay any attention to these caricatures of personal responsibility.

Eastman and DeHaven mined the relevant information, found common causes across accidents of wildly different types, and discovered how to prevent them by controlling the built environment. In a 1960s rise in work accidents, we see a potent example of what happens without this intervention, when the people who suffer accidents gain, and then lose, control of the dangerous world around them.

There Is Power in a Union

Workplace accidents first declined when accidents began to cost employers money, because then, for a corporation, making the workplace safe was cheaper than paying for accidents. From the 1920s to today, thanks to workers' compensation and safety laws, and the widespread unionization that helped enforce them, the likelihood of accidentally dying on the job decreased. However, accidental injury did not follow the same downward trajectory. Rather, worker injuries fell from World War II to the late 1950s, and then rose by equal measure until 1970. This rise brought the passage of the Occupational Safety and Health Act—the first nationwide federal regulation of workplaces to mandate and enforce safe working conditions. Regulators defined what was and was not a safe environment for workers, inspected workplaces, and issued penalties for noncompliance, but the rise in accidental injury that came before the U.S. government set those rules in motion resulted from workers losing control of dangerous conditions. Work accidents rose again after the 1950s due to a shift in the power of unions.

It wasn't workers' compensation laws alone that brought about that first decline in workplace accidents following the 1920s but an era of massive strikes where workers semi-regularly ground the economy to a halt for their own protection. The number of unionized workers rose massively from 1935 to the 1950s as the work accident rate declined. Accidents didn't just cost employers; workers had the means to ensure their own safety.

Here's how it worked: Before the 1960s, the safety of any worker could be negotiated on the factory floor between foremen, who represented the company, and shop stewards, who represented the union members. If you were a worker whose job felt unsafe, you could tell your shop steward, and your shop steward would negotiate with your foreman to add safety to your workstation or slow down the production line. Backed by the union, the shop steward had power, and the prospect of work stoppages or slowdowns gave foremen the incentive to negotiate. This was how things worked for decades, until an economic downturn in the 1950s, when companies began to insist that these small, local negotiations about specific safety issues cease.

Where workers had managed assembly line procedures before, they were now subject to formal "productivity enhancement" and "waste reduction" protocols. They weren't just working harder now; they had less say in the best way to work. Employers began to speed up production and spend less on safety. The opportunity to question these decisions came only once a year, during collective bargaining negotiations, instead of in real time. Before, any threat to one worker's safety could have been cause for a strike; now it was something to negotiate in next year's contract.

This shift, a loss of control over workplace conditions, coincides precisely with the rising accidental injury rate of workers. The shift also made the debate over whether accidents were caused by dangerous conditions or worker error into a fight about communications and control. Denied the power to communicate individual hazards, workers could no longer tell their stories before accidents happened—and in time to prevent future ones. It was a loss of control that resulted in more of the accidents that came in ones and twos—the little deaths no one notices until someone like Crystal Eastman or Hugh DeHaven gathers them up.

But the results are the same when accidents are big and catastrophic, too. You can always point out a danger in the built environment, even a jumbo-sized danger, but an accident will be the predictable result if no one listens to you.

Investing in Plane-Crash Futures

On June 12, 1972, the cargo door blew off an American Airlines DC-10—a recently introduced jumbo jet—somewhere high over Ontario. It was lucky that they hadn't flown too far from Detroit. It was also lucky that one of the pilots, Captain Bryce McCormick, had spent hours in a flight simulator learning his way around the new jet. He righted the plane. The plummet stopped. Every passenger survived the emergency landing of American Airlines Flight 96. The landing was a triumph of coincidences, the fact that Captain McCormick had put in voluntary hours in the flight simulator and a miraculously clear runway in Detroit among them.

But according to an airplane engineer named F. D. Applegate, what necessitated the emergency landing was no coincidence or miracle. It was a warning.

The plane that blew its cargo door was built by McDonnell Douglas, but a subcontractor, General Dynamics, built the door latch, and F. D. Applegate was the director of product engineering for General Dynamics. Fifteen days after Captain McCormick barely put a broken DC-10 back on the ground, Applegate wrote a two-and-a-half-page memo to his supervisor, J. B. Hurt, project chief for the subcontract between General Dynamics and McDonnell Douglas.

"'Murphy's Law' being what it is, cargo doors will come open sometime during the twenty years of use ahead for the DC-10," Applegate wrote. "I would expect this to usually result in the loss of the airplane."

Applegate recommended grounding all DC-10 aircraft until engineers at McDonnell Douglas and General Dynamics could redesign and rebuild every plane. Before signing his name, he laid his threat plain, person for person, dollar for dollar.

"This corrective action becomes more expensive every day as production continues. However it may well be less than the cost of damages resulting from the loss of one planeload of people," he wrote.

Hurt declined Applegate's suggestion on two counts. One, grounding the planes would put the blame on them, an admission to McDonnell Douglass that General Dynamics' design was faulty. And two, any conversation about a malfunction would muddle the negotiation the two companies were having about liability.

Two years later, in 1974, the cargo door on Turkish Airlines Flight 981 failed mid-flight out of Paris. The plane was another DC-10. All 346 people on board died. It was the heaviest death toll of any plane crash to date.

Applegate had predicted this exactly. He had even titled his memo "DC-10 Future Accident Liability."

Just as with cars and industrial work before them, the introduction of jumbo jets—larger in size than previous aircraft and more complex to operate—propelled the airline industry into a new realm of both accident risk and profit. A single plane, seating far more people, could net a much larger sum with every flight. And a single mistake at any stage of the process, from the drawing board to the assembly line to the cockpit, could produce massive loss of life. These factors grew in tandem. The jumbo jet, more complicated to fly and to build than earlier generations of aircraft, multiplied the dangerous conditions that could lead to an accident and in turn multiplied the number of people who would die when Murphy's Law inevitably kicked in.

Chapter Three

Scale

A dvances in technology can create built environments that are larger in scale and more complex in operation. The accidents that happen in these environments tend to grow to match. The Triangle Shirtwaist Factory fire was one of the worst accidents in its day; it destroyed one building and killed 146 workers. The explosion of the Monongah mine in 1907—known as the worst mining disaster in U.S. history—killed more than 300. The Chernobyl nuclear power plant meltdown occurred seventy-nine years later, bringing an almost unimaginable increase in the scope of destruction. The range of radioactive contamination includes 40 percent of Europe and parts of Asia, Africa, and North America. Researchers estimate that 41,000 people will develop cancer related to the accident by 2065; it will kill more than a third of them, some 16,000 dead. When we talk about large-scale accidents today, we mean mass death and destruction—commercial plane accidents, oil spills, nuclear accidents—ecosystems decimated and hundreds or thousands dead in one fell swoop. These aren't just accidents but accidental disasters.

Arnold Gundersen, whom everyone calls Arnie, is an expert in the most enormous of all these, the nuclear accident. He worked as a nuclear reactor operator, nuclear engineer, and manager coordinating projects at some seventy U.S. nuclear power plants for decades. That all changed in 1990. Arnie was a senior vice president at Nuclear Energy Services when he came across radioactive material, unguarded and misplaced, that someone had shoved in a safe in the company's accounting department. He blew the whistle, reporting the risk of accidental radioactive exposure up the chain, and the company fired him three weeks later. Gundersen would leave the industry, and with his wife, Maggie, a nuclear power communications specialist, dedicate his life to educating the public about the threat and scale of nuclear power.

"It's not just nuclear. It's the Deepwater Horizon. It's any of these high-technology systems that we take for granted. When they go wrong, they really go wrong big-time," Gundersen tells me. "Sooner or later, in any foolproof system, the fools are going to exceed the proofs. It's inevitable as you build more proofs into the system—it delays, but cannot prevent, an ultimate catastrophe."

Accidents in America come in two sizes, relative to likelihood. Most are small and frequent—a drug overdose, a traffic crash. Some are big and rare—an oil spill, a plane crash. Crystal Eastman's message from Pittsburgh was that the minor accidents, being unsensational, were ignored and thus added up to a massive toll. Whereas the sizable and infrequent accidents are not so easily forgotten—not in Eastman's day, when an accident such as the Triangle fire dominated headlines for weeks, and not today. For example, in 2020, small and frequent car accidents are estimated to have killed more than 42,000 people. Still, few were news outside the occasional drunk celebrity or the rare sensation, such as the bus that drove halfway off a ramp in the Bronx and dangled there until the next day. But in 2018 and 2019, when two Boeing 737 Max aircraft crashed—each a big, rare accident—they generated months of news stories, a series of public hearings, and multiple investigations into the regulatory system that allowed the malfunctioning planes to fly. Those two crashes combined killed only 0.8 percent as many people as died in one year of car accidents.

However, since Eastman's day, the scale of the big, rare accidents has also grown in a more technologically complex world. The oil spills and nuclear meltdowns of today are so massive that, even under the public spotlight they attract, the amount of destruction they cause remains hard to measure and ripe for manipulation.

The Near Loss of Harrisburg, Pennsylvania

Maggie and Arnie Gundersen are both on the phone when I ask about the likelihood of a nuclear accident today. Maggie cuts me off.

"You mean of nuclear meltdown or disaster or catastrophe?" she corrects me.

Arnie tells me his wife does not like the word "accident," and that he tries not to use it. When he gives a presentation, he asks the audience to make a buzzer sound whenever he says "accident." But in the work they left behind, the word is still revered.

"The industry, and by industry I do not just mean the nuclear industry—oil and gas, and some chemical industries, all use the term 'accident,' because that gives them a path: *Oh, it was an accident; we couldn't help it*," Maggie says.

And they can definitely help it. "At Fukushima," Arnie explains, "there were warnings for decades that a forty-five- or fifty-foot tsunami could hit the coast, but they built a fifteen-foot wall because building a higher wall costs a boatload of money. The same thing with the Deepwater Horizon—they knew that the shut-off valve was not working, but they didn't want to spend the money to do it right. When you're looking at large accidents, it's a matter of management. In their minds, they discount the probability of failure and focus on the short-term gain."

Two factors increase the risk of a nuclear accident today. One is that aging plants are malfunctioning more often. The other is that the renewable energy and natural gas industries are booming, putting financial pressure on the nuclear industry and leaving less money to keep those aging plants in good repair. The likelihood of a disaster is higher now than it has been for twenty years, Arnie tells me, and he suspects that the stakes will keep ratcheting up until the worst occurs.

Maggie and Arnie have sounded the alarm on this risk for decades. But in the beginning, when they met, both were working in the nuclear industry, believing wholeheartedly that atomic power was the safest use of the atom. Their beliefs would start to waver the year they went on their first date, in 1978, a year before Three Mile Island experienced a partial meltdown. At the time, Arnie worked for a different nuclear power company, where he was in charge of buying a reactor. He looked at one designed by a company called Babcock & Wilcox. He recognized that it met all the regulatory criteria but that it was also fragile, in ways he understood as a nuclear engineer. He passed on buying it. But at Three Mile Island, a Babcock & Wilcox reactor was already running.

A year later, on March 28, 1979, at 4:00 a.m., the Three Mile Island nuclear power plant shut down. This was normal—a designed-in safety measure that indicated something was wrong. Shutting down stopped more atoms from splitting, but unlike turning off a hair dryer or the gas on a stove, turning off a nuclear reactor doesn't eliminate all the heat and radioactivity generated. The reactor still needed to be cooled down.

Then other things went wrong. For example, like most nuclear reactors, the Three Mile Island plant contained a system to pump water to keep the plant cool—the auxiliary feedwater system. That system failed. Nothing was cooling the reactor.

Temperatures went up, pressures went up, and a relief valve opened—letting out steam like the jangly bit on top of a pressure cooker. Except this pressure cooker was venting radioactive steam. And that relief valve got stuck open. And the mechanism meant to report a stuck-open relief valve to the plant's operators failed. No one knew that the valve was stuck.

How did no one know that a valve was open and releasing radioactive steam for hours? In the control room, the switch indicating the status of the valve was marked red and green. Since the valve was almost always closed, green should have meant closed—safe, normal, all is well—as with traffic lights, where green means proceed and red means halt. But the designers of this nuclear reactor had chosen green to mean open. So when the operators looked at the valve indicator light, in the pressure of the moment, with alarms going off on all sides, they saw green and thought it was closed, working correctly, and that they could proceed without caution.

At this point, there were three related problems: The reactor could not cool down, the plant was blowing radioactive steam out its relief valve, and the plant operators did not know about the open valve. Radiation leaked for hours, starting at 4:00 a.m. By 7:00 a.m., radiation levels were lethal inside the reactor containment building. A meltdown was underway. At 9:00, the plant operators finally got water pumping in. But by 1:00 p.m., hydrogen that had built up inside the reactor exploded, cracking the concrete wall of the reactor containment building and expelling a massive amount of radiation. The explosion changed the equation—the difference between exposure to a small radiation leak and a huge radiation dose can be the difference between life and death. Still, at 2:00, the plant owner told the governor of Pennsylvania that everything was under control and that there was no reason to worry.

Arnie would meet the governor thirty-five years later, when both were keynote speakers at Pennsylvania State University's commemoration of the accident. The day of the commemoration, Arnie told the governor that he had been lied to all those years ago and the governor acknowledged it—yes, he had been lied to. Then, Arnie asked him a critical question: "Knowing what you know now about how close you were to essentially losing Harrisburg, would you have called an evacuation?" The governor's response had not changed in those three decades. He would not have evacuated, he told Arnie, because that is not the type of person he is. "Even now, as we talked about this low-probability, high-risk situation—he was down to one last line of defense. Out of six, five of the six had failed, one was left—and even now he would still not evacuate."

What the governor meant, I think, was that he was no Chicken Little. Three Mile Island was a large and unlikely accident—many individual things went wrong, adding up to a meltdown—and for the governor, *unlikely* mattered more than *large*. He did not feel at risk, so he decided that the city was not at risk.

Focusing on the unlikelihood of an accident, especially when mass destruction could result, is common. A lot had to go wrong for the meltdown at Three Mile Island to occur, and the rarity of large-scale accidental disasters is deceptively reassuring. But around the time of this meltdown, there was a then-unprecedented confluence of large-scale accidents. Those disasters inspired a few pioneers in the fields of sociology and organizational psychology to ask why, when these big accidents happened, we thought the likelihood mattered so much. When Arnie talked about the governor being down to his last line of defense, he was referencing the theory of one of those pioneers—a psychologist named James Reason who developed a new way to understand large-scale accidents called the Swiss cheese model.

Shot Full of Holes

Imagine a stack of Swiss cheese. The cheese is full of holes, right? But the holes are unique to each slice, so those holes rarely line up when you stack slices on top of one another. This stack of cheese was James Reason's analogy for how, in complex technologies, large-scale accidents occur. For example, in a nuclear power plant, each safety system is a slice of Swiss cheese. An alarm is a slice, a cooling system is a slice, and each indicator light is a slice, too. A well-trained operator is a slice of cheese, and so is their boss, who listens when the operator warns of danger, and their union, which makes the boss listen. The holes in all the slices rarely align, but when they do, catastrophe results.

One hole in one slice won't bring down the whole house. Ideally, in a safe system, disaster will be prevented by the other slices. When a failure slips through a hole in one slice, the malfunction should smack firmly into the next slice, halting the progress of disaster. Today, we build the most technologically complex parts of our built environment so that if one system fails, it doesn't cause all other systems to fail—a faulty indicator light will not by itself cause a nuclear meltdown. But in Reason's model, accidents happen when all the holes, by chance, line up—the failures cascade, and the nuclear power plant melts down. Safety systems fail individually and in failure are discovered to be connected in unpredictable and surprising ways. Reason called this alignment "a trajectory of accident opportunity."

For example, the most straightforward story of what went wrong at Three Mile Island might be about red and green lights. But you could see the meltdown as beginning far earlier, with the purchase of a fragile nuclear reactor, as Arnie recognized the Babcock & Wilcox reactor to be, or the training of the person who made that purchase. In Reason's model, the Three Mile Island meltdown occurred for two reasons: First, multiple things went wrong, and second, those various things interacted in unexpected ways. The designers of a nuclear power plant would consider the cooling system, the relief valve, and the control room indicator lights each a layer of safety if functioning correctly. And at Three Mile Island, each protective layer failed in a way that affected all the others.

This model applies to every large-scale accident, even accidents far less complex, such as the Triangle Shirtwaist Factory. The story says the fire began when a cigarette set some rags alight. But the outcome, all those women jumping to their deaths, could be traced back to layers of safety failures from piles of scrap fabric filling the floors, to the locked doors, to a lack of laws mandating that those doors be unlocked. Before the fire, no one would have suspected that the anti-theft policy of the Triangle Shirtwaist Company had anything to do with the cleanliness of floors—and this was, in part, Reason's point. The Swiss cheese model is not just about systems failing but also about the weird links among those systems that produce catastrophe—a wealth of surprisingly interconnected dangerous conditions.

The role of human error in all this, Reason wrote, is "that of adding the final garnish to a lethal brew whose ingredients have already been long in the cooking." The worker who supposedly dropped the cigarette at the Triangle Factory, or the nuclear engineer mistaking the meaning of a green light on the control board at Three Mile Island, are not instigators of accidents. Instead, they are "the inheritors of system defects created by poor design, incorrect installation, faulty maintenance and bad management decisions."

The Swiss cheese model is a method for understanding accidents and also preventing them. What we do after an accident dictates whether the same accident will happen again. The sinking of the *Titanic* and what happened afterward provide an apt example.

The most basic story of that tragedy goes like this: People died when the *Titanic* sank because there were not enough lifeboats (and Rose would not share her door with Jack). After the sinking, in 1914, the International Convention for the Safety of Life at Sea offered a simple solution that responded to this most basic story. Big ships were required to have enough lifeboats for every butt on board. Of course, the reasons people died on the *Titanic* are not simple but layered: not enough lifeboats, a ship so large that it was unstable, problematic navigation, Rose not sharing her door, etc. As each failure passed through hole after hole, the failures interacted in surprising ways.

Evidence of the problem with applying a simple solution to complex accidents arrived three years later, when a tour boat called the *Eastland* prepared to leave port in the Chicago River, with 2,500 people on board and plenty of lifeboats. On the morning of departure, most of the passengers were on one side of the ship, waving farewell to those on shore, as one did at the time—and that happened to be the same side where the ship's designers had located all the new lifeboats. As a result, one side of the boat weighed too heavily toward the river, and the *Eastland* capsized in port. Some 840 people died, primarily immigrants in heavy clothes who could not swim, shocked by the freezing water.

Seeing the *Titanic's* demise as the result of a single failure—one hole in one slice of cheese—actually caused more fatal accidents. Similar to nuclear reactors, giant ships are complex systems. To understand why complex systems fail, we need to track backward through systems that should have kept people safe—lifeboats, hull strength, navigational procedures, sharing doors as flotation devices—and see how the failures interacted to lead to a catastrophe.

Reason was using a stack of Swiss cheese to explain what is known as a complex system accident. A sociologist named Charles Perrow first conceived this concept—that accidents were not chance mishaps but systemic inevitabilities—as the dust settled on Three Mile Island. Ten years before James Reason pitched his Swiss cheese analogy, Perrow investigated the organizational issues that had led to the meltdown. While the commission formed by President Carter to investigate the accident chalked it up to "operator error," Perrow's analysis would birth a new understanding of the accidental by rejecting the idea that a single human error could cause a large-scale accident.

Accidents Happen

The 1970s saw an epidemic of large-scale accidents. More major oil spills occurred in the 1970s than in any decade before or since. In 1972, fatal airline accidents hit a twenty-year high, and in 1977, two 747s crashed into each other—the worst airplane accident in history. Before Charles Perrow investigated Three Mile Island, the story of these accidents was all about human error, acts of God, and pure randomness. Each was tracked back to the last person involved—the pilot who pulled the wrong lever or the nuclear plant operator who failed to notice a warning light—and that was the end of the story.

In analyzing Three Mile Island, Perrow wished to avoid this oversimplification. What went wrong at the nuclear facility was not a problem of human error, he concluded, but of the complex interactions of dangerous conditions and fragile safety systems. From his analysis of Three Mile Island, he developed a framework for understanding large-scale accidents called Normal Accident Theory. It said, in short, that accidents were inevitable in systems of a certain complexity.

Perrow defined complexity in terms of coupling. In a "tightly coupled" system, it is hard to separate one failure from the next. In a "loosely coupled" system, this is easier. A factory, for example, is a loosely coupled system—if rags catch fire, and you put out the fire, disaster is averted. A nuclear reactor would be a tightly coupled system; its workings are so hidden and complex that one mistake is likely to trigger another unanticipated error. The more complex and tightly coupled the system, the more likely that one problem would connect to another problem in a surprising way that may result in catastrophe.

After his Three Mile Island investigation, Perrow would look into major accidents in petrochemical plants, hydroelectricity, and oil transport. He found patterns and published a book about them all, *Normal Accidents: Living with High-Risk Technologies*—applying his theory about Three Mile Island to large-scale accidental disasters of all stripes. It held every time. There was a connection between chemical plants, dams, big ships, and airplanes—a complexity of interactions that made accidents inevitable, or "normal," as Perrow put it. No single human error was to blame for a large-scale accident. To meet growing needs for goods, transportation, technology, and energy, we build systems so complex that accidents must be expected. All these accidents were born of systemic conditions. Since Crystal Eastman went to Pittsburgh, no one in the United States had so comprehensively demonstrated that so many very different types of accidents were in fact rather alike.

Perrow's book was published in 1984, the same year Union Carbide (today a subsidiary of the Dow Chemical Company) accidentally leaked gas from pesticide production into Bhopal, India, poisoning half a million people, two years before the Chernobyl nuclear reactor meltdown and the *Challenger* space shuttle explosion, and five years before the *Exxon Valdez* ran aground in Prince William Sound. These accidents were bigger and badder than anything the world had seen before by an order of magnitude—but still, they were relatively rare. Even in this era of accidental disasters, the worst was occurring just once or twice a year.

This rarity can dilute our perception of the severity of a large-scale accident—when in reality these accidents are very, very severe.

What We Mean When We Say Large

Nuclear meltdowns are uncommon, but the outcomes are outsize and earthshaking—one is enough to produce widespread death and destruction. But those outcomes are dispersed over hundreds of miles and trickle out over decades, so the scope of the damage is difficult to perceive.

Take Three Mile Island, which was a partial meltdown. Engineers eventually halted the meltdown—no harm, no foul, right? The official narrative, for eighteen years after the accident, was that no one died.

This, Arnie Gundersen says, is a myth: In the six years after the meltdown, the cancer rate doubled in the Susquehanna River Valley. And the outcome of accidents of this magnitude is more than death and injury. Cleaning up Three Mile Island began in 1979 and did not conclude until 1993. Property damages cost an estimated $2.4 billion.

Arnie tells me about the day of the meltdown; a calm, windless afternoon. The moderate weather trapped all the radiation in the valley—the stuff that leaked out for hours and the stuff that blew out all at once when the reactor containment shell cracked. No one died immediately from the events of that day, but in time, people would die. He points me to the work of the late Dr. Steve Wing. In 1997, Wing, an epidemiologist at the University of North Carolina, reevaluated previous studies of cancer incidence surrounding Three Mile Island. He found that the radiation dose received from proximity to the accident was significantly associated with increased cancer rates—leukemia most of all. Another study two decades later found significantly higher levels of a type of thyroid cancer caused explicitly by radiation exposure among people near the plant when it melted down. The nuclear industry denies this research.

"Not to say that there weren't any radioactive releases during the accident, but they were at such a low level that they would not be expected to have any sort of ill health effects," Neil Sheehan, a spokesperson for the Nuclear Regulatory Commission, said in 2019. He was responding to new reports that Pennsylvania had some of the highest thyroid cancer rates in the country.

Of course, we are all limited in what we know because Three Mile Island was the world's first large-scale nuclear reactor meltdown. But when the Fukushima Daiichi nuclear power plant melted down in 2011, scientists were primed to track the outcome of such an accident, and what happened there can tell us a lot about what happened at Three Mile Island and what could happen again at reactor sites all over the country.

One year after Fukushima melted down, Arnie went to Tokyo. While he was there, he collected five samples, digging dirt from random sidewalk cracks. Back in the states, he measured the radioactivity. Every sample he took would be classified as radioactive waste in the United States—and this was in Tokyo, more than 150 miles from the source, almost 50 miles farther than Three Mile Island stood from Washington, DC.

I ask Arnie what would have happened if someone hadn't shut down Three Mile Island—if the meltdown had been complete, as in Fukushima. He says, "You're in a situation where you'd have to declare Washington, DC, a nuclear waste dump from the radioactive particles that rain down on the city."

Arnie applied Wing's math from Three Mile Island to Fukushima. His results point to an estimated 100,000 fatal cancers in the first generation, not including those caught and cured, not including the mutagenic effects on later generations, the noncancerous heart diseases and lung diseases. It could have happened here. But of course death by disease is not often counted as an outcome of accidents. Arnie notes that the nuclear industry counts on this epidemiological murkiness—how deaths spread out over a total population and a few decades are difficult to trace.

These consequences add up in ways that are difficult to comprehend: the shuttering of whole cities, mass death, but also the quiet creeping death from diseases ten or twenty years down the line. When oil spills, the outcomes can be just as incomprehensibly large and long-lasting. The *Exxon Valdez* dumped 11 million gallons of crude oil into the Gulf of Alaska when it ran aground in 1989. Researchers estimated the death toll to be at least 2,800 sea otters, 300 seals, 250 bald eagles, 22 killer whales, and 250,000 seabirds, along with billions of salmon and herring eggs. But the effects of the accident have lasted far longer and are far more wide-reaching. It took until 2014, for example, a full quarter century, for the otter population to recover.

The *Exxon Valdez* was the largest oil spill on record, until twenty-one years later. When the Deepwater Horizon drilling platform exploded and sank, at least 134 million gallons of oil poured into the Gulf of Mexico. Researchers estimate the death toll at between 300,000 and 2 million birds from at least 102 species, close to 26,000 sea mammals, and a number of fish and crustaceans that is too large to estimate. An estimated more than 320,000 sea turtles are thought to have swum through the spill. People reported finding oiled birds from Texas to Florida. Four years later, dolphins and turtles were still dying in record numbers. In 2019, nine years after the spill, dolphins began to wash ashore, covered in lesions, part of another die-out. Researchers are concerned that this recent die-out is actually just a continuation of the same dolphin die-out, making another new record.

"We have reduced the frequency, but we have increased the consequences," Arnie points out. "That seems to be what happens with these high-risk endeavors, like space shuttles and oil rigs. They're farther apart but the consequences become more severe."

We are solving problems over time in all the stacked safety systems that make up our most complicated technologies—better training, better control room designs, all of it. But all those layers of safety are being added less quickly than our energy demands are growing. While we invent individual survival mechanisms for extremely unlikely accidents—such as a life vest that can fit under the seat on an airplane— we still accept potential group risk so significant that mere exposure is not survivable. We do this, allowing for accidental horrors that are both massive and inevitable, in part because our moods and emotions distort our perception, and we cannot grasp what "likely" really means.

The Likelihood of an Accident

Even if we understood scale and likelihood in these giant accidents, we might ignore it. David DeSteno, a professor of psychology at Northeastern University who studies how emotions guide decision-making, explains that in a large-scale accident, the sheer magnitude of shock and horror can make us subconsciously repress thinking about it. This is called empathy fatigue.

"As the magnitude of the tragedy of an event goes up, the level of compassion people express for it doesn't track," DeSteno tells me. "What's happening is people begin to feel overwhelmed by the size of the tragedy, and they want to turn away. They want to ignore it."

But even if we had a handle on scale, and withstood its overwhelming nature enough not to look away, we would still struggle to understand the likelihood of an accident.

When we lack the information to explain a complex accident, DeSteno explains, our brains estimate based on what we do know. And without clear memory or factual information, we lean on feeling. This is evolutionary—if you learn to fear when you see a tiger, you are less likely to be killed by a tiger. Emotions shape predictions about what comes next in hopes of steering us toward survival. But the rarity of large-scale accidents means that we likely will not have a memory to cite, and our predictions will veer off course.

Studies of how predicting likelihood can go wrong began in 1983, with the work of a psychologist at Carnegie Mellon University and another at Stanford. The pair conducted an experiment to test whether our feelings affect how accurately we estimate the likelihood of an accident. In the study, 557 subjects read newspaper reports of various accidents. Later the psychologists asked the subjects to estimate how likely it was that other specific accidents would happen to them and how often those accidents occurred in the world at large. If the subject read a story of a fatal accident, they were more likely to think that the accident would happen to them—and to other people. Reading the story of that one fatal accident also increased the subject's estimation of how likely it was that they would be involved in a number of other kinds of accidents the psychologists prompted them with. The inverse was also true, and this is important. Reading about an accident that turned out all right made the study subjects predict that all accidents were less likely to occur. The psychologists could use the outcome of one accident to affect their subject's perception of the likelihood of another. Manipulation of our mood affects our judgment about likelihood. When you feel sad, DeSteno tells me, you are more likely to think that whatever comes next will be bad. The opposite is true as well.

Large-scale accidents are roundly awful, so according to these studies, once we live through one, it should convince us that the sky will fall every time—except that politicians and officials in industries prone to large-scale accidental disasters know how to manipulate our feelings, as the nuclear industry did and does in response to increased incidents of cancer surrounding Three Mile Island. The story of a nuclear meltdown may begin with an unmitigated environmental disaster, but when the middle and end of the story are as yet unwritten, we are susceptible to suggestion.

Manipulating our feelings about a nuclear accident was part of Arnie Gundersen's job when the nuclear industry still employed him. In the days following the Three Mile Island meltdown, he got on TV and told everyone in Pennsylvania that it was safe to go outside. You can track this narrative-setting after oil spills as well, first with politicians and industry officials reporting that the accident was not so bad, and then with volunteers gathering to "clean up" the mess—even though cleaning up an oil spill actually does little good. But if these displays make us feel less gloomy about oil spills, then we will think an oil spill is less likely to occur again.

Sometimes, to manipulate our feelings after an accident, officials will stretch the truth to extreme limits of optimism. Less than a month after the Deepwater Horizon exploded, BP CEO Tony Hayward described it this way: "The Gulf of Mexico is a very big ocean. The amount of volume of oil and dispersant we are putting into it is tiny in relation to the total water volume."

Officials will also straight-up lie to change our perception of the accident. David Rainey, a vice president at BP, reported to a congressional subcommittee that the spill rate was around 5,000 barrels a day; he ignored the estimate he received from BP engineers, which was 146,000 barrels a day. After BP capped the well, officials estimated that 3.19 million barrels had spilled, at a daily rate more than seven times Rainey's lowball. In the month and a half following the spill, Mississippi governor Haley Barbour insisted that his state had not seen enough oil to fill a milk jug. "If you were on the Mississippi gulf coast any time in the last 48 days you didn't see any oil at all. We've had a few tar balls, but we have tar balls every year as a natural product of the Gulf of Mexico," he told reporters.

Like the employer blaming the accident-prone worker in the small accident, the politician or corporate CEO insisting *this is no big deal* is a fixture of the large-scale accident. You could say, of course, that it's essential to calm the public. Except that diffusing our panic can also diminish how much we care about a disaster. Our empathy fatigue is a gateway, and powerful people walk right through. When we listen to a politician or an industry official explain why an accidental catastrophe is actually minor or how volunteers are standing by for the cleanup, we are relieved of upsetting feelings about the disaster. As a result, we're less concerned with how and why the accident began.

All of this—the cleanup, the lies, the hyperbole of politicians and executives—is an equivalent of the accident-prone worker and the nut behind the wheel. However, the large-scale accident is too big and too public to shift the blame to one person making one mistake. Yet there's still a need to distract from the dangerous conditions of generating nuclear power and pumping oil, so instead you get powerful people mucking with your perception of the problem.

We can find a small example of the danger of our diffused panic in the routine practice of oil spill cleanup. For all the news coverage of oil recovery efforts, volunteers in rubber gloves, and the miles of oil booms spread across the ocean to contain the spill, researchers determined that Exxon's cleanup effort only recovered 14 percent of the *Valdez* spill. BP said they recovered 25 percent—but that is self-reported, so even that small number is potentially dubious.

In general, after an oil spill, cleaned birds suffer higher than average mortality rates. Less than 1 percent survive. Scientists found that cleaning oil off a bird could cause as much injury as the oil itself. The majority of brown pelicans cleaned and released after an oil spill in California never mated again and died. After a 2002 oil spill in Spain, scientists and volunteers cleaned thousands of birds; the majority died within a week. In one horrific scientific experiment out of Canada, researchers intentionally spilled oil into the Beaufort Sea to help guide a decision about whether or not to drill for oil there. The local polar bears died of kidney failure, and so did the birds. The researchers failed to contain the oil. The project concluded that cleaning up oil spills was largely ineffective. Canada still permitted drilling in the Beaufort Sea.

Still, all this scrubbing serves a purpose. It is oil spill response theater, with the message that these accidents are fine *because* they can be cleaned up. Pretending that we can clean up an oil spill is one way that oil companies make the risk of an oil spill feel less dire.

But what that risk encompasses may also be a mystery, even to the experts. Large-scale accidents come with an unknown number of small ones. To look at the "little" in big accidents, we need to talk to the person with the best job title in this book: Prosanta Chakrabarty, curator of fishes.

Little Deaths in a Big Accident

After an oil spill, all the attention goes to what Prosanta Chakrabarty, curator of fishes at the Department of Biological Sciences at Louisiana State University, calls "charismatic mega-fauna": charming whales, clever otters, intoxicating pelicans—the eye-catching ocean dwellers. That is not his area of study. Chakrabarty, an ichthyologist, speaks for the fishes.

In 2008, two years before the Deepwater Horizon exploded, on his first trip out in the Gulf of Mexico, Chakrabarty discovered two new species of a small bottom-dwelling member of the batfish family known as the pancake batfish.

Before he arrived in Louisiana, Chakrabarty had studied batfishes, and he'd noticed something funny among the limited preserved specimens owned by the American Museum of Natural History. The museum listed only one species of batfish among its specimens from the Gulf, but those specimens appeared to him to be a bit different from one another, possibly distinct species, he thought. But these were old preserved fish, faded in their color, so he simply noted the oddity and moved on. Then he got a chance to go out in the Gulf. On that trip, Chakrabarty's suspicions about the batfish were borne out. He discovered two new species of batfish, and learned that the one species that ichthyologists had thought to be widespread throughout the Gulf was actually three.

By the time his findings were published, the worst had occurred. The Deepwater Horizon had exploded, and all of a sudden, reporters were calling Chakrabarty. The pancake batfish was on the front page of CNN. The Gulf was filling with oil, and reporters wanted to know what effect it would have on the newly discovered fish.

Thanks to GPS data, Chakrabarty could estimate about how many fish could be affected—and not just batfish. He looked at 124 species known to the Gulf, of which 77 were endemic—meaning they lived there and nowhere else. Of all those species, the territories of 64 percent overlapped with the oil spill. Among the endemics, more than half now lived inside the spill area. What's worse, five years later, Chakrabarty found that no one had seen more than half of the fish endemic to the Gulf of Mexico again since the spill. But not catching a tiny fish—some smaller than your palm—in a giant ocean does not mean the fish no longer exists. Chakrabarty tells me that he can't say for sure what the oil spill did to the pancake batfish, because before the oil spill, it was also a mystery—he'd just discovered them. Happening to find new species of pancake batfish helped him better understand how little we really know about the Gulf—and in a catastrophic accident, knowing so little means we could be losing entire life-forms we have yet to even discover.

In 2020, researchers uncovered the fact that the spill and the affected population were much larger than previously suspected. While the oil slick, as seen in satellite images, measured 57,000 square miles, researchers tracking concentrations of oil below the surface found a footprint 30 percent larger than that—"potentially exterminating," those researchers wrote, "a vast amount of planktonic marine organisms across the domain."

Planktonic marine organisms are perhaps the smallest death to result from the spill. The discovery of their potential mass extermination a decade later shows that Charles Perrow and James Reason were right. Accidents are layered, and when things go wrong, the failures intersect in complex, surprising, and often unseen ways. This is true of large-scale accidents such as nuclear meltdowns and oil spills, but it is also true of accidents that, at first, might not appear layered, complex, or large-scale at all.

All Accidents Are "Normal" Accidents

Many of the systemic accidents in this chapter start on a ship or a drilling platform, within the four walls of a factory, or inside the confines of a nuclear reactor. The theories and models—Normal Accident Theory, the Swiss cheese model—were meant to apply to these large but physically confined systems.

But the more accident stories I read, the more I became convinced that all accidents are systemic and normal—routine failures of design, management, and organization in complex settings—and that a system could be far less tangible than a single factory or reactor. A network of highways could be a system, or an ocean, or an energy market. To really understand accidents, I realized, I needed to apply Perrow's and

Reason's theories to systems beyond just physical, confined spaces—to social systems, economic systems, and the entire built environment.

At Three Mile Island, the decision to purchase a fragile reactor lined up with a routine shutdown lined up with a locked cooling system lined up with a control board that made it look like an open valve was closed—a tightly coupled, complex system. But isn't the entire apparatus of energy production the same? The design of a blowout preventer is a slice of Swiss cheese, yes, but so is the decision to allow deepwater drilling in the Gulf, and so is the politician who, after the fact, swears it's not that bad, really. The life and death of a pancake batfish may rest on the prevention of an accident on the Deepwater Horizon, but it also rests on the decision to seek energy from technology where accidents are normal and hugely consequential.

Before you accuse me of a case of conspiratorial paranoia, tacking newspaper articles to my wall connected with red string, consider the Permian Basin—not a plant or a factory or a corporation but the location of a bustling new energy market, born of fracking technology. If we view the energy market as a system, a stack of Swiss cheese slices, we can see all the complex ways that it might drive little accidents, too. For example, the accidental fatality rate for workers in the oil and gas industry rose as fracking in the Permian Basin escalated and by 2010, was seven times as high as in every other industry combined. And this, perhaps, could be expected—work accidents follow new and dangerous work.

But other accidents followed this new energy market, too—accidents that had surprising intersections. In one Permian Basin county, traffic accidents rose more than 70 percent. The rise in oil production directly correlated with a dramatic rise in police seizing large amounts of methamphetamines and an opioid overdose epidemic. The drug problem was a by-product of more money in the area as workers were better paid for dangerous work and of independent contract workers without health insurance self-medicating after days of painful work.

These are normal accidents that grow out of complex and surprising interactions of large-scale systems—the energy market, the drug market, the rural highway system unprepared for an influx of people. The four walls of a factory do not confine these systems. Instead, they are social systems, economic systems, and organizational systems. All accidents are systemic, but to understand some of the systems, we will need to zoom far out from one man falling off an oil rig, or another, flush with cash, taking too much of a drug. Racism is a system, and so is stigmatization, and so is the federal infrastructure budget. The accidents themselves will not get larger in scale than the accidents in this chapter, but the systems that can cause accidents will get more encompassing, and the risks will get harder to control.

Chapter Four

Risk

One way to measure the risk of a person being killed or injured in an accident is to estimate crashworthiness—crashworthiness being the degree to which any container you may be strapped inside, be it a car or boat or plane, is resistant to allowing injury to occur. This can be measured in the presence of protections, such as airbags and cushioned seat backs, and in the absence of dangerous conditions, such as sharp knobs or cockpits that disintegrate on impact. Hugh DeHaven perfected a test of this in the 1950s as part of the Automotive Crash Injury Research project he founded at Cornell University. First, he would put crash test dummies inside a car, and then he would crash the car. How those dummies fared in the crash told him how at-risk you or I would be in a similar car at a similar impact. This sounds straightforward, but it's not.

Engineers build almost all crash test dummies to model a 171-pound, five-foot-nine "male" body. At the National Highway Traffic Safety Administration, which tests and regulates the risk of cars sold in the United States, the only "female" crash test dummies are not female-bodied at all—just smaller versions of male crash dummies, and, at four foot eleven and 108 pounds, so small they represent only 5 percent of the female population. No crash test dummies account for the physiological differences between male and female bodies—in chest, shoulders, and hips—or the presence of breasts, or most females' physical size. Risk for female bodies in car crashes *is built in* because it is simply not measured. Perhaps it's no surprise, then, that women are up to 73 percent more likely to be injured and up to 28 percent more likely to be killed in a front-facing car accident. Even the experts who test crashworthiness know little or nothing about the risks faced by more than half the population.

Ignorance of risk appears across the spectrum of accidents. Experts make risk decisions—decisions that shape our built environment— with bias and without actual expertise. As a result, the systems used to measure risk, like crashworthiness testing, intersect with other systems, like sexism, in surprising ways. Women are more likely to be killed and injured in car accidents because we don't have female-bodied crash test dummies. We lack female crash test dummies because sexism is systemic. And all this is beyond the control of any one female driver—though she may, after an accident, be blamed for driving like a nut.

"People do things that are not optimal because they are trapped in situations where they do not have the information or the tools that they need, and then they are held responsible for things that were really outside their control," explains Baruch Fischhoff, who with Paul Slovic and the late Sarah Lichtenstein founded a think tank called Decision Research in 1976, which pioneered the study of risk perception. "Conversely, the pressure is taken off of the people who should be providing them better information in a more realistic and readily accessible form, and empowering them to run their own lives better."

Risk perception experts like Fischhoff and Slovic would argue that we as individuals are pretty good at perceiving and avoiding risk. More often than not, however, when accidents happen, the risk is taken out of our control. Consider the passengers on the DC-10, who didn't know about the whistleblowing engineer who tried to ground their plane. Or the chicken processing plant workers who had nowhere else to work if they were unwilling to work behind a locked door in a factory never inspected by OSHA. Or the driver in 1956 who could buy a Ford but only one with a steering column that would impale them in an accident.

The risk was not just taken out of these people's control—these people didn't know the danger they were exposed to or the resources available to avoid it.

We can understand these two factors as actual risk and risk perception—the dangers we face and how we understand those dangers—and the way that these two factors interact is very important. Risk perception experts have found that feeling in control of a situation makes us feel less at risk—regardless of actual risk. Because the DC-10 passenger or the chicken plant worker or the Ford driver did not know about the dangers they faced, risk was both present and imperceptible, doubly unavoidable and out of their control.

The Benefit of Feeling in Control

In the past forty-five years, researchers who study how we perceive risk have pinpointed a few internal biases in what makes us feel that an activity is risky or not, and feeling in control is high on the list of things that make us feel safe. We tend to underestimate the risk of a car accident, for example, in part because, as drivers, we feel we're in control. Feeling in control is also why most of us are more comfortable driving than being a passenger and why people who own a gun feel that guns are less risky than people who don't own one.

"You feel if you own a gun that you are in control of your safety," Paul Slovic tells me. "There are a lot of elements that are out of your control, but that *sense* of control is very powerful in both diminishing your perception of risk and increasing your acceptance of risk."

People are also more willing to tolerate a risk if it comes with benefits attached—another reason we underestimate the risk of a car accident. Consider our strong and opposing reactions to two chemicals: pesticides and medicine. Surveys conducted by Slovic and Fischhoff found that most people considered pesticides to have little benefit and high risk. People thought of medicine in the opposite way—little risk and high benefit. In reality, both are chemicals. Both are beneficial, and both are dangerous. Arguably, in terms of our individual survival, pesticides are statistically less risky than medicine—an average of twenty-three deaths a year are directly attributable to pesticides in the United States, while around thirty-eight people die *every day* from prescription opioid medication alone. But because we have bad feelings about pesticides, including the fact that exposure to them is out of our control and we don't directly observe their benefit (unless we are farmers), we judge them as riskier. With medicine, we get the direct benefit of feeling better, and we are entirely in control of when we take it, so it feels like less of a risk. In this light, it's easy to see why the risk of a gun, which conveys a sense of security, and the risk of driving, which offers the benefit of convenience, are both underestimated by most people.

Slovic and Fischhoff identified other factors that skew our perception of risk. We feel a thing is riskier if we dread it—say, fear of a plane crash versus fear of driving to the store. If it is man-made, it feels more dangerous than something in nature, like a nuclear meltdown versus an earthquake. If we don't have a choice in the matter, or it requires trusting someone else, or it involves children, or it is novel and uncommon, or it gets a lot of publicity, it feels riskier. If the risk threatens us, it feels scarier than if the risk threatens someone else. When these conditions overlap—the dreaded, man-made, out-of-our-control, novel, highly publicized accident, like the concurrent crashes of two Boeing 737 Max airplanes in 2018 and 2019—it can increase our perception of risk even further.

Of course, these are only perceptions. Whether we are purchasing firearms or taking a pill, we *feel* more in control and less at risk, but that does not mean we *are* more in control and less at risk. The people who design the road and manufacture the gun and package the medicine primarily determine our *actual* risk—but those people have the same problems perceiving risk as the rest of us do.

Knowing what we know about systemic accidents, the mismatch of risk and perception in the hands of experts is a frightening premise. Applied to a whole system—whether that system is how engineers design roads or weapon companies design guns—the consequences of misperceiving risk get multiplied across the population. If you drive too fast, for example, because you feel in control and stand to benefit from it, you minimize your perception of the risk and then expose yourself and maybe a few people around you to increased risk. But if you're a traffic engineer designing a road, your risk perception could affect far more people and result in countless accidents over the decades-long life cycle of a road. The risk perception of a person with power can create dangerous conditions for us all.

Speed Limits Are Just a Feeling

There is loads of evidence that traffic accidents repeat in similar places and similar ways until conditions change. When a traffic engineer changes the design of a street—say from one that makes drivers feel comfortable speeding to one that makes drivers feel at risk unless they slow down—accidental deaths and injuries on that street decline in dramatic ways. This tells us that a traffic engineer can prevent accidents. Still, the risk of dying in a traffic crash remains very high—the second most common cause of accidental death in 2020, killing more people than guns, or fire, or any other dangerous machinery.

Eric Dumbaugh, a civil engineer who teaches urban and regional planning at Florida Atlantic University and is associate director of the Collaborative Sciences Center for Road Safety, explains this dissonance as a matter of bad information about risk. He tells me that many of the rules that traffic engineers use to design roads are old, misapplied, or based on false information.

The problem is that most U.S. road engineering guidelines were written in the 1950s and '60s, when the U.S. government was in the process of building 41,000 miles of interstate highways as part of the Federal-Aid Highway Act of 1956. At the same time, Ralph Nader was rallying a case against automakers. One tactic automakers used to redirect the heat they faced then was to blame the nut behind the wheel, as we've seen. The other tactic was to insist that cars were not inherently dangerous; road design was. Automakers elevated the importance of traffic engineering. But the authors of America's earliest traffic engineering rule books had limited ability to measure the risk of the roads they were building. The guidelines used to design roads today were written at this intersection: limited ability to measure risk, an elevated focus on road design as the secret sauce of traffic safety, and a well-funded and myopic focus on interstate highways.

At the time, no federal agency was in charge of traffic safety and crash-counting was an inexact state-by-state affair, so data on the risk of accidents was scant. But early traffic engineers did know that the interstate highways they were building had lower rates of accidents and injuries than other roadways. Newspapers were also reporting heavily at the time on one particular type of dramatic, memorable accident occurring on roads nothing like interstates: when a driver lost control, left the roadway, and wrapped their car around a tree or telephone pole. The loss of control would have made these accidents feel especially risky, as would the publicity and the dreadful pictures of these violent crashes. From these two factors—memorable accidents involving roadside trees and telephone poles, and the low crash rate on interstates—came the idea of the "forgiving roadside," or a street design that would "forgive" a driver when they made a mistake.

In theory, the forgiving roadside appeared to reduce risk. In practice, it meant that engineers started designing other roads like interstates. Compared to other roadways, interstates were straight, wide, and had broad clearance on the roadside—there were no trees, no telephone poles, no shops or driveways. You can't wrap your car around a tree if there's no tree, right? Without much data, this soon became the rule. Engineers decided that stuff on the roadside was a "roadside hazard." The rules written into early American engineering design standards—that roadsides should be clear, and roads straight and wide so you could not lose control and swerve off of them—were based on the perception of risk from these hazards. In time, mandated airbags, seat belts, and collapsible steering columns would reduce the risk of death and injury in these accidents, but the rules stuck. Engineers today still learn that a curvy rural tree-lined highway is risky, as is a curvy urban street lined with shops and benches.

These guidelines puzzled Dumbaugh, who had spent enough time on shop- and bench-lined urban streets to know they sure didn't appear hazardous. Investigating the disparity between the rules and reality became the subject of his dissertation. It turned out that the theory behind the "forgiving roadside" was inaccurate, or at least wildly over-applied. Dumbaugh found that urban streets that looked like interstates actually increased accidents, while those that looked like they belonged in a neighborhood reduced them. He searched out main streets adjacent to suburban areas, prime tree-lined street locales, and found that accidents were not occurring on these streets at all. They were as safe as they looked to Dumbaugh, countering the lessons that came with his engineering degree and are still taught today.

"Most urban roadside crashes are not the result of random error," Dumbaugh tells me, "but are instead systematically encoded into the design of the roadway."

Dumbaugh found that most accidents on city streets happened because cars were driving and turning too fast onto driveways and side streets. It turned out that when traffic engineers built straight, wide roads that looked like interstates, drivers felt encouraged to drive at interstate speeds. Those curves, trees, and benches that engineers removed had actually been making drivers slow down to avoid the risk these hazards presented—without all that, drivers felt less at risk and more in control driving faster, and driving too fast, people died in traffic accidents. The design of the road induced the errors.

Dumbaugh continued this research into his career. In 2020, he took a similar approach to examining some fifty thousand traffic accidents over three years near Charlotte, North Carolina. While, he notes, his fellow traffic engineers would likely blame these accidents on driver error, what he found was that, far more than accident-prone people, the characteristics of the road put everyone at risk. The worst crashes—where people were killed or injured—happened on streets with more than four lanes, where the speed limit was more than 35 mph, where lots of commercial driveways cut in and out of the road, and where bus stops lining the street brought pedestrians in conflict with people driving. Applying interstate rules to these roads full of interaction was deadly.

Most of the time, when a traffic engineer designs a new road to connect two places, there is nothing in between, at least at first. Traffic engineers make all the big decisions about road design—how wide, how fast, how straight—by prognostication. They forecast traffic and land development thirty years into the future and design high-speed roads connecting that new development to the rest of the region. The road is perfectly safe when there is nothing much on it, but as development fills in the spaces between with shops, homes, and schools, the empty high-speed road becomes a busy—and hazardous—high-speed road. Dumbaugh had been taught that roadside hazards were the risk, but the actual hazard is the shape of the street and the speed it encourages. The risk that engineers build into a new roadway only increases over time as development fills in the area around the road.

Once engineers design that fast road, they set a speed limit. This, Dumbaugh explains, is also based on those old rule books. The rules recommend setting a speed limit based not on safety or accident prevention but on a combination of factors that engineers should consider equally. As one engineering rule book puts it, "In selection of design speed, every effort should be made to attain a desired combination of safety, mobility, and efficiency within the constraints of environmental quality, economics, aesthetics, and social or political impacts." Or, traffic engineers should consider whether people can get to Walmart without a traffic jam to be *as crucial* as whether people don't die on the road.

As development arrives on a new road, congestion follows, and the road slows down. Chief among the rules taught to traffic engineers is that congestion is a problem and slow is inefficient, so postdevelopment, traffic engineers will reevaluate the speed limit. They decide the new speed limits by conducting a study that looks at how fast everyone is driving on the street. Then, they chart those speeds by frequency. Almost always in these studies, the majority of people are found to be driving at a similar pace, but around 15 percent are found to be driving much faster than everyone else. Traffic engineers use this latter group as their limit—setting the speed limit at the low end of how fast the fastest 15 percent drive, which is the high end of how quickly the other 85 percent drive. They call this the 85th percentile speed. It is how engineers set speed limits on major roads nationwide.

"We look at how fast cars are going and we assume that is the safe speed of the roadway," says Dumbaugh. "Note that this has no safety basis: it's simply assumed that most people don't want to get into a crash and are thus doing what it is safe for them to do."

Most speed limits are not based on physics or crash test expertise but simply the upper limit of what most amateur drivers *feel* is safe. A speed limit is the *perceived* safe speed of a road, not the actual risk of traveling that speed on that road. The experts, the engineers, those in control, do not set speed limits to limit the risk of a road or design the road to limit speed. Instead, the experts design a wide, straight road that encourages speeding and decide the speed limit based on how fast nonexperts drive there. One reason that this problem goes unnoticed is that it is not classified as a problem. For example, in 2018, the National Highway Traffic Safety Administration attributed the deaths of about 9,000 people in traffic crashes to speeding. More than 36,000 were killed that year, but if any of those were attributable to a speed limit *set* too high, those deaths would not be attributed to speeding—those drivers, after all, were just following the rules of the road.

When designing roads based on drivers' faulty perceptions of risk or the misleading lessons of the interstate highway system, engineers are drawing on guidelines drafted decades ago. These rule books, such as the *Manual on Uniform Traffic Control Devices for Streets and Highways*, and *A Policy on Geometric Design of Highways and Streets*, are so divorced from safe outcomes that the rules actually discourage installing

crosswalks or pedestrian walk signals at intersections unless the risk of
an accident is extreme. According to those rules, a lower-risk way across
a street—like a crosswalk and traffic signal—is only warranted if one
hundred people cross a street every hour for four hours. Ninety-nine
people running across the highway is not enough of a risk.

Engineering schools across the country still teach these rules, and the
graduates of those schools still believe that following them will reduce
risk for drivers. But these guidelines also give engineers protection. By
following the rules, however outdated or unproven they may be, engineers
shield themselves from lawsuits. Engineers build roads that put us all at
risk of an accident and thus protect themselves from the risk of legal action.
When a traffic accident kills someone on an unsafe street, the engineer can
claim, accurately but dangerously, that they were just following the rules.

"I say this as somebody with a PhD in civil and environmental engineering from a wonderful university. Traffic engineering is a fraud discipline," Dumbaugh declares. "It presumes knowledge on road safety
that it doesn't have and it educates people generation after generation
on information that is incorrect. So it allows people to graduate with
this degree, with a designation that they are an expert in the field and
which they have no substantive knowledge of whatsoever. Most traffic
engineering programs in the U.S. do not have a single course that covers the issue of road safety. If they get it at all, they get it, at best, as a
lecture—it is part of a class on traffic engineering, on building streets
for high speeds."

Research corroborates this. One study surveyed 117 transportation
engineering programs in the U.S. Less than 25 percent self-identified as
offering a safety course, and when the researchers looked into it, a third
of the courses were actually just traffic engineering and highway design
courses—teaching the same old rules, not safety at all.

Instead of controlling dangerous conditions, traffic engineers lean
on human error to excuse accidents. For example, here is how one traffic engineer described to me the cause of accidents on an interstate
highway—and not just any highway, but an interstate that they helped

design: "There are still crashes, because some people are just nuts. I don't know what it is about it, but they are nuts. They are going way above the speed limit there."

If you look only at the moments leading up to a traffic accident, you can almost always pin the blame on some nut behind the wheel—that risky driver. But if you zoom out, you will find risk at every level of the system—well beyond the driver's control.

Risk is rooted deeply in our roads because of the prejudices and misperceptions underlying their design and use. But there's another realm where the roots of risk go even deeper: the founding fathers embedded them in the Constitution.

Perfectly Legal Guns That Can Fire at Random

The men wear camouflage and safety goggles or bulletproof vests over gray t-shirts in the videos. They stand in backyards or garages and look at the camera as they talk about the gun they are about to drop. Then, they drop the gun—from three feet, from four feet, from five feet. The gun hits the ground and fires a shot. On YouTube, there is drop test after drop test, amateur and produced—I stopped counting at one hundred. The men hit the gun with a hammer and drop the gun on carpet, wood, and dirt. No one touches the trigger. It fires again and again.

The gun is a SIG Sauer P320. It is the subject of YouTube experiments not only because it can fire at random but because it is a widely owned weapon. Or at least it was. After SIG Sauer signed a half-billion-dollar contract with the U.S. Army to make the P320 a service weapon, police forces around the country adopted it, too. Gun enthusiasts followed suit. The problem was that in the rigorous testing done before the purchase, army officials found that when you drop the P320 so that it hits the ground right around its rear sight—that outer corner of the L of a handgun—it can fire a bullet without anyone pulling the trigger.

The army called out the defect before SIG Sauer delivered on the order, and SIG Sauer fixed the problem in guns delivered to the army.

However, the other P320s were shipped without the fix—the company sent over 500,000 to police precincts and others eager to own the gun endorsed by the U.S. Army. Soon the accidents began.

In Stamford, Connecticut, a police officer dropped a holstered P320 outside the trunk of his car and took a bullet through the knee. In Orlando, a cop let his holstered P320 slip and the gun discharged into his leg. A sheriff's deputy in Virginia did not even drop the gun; she just removed her holster and the P320 fired and shattered her femur. She may never walk unaided again.

As lawsuits mounted, SIG Sauer launched the P320 Voluntary Upgrade Program. On their website, the FAQ began with the most crucial question:

Q: *Is my P320 safe in its current configuration?*
A: *Yes. The P320 meets and exceeds all US safety standards. However, mechanical safeties are designed to augment, not replace safe handling practices. Careless and improper handling of any firearm can result in an unintentional discharge.*

It is a bit less pithy than "the nut behind the wheel," but we can add "careless and improper handling of any firearm" to the list of ways to blame human error after an accident, alongside the jaywalker and the accident-prone worker.

SIG Sauer trotted out the human error story when Jeff Bagnell sued the company in 2019 on behalf of his client, Deputy Marcie Vadnais, a deputy sheriff in Loudoun County, Virginia, and a seven-year veteran on the force. In February 2018, her holstered weapon fired into her leg. Her injury was so severe that she could never return to police work. SIG Sauer settled with Deputy Vadnais on the second day of her jury trial. That did not change their response to her or anyone else.

"They basically state that all these people are somehow negligently pulling the trigger, which is a tremendous insult—not just to a law enforcement officer, it is an insult to anyone who has any weapons training whatsoever," says Bagnell, who is now representing many injured P320 owners, including law enforcement agencies, across the country.

Semiautomatic pistols are classified by what makes them fire. Unlike a pistol with an external hammer, a striker-fired weapon like the P320 is under spring pressure to fire. Once a striker-fired weapon is cocked and loaded, Bagnell tells me, it is a high-risk situation, very much like a bow pulled back with an arrow in it, and any mechanical or design defect is an accident waiting to happen. Then he interrupts himself. He doesn't want to call it an accident.

"Not when it happens this many times. The word 'accident' is gun industry jargon that serves to disguise negligence in design and manufacturing—negligence on the part of the manufacturer, the corporation, not the law enforcement officer, not Marcie, not any civilian," he tells me. "It has happened so many times that this weapon should have been recalled years ago."

Corporations recall products, from Tylenol to Cheerios, all the time—by government force, or voluntarily, in anticipation of government force. Yet guns never are recalled, because they have a unique privilege: no government agency polices their safety. There are no federal standards for gun design. In 1972, the National Rifle Association and gun manufacturers convinced Congress to forbid the Consumer Product Safety Commission—which sets safety standards for commercial products and issues bans and recalls for hazardous ones—from including gun safety in their remit. Guns are permitted to go off by accident. This completely upends a gun owner's perception of risk. A trained gun owner understands risk as a matter of how they handle their weapon, but training made little difference for someone like Officer Vadnais. SIG Sauer took the risk out of her control because her weapon fired when she wasn't even handling it.

"My mission as a lawyer right now is to get the word out to everyone out there who is carrying this weapon, who owns it, that it needs to be put into a safe and never touched again, because it can fire without a trigger pull. That cannot happen. You cannot have a semiautomatic pistol that can fire if it is bumped the wrong way, if you lean against the wall, if you turn the wrong way," Bagnell explains—except that is what the P320 does. "They basically have no control over when this calamity may occur."

Remember what Slovic and Fischhoff uncovered about risk and feeling in control? Owning a gun or driving a car makes us feel in control. Those are *our hands* at two and ten. *We decide* when to pull out into traffic. *We* buy the bullets. *We* pull the trigger. With guns, this feeling extends beyond the physical aspects of controlling the weapon. Owning a gun also makes people feel in control of more intangible things, such as their own safety. In fact, most gun owners cite protection as their prime reason for owning a gun, and this has increased over time in inverse to the crime rate—people are more likely to buy guns for safety the safer our country gets.

Psychologists researching why people buy guns have identified two common feelings among the purchasers: a specific perceived risk of being attacked and a diffuse perceived risk of a dangerous world. These are not actual risks but perceptions—which is why gun ownership increases in times of well-publicized civil unrest, like the sustained period of Black Lives Matter protests in the summer of 2020, which brought about an all-time high in background checks, the main metric for gun sales. And even though gun owners may be deciding to purchase guns to increase a sense of control, gun owners are more at risk of accidentally shooting someone or being accidentally shot. Two researchers in Massachusetts tracked a spike in background checks for gun purchases *and* accidental shooting incidents five months after the Sandy Hook massacre. Gun shops sold 3 million more weapons in that period compared to the same period in previous years, and accidental shootings killed sixty more people than usual. Of the dead, around twenty were children.

Guns purchased in response to perceptions of risk and a desire to be in control left people at greater risk. People might feel less in control in states with the strictest gun control laws because the government limits gun ownership there, but the risk of accidental shooting is lowest in these states. In perceiving risk and buying guns to control risk, we increase risk.

When we measure risk in our brains, we measure *our perception* of control as much as anything. But not only are our risk perceptions sometimes wrong, we also may not actually be in control. With the SIG Sauer P320, the risk was out of the control of owners of that one gun because gun lobbyists successfully exempted all firearms from the U.S. regulatory system. Medicine is the opposite—comprehensively regulated in a way that makes people generally feel safe about having medications in the house. But regulation can't make medicine safe if regulators ignore known risks.

Built to Spill

There might be no group of people in American life more concerned with accident risk than parents. This concern encompasses trivial dangers, such as the risk of an accident when leaving the house during diaper-less potty training, and life-threatening dangers, such as the risk of babies accidentally strangling themselves if allowed to sleep with a blanket. Parental risk perception is evolutionary; human babies are not born with turtle shells or hunting instincts. We are a species that would die if abandoned in the wilderness anytime in the first few years of life—in those years, parents manage risk.

We also live in a society, and part of that arrangement is trusting that people with power over risks that affect all of society will guard us from hazards that are known. Where protective solutions against risks exist, we expect government officials and corporate executives to implement those solutions. That is not what happened for Maisie Gillan.

Adam and MaryBeth Gillan took no risks before their nine-month-old baby, Maisie, died of accidental drug poisoning. The risk was out of their control in more ways than one.

During dinner at their neighbors' house, Adam and MaryBeth

allowed Maisie a few minutes of crawling on the floor. Her parents and their neighbors watched her closely the entire time. But somehow, in that time, she ingested a methadone pill dropped at some point days earlier by an elderly parent of their neighbor who was taking the medication for pain. Maisie's parents suspect the tiny pill stuck to her hand unseen and then she put her hand in her mouth, as babies do. Maisie went to sleep that night and never woke up.

When we spoke on the phone, Adam and MaryBeth were both home on parental leave. They recently had a baby. With a newborn in the house, after losing Maisie, they explain that risk feels different now. If before they were cautious, now they parent under conditions of post-traumatic stress. Adam talks about the stories you hear of parents accidentally leaving kids in their car seat—forgetting, somehow—and these haunt him.

"I'm in the car on a ten-minute trip to the grocery store at a stoplight, and I am poking him to make sure he is moving, that type of thing," he says. How he thinks about risk with his older child has changed, too. "If she's watching TV in the living room and I'm in the kitchen and I hear her cough because she is eating an apple or something like that, it is a dead sprint. The rarity of what happened is now much more present for me."

Rare as it was, what happened to baby Maisie was not providence or coincidence. Her parents took no risks, but others did: the older woman who dropped the pill but failed to pick it up, the neighbors who owned the home. But this risk, too, is baked into the system in the way that high-risk drugs such as methadone are distributed and packaged.

In this case, and for the more than sixty thousand children under age five who end up in the emergency room every year for drug-related poisoning, the risk is not hidden in tradition, as it is for traffic engineers, or protected by lobbyists, like the manufacturing mistakes of SIG Sauer. Instead, the risk persists due to inaction by government officials and drug companies to protect people from high-hazard drugs. The phrase "parents know what's best for their children" is often invoked to drive home the point of who is responsible when children get hurt, but in an era when prescription opioids are aggressively marketed to all Americans, children are killed by accident because of risks far outside their parents' control.

Dr. Milton Tenenbein is a pediatrician focused on emergency pediatric toxicology and injury prevention. I tell him about the Gillan family, how they do not like the word "accident." He also disapproves of its use.

"The term 'accident' is a four-letter word for those of us that practice the discipline of injury prevention," he tells me. "Whenever we are meeting or writing policy or advocating for improvement, that word will never appear in any of our documents, policies, or talking points."

For four decades, Tenenbein has been trying to change policies such as the one that allowed Maisie Gillan to come across a methadone pill. He tells me about a law passed almost fifty years before Maisie was born, in 1970—the Poison Prevention Packaging Act. Under the law, medicine would be under the jurisdiction of the Consumer Product Safety Commission. The law required the commission to develop child-resistant closures for hazardous products to reduce accidental poisoning risk.

Before this, when a child died because they got hold of medication, the medication's manufacturers would have just chalked the accident up to parents who weren't careful enough—another human error story. But the Poison Prevention Packaging Act created a system for designing and testing pill containers. The designers brought in little children and older adults to see if they could open the pill bottles—to pass, a design would need to be impossible for the first group but feasible for the second. These tests set criteria for packaging pills and the Consumer Product Safety Commission tested every new pill bottle design on those criteria.

This legislation was a huge success—proof that this was not a problem of parent error. In the first twenty years, the rate of children poisoned by accidentally eating medication fell by half; the number of children accidentally killed declined by 75 percent. Researchers would later estimate that the law prevented 200,000 accidental child poisonings in the first decade. But from the 1980s to today, the law accounted for no more major decreases. The law didn't become less effective; high-risk pharmaceuticals became more common—and with high-risk drugs, such as the opioid methadone that killed Maisie, it only takes one pill to kill a child.

The Poison Prevention Packaging Act created containers that children could not open, and this would have included the opioid that Maisie ingested. But Maisie did not open a pill container; the older woman prescribed the drug dropped the container or otherwise spilled the pill. The child-resistant bottle does not help if your pills spill and you fail to pick one of them up. Instead, Tenenbein says, we need new strategies for high-risk drugs like methadone. More than six hundred children under the age of five have died this way in the last twenty years, poisoned by accidental ingestion of opioids.

In 2005, Tenenbein set out to find a more effective approach. He found it in iron pills. After a rash of iron poisoning deaths in young children in the 1990s, the Food and Drug Administration (FDA) mandated blister packs for iron tablets—the ones that only pop out one pill at a time. Tenenbein notes that this is a form of passive safety—like an airbag, compared to a seat belt that works only if you buckle it. A person doesn't need to do anything to be made safer by an airbag or a blister pack. Of course, we cannot know what would have saved Maisie, but if a known dangerous pill is popped out one at a time, we can safely say that the risk of a misplaced pill would decline quite a bit. The evidence shows a direct risk reduction. Tenenbein examined iron poisoning deaths in young children before and after blister packs were introduced and found a dramatic decrease. Calls to poison control centers for kids who had accidentally eaten iron pills fell by a third, and a few years after implementation, annual iron poisoning deaths fell from twenty-nine to one.

In the aftermath of Maisie's death, Senator Chuck Schumer met with Adam and MaryBeth at their home in Rochester. Together, the parents and the senator called on the Food and Drug Administration to require blister packaging for opioids and other high-risk drugs. The FDA would be able to enforce this regulation, Schumer noted, thanks to a law passed by Congress the year before—the Substance Use-Disorder Prevention that Promotes Opioid Recovery and Treatment (SUPPORT) for Patients and Communities Act—which granted new powers to the FDA to regulate opioid packaging, among other things. For Tenenbein, this regulation is the key. Drug companies will not volunteer to change anything, he tells me, without the government forcing change upon the entire industry. No corporation will risk spending money where others do not, preventing accidents but losing their market share, not even to save lives.

Even if the government does soon force drug companies to reduce the risk of a child accidentally ingesting an opioid pill, it is important to recognize that these are not the only drug-related accidents; there are others that the government is far less interested in preventing. Consider the time line here: Within a year of Maisie's death, Senator Schumer arrived at the Gillan's house with a plan to prevent what had happened to her from happening again. But it was only the year prior, in 2018, after the opioid epidemic had been growing for two decades, that Congress passed the SUPPORT Act. The U.S. government only declared the opioid epidemic a public health emergency the year before that, in 2017. Congress passed the very first piece of national legislation in response to the crisis in 2016. In the seventeen years before that, close to half a million people were killed in accidental drug overdoses, and drug poisoning went from being the third leading cause of accidental death to being the first.

The government's interest in protecting people from an accident differs depending on the person to whom it happens—an innocent child accidentally ingesting a pill merits a response different from that accorded an adult who uses a drug and who accidentally overdoses. In this way, risk exposure can be a moral judgment. The difference between a rapid response to one accident and a seventeen-year wait before responding to accidents that were killing tens of thousands a year represents how we feel about the people having those accidents. We are especially willing to let accidents happen to some people.

Chapter Five

Stigma

Since Maisie's death, Adam and MaryBeth Gillan have sought to pass a number of pieces of legislation at the county, state, and federal levels—including one to mandate blister packaging for opioids nationwide—to prevent what happened to their daughter from happening again. This is not a role they want to play, they tell me, but as they see it, this is how they parent Maisie now. In 2021, one of those efforts became law in Monroe County, New York, where they live: Maisie's Law would require pharmacists to offer a dose of naloxone, the opioid overdose reversal drug, with every opioid prescription.

When the law was first proposed, however, it was slightly different. At first, the law required pharmacists in Monroe County to *distribute* a dose of naloxone with every new opioid prescription. This was a way to provide a parachute with every pill, should the worst occur. But lawmakers revised the legislation a number of times before it passed. By the time it was signed by the county executive, Maisie's Law would instead require pharmacists to *have a conversation* about naloxone and offer patients the option to purchase it.

While this version of the law will undoubtedly still save lives, the excuse for the revision tells us something about how some accidents are understood. The legislators said they revised the law because distributing the drug, which is safe for children and can reverse an accidental opioid poisoning, would burden pharmacies and risk leaving unused naloxone around.

The reason that leaving unused naloxone around is problematic is *not* that it can cause harm—there is no risk; unlike an opioid, accidental naloxone ingestion is harmless. Instead, government officials argue in favor of restrictions on naloxone because, they say, it may encourage drug use. This is similar to the debunked idea that giving teenagers condoms will encourage them to have sex. What is behind both of those arguments is stigma, in this case in the form of government officials who believe that teenagers and drug users are insatiable and without willpower. At least when it comes to drugs, most Americans believe the same—that access to naloxone encourages drug use. Unspoken in this belief is the idea that some accidental overdoses might actually be a bit intentional.

If someone unintentionally crashes a car, you might call it an accident. But if someone overdoses on drugs—is that an accident, too? Does it make a difference if the accidental overdose happens to a child or an adult? What if, sharing needles to use drugs, someone unwittingly transmits a disease? Can that be an accident, too? Your answer matters less than your awareness that we do not judge these accidents by the same standards. We view them differently because of stigma—bias against a person for a characteristic that distinguishes them from the rest of society.

Stigma is slightly different from the human error we've discussed until now. In previous chapters, when we saw automakers and factory owners blame human error for accidents, it was related to the task at hand—the nut behind the wheel is only a nut while driving, and "accident-prone worker" is only a relevant insult at work. Stigma is less conditional, an intrinsic flaw that extends beyond the task at hand to define who you are in all circumstances. Race, class, and gender are often stigmatized, as is drug use. Unlike the accident-prone worker or the nut behind the wheel, we may consider a person who uses drugs to be "a drug addict" even when not using drugs—this is why you may feel that a car crash is an accident but that an overdose is not.

We have covered how accidents happen. Stigma is one reason why we let them happen.

While you may see an accidental overdose as different from a car accident, in many respects it is not. An accidental overdose happens when dangerous conditions stack up—addictive drugs marketed as nonaddictive, a lack of access to health care, or the threat of criminal prosecution if you call for help. In this chapter, we will look at how stigma causes those dangerous conditions to stack up for people who use drugs.

Stigma is what doctors call a "fundamental cause" of health disparities—an inescapable reason why some people die by accident and others do not. Drug-related accidents can occur in different ways and have different outcomes, such as accidental overdose or accidental disease transmission from shared equipment. There is also "accidental addiction," a term used to describe some less stigmatized people who use drugs (namely white people whose addictions began with a prescription) to absolve them of the stigma of drug use. The "accidental addict" is an example of how powerful the stigma of drug use is—so powerful that there's a special term to absolve certain people of it.

We Don't See the Pain of People We Don't Like

Erving Goffman is the psychologist who coined the modern understanding of the term "stigma." He defined it as a "spoiled identity." Society ostracizes stigmatized people for a characteristic that becomes all-encompassing—a single trait dictates how we judge a whole person. And, importantly, when something goes wrong, the stigmatized, because of their flawed character, are blamed.

Goffman also defined two types of people who interact with the stigmatized: the normal and the wise. By "wise," Goffman meant people who see and understand the reality of the stigmatized; the wise empathize with their pain. The "normal" are people who see the stigmatized by the word's definition—as tainted and at fault. Goffman considered most people to be "normal." Research shows that he was right.

A study by cognitive neuroscientists at the University of Chicago found that people had less empathy for pain when they stigmatized the person in pain. Subjects watched videos of people portraying expressions of pain while an fMRI machine tracked the areas of their brains that process pain and distress. Subjects in the study also self-reported their feelings, ranking the degree of pain the person in the video appeared to be experiencing and their own degree of distress from watching. The people in the video were identified as (1) healthy, (2) having AIDS contracted by blood transfusion, or (3) having AIDS contracted by intravenous drug use—and effectively were otherwise the same as one another. All made similar facial expressions. Of the three types, participants reported the lowest pain and empathy rankings—both self-reported and in their brainwave readings—for the people who they were told contracted AIDS by drug use. Though contracting AIDS in either case would be an accident, the subjects both saw less pain in the faces of these people and felt less distress watching their pain. In a survey afterward, subjects ranked the drug-use-related AIDS patients as most responsible for their condition, and the researchers found that the more someone blamed an AIDS patient, the less pain they could see in their face.

But as Goffman said, this is "normal." Even twenty years into the opioid epidemic, where more than one in ten Americans know someone killed by the drug, these stigmas are common. Only a slim majority of Americans see drug addiction as a disease. Less than 25 percent would accept a drug-addicted colleague. Less than one in five would associate with a friend or neighbor who was addicted to prescription drugs. A sizable majority believe that people who are addicted to drugs do not deserve the right to equal employment. Four in ten say that health insurers should deny the addicted equal coverage. One in three people say opioid addiction is a character defect or the by-product of shoddy parenting. Two in five say that the addicted simply lack willpower.

These statistics illustrate the ways that many Americans believe that the stigmatized deserve their fate. But if you talk to the stigmatized, you hear a very different story. I asked Amanda Leigh Allen to explain this, because she is stigmatized twice over. She has used drugs, and she has sold them.

The Criminal Addict

Amanda Leigh Allen's story is inseparable from the story of Billy Ray Bullabough. Allen is in prison, and Bullabough is dead. In the spring of 2017, in Huntersville, North Carolina, after a family barbecue, Bullabough, a young father, called Allen and bought $20 of opioids from her. He came home to the house where he lived with his parents. He left the lights on in his room. He did the drugs.

Those lights made his mother worry. When she spotted them at 2:00 a.m. and came into her son's room, she found him facedown on the bed. He had his phone in his hand. He was pale. He did not respond. It was an accidental fentanyl overdose, part of a poisoned opioid supply, tainted with a substance up to a hundred times as potent as the opioids a drug user may be used to, and often unknown to the people who sell and consume it.

On his phone, Bullabough had a message from Allen. "Hey Billy, I was supposed to cut that run, and I didn't. So be careful," she says in the recording. "Don't do too much of it. I think it's got a little fentanyl in it. Just be careful."

Bullabough didn't know about the fentanyl. As a drug user, he had an understanding of the risk that did not match the actual risk. But Allen did know. Her story is interesting because she incriminated herself in an effort to prevent an accidental overdose. She revealed her role as a drug dealer in hopes of avoiding an accident. This act appears a marker of goodness and redemption that should be powerful enough to erase some of the stigma of being a drug user and a drug seller, but it was not. A judge sentenced Allen to involuntary manslaughter and drug sales, ten years.

From a women's correctional facility in North Carolina, Allen tries to explain to me what it is like to be addicted to drugs. "Regular people don't understand the complicated, chaotic lives that addicts lead," she writes. "No needle junkie goes out to cop a bag thinking, damn, I hope this is the one that kills me! But fact of the matter is, deep in the back of your rational mind you know it could be."

She calls this at once "junkie logic" and "the disease," meaning addiction. That logic reinforces the belief that the accident won't happen to you, she says—it also tells you that if a small dose makes you feel good, then a big one will make you feel great. Allen says she sold drugs to manage and support her own drug use, and she understands the stigma she bears as a result.

"There seems to be some basic need at the core of human beings to (1) assign blame and (2) persecute others," she writes. "It's how we cope with our problems, relate to one another, feel superior, forgive ourselves, protect our beliefs, and accept our situations."

She also notes that it is not particularly easy to be on the wrong end either of this stigmatization or of the opioid epidemic. From prison, Allen writes that Bullabough was her friend, that every day she hears of another acquaintance coming close to death, and that since her arrest, two or three people she knew have died every month. Her imprisonment hasn't improved the situation; indeed, it's gotten worse.

Allen's prosecution is part of a trend that has risen with the opioid epidemic. Prosecutors treat accidental drug overdoses as murders and charge the friends, partners, and dealers who sold or shared the drugs with that crime. The simple fact that we stigmatize Allen, that we are less likely to see or empathize with her pain, also supports sending her to prison.

And this is no accident. The criminalization of drug use and drug sales directly aids corporations that sell addictive drugs. When a rising number of OxyContin overdoses threatened to affect Purdue Pharma's profits, even though executives at the company knew the drug was addictive, they blamed people who overdosed. By 2001, there was clear evidence that OxyContin, the gateway drug for the opioid epidemic, was very addictive and was being diverted into the illegal drug market, and that accidental overdoses were rising. Richard Sackler, then president of Purdue Pharma, wrote an email about how the company should address the problem. "We have to hammer on abusers in every way possible," Sackler wrote. "They are the culprits and the problem. They are reckless criminals."

The company would continue to advertise the drug explicitly as non-habit-forming for years until the federal government prosecuted them for that lie. But Richard Sackler understood that stigma was strong enough to let him continue to profit from an addictive drug. His "criminal addict" is not so different from the jaywalker, the accident-prone worker, or the nut behind the wheel. Each is a way to blame human error to distract from dangerous conditions that lead to accidents.

And people who use drugs are faced with impossibly dangerous conditions. Known addictive drugs such as OxyContin are marketed and sold as nonaddictive, making accidental addiction more likely. Illegal substitutes for those drugs come with unknown additives and potencies, such as the fentanyl that killed Billy Bullabough, making accidental overdose more likely. Tools needed to use drugs safely, such as clean syringes, are often illegal to own, making accidental disease transmission more likely. Medication to stop an overdose, such as naloxone, is often impossible to buy. Drug illegality makes people feel unsafe calling for help, making accidental overdose more likely to be fatal. And medication that helps control addiction, such as methadone, is extremely restricted in who can administer it, and when and where it is available, so assistance may require two hours of driving a day, making continued drug use simply a more plausible choice for an addicted person.

In her letters from prison, Allen tells me that she sees what happened to Bullabough as an accident, and that as a person who uses drugs, she sees all drug overdoses as accidents. In fact, every expert I spoke to agrees that drug overdoses are accidents. Researchers estimate that, at most, 4 percent of fatal drug overdoses are intentional. And researchers have also found that the word "accident" can act as kindness in mourning.

In a comparative survey, parents who lost a child to overdose suffered more grief and worse mental health outcomes than parents of children who died of other accidents. The study authors concluded that these parents' post-traumatic stress symptoms were a direct product of stigma against drug-use accidents.

When I say that there are no accidents, I mean that everything we call an accident is predictable and preventable. When a person who uses drugs says that an overdose is an accident, they mean that what happened was not intentional and was regrettable, and that no one wanted anyone to die. If anyone should be allowed to say "it was an accident," it's people who use drugs and the people who love them, if it offers any comfort.

When we protest the word "accident," it should matter who has been hurt and who is telling the story. This book is full of powerful people who say "it was an accident" to keep making money, to avoid admitting fault, and to not have to be accountable for the people they kill and injure. In so many cases, "it was an accident" is a phrase that absolves powerful people of responsibility for dangerous conditions. And these people allow accidents to happen again and again.

But when a powerless person says "it was an accident," the phrase can take on other meanings. It can mean that an overdose was unintentional or that any consequence was regrettable—it can be a way to say: *I didn't mean it*. And if "accident" can offer that person some kindness and absolution, that is a story that I want us all to hear.

Systemically, however, there is nothing unpredictable or unpreventable here.

Addiction is not an accident when a drug company markets a drug known to be addictive as nonaddictive. Overdose is not an accident when overdose reversal and addiction mitigation medication are made intentionally unavailable. Disease transmission is not an accident when clean equipment to avoid transmission is illegal. People who use drugs face impossibly dangerous conditions. These conditions are also not the fault of a person who uses drugs. If using the term "accident" helps them or their loved ones in psychic terms, then that term is the least we can give them.

What's at stake is whose story we hear when we talk about addiction and drug use—what drug companies, police, prosecutors, and government officials want us to hear or what people who use drugs are saying. One reason the modern opioid crisis was allowed to get so bad was that we all spent too long listening to these powerful people, and not people who use drugs, about what was going wrong, and those powerful people insisted that it was not a crisis of accidents but one of bad people.

A Crisis of Bad People

David Herzberg has the second-best job title in this book: historian of drugs. He is also a history professor at the University at Buffalo and the author of *White Market Drugs: Big Pharma and the Hidden History of Addiction in America*. He notes that one of the reasons that the modern opioid epidemic has gotten so bad—bad enough to decrease the overall U.S. life expectancy—is that Purdue Pharma aggressively marketed the false claim that OxyContin is nonaddictive.

Maintaining this lie was Richard Sackler's point about needing to "hammer on abusers." And for a long time, that stigmatizing strategy worked. Purdue blamed human error for the opioid epidemic, distracting from the dangerous condition of an addictive drug marketed as nonaddictive. All the while, addictions and accidental overdoses grew and grew. Between 1995 and 2001, the number of people treated for opioid abuse in the state of Maine grew by 460 percent. In 2000, West Virginia opened its first methadone treatment program, and then, in the next three years, the state would need to open six more. In 2002, OxyContin prescriptions climbed over 6 million. By 2003, accidental fatal prescription overdoses had grown by 830 percent in one corner of Virginia. The Drug Enforcement Administration did not begin to crack down on pain clinics and distributors until 2005. By then, for the addicted, it was too late. In 2021, the vast majority of accidental overdose deaths are still due to opioids. Between 1999 and 2020, well over 840,000 people died of an opioid overdose. As the death toll rose too precipitously to be ignored, the drug companies leaned into this idea: *There are no accidental overdoses. There are only reckless criminal addicts.*

"Once it became clear that addiction was a problem, the drug companies' first line of defense, and an incredibly successful one, was to say: Look, our products are good, the doctors are good, the patients are good, but there are these evil abusers," Herzberg tells me. "They are becoming addicted and giving our drug a bad name. So, we should respond to this, not as if this is a crisis of accidents, we should respond to this as if it is a crisis of bad people."

What distinguishes a good person from a bad person in this logic is legitimacy—a factor that stigmas around legality, race, and economic class can dictate. Let's imagine a scenario in which prosecutors would not have charged Allen with Bullabough's murder. It would require that she be Dr. Allen and that Bullabough buy his opioids at a pharmacy with a prescription and accidentally overdose that way. Looked at broadly, in taking the same actions, some people have accidents and some commit crimes—stigma is the decider. In this way, stigma is a weaponized version of the human error stance. It is the same old story of finding fault with human error, but the stigma of crime ratchets up the stakes. The victim is labeled not just an addict but a criminal addict.

The drug companies endorsed this message—to arrest more people for the crime of illegal use—and disseminated it by planting articles and op-eds, funding think tanks, and hosting anti-addiction websites that all pointed to human error as the problem. As one essay in the *New York Times* put it, "When you scratch the surface of someone who is addicted to painkillers, you usually find a seasoned drug abuser with a previous habit involving pills, alcohol, heroin or cocaine." A doctor who worked for a think tank funded by Purdue wrote that piece, wherein she cited studies funded by Purdue, and quoted doctors who worked for Purdue. As long as the criminal addict message prevailed, the opioid epidemic was a crisis of bad people, human error was to blame, and the conditions did not change.

But over time the epidemic became so widespread that the "bad people" story no longer made sense. Or rather, the bad people story became harder to sell as more white soccer moms and clean-cut suburban teens became addicted to opioids. To get around this, the drug company drew another line: the accidental addict—a blameless person who stumbled into addiction "by accident." The drug companies put forth a new narrative that there can be, at once, criminal addicts and accidental addicts.

"Some of the work that gets done when you call something an accident is about the innocence or guilt of the person who suffers the problem," Herzberg points out. "We consider some people to be blame-free and others to be guilty. There are very strong patterns about who we apply those to."

This is stigma exactly—the exact same human errors defined in different terms. One is criminal, one is accidental, and which is which defined by other stigmatized characteristics, such as race and income, and one you might not have heard of: *the doctor-visiting class.*

Using crime to stigmatize drug use is a tradition as old as the mass production of drugs, and that story gets interesting at the same moment Crystal Eastman is prowling the morgues, factories, and coal mines of Pittsburgh.

The History of Bad People

America's first opioid epidemic arrived with the Industrial Revolution. While we mined more coal, built more factories, and had more accidents, we also took more drugs. The accidents that followed the expansion of coal mining and factories resulted in wholesale laws that created systems of safety and restitution for all workers. But the response to the concurrent addiction crisis instead divided drug users into two classes of people. Some overdoses were accidents, some were crimes, and there was no overlap between the two—race, money, and power decided which side your addiction fell on.

One group of people using addictive drugs—the majority—were called patients, people who went to see doctors. These were middle-class white people born in the United States; they are the people Herzberg refers to as "the doctor-visiting class." Doctors and lawmakers understood this group of people as deserving of cures, and their addictions as the by-product of trying to recover from illness. Their overdoses were seen as tragic accidents. This is the earliest iteration of the accidental addict. The answer to these accidents was better education for doctors and pharmacists, and tighter controls over the supply chain.

The other crisis belonged to the people who couldn't see a doctor for reasons of money or race: Chinese immigrants on the West Coast, southern and eastern European immigrants in northeastern cities, Black people in the South. This group gained access to cheaper and more powerful drugs in the late nineteenth century as well, but were seen as willfully, criminally deviant. Doctors and lawmakers saw the accidental addict as deserving a cure but considered this group to be seeking pleasure rather than health.

"Long before smoking opium was illegal, you had oceans of ink spilled on talking about the 'yellow peril' and the threat to America from these Chinese men lured into opium slavery—all these prurient tales about them selling their bodies and souls to the yellow devils," Herzberg explains. "You can look in the New York Times in the same day of the same year of 1874 and you'll see this vicious takedown of the horrible people that are going to the opium den, then at the same time, these sensitive pieces about the tragic miseries of the unfortunate innocents who had become addicted when they just innocently trusted their doctor."

Less than forty years after that issue of the New York Times came out, the government would write this divide into law. In response to the opioid crisis of that day, they passed new laws, and different laws for stigmatized and non-stigmatized drug use. These laws followed the human error–dangerous conditions divide exactly—fixing dangerous conditions to prevent accidents in some cases and blaming human error, which disregarded and exacerbated the same conditions, to increase accidents in others.

The first drug law, the Pure Food and Drug Act of 1906, protected the doctor-visiting class, and it did not outlaw the possession of anything. It just required an honest label on the container of a doctor-prescribed or pharmacist-bought drug, detailing what they'd put inside. The second drug law, passed in 1914, was for people who were unable to access or disallowed access to a doctor—the Harrison Narcotics Tax Act. This law made it illegal to possess drugs without a prescription from a doctor. One law was a consumer protection that identified drug risks for people with access to doctors; the other was a criminal prohibition that made it riskier for people without access to doctors to use drugs. While the government declared the stigmatized drug user to be a criminal, they guaranteed that the non-stigmatized drug user was safer *and* less likely to overdose. In this way, whether or not your drug use was stigmatized became a slice of Swiss cheese protecting you or a hole through which an accident might slip through.

By these laws, a person who *could* visit a doctor could legally obtain a prescription for an opioid—say, morphine—and be legally addicted to morphine. The government would consider both their addiction and their overdose an accident. And both accidents would be less likely to occur, because their drug now had an honest label and a doctor's observation—and we know that overdoses are more likely when drug potency is unknown and use is unmonitored. On the other side of the coin, a person who *could not* visit a doctor could be thrown in jail for possessing the same drug.

The "war on drugs" may have been invented by Richard Nixon, but it began far before. By 1928, one-third of America's federal prisoners were there for violating narcotics laws, just fourteen years after the government first criminalized drug use. Even as the drug war intensified through to the 1950s, doctors continued to prescribe morphine to people who had become addicted to it—because it was an "accidental addiction," thus innocent and deserving treatment. It was not their fault, the story went, and they should continue to get morphine.

This divide matters in a multitude of ways that define who lives and who dies by accident. Stigma does not just draw a line between an accident and a crime; stigma can be the difference between life and death.

How Stigma Causes Accidents

When drug use is stigmatized, the risk of overdose increases in myriad ways, explains Dr. Kimberly Sue, medical director of the Harm Reduction Coalition, attending physician at Rikers Island correctional facility, and author of *Getting Wrecked: Women, Incarceration, and the American Opioid Crisis.*

Take a person who is in treatment for opioid use but then relapses. Anticipated and internalized stigmas may drive that person to use drugs in riskier ways, such as not informing loved ones of the relapse, using drugs alone, and hiding their use. In this way, stigmas create holes in that person's layers of safety. That person is at very high risk of dying of an overdose—they would not have naloxone, or anyone to get help, or anyone to revive them, or anyone who knows to check on them.

But even if people are using together, the way stigma appears in laws and policies can increase the risk of accidental death. A person might not call 911 during someone else's accidental overdose for fear the police will arrest them under drug-induced homicide laws. A law restricting drug paraphernalia such as syringes could make it illegal to use drugs without risking accidental disease transmission.

It's also much easier for a doctor to prescribe an addictive drug than a drug that treats addiction. To prescribe OxyContin, doctors require no special training or certification beyond their medical degree. To prescribe buprenorphine—an opioid substitute treatment that helps a person addicted to opioids off their edge, allowing safe recovery in the privacy of their own home—doctors must fill out a pile of paperwork, get a special waiver from the Drug Enforcement Administration, and undergo an eight-hour training session. After all that, they're only permitted to prescribe to a limited number of patients.

"Most physicians are not able to prescribe this highly effective medication. That's an example of what I would say is stigma writ into law," Sue explains. "There is no other medication that we cannot write a prescription for unless we do special training."

Without addiction-mitigating drugs, cold turkey may be your only option. That is a major risk, because it shocks your body, and a factor for accidental overdose, because if you relapse after withdrawal, your tolerance will be significantly lower. However, often this is the only brand of healing allowed. Buprenorphine, as Sue described, is limited. Methadone, the other safe substitute for people addicted to opioids, can only be distributed at a clinic, requiring daily visits, and the government restricts how many of these can operate in a given region, and for how many hours of the day.

Overdosing may not only be more likely because of stigma; it may be less survivable. For example, naloxone, the drug that can arrest an overdose, is often inaccessible. One study of Tennessee pharmacies found the average price of a single dose to be a whopping $132.49. In a study of California pharmacies, fewer than one in four pharmacists were willing to distribute the drug without a prescription even though that is perfectly legal there. In a Texas study, 31 percent of pharmacies did not have naloxone in stock, and half the pharmacists refused to bill insurance for the medication. Three years after New York State made naloxone legal without a prescription, fewer than 38 percent of New York City pharmacists both stocked the drug and were willing to sell it. And, because these structural stigmas overlap with our own personal stigmas, it is essential to point out that well over half of Americans approve of these tight restrictions on access to a medication that can stop an overdose.

Government officials can also stigmatize drug use in a way that causes accidents, as in 2015, when the state of Indiana had an HIV outbreak. There is no reason that any place in the United States should be having an

HIV outbreak in 2015—we know what causes HIV and how to prevent it. But in Indiana, it was illegal to have a syringe. Thus syringes were in short supply, so people who used drugs were reusing and sharing syringes, leading to accidental HIV transmission.

At first, Sue explains, the response to this crisis appeared good. Instead of blaming human error, the state changed the dangerous conditions by legalizing some programs that gave people who use drugs access to syringes. But the stigma of the criminal addict won out.

"A public health emergency was declared. Syringe exchange was 'made legal.' But there were all these restrictions, all these hoops to jump through. People might have a card that authorized them to carry a syringe, but they were still getting arrested for having them," Sue points out. The law partially removed a structural stigma on paper but not in the practice of those who enforced the law.

Even this limited dose of assistance for drug users did not last: the rural Indiana county where that HIV outbreak began shut down their needle exchange in 2021. These stories are all too common. West Virginia passed a law in 2021 limiting access to syringe exchanges to those with a state identification card, and forcing staff at the exchanges to refuse clean needles to those who do not show up with dirty ones to swap out. New Jersey evicted its largest syringe exchange in 2021 because, officials said, too many people were using it.

This practice of offering forgiveness to the addicted only in tiny doses derives from another stigma—that people who use drugs are weak-willed and insatiable—and this, too, causes accidents. One example is when states legalize only some of the equipment drug users need to avoid an accident—say, syringes, but no other paraphernalia, such as cookers. Drug users have clean needles but have to share other contaminated equipment, and the risk of disease transmission remains.

We also find stigmas baked into the federal budget, which devotes billions more to the enforcement and prosecution of drug laws than it does to research and to treatment of people suffering addictions. Researchers have found that these policy decisions increase the likelihood of accidental death—increased spending on drug law enforcement increases the number of people who die of an overdose.

Other studies have found that stigmas around drug use affect every facet of interaction with legal and illegal drugs. Opioid stigmas make it hard for people with chronic pain to obtain treatment for their pain *and* make patients seeking addiction treatment more likely to quit their treatment. These stigmas also influence doctors, making them more likely to set up onerous rules and policies (say, restricting patients from smoking cigarettes) and punitively terminate treatment for the addicted as punishment (for, say, violating the no-cigarettes rule). People who use drugs cite the stigmatization they feel as the primary reason for not getting help.

It is no accident that mechanisms that can prevent overdose and disease transmission are inaccessible; it is a direct result of a lack of empathy and perhaps even a desire to punish people who are addicted. The outcome of making known methods of prevention inaccessible is that accidental overdose crises are allowed to grow for decades. And while the stigmas that attend addiction are particularly deadly, these are hardly the only dangerous ones. For too many people, stigmas stack up.

Criminalization Makes You a Criminal

Say you become addicted to opioids. Addiction can mean that you need to use them every few hours, forever.

If those opioids are legal, your addiction may still be annoying and expensive, and a part of your life you're probably not happy about, but you can handle it, as many people do. If you have a prescription, you'll likely have a reliable supply of the drug you need on hand.

If you don't have a prescription, it's less likely your supply would be reliable. And if the opioids you need are illegal, or only accessible to you illegally, then addiction and social stigma would force you into other stigmatized situations not directly related to drug use. For example, you might need to live near where people sell illegal goods, which may not be the safest place to reside. You may have trouble keeping a job if you regularly have to disappear on a time-consuming search for your drug. If you are constantly in the company of people doing illegal things, it may be easier for you just to get a job doing illegal things, a job from which they won't fire you if you have to go and buy drugs. When one part of your life is stigmatized, you can quickly amass other stigmas, too.

The "yellow peril" that Herzberg explained is a prime example. That was a stigma about being an opioid user and a stigma about being a Chinese immigrant. The yellow peril wasn't just people who used opioids but poor Asian immigrants who used opioids. Drug laws did not develop to address drugs alone; otherwise, they would have applied equally to everyone. Rather, the government made and enforced the laws with the goal of creating two classes of drug use.

"Those socially marginalized people, those communities were already ones that authorities wanted to police, and were policing in a bunch of other ways already," Herzberg says, "so a drug law just added a new tool, new money to hire cops, and new ways to control those neighborhoods and the people living in them."

In the 1970s, 1980s, and 1990s, the U.S. government supercharged that so-called war on drugs with new laws expanding criminalization, setting minimum sentences, and outsizing budgets for policing and prison expansion. Over the past forty years, the United States has overall increased the number of people in prisons and jails by 500 percent, to more than 2 million—more than any other country in the world. Significantly more federal prisoners are convicted of drug offenses than any other offenses—more than for weapons, sex crimes, or burglary.

In 1980, fewer than 41,000 people were incarcerated for drug charges. Today, more than 430,000 are. But the U.S. government had already been ratcheting up the war on drugs for some time. Between 1925 and 1954, legislators, police, prosecutors, and judges doubled the prison population. Between 1954 and 1982, they doubled it again. Then, they picked up the pace. By 1992, they doubled the population again, and then again by 2008. The government holds more people in prison for drugs today than all people incarcerated for any crime in 1980. Judges and prosecutors increased the length of federal prison sentences for drug offenders by 36 percent between 1980 and 2011. Between 1988 and 2012, the average time that a person sentenced to federal prison for drug offenses spent incarcerated rose by 153 percent. And considerably more Black people than white people are imprisoned for drugs. "It is no accident that eras of drug and pharmaceutical reform have so often paralleled each other, nor is it an accident that they map so well onto civil rights history," Herzberg points out.

More than one in every four people that police arrest for drugs are Black. More than one in every three people that judges incarcerate for drug offenses are Black. But only around one in eight Americans are Black, and both Black and white Americans use illegal drugs at about the same rate. Doctors are significantly more likely to test Black women and their infants for drugs during pregnancy or delivery than they are to test white women and infants. And the results of these tests prove that the choice to test is a racist stigma: Black women are not more likely to receive a positive drug test during labor; they are just more likely to be tested. Dr. Kimberly Sue sees this as drug-use stigma exacerbated by racial stigma.

"We know that, at least in health care, and as well as our social services and legal systems, racism is pervasive. In all of our systems, institutional and structural racism is present, and it is at play in these microlevel interactions for cognitive decision-making processes for individuals on the front line—doctors, cops, social workers," Sue notes.

Drug use is generally equally prevalent across race and ethnicity. But for decades prior to the modern opioid epidemic, accidental drug overdose in the United States disproportionately affected Black people. This is a measure not of drug use but of stigma—Black drug use was more often considered criminal and less likely to come with a doctor's prescription, so use came with higher risk. Proof of this arrived when the most popular opioids in America again came with a prescription and were prescribed in record numbers to white people. For at least twenty years, from 1979 to 2000, Black people died from accidental opioid overdoses at a higher rate than white people. When Purdue Pharma released OxyContin and aggressively marketed it to doctors as a nonaddictive opioid pain medication, the rate of accidental opioid overdose in America skyrocketed among white people. Black people were protected in part because OxyContin was made for and marketed to the doctor-visiting class.

Other stigmas stacked up to protect Black people from these overdoses as well, such as the fact that OxyContin is a pain medication. Researchers have found that some doctors and medical students believe racist mythology about Black patients to a significant degree—thinking Black people have thicker skin and less sensitive nerves than others, are less likely to follow doctors' orders, and feel less pain. As a result, doctors and medical students disregard pain of Black patients twice as often as they do that of other races and are significantly less likely to treat it. Had white and Black prescription opioid rates been similar between 1999 and 2017, researchers estimate that more than 14,000 Black Americans would be dead today—killed by accidental opioid overdoses.

In 2010, white people were dying of accidental drug overdoses at nearly twice the rate of Black people, in large part because OxyContin prescriptions still dominated the overdose epidemic. The epidemic was significant enough to shift the statistics of the entire history of accidental death in America—in 2002, white people began to be killed by accident, all accidents total, at a higher rate than Black people for the first time in recorded history because of the way white overdose deaths shifted the numbers. It was not the pile of bodies that made the public see the opioid epidemic as an epidemic, but that suddenly the bodies were white.

Today, that gap is shrinking. White opioid overdoses are leveling off, and Black overdoses are rising sharply. In 2019, accidental drug overdoses returned to their old pattern, with Black people dying at a rising rate, and at the same rate as white people, for the first time since 2002, because with OxyContin finally regulated, most accidental overdoses now come from illegal, not prescription, opioids. But stigma has not changed as an arbiter of accidents. Doctors prescribe buprenorphine, which lowers the risk and rate of accidental overdose by managing the urge for the drug, almost exclusively to white people. Researchers investigated some 13 million doctor visits between 2012 and 2015 and found a surge of physicians prescribing the medication to white people and no change in the number of prescriptions for Black people. Even while Black overdoses are rising faster than white ones, doctors are thirty-five times more likely to prescribe buprenorphine to white people.

Buprenorphine is better than methadone because it doesn't require daily visits to a clinic—but that only helps if you're white enough to get a prescription. For Black people without a prescription, there is the risk of the accidental overdose or the daily burden of the methadone clinic. As a result, white opioid use has begun to taper, while the crisis for Black people rises at a disproportionate rate.

In accidents, stigmas stack up, and race trumps them all.

Chapter Six

Racism

W hen we tell a "human error" story—when we blame the jaywalker, the accident-prone worker, the nut behind the wheel, or the criminal addict—we are being duped into distraction from the ways that we can prevent accidents. And this allows the same accidents to happen again.

Finding fault in a person smells like justice and feels like a book being closed. It makes sense that we seek it. But failing to prevent the preventable results in a vast and deadly unfairness—and one outcome is the wildly unequal rate at which people are killed by accident because of racism.

In his book *The Field Guide to Understanding 'Human Error,'* Sidney Dekker—the pilot and safety expert who invented the "Bad Apple Theory" and "New View" framing of the human error–dangerous conditions debate—argues that for us to understand how policies, practices, and the built environment can cause accidents, we must see the world from the perspective of the people involved in those accidents. He uses a tunnel to explain.

Picture a tunnel as seen from the outside. On one end is a person just before an accident. On the other end is the accident's aftermath. From your perspective, everything about the accident is hidden inside the tunnel, except for the person it began with, their possible error, and the outcome. This is the common perspective from which an accident is interrogated, far away or high above, looking at the beginning and the end and nothing in between. From this perspective, we can reach the wrong conclusions in a lot of different ways.

For one, we could assume that the bad outcome must have started with a bad action—if *something* went wrong, then *someone* must have done something wrong. If that's our conclusion, then the way to fix the accident is to stand outside the tunnel, holding up a safety manual, such as the managers at the Georgia-Pacific paper plant did in chapter 1, imposing those rules and procedures on something that already happened as though you could go back in time.

Or we could detail all the ways a person could have avoided an accident, as though each detail was a fact—for instance, if we were to say that the cause of the accident that killed Irwin Ouser was that he *could have* played somewhere else and his parents *could have* been more responsible. We'd work backward through what happened to ask why a person zigged when they should have zagged. The issue with this approach is that by focusing on what we wish happened, we learn nothing about what actually happened.

"The problem about taking the position of retrospective outsider is that it does not allow you to explain anything," Dekker wrote. "From that position, all you can do is judge people for not noticing what you find so important now (given your knowledge of the outcome)."

None of this helps us understand the accident itself.

Dekker encourages us instead to get in the tunnel and see an accident from the perspective of the person inside it. If we can see an accident unfolding from inside the tunnel, not from outside or in hindsight, we can more easily grasp why someone's decisions made sense to them at the time.

Let's be clear: to err is human. People make mistakes. But we have avoided focusing on that fact, because it doesn't help prevent accidents and instead encourages the sort of sham conclusions that Dekker outlines with his tunnel metaphor. We have also avoided focusing on human errors because many accident experts believe that they don't really exist—rather, every human action in a built environment is a product of that environment. Dangerous conditions *cause* mistakes, the thinking goes, so *if* the conditions were not dangerous, then there would be no mistakes, or at least none that resulted in death or serious injury.

Keeping this front of mind, we will turn to *who* has accidents and how that feels. People do not die by accident equally in America. Racism and stigma, for example, both excuse and cause accidents. For this reason, I would take Dekker's idea a step further: We need to see accidents from the perspective of those involved, and we especially need to see accidents from the perspective of those harmed. By doing this, we can trace an accident beyond the built environment—the fragile nuclear reactor and the wrong color of the indicator light—and see the intangible systems that lead to accidents, too. Racism defines who feels at risk from accidents and who is at risk, whom we blame and whom we punish, who lives and who dies, and for whom the most dangerous systems lie in wait.

But it is important to note that the same rules about human error apply to race as well. Just as accident-proneness is not an indelible trait, race is not genetic. If more people of a certain race die by a certain accident, blaming accidents on human error would just be racism.

If, for example, we know that Black people are more likely to be struck by a car, we could think that Black people make more errors when walking—an assumption of human error based on racism—and issue them summonses for jaywalking. (As we will learn, this is what actually happens.) But the truth is that Black people are more likely to be struck by a car for a stack of reasons that intersect, including drivers who make split-second racist decisions and racist planning policies that leave streets more dangerous where Black people live—exactly what William Bunge was pointing out when he mapped *Where Commuters Run Over Black Children* in Detroit in chapter 1.

Racist people and systems create hazardous conditions that cause accidents and then blame the victims of those accidents, a human error conclusion we may be more likely to accept because we, too, may be racist. In this way, accidental deaths land unequally along racial lines, and so does what happens next. White people are more likely to have their mistakes absolved as "accidents," and Black people are more likely to be blamed, often criminally, for the same mistakes. Racism defines which outcome we allocate to which people. This cycle creates stigma and an illusion that racial differences are real. The sociologist-historian team Karen Fields and Barbara Fields call this "racecraft"—when racism makes it appear that race is more than a construct.

In accidents, racecraft can come into play if we use race or ethnicity to explain unequal outcomes. Let's look at one way this could work: Nationwide, Latino people are more likely than white people to be killed in bike accidents. In New York City, Latino people are also more likely to be ticketed for bicycling on the sidewalk. Knowing these facts, we could develop a racist stigma that expects Latino people in New York City to be risky and lawless cyclists. That stigma would reduce empathy for a Latino cyclist killed in a bike accident. As a result, police may enforce laws against people biking in Latino neighborhoods more strictly, and taxpayers, in general, could be less supportive of building bike infrastructure in these neighborhoods. If you believe the stigma, why would you want to give good things to lawless people? A racist New York City community board member made a similar argument in 2017, arguing to halt construction of bike lanes in the majority Latino immigrant neighborhood of Corona, Queens. "Once Trump removes all the illegals from Corona," she said, "there won't be anybody to ride bike lanes."

You can see how this could create a vicious cycle: accidental death is more likely because of dangerous conditions, which are distributed across society in a racist way, and which are justified to remain dangerous by a racist interpretation of the cause of accidental death. The response to a white person killed in a bike accident, absent racecraft, might be more sympathetic, less focused on human error and more on dangerous conditions—leading to solutions for the actual problems.

Like all stigmas in accidents, these thought processes are about othering the killed and injured, indelibly marking the differences between "us" and "them." Overcoming this requires putting ourselves in the shoes of the harmed. And when we do that, we can see that the threat of an accident is different *and feels different* if the person at the start of the tunnel is not white. There we find people who are very aware they are at risk.

The White Male Effect

In the late 1980s, a first-of-its-kind mapping study (which we will examine at the end of this chapter) demonstrated that people of color faced heightened risk for accidental chemical exposure based on where they lived. That study inspired Paul Slovic, the risk perception expert from chapter 4, to ask questions about how that heightened *actual* risk manifested in *feelings* about risk. The unequal risk of accidental chemical exposure was real, but, he wondered, how was it perceived?

In a nationwide survey, Slovic asked a group of subjects, male and female, white and "non-white," a series of questions about twenty-five hazards, largely accidental—including big risks, such as a nuclear disaster, pollution, or rapidly accelerating technology, and everyday risks, such as car accidents and home fires. Slovic's survey asked respondents to rate these risks on a scale of "almost no health risk" to "high health risk," and then broke out the respondents by race and gender.

Non-white people felt at risk more often and to a greater degree than white. While white women perceived more risk than white men, the perception of risk was nearly the same across gender lines for non-white people. White men felt the least threatened by everything, from nuclear waste to suntanning to plane crashes.

To determine the "why" behind all this data, Slovic asked other demographic questions, and a clear pattern emerged among the white men who were wealthier, more educated, and more politically conservative. This group reported feeling least at risk from the listed hazards. They also answered yes to questions such as "Do you feel it is acceptable for society to impose small risks on individuals without their consent?" and

"Has America gone too far pushing equal rights?" This same group said no to the question "Should local residents have the authority to close a nuclear power plant they think is run poorly?" That question, of course, is another way of asking whether the power to change dangerous conditions should rest with the people who are at risk from an accident.

In 2000, Slovic reran the study and found similar results.

In 2004, another researcher published a similar study but focused on Black and white men and women who lived along the stretch of the Mississippi River from Baton Rouge to New Orleans, Louisiana—a region with such frequent chemical accidents that it's known as Cancer Alley. The people exposed to these accidents are disproportionately Black, despite racial diversity within Cancer Alley. The 2004 study found the same—Black women perceived the most risk, followed closely by Black men, followed closely by white women, and followed not at all closely by white men.

Risk perception researchers have found similar results so often they've branded this the "white male effect." White men feel significantly more comfortable with risk or are just acutely aware that their risk exposure is relatively minimal. They aren't simply more willing to accept risk; they accurately perceive that *they alone* are at less risk. Slovic, writing in 1997, makes a similar point:

> *Perhaps White males see less risk in the world because they create, manage, control and benefit from many of the major technologies and activities. Perhaps women and non-White men see the world as more dangerous because in many ways they are more vulnerable, because they benefit less from many of the technologies and institutions, and because they have less power and control over what happens in their communities and their lives.*

In these studies, Black people accurately perceived a lack of control over the dangerous conditions that lead to accidents. But the same powerlessness is present *after* an accident. Another reason non-white people may feel more at risk is that, after an accident, they are more likely to be blamed. (And based on what we know about stigma, that blame can increase the likelihood of the next accident.) Evidence of a racist divide—where some accidents are mistakes and others are violations—is not hard to find, even from the very first moments of life.

Racism for Babies

Doctors generally diagnose two ways that babies die in their beds, both classified under the subgroup sudden unexpected infant death. One is a medical condition—the mysterious and innocent sudden infant death syndrome, also known by its acronym, SIDS, where a child succumbs for unknown and unexplainable reasons. The other is an accident, or an "unintentional injury death" in Centers for Disease Control and Prevention parlance: accidental suffocation and strangulation in bed, or ASSB. The rate of the latter, accidental suffocation, as a cause of death for babies under the age of one is 36 percent higher for Indigenous people and 132 percent higher for Black people than for white people. But there is evidence that this disparity may be a product of imperfect and racist diagnoses.

In 2019, researchers at Sanford School of Medicine in South Dakota began to explore racial disparities in the number of sudden unexpected infant deaths and recent shifts from SIDS to ASSB. They found reason to be concerned.

SIDS rates have been in decline since the early 1990s, when doctors began to tell parents that babies should sleep on their backs in hard, blanketless beds. And ASSB rates have risen in tandem, though the reason why is uncertain—it could be that the latter diagnosis is applied increasingly as doctors begin to understand what is and is not SIDS, or it could be some other factor. However, neither the rise nor decline in these diagnoses is occurring evenly across the population. The rate of SIDS diagnoses is declining among people of color at a much faster rate than among white people, and the rate of ASSB diagnoses is increasing among people of color at a faster rate than among white people. ASSB diagnoses in sudden infant deaths are going up for all races but are rising faster for people who aren't white.

The lead researcher on the Sanford School of Medicine study hypothesized that whoever is diagnosing the cause of death in these infants might at once be less willing to call the death of a non-white child SIDS and less willing to diagnose asphyxia deaths in white babies. It appears that—because SIDS is the more innocuous diagnosis, free of human error—doctors are less likely to diagnose non-white babies with the syndrome. And because ASSB is the more stigmatized diagnosis, bordering on neglect, with definite implications of human error, doctors are less willing to give that explanation for white babies' deaths.

One reason for this disparity may be that the medical professionals marking these deaths are more willing to tell white parents that their child died of an unpreventable syndrome and more inclined to blame the parents of non-white babies for their children dying of you-should-have-known-better accidental strangulation. By this count, non-white babies appear to die more often by accident because medical professionals absolve white parents of the shame of a child's accidental death.

A Taste for Vengeance

The tendency to divide forgiveness and blame for accidents along racial lines is also present in everyday circumstances, such as jaywalking—a violation selectively enforced along racial lines.

In Jacksonville, Florida, one of the top ten U.S. cities where pedestrians are most likely to be killed by drivers, police disproportionately issue jaywalking citations to Black people. Researchers at ProPublica found that in a five-year period ending in 2016, police issued 55 percent of the city's jaywalking citations to Black people, who make up only 29 percent of the population. Black people were three times more likely to be cited for crossing the street than were white people. Similar studies have found evidence of racist enforcement of this violation in cities much safer for pedestrians, such as New York. In 2019, police issued almost 90 percent of jaywalking summonses to Black and Latino pedestrians, who make up about half of New Yorkers. In the first three months of 2020, New York City police issued 99 percent of the jaywalking summonses they wrote to Black and Latino people.

Racism is prevalent, too, in sentencing for vehicular homicide. But where being Black means that you are more likely to have to pay a fine for jaywalking, if a driver kills you while you are crossing the street, being Black means that your killer pays less of a debt to society than if the driver had killed a white person. Researchers have found that vehicular homicide, essentially the unintentional but negligent killing of a person with a car, is a crime with a shorter sentence when the victim is Black.

In 2000, researchers at Dartmouth and Harvard University cataloged U.S. Bureau of Justice Statistics data on sentence length for vehicular homicide—largely drunk driving accidents—based on the victims' characteristics. They looked at reams of sentencing data from courtrooms across America and found that when prosecutors charged a person with vehicular homicide, the prison sentence was 53 percent shorter if the victim was Black.

If a prison sentence measures the value of the victim's life, Black life is worth less than white life. The authors of the study concluded that there was something more sinister to sentence length than a measure of justice—they called this "the taste for vengeance."

"I Just Don't See Race"

When a Black or Latino person crosses the street outside a crosswalk, they are more likely to be found at fault for that violation. And when a Black person is struck and killed crossing the street inside or outside a crosswalk, the crime weighs less. The event before that accident and the outcome after that accident are both dictated by racism. What occurs between these events shows the same pattern.

In 2019, on average, U.S. drivers killed twenty-one pedestrians every day. Disproportionately, the dead were Latino, Black, and Indigenous.

The rate of accidental pedestrian death is 87 percent higher for Latino people, 93 percent higher for Black people, and 171 percent higher for Indigenous people than it is for white people. Black people are more likely to be found at fault walking in the street, less likely to be offered justice if killed there, *and* more likely to be killed there.

Even the moment after stepping into the crosswalk but before being struck and killed in the crosswalk is determined by racism. Researchers at Portland State University have found that drivers yield the right of way significantly less often to Black pedestrians.

Tara Goddard, who led this study, modeled her research on earlier studies of racial bias in decision-making, most of which exist outside the realm of transportation, along with one transportation study about canes and umbrellas. That study looked at whether drivers' decisions to yield were affected by whether a person waiting to cross the street carried an umbrella or a cane. Drivers yielded more often for those holding the item that implied disability, evidence that people made biased decisions while driving. Goddard wanted to know if racism could bias those decisions and if that's why Black pedestrians are so much more likely to be killed—a disparity that exists even after you control for socioeconomic status, alcohol use, and the fact that more Black people may live in pedestrian-dense urban areas.

Downtown in Portland, Oregon, in 2015, Goddard and her team hired six men, chosen for their height and weight—same age, same build. She had the men dressed in identical clothes. Three were Black and three were white. Each man was sent out to a busy one-way, two-lane street with a crosswalk that did not have a Walk signal. With the researchers watching, the men waited to cross the street. For them to cross the road safely, a driver would need to yield.

"This is what's referred to as a quasi-experiment. Because it wasn't in a lab, we couldn't control everything that was happening," Goddard explains. "We wanted to filter out as much noise as we could to ask if, all other things being equal, drivers are yielding differently based on whether the person trying to cross was white or Black."

Goddard ran the experiment in the field, telling the pedestrians when to step up to the crosswalk so every driver would have about the same amount of time to decide whether to yield or not. She instructed the pedestrians not to look at their phones. At the intersection, she told each to step forward and face the oncoming cars. The pedestrian would face the driver, try to make eye contact, and indicate that they planned to cross. Goddard checked not only whether the first car stopped but if they did not stop, how many cars went by and how long the person had to wait to cross.

Many drivers passed all the men. But when drivers did yield, it depended on who stood in the crosswalk. In eighty-eight attempts to cross the street, on average, twice as many cars passed the Black pedestrians without stopping. If the first person didn't stop for the Black pedestrian, five times as many cars would pass. Drivers yielded to the white men 24 percent quicker. On average, Black pedestrians waited 32 percent longer to cross the street. Whether this was implicit or explicit bias, the decision to yield was distinctly racist—and could lead to accidents.

"One potential outcome of that is that if you don't think that people are going to stop, you may be more likely to try and force the issue by taking a risk that you wouldn't normally take, stepping out in the gap between cars because you think nobody is going to stop," Goddard explains to me. This racism could even affect the simple health benefit of walking to one's destination. "People may just opt not to go out or to walk because they are not going to get stopped for."

A man could wait so long for someone to yield that he is late for work. A man tired of waiting could rush across when it's unsafe to do so. In any case, one result is that drivers kill twice as many Black pedestrians as white ones.

Failure to yield is inherently a nonaction, just a blip of a decision to continue on as before. In this, it could appear to be a less vile form of racism. But it's just a more insidious form of discrimination. It is a matter of Black lives mattering less, hidden behind a mask of "oops" and "I didn't see him."

Not seeing someone is a classic and false explanation for a car accident. Proof that racism can be the actual explanation is reinforced—
beyond these statistics—by changing the context in which a person is
or is not "seen." To a person in a car, a Black pedestrian disappears. To
a person with a gun, a Black pedestrian is especially visible—so much
so that they get shot more often, no matter what the context.

Open (Kitten) Carry Permit

Compared to traffic accidents, accidental shootings are uncommon—
tens of thousands a year compared to a few hundred. (However, as
discussed in the introduction, these accidental shooting counts may be
significant underestimates.) In these uncommon accidents, Black people
do not disappear the way they do while waiting to cross the road. Rather,
in laboratory studies and real life, Black people appear as a target. The
rate of accidental shooting deaths is relatively low, but it is 29 percent
higher for Black people and 19 percent higher for Indigenous people
than it is for white people. Here, too, there is ample evidence that the
accidental death toll is a product of racism.

In 2003, researchers at the University of Washington seated about
one hundred subjects at a computer screen showing an alley with two
dumpsters. The researchers asked the subjects to play the role of a police
officer and react to a figure emerging from behind one of the dumpsters. One of three figures might emerge: a criminal, a cop, a civilian,
all dressed in the same casual clothes. The civilians carried innocuous
items (a kitten, a camera, a beer, or a flashlight). Both the criminals and
the cops had guns. The researchers instructed the subjects to distinguish
between the cops and the criminals, otherwise identical-looking, by race.
In one version, they were told, white figures with guns were criminals,
and Black figures with guns were cops. In the other version, they were
told to reverse the roles. The researchers ran the test twice, so the subjects
did both versions. Point and click to shoot a criminal, hit the space bar
to give a safety signal to a fellow cop, or do nothing to let a civilian pass.

It didn't matter if the researchers told the subjects that the Black figure was the civilian, the criminal, or the cop. Black skin meant to shoot. Subjects struggled to notice that the kittens were not guns when the figure was Black and shot more kitten-carrying Black civilians. Even when they knew the figure had a gun, subjects shot more Black cops.

Two social psychologists did a meta-analysis of forty-two of these "shoot/don't shoot" studies conducted over a decade. Across the board, Black figures were shot more quickly and more often, including more often while not carrying a gun. In studies conducted in states with fewer gun laws and therefore more guns, Black figures were even more likely to be shot and for less reason.

This trigger-happiness is also present in real life. Black, Latino, and Indigenous people are more likely than white people to be killed by police. While these shootings may come with an excuse, some threat claimed by the officers, one study found that around 6 percent of police shootings are described as accidents by the officers involved. In these, too, the people shot were disproportionately Black. Consider Breonna Taylor in Kentucky in 2020; her killing was called a "miscalculation." Or Daunte Wright, killed in Minnesota in 2021 by a police officer who said she accidentally pulled a gun instead of a Taser. Or Eurie Stamps, a sixty-eight-year-old grandfather, killed in Massachusetts in 2011, unarmed and lying on his stomach, by police officers who broke into his home with a no-knock warrant for someone else. Or Aiyana Mo'Nay Stanley-Jones, a seven-year-old child killed in Michigan in 2010 by police officers who had the wrong apartment number on their no-knock warrant. Or Iyanna Davis, who woke up to the sound of her door being smashed open in New York in 2010 and hid in a closet. A police officer with an assault rifle said he accidentally tripped before he shot her. He, too, had accidentally gone to the wrong apartment with his no-knock warrant. Or Alberta Spruill, a fifty-seven-year-old employee of the City of New York who died of cardiac arrest in 2003 after police officers threw a concussion grenade into her apartment while accidentally executing a no-knock warrant on the wrong address.

Racism influences almost every way to die by accident in America, and has for a long, long time. Black people died by accident at a higher rate than white people every single year since the earliest counts of accidental death in America, as far back as 1900, and through 2002, when prescription opioid drug overdoses shifted the dominant paradigm.

Today, Black and Latino people are killed by accident on bicycles at a higher rate than white people. Drivers accidentally kill Black, Latino, Asian, and Indigenous people crossing the street at a higher rate than they do white people. For Black and Latino people, the rate is nearly double the rate of white people; it is nearly three times as high for Indigenous people. In fact, Black and Indigenous people are disproportionately killed in all traffic accidents, and for Black people, this inequity has been growing, with traffic accidents that kill white people declining since 2005 and those that kill Black people rising since 2010. And this is true of all accidents, not just limited to traffic. Black people are more likely to die by any accident than white people from the time they are born to age fourteen, and from their forty-fifth birthday to their seventy-fifth. Black babies die by accident at more than twice the rate of white babies. Black and Indigenous people are more likely to drown or be shot by accident than white people, the latter including but not limited to being shot by police. Black and Indigenous people are more than twice as likely as white people to freeze to death or burn to death by accident. Black people and Indigenous people are more likely to be killed by "unintentional natural and environmental causes." This broad category of accidental death includes rat bites and starvation, among other horrors.

No one in America is more likely to die by accident than Indigenous people. This is true of every cause of unintentional injury tracked in the CDC's Web-based Injury Statistics Query and Reporting System, except two: death by accidental exposure to smoke, fire, and flames, where Black people edge out Indigenous people by a small margin, and death by falling, a subcategory which is fatal mainly for older adults.

To die by accidental fall, you need to live a long life, which is less likely if you're Indigenous.

The way that racism produces unequal death is what epidemiologists call a social determinant of health. Determinants are tangible and intangible—social structures, built environments, and economic systems differentially distributed—and can essentially be understood as your personal stack of Swiss cheese, one that you carry with you into any risk. The holes in the Swiss cheese may line up for us all, based on how a medicine is packaged or a gun is designed, but they also may be more likely to line up precisely for you, based on who you are or how you are perceived.

Racism stacks dangerous conditions against some people and drives holes in their layers of safety to such a degree that it would be useless to ask what any one person could have done differently to alter their fate. The inevitability of these accidents becomes even more apparent if we pay attention to *which* accidents are most starkly divided by race. We can see the racial divide in accidental death most prominently in the most common and preventable accidents, resulting when the safety of the built environment is full of holes.

For example, people accidentally choke on food at pretty even rates across racial lines. But Indigenous people accidentally drown at a 50 percent higher rate than white people. And people are also more likely to drown if the place to swim nearest where they live is a lake or river, compared to those who live near a swimming pool with lifeguards. The difference between accidentally choking and accidentally drowning is that the built environment dictates the survivability of only the latter. And it is in these accidents that outcomes are most starkly divided by race.

We can follow this pattern in fires, too. Black people are more than twice as likely to die of accidental burns as white people, and they die in accidental house fires at more than twice the rate of white people. But when we talk about the racialized outcome of accidental fires, we must also talk about the fact that a person is more likely to die in a house fire if they don't own their home, if their home doesn't have fire safety devices, and if their home is built of cheap composite wood rather than safer, more expensive materials.

Where a seat belt or a life vest is an obvious layer of safety that can make the difference between life and accidental death, these examples—a pool versus a lake, a house of bricks or a house of particle board—are less apparent. What we call accidents can be a matter of geography and resource allocation, and this, too, is racialized.

To better understand how resources and locations affect accidental death and how racism decides who survives, let's look at accidents on the job—where life and death are decided not just by which type of job you do but by who you are and where you do it.

What a Way to Make a Living

There is a long history of job risk relating to race, wherein people of color have access largely to only the most dangerous of jobs. A hundred years ago, Black workers were so much more likely than white workers to be killed at work that the most dangerous jobs were known as "Negro work." This remains true today. In the past decade, the number of Black workers killed on the job rose by 51 percent. And Latino people, especially Latino immigrants, suffer the highest rate of accidental injury at work.

These statistics may seem obvious: Black and Latino people have less access to work, and so are forced to take more dangerous jobs. What's interesting about these statistics appears when we try to even the stakes—comparing apples to apples and coal mining to coal mining. Then we find not only that accident risk at work is unevenly divided by race, but that racism so thoroughly dictates differences in the built environment that race can be used to predict accident likelihood at the same job.

In the 1980s and early '90s, before Latino people began to dominate America's most dangerous and undesirable jobs, Black men were still more likely to die by accident at work, with a rate of occupational fatality more than 12 percent higher than for white men. (And these differences were even greater in some states, such as North Carolina, where the Hamlet fire burned, where Black men were killed at work at a 32 percent higher rate.) This was, in part, a matter of Black men doing more dangerous jobs, but Black men were also killed more than white men even when doing the same job. The crucial difference lay in the conditions offered to each group of workers. Coal mining was dangerous, but not all coal mines were equally dangerous, and you could figure out which was which by the number of Black people who worked there.

Latino workers would begin to dominate America's worst jobs a decade later. In 1990, the rate of fatal accidents for Latino workers hovered somewhere between that for Black and white workers. By 1996, Latino workers exceeded Black workers in this measure. The disparities again held even after adjusting for the relative danger of different jobs. As for Black workers a generation before, even in the same occupation, you could measure the danger of a workplace by the number of Latino people who worked there.

It's a stark portrait of risk and dangerous conditions, where some people have only two bad choices. You could work, and eat, and pay your gas and electric bill, and risk accidental death on the job, a place where the built environment is out of your control. Or you could not work, and not eat, and not pay your utility bills, and risk accidental death at home by not being able to afford to control that built environment. Then your risk would be unintentional starvation, or a wide array of other dangerous conditions that cause accidental death and come with not having money: fire, freezing, overheating, rat bites. None of those would be considered work accidents, but we could call them all accidents risked in order to avoid risk at work. In either case, the outcomes are the same—racism defines the risk of an accident by defining your conditions at work or your conditions at home. In the latter case, one of those conditions is where your home is.

The Toxicity of Our City

The United States has about 13,500 chemical facilities. These are sites where corporations store petrochemicals and fertilizers or make plastic resins, synthetic rubbers, household cleaners, or pesticides. All in all, these sites create hundreds of millions of pounds of toxic emissions and hazardous waste a year. Accidents at these facilities are not random or unpredictable—nor is who suffers when they inevitably occur.

The first thing that happens in a chemical accident, long before any one discrete failure, is that a facility is built, or someone moves into a home near the facility. Of course, people who live near a chemical facility are more likely to be killed or injured by an accidental chemical release. It is also predictable whom those people will be. One study by the NAACP found that Black people are 75 percent more likely than the average American to live near a toxic waste facility. Researchers have also found that the more high-risk the facility, the more Black people live nearby. People of color are almost twice as likely as white people to live near the most dangerous chemical facilities—those facilities have twice as many accidents as the ones in white neighborhoods.

The first finding of this kind came in 1987, when the United Church of Christ Commission for Racial Justice published *Toxic Wastes and Race in the United States* (and prompted Paul Slovic's survey on risk perception discussed at the start of this chapter). It was the first-ever national investigation into the overlap between where America's chemicals are made, mixed, stored, and sold, and where people of color live.

That study was inspired by perhaps the most significant demonstrations of civil disobedience in the U.S. South since the death of Martin Luther King Jr. In 1982, some 550 people sat down to be arrested over plans to locate a polychlorinated biphenyl (PCB) landfill outside a rural Black community in Warren County, North Carolina. For six weeks, the protesters lay in the street, blocking the path of dump trucks full of toxic soil. It would be the inception of what is now known as the environmental justice movement.

In maps, the Church's findings appear especially stark. Patterned across the country is the overlap between toxic industries and places where people of color predominate. The Church's study found that poverty mattered, too. The places where accident risk and race intersected were also exceedingly poor. In areas where there were multiple hazardous waste facilities, there were three times as many people of color as in areas without any hazardous waste facilities. These figures held even after controlling for urbanization and regional economic differences. Of every five Black and Latino people in America at the time, three lived in a community with a toxic waste site. The same was true for half of all Asian Americans and American Indians.

Dozens of studies would follow, and the results held. No source of environmental danger is fairly distributed across America—not refineries, incinerators, chemical plants, power plants, or waste dumps. Every time, researchers found that most often, these dangerous places were closest to people of color.

In 2007, that first study—*Toxic Wastes and Race in the United States*—was replicated. In the two decades that had passed, data had become more widely available and methods of interpreting it had improved. The results had not. In fact, in twenty years, the problem had grown worse. In the modern era, poor people and people of color are even more likely to live near hazardous places that are likely to leak or explode in spectacular, horrible fashion.

But the accidents aren't always sudden. Superfund sites are locations of toxic chemical spills so extensive that massive funds are needed to detoxify them. Typically, Superfunds are created gradually over months or years, chemicals accidentally and intentionally spilling again and again. For instance, the owners of a PCB transformer company dumped toxic oil on the edge of a North Carolina highway night after night for a year to save on the cost of properly disposing it (which is why that PCB landfill was being built in Warren County, North Carolina, in the first place).

One study of nearly 1,700 Superfund sites found that Black and Latino people disproportionately lived nearby compared to their portion of the population and were more likely to get cancer. Another study of over 1,800 Superfund sites found that Latino, Black, and Asian American people disproportionately lived within three miles of them. The results are the same if you look at Superfund sites nationally, in cities, or in states.

When you live near a Superfund site, you are more likely to get cancer. Now, cancer is not an accident, nor is it accidental who lives near Superfund sites—but it is often accidents that make the lands toxic. In this way, the Superfund site, which gathers many small, repeated accidents, creates a dangerous condition that we might not feel for years or decades.

Racism Is a Hole in the Swiss Cheese

Not all accidents kill more people of color, just the ones where conditions really matter. Rates of accidental death in house fires are 43 percent higher for Indigenous people and 112 percent higher for Black people than for white people. Rates of accidental drowning are 22 percent higher for Black people and 51 percent higher for Indigenous people than for white people. Rates of accidental death on a bicycle are 11 percent higher for Black people and 30 percent higher for Latino people than for white people. These are accidents where the only difference between life and death is the nature and quality of the built environment.

In the United States, racist decision-making can define public policy, direct budget allocations, and allocate governmental resources. One-on-one human interaction alone does not cause accidents, but rules and policies may expose some people to more dangerous conditions than others.

And these decisions can have historical reach. Redlining in the 1930s and 1940s undermined Black homeownership and empowered the (racist) builders of America's early highways to build those roads straight through Black neighborhoods. Then, the highways were a segregationist tool. Today, Black people are still less likely to own their homes and more likely to live near a highway. Those historic policies cause accidents now.

People who don't own their homes are more likely to die in an accidental fire. Extreme heat is worse in redlined neighborhoods because of highway pollution, so people who live near highways may be more likely to die of accidental overheating. Living near highways delivers more drivers traveling at highway speeds to residential streets, and people who live near highways are more likely to be killed in a car accident.

Researchers have even found that any given urban or suburban rail project is more likely than not to get built if it will serve white people and more likely than not to get canceled if it will serve people of color. And the per-mile accident risk of rail travel is more than twenty times lower than driving. Decades after the decisions to build or not build a train, people of color are more likely to lack an alternative to driving, walking, or biking on or near unsafe roads, and thus suffer the accidents that result.

In this way, policies of economic and racial segregation of one generation can lead to accidents in the next.

The layers of safety that protect us from an accident—and the holes in the Swiss cheese that allow accidents to slip through—can be far less concrete than a seat belt or a broken indicator light. The history of infrastructure financing, the design of the road and the design of the car, the race of the person driving, the race of the person walking, and the neighborhood where they meet—all of this affects whether or not an accident happens, who lives and who dies. When James Reason developed the Swiss cheese model, he believed that the holes were unintended lapses and failures, and that what led to what he called "a trajectory of accident opportunity" was a matter of random convergences. But accidents are a matter of being a certain person at a certain place at a certain time. Whiteness protects. And the one thing that can change the fate of the "accident-prone" is cash.

Chapter Seven

Money

In 1999, Dr. Deborah Girasek, an epidemiologist at the Uniformed Services University of the Health Sciences, realized that while her fellow public health workers were eschewing the word "accident," no one had ever bothered to ask the public what they thought it meant. Through a telephone survey of 943 adults, she found some answers: Most people viewed accidents as preventable *but* unpredictable—and there was little discomfort with this dissonance. However, the strongest feeling of agreement, and most relevant to our work here, was by far that people felt accidents were unintentional. More than 94 percent of those surveyed agreed that accidents were "not done on purpose."

Girasek has a theory about why the respondents homed in on intentionality. Public health professionals like herself watch accidents happen to populations as a whole, counting rates by demographics like age, gender, race, and income. But the public doesn't deal in such large numbers. Instead, by and large, when we explain accidents, we are seeking to make sense of a single tragedy. Focusing on intention came from looking at one accident at a time.

This focus helps us better understand why human error so often rises to the top to explain accidents. If you hear "accident" and think "they didn't mean it," then the solution to the problem is to help a person better match their actions to their intentions.

Tellingly, the focus on intention was not entirely universal. When Girasek broke down her survey respondents by race and income, the results shifted to reveal that it was largely wealthy and white people who believed in the idea of the *unintentional* accident. She found that people who associated "accident" and "unintentional" were more likely to be white and make more than $25,000 a year (around $40,000 today). Black people were twice as likely as white people to say that accidents were actually *intentional*, and low-income respondents were nearly two and a half times as likely to say the same. These figures mirror accidental death rates—Black people and low-income people are more likely to be killed in most accidents. For the people most at risk of accidental death, accidents did not appear unintentional at all.

The reason for this may have been that people who called accidents intentional were focused not on one accident at a time but rather on the clear and present danger to their group, because from that perspective, where race and class define the likelihood of accidental death, there's no way to see accidents as unintentional. If we want to prevent accidents, this perspective matters—not who did it (human error) and not the fact that they didn't mean to (intention). Everything we need to know about accidents, why they happen, and how we can stop them can be understood from the perspective of who bears the brunt of the harm.

Economic inequality, like racism, is used to rank and subjugate America. The accident is another, less blatant tool—a manifestation of ideologies about wealth and whiteness that nest with the U.S. social order and determine what layers of safety people can access at home, at work, and on the road, based on race and class. In this way, while appearing unintentional, accidents perpetuate a caste system, advancing what the institutions of debt, capital, slavery, and Indigenous ethnic cleansing began hundreds of years ago—all while disguised by the excuse preferred by the wealthy and white: *I didn't mean it.*

Race or Class

Dr. Chukwudi Onwuachi-Saunders was an agent of the U.S. government at the Centers for Disease Control and Prevention when she presented a paper—"Black-White Differences in Injury: Race or Social Class?"—with sociologist Darnell F. Hawkins at the Tenth Annual Scientific Meeting of the American College of Epidemiology in 1991. She recalls it being a difficult paper for a government employee to get through government approval processes at the time, in part because no one wanted to talk about racism, and in part because it demonstrated that the go-to government answer to accidents did not work.

At the time, Onwuachi-Saunders explains to me, the favored governmental strategy for addressing race-based differences in injury-related death was to treat the disparity as a human error problem, offering education and enforcement as a solution. Black people were killed more often than white people in house fires, and in response, government officials urged Black people to not smoke in bed and charged them with murder when their child died in an accidental fire.

To Onwuachi-Saunders, it was obvious that this approach was not just wrongheaded but also not working; race-based differences remained. She looked at all the ways that Black people died by accident at a higher rate than white people. At the time, you could isolate much of the difference by examining three types of accidents: drownings, house fires, and being hit by a car. But despite the fact that the fatality rates in these accidents were clearly divided along racial lines, she found that the way to reduce the number of those accidents appeared to be not behavioral but financial. For some people, Onwuachi-Saunders found, the safety system wasn't failing; rather, no one had ever spent the money needed to create one.

In accidental home fires, Onwuachi-Saunders found, the risk factors for death were living in substandard housing that burned quicker, living in homes that did not have smoke detectors, and living in poor, rural areas that lacked firefighters or modern firefighting equipment.

She found that the risk factors for accidental drowning were swimming without having taken swimming lessons and swimming in unsafe places in the natural environment or where there were no lifeguards. As for being hit by a car, the risk factors were also matters of economics and access: no safe play areas for children, no pedestrian crossing signs in hazardous locations, and no street lighting.

"What we found is that race is a proxy for socioeconomic class," she tells me, "that many people, because of racism, live at a lower socioeconomic class."

No amount of education or enforcement would patch these gaps in the built environment. In fact, behind each of these catalogs of accident causation, Onwuachi-Saunders found the same conclusion: yes, this is how Black people die by accident, but this is also how poor people die by accident. To solve racial disparities in accidental death, she wrote, we need to take economic measures: fixing substandard housing, installing fire detectors, purchasing modern firefighting equipment for use in poor, rural areas, creating safe swimming areas, and modifying the streets people need to cross.

"If people live in dilapidated housing or slum housing and they don't have fire or smoke detectors or even carbon monoxide detectors, their death is not an accidental death. Even though it may fall into this category of 'residential fires'—that's not an accident," Onwuachi-Saunders points out. "There are greater societal issues that are causing that particular death."

What Onwuachi-Saunders uncovered in 1991 has not changed. Today, Black people and people living in poverty still die at disproportionate rates—and of the exact causes she uncovered three decades ago.

Recessions Save Lives

Onwuachi-Saunders found a direct link between racism, money, and any one accidental death, but economics also influences how accidents happen in much more expansive ways. The Great Depression and the Great Recession both brought a decline in accidental death. Throughout history, when the economy was booming, accidental death also peaked. Nationwide, more income inequality means more accidental death.

Patterns repeat if you zoom in. Researchers have found that, traditionally, for every 1 percent that unemployment increases, the traffic accident fatality rate falls by 2.9 percent. In a recession, fewer truck drivers deliver fewer goods, and with unemployment up, everyone travels fewer miles, and the number of traffic accidents goes down. The reduction in vehicle traffic in a recession plugs one hole in the Swiss cheese of any one person's drive to work.

(The coronavirus pandemic complicated this idea—where fewer cars on the road in a recession typically meant fewer accidents, in 2020, the nationwide shutdown reduced congestion so dramatically that accidents actually increased. On those unusually empty streets—which, as Eric Dumbaugh taught us, were built for speed—drivers sped and accidents happened. The fatality rate rose 8 percent, the highest year-to-year jump since 1924. Notably, this increase was racially uneven because of economic consequences: Black people suffered a rise in traffic accident fatalities between 2019 and 2020 that was 19 percentage points higher than the rise for white people, which experts cite as evidence that when the world shut down, Black people still had to leave the house to go to work.)

It is more than a one-to-one relationship between work and accidental death. If people often die making widgets and, in an economic downturn, the widget factory shuts down, those people will not die on the job, but they will also not die on the drive to the widget factory, or from falling off a high place (drunk after their shift, because making widgets is so depressing). This is a measure of risk exposure: less work equals less risk everywhere.

Time is also worth more in a booming economy. That means that the cost of risks taken or declined is higher. If your time is worth more money, speeding, for example, is a risk you may be more likely to take, and the same goes for a more dangerous job. In this way, the dangerous condition isn't just America's roads but American capitalism.

These economic intersections ripple outward. Speeding to work may be a personal economic decision, but its costs—a trip to the hospital, fixing a roadside barrier after someone crashed into it, Medicare—impact all of society. The National Highway Traffic Safety Administration estimates that the immediate costs of traffic accidents to society—the busted cars and property, the people killed and injured—add up to $277 billion a year. And the long-term costs—such as living without a loved one or without a leg—add up to another $594 billion annually. And those are just the car accidents.

Whether we live or die by accident is an economic policy decision. Such decisions cost money either way—but the outcome of money spent now can prevent accidents later. Building a local pool and hiring a lifeguard, for example, is a financial decision that can prevent accidental drowning in a river or lake. Not building a pool and hiring a lifeguard ultimately costs more: paramedics, hospital bills, lawsuits, warning signs and barricades, and cops to patrol after a child drowns at an unofficial swimming area. We can pay the cost to avoid an accident or pay more for the consequences after an accident—but because we consider these accidents, we rarely do the math.

The costs of accidents are incurred not just at the site of an accident but by society. And these costs are baked into our economy. By and large, we don't measure them because we're so accustomed to paying them. Any given city or state has a certain number of emergency responders or a certain percent of the budget devoted to roadside barrier repair *because* they have a certain number of accidents every year.

Failing to pay these costs can also result in further accidental death. Medical expenses, for example, are a major component of what drives poverty in the United States. Increasingly, hospitals are closing, especially in rural areas, because their patients are poor. Keeping a private hospital open is a cost to society, in part, but mostly it is a cost to a corporation seeking profit. When the profit margin disappears, so does a hospital, and so does the most efficient route between an accidental injury and treatment—and in that time, the accidentally injured might die.

Dying en Route

In 2019, Dr. Kyle Hurst, a medical director at United Hospital Center in Bridgeport, West Virginia, became the second emergency medical service–certified physician in the state. As an EMS physician, he understands when rushing matters. And in West Virginia, rushing to the hospital is a matter of money, space, and vulnerability to accidental death.

Bridgeport is not a big city, with a population of only around 9,000, but United Hospital Center, where Hurst works, has a big catchment area—it is the destination hospital for all the counties surrounding it. This is true of a lot of West Virginia hospitals. And those hospitals see a lot of action. Every year, West Virginia hospitals discharge nearly as many patients and record more patient days than Utah, a state nearly twice as populous. The problem in West Virginia is that the population is small and the state is not—it is the third most rural state in the nation, and one of the poorest. Its hospitals are often losing money, and the nearest hospital can be a long, long way away from an accident—and that route is getting longer.

In West Virginia, about half of rural hospitals are at risk of closing. Of the hospitals at risk, 80 percent are considered "essential"—a factor defined by the frequency of accidents and injuries in the catchment area, the number of vulnerable people they serve, how far it is to the next hospital, and how hard it will be for the people employed there to find a new job should this one disappear. If an essential hospital closes, transit time to the next one is long, which is another way to say that when these hospitals close, there is no next slice of Swiss cheese to back them up.

In Bridgeport, United sees more than seven times the city's population in patients every year—around 60,000. Those patients come in with abdominal pain, cough, and flu, and injured by accidents, of course. In the emergency room, Hurst and his colleagues treat small accidents, where people fall or cut themselves but don't suffer any major injuries, and big ones, where someone falls down and breaks a hip and then never leaves the hospital, a common occurrence among the aging population of West Virginia. Patients arrive with gunshot wounds, but these are less often from violent crimes than from hunting accidents, and gun cleaning accidents, and using-the-waistband-of-your-pants-as-a-holster accidents. It used to be common to see people crushed by coal ceiling collapses or mauled by mining machines, Hurst says, but now more people suffer burns from shale drilling explosions.

But the accidents Hurst most often sees in his emergency room involve drugs, cars, and all-terrain vehicles. These are a matter of geography and space. If a person in a big city gets hit by a car crossing the street, it may be because the people and the cars are so close together. In West Virginia, vehicular accidents happen because of the rural state's open spaces, which allow more room to go fast and get hurt and more distance between an accident and medical help.

"The problems that we have are completely different than what the metropolitan areas have—especially the transit to our hospital. On any given day we will see patients that are transferred here from an hour and a half to two hours out. A normal transit to the hospital here may be up to one hour," Hurst tells me.

Transit times might mean the difference between an overdose and an overdose death—and this risk is rising. Hurst watched as the opioid overdoses he treated changed from prescription pain pills to heroin to heroin cut with fentanyl, which people often didn't know was in their drugs. Even for a normal overdose, an hour or two is a dangerously long time to wait for treatment. For fentanyl, which is much more potent, it's fatally late. The state relies on aeromedical procedures for these accidents, which Hurst says are particularly advanced in West Virginia, with trained flight medics and medical evacuation helicopters located strategically across the state.

"A lot of times if there's a bad accident that is far away from our facility, it is usually a helicopter that's gone to pick them up," Hurst says. "Of course, there are incidents where there's cloud cover or an issue where a helicopter is unable to get into the air to go get them safely." In West

Virginia, help is so sparse that surviving an accident could depend on the weather.

Often the accidents Dr. Hurst treats are related to fire. Fires are the sixth most common cause of accidental death in West Virginia, and the state ranks tenth in the nation for the highest rate of fire-related accidental deaths. This prevalence is a matter of rurality and poverty—the time it takes a firefighter to arrive at a rural home, the time it takes to transfer a burn victim to the hospital, and the speed at which cheaply built homes burn. People living in poverty might also be more likely to heat their home with a woodstove or propane, Hurst suggests, increasing the likelihood of carbon monoxide poisoning. They might not have a working smoke detector or one with a carbon monoxide add-on—another cost that if paid can prevent accidental death. Dr. Hurst has seen these patients: a headache turns into confusion, which turns into carbon monoxide poisoning, and by then it can be too late to get help, at least in West Virginia.

Carbon monoxide poisoning is an accident that society has already put an end to, at least in theory, by the invention of carbon monoxide detectors. As such, it is also an accident that costs people money to prevent and, if not prevented, costs a community money to address in an emergency. And when that money runs out, you may have no hospital close enough to save your life. This is a problem for accidents more than disease because in accidents, the difference between injury and death can be a matter of minutes.

Among rural states, West Virginia is not alone in its dwindling access to care. Since 2005, 180 rural hospitals have closed across the United States. This appears to be accelerating, with 136 of those closures occurring since 2010, and closures in 2020 reaching a record high. Nationwide, half of rural hospitals were operating at a loss before the 2020 recession. One in four rural hospitals are at risk of shutting down. And the volunteer emergency medical services that shuttle injured people to the hospital are shutting down in rural areas, too, when they can't find enough people to staff them or have run out of money to pay for the required training. A third of rural EMS providers were at risk of closing in 2021—which means if the hospital is an hour or two away, you may have no treatment en route and, if you do not have access to a vehicle, no route at all.

These closures, which are the result of economic decline, in turn exacerbate economic decline. When a local hospital closes, unemployment rises, and income falls by as much as $700 a person.

The math here is not complicated: Hurst's patients are older and lower income than most of America. From Medicare reimbursements to food stamps, every cut to government care can add to a hospital's budget. We can see proof of this when some states cut social services while others expand them. The Affordable Care Act (ACA) offered funding for states to expand Medicaid access to nearly all low-income people, including anyone at or below 138 percent of the federal poverty line. But twelve states refused to participate in protest of the legislation, which meant that in those states, access to Medicaid remained limited to low-income people at or below 41 percent of the poverty line. That's an annual income of $8,905 for a family of three in 2020 dollars—make more than that, and you get no medical assistance in these twelve states. Researchers tracked rural hospitals in the decade after this decision and found that those in states that expanded Medicaid were 62 percent less likely to shut down. The researchers also ranked the 216 rural hospitals most vulnerable to closure—three out of every four were in a state that refused to expand Medicaid. The nine states with the greatest number of rural hospital closures since 2010 all refused to expand Medicaid in protest of the Affordable Care Act (ACA). Texas and Tennessee top the list of rural hospital closures, with 21 and 16 closings, respectively, since 2010. Both refused to expand Medicaid.

West Virginia is not on this list. The state expanded Medicaid when the ACA passed in 2014. But even with that boon, in 2020, somewhere between 40 and 60 percent of the rural hospitals in West Virginia were operating without a profit. In 2019, the only hospital in Mingo County, West Virginia, (south of Bridgeport) closed. That year, Ohio Valley Medical Center, a hospital in Wheeling, West Virginia, (north of Bridgeport) shut down as well. The only hospital in Fairmont, West Virginia, (just twenty miles from Bridgeport) shut down in 2020. One of these would reopen as a temporary twenty-two-bed emergency department in the coronavirus pandemic—the others would not. Neighboring hospitals, such as United, will absorb their accidents, and in this poverty of care, every accident will become more dangerous.

The Most Accident-Prone Place in America

I sought out Hurst for a reason. West Virginia has had the nation's highest rate of accidental death per capita since 2010, when the state began to edge out New Mexico. The rate of accidental death in West Virginia is 70 percent higher than it is across the state line in Virginia.

Looking at the state-by-state rate of accidental death from the last two decades, little has changed from 1999 to today, even during the Great Recession. Year after year, California, New York, and Hawaii are, in that order, the places in America where you are least likely to die by accident. These states are also in the top fifteen highest in per capita government spending and the top ten highest in tax collection. The states where you are most likely to die by accident are West Virginia, Kentucky, and New Mexico—three of the five states with the highest poverty rates in America.

These statistics are a result of an unprecedented nationwide economic divergence. Economists traditionally measure the state of the economy by the national *convergence* of employment, tax revenue, and the like. Increasingly, they are starting to track what they call "spatial inequality"—place-based trends of economic downturn and stagnancy masked by economic ascendancy of other places. If you look nationwide, all appears fine, but if you break things down by state and county, some

places are falling behind as never before. For example, the life expectancy gap between wealthy places and poor places is larger than it's ever
been—by as much as twenty years—and growing.

We often think of the life expectancy gap as one man dying at sixty
and another, across the state line, dying at eighty, but life expectancy
is an average, and that average is dragged down in the places with the
lowest life expectancies by people dying of accidents far before their time.
One reason the life expectancy is so low in impoverished places is that
so many people there are dying not at sixty but at eighteen or twenty.

The correlation between accidental death and the economics of a
place indicates that, at least in some places, money can buy prevention.
Researchers have found a correlation between deadly work accidents, for
example, and high state debt, meaning that states that spend money—
whether on infrastructure or social welfare programs—are also places
where you are less likely to die by accident. Other research, which correlated greater income inequality with higher accidental death, also
found that the cities that spent more on roads had a 14 percent lower
rate of accidental death.

And the opposite is true: preventable accidents happen because of
money not spent on the infrastructure that can prevent accidents. One
study that investigated the sixty U.S. roads where the most pedestrians
are killed found that three out of every four bordered a neighborhood
where incomes were lower than the U.S. average. And this remained true
even if you zoomed in further—nearly nine out of every ten of those
most deadly streets bordered a neighborhood where incomes weren't
just lower than the U.S. average but also lower than the average for that
specific area of the U.S.

Perhaps nowhere is the decline of American infrastructure more
evident than in West Virginia, where public works spending fell for five
years running. In the state's 2020 budget, the governor's office noted
that highways were deteriorating for lack of funding, that $3 billion was
needed to replace bridges that were more than sixty years old, and that
more than $400 million was needed for repaving. Moreover, there were

so many spots where rocks and landslides were likely to accidentally ruin a road or kill a person that it would cost tens of millions of dollars to shore them up. And that was looking only at transportation issues.

You could say that West Virginia is poor. Or you could say that many West Virginians live in poverty because West Virginia is built for accidents to happen, and accidents come with a cost that states, counties, and residents bear. One study found that the per capita cost to states of a fatal opioid overdose was highest in West Virginia, where fatal overdoses are driving an epidemic of accidental death, and lowest in Hawaii, where per capita accidental death is least likely. This is the cost of health care, treatment, criminal prosecution, and less tangible things: work missed, pain, suffering. And the researchers found that the difference in cost is massive—the cost that states pay per capita in coping with these accidents is more than 1,134 percent higher in West Virginia ($5,298) compared to Hawaii ($429). One way to understand this is that accidents beget accidents, and the cost of accidents rises as the resources to respond to accidents are used up by other accidents—if all your EMTs are busy, you need to pay to train more EMTs, and in the time that takes, more people die by accident who otherwise might have survived.

There is a catch-22 here: If the economy declines in your hometown, you need to drive farther to find work, increasing your risk of accident by exposure at the same time that your hometown has less money to pave roads. You are also more likely to take more dangerous work in desperation. If you get into an accident, you are saddled with medical debt that directly affects your ability to pay state taxes so the state government can pave the roads. Even this example skips over many factors that can multiply risk: less-safe older cars, exhaustion and stress brought on by longer commutes and life in poverty, distance to medical care, and the fact that your income might be so low that you have to walk or bike to work, an especially dangerous condition. An accident can make you vulnerable to poverty, living in poverty makes you more likely to die by accident, and poor places do not have money to spend to prevent accidents.

This all remains true even at a more local level. Nationwide, the census area whose residents are most likely to die by accident is rural Lake and Peninsula Borough, Alaska, which is 76 percent Indigenous. Looking at data from 1999 to 2016, the most recent year tabulated in the Centers for Disease Control and Prevention's county-level mortality database, the first sizably populated runner-up is Oglala Lakota County, South Dakota. Oglala Lakota County, with a population of more than three quarters of a million people, is entirely inside the Pine Ridge Reservation. It is one of America's biggest and poorest reservations, a place of devastating superlatives: lowest life expectancy, lowest per capita income, home to two of the poorest communities in America.

In Oglala Lakota County, dangerous conditions stack up. A majority of homes lack water, electricity, insulation, and sewage. Work for most is at least an hour's drive away in the nearest city, and weather is extreme, sometimes getting up to 110 degrees in the summer and as low as 50 degrees below zero in the winter—conditions primed for accidental death by "unintentional natural and environmental causes." But conditions are also primed for more common accidents. For example, to maintain tribal roads and bridges managed by the Bureau of Indian Affairs, the Oglala Lakota Nation receives more than 95 percent less per mile than the nationwide average per-mile spending on state roads, and more than 82 percent less than what the rest of South Dakota spends. In 2019, backlogged road maintenance needs reached $60 million, and routine bridge maintenance only occurred once bridges reached a state of emergency. And tribes cannot implement taxes, such as a gas tax, which states often use to make up the difference between costs and federal funding.

Of the U.S. counties with the highest accident rates, nine of the top ten are majority Indigenous. Per capita income in these areas is half the U.S. average, and the poverty rate is three times as high. Officials at the congressional Government Accountability Office have marked the Bureau of Indian Affairs—the agency tasked with protecting Indigenous people in the United States and managing all the conditions that could cause or prevent an accident on tribal lands, from health care to road paving—as "high risk" on account of "vulnerabilities to fraud, waste, abuse, and mismanagement." In 2015, the Bureau of Indian Education skipped safety inspections at a third of the schools in its system, a rate of negligence that had risen by almost half since 2012. This included one school where there was a natural gas leak and four boilers failed inspection due to elevated carbon monoxide levels—an accidental explosion risk and an ongoing accidental poisoning—and it all stayed that way for eight months, because there was nowhere else for them to go. In 2018, the Indian Health Service spent around two-thirds less per patient ($3,779) than the national average ($9,409). In the Indian Reservation Roads program, 80 percent of streets are unpaved and over one in four bridges need major structural repairs.

Compared to the rest of the country, the Federal Emergency Management Agency (FEMA) approves fewer grants to Indigenous people to prepare before disasters and approves fewer grants to tribes to repair after disasters. This could lead to little accidents, such as accidental deaths by drowning or fire or freezing or overheating that may follow a flood, wildfire, blizzard, or heat wave, but also the large-scale accidents in FEMA's remit: dam, levee, tunnel, and bridge failures; explosions; and accidents involving biological, chemical, or other toxic substances. Both before and after large-scale accidents on tribal land, Indigenous people are granted less funding to protect themselves and to solve the problems that allowed the worst to occur. It is under these dangerous conditions that Indigenous people are killed by accident at such a higher rate than other Americans, killed twice as often in car accidents, fires, and drownings, and three times as often while crossing the street.

This problem, which is worse on tribal land, is bad everywhere. Infrastructure spending has been falling in the United States for decades. In 2018, public construction spending reached a twenty-five-year low. Two of every five U.S. bridges are more than fifty years old; one in eight are eighty years old or more. Water mains, some so old they were laid in the nineteenth century, are breaking at an increasing rate. U.S. levees are, on average, fifty years old; the average age of drinking and wastewater pipes is just five years younger. More than 2,300 dams in the United States have major structural problems—these continue to hold back lakes and rivers, however tenuously, all in locations where human death is near guaranteed in the event of an accidental dam collapse. Local officials have shut down more than four hundred bridges in Mississippi alone for fear that continued use will end in accidental collapse. In the accident-prone locales of West Virginia and South Dakota, around one in five bridges are structurally unsound. Rural roads are in such bad condition that the fatality rate per mile traveled is more than twice as high as on all other roads. Half the oil and gas pipelines in the United States are at least fifty years old, and more than 2,000 miles of pipeline are over one hundred years old.

These are just a few of the many, many holes in the safety systems of our day-to-day lives. The holes are known; the government chooses not to spend the money to repair them. Federal government spending on America's road and water infrastructure is the smallest percentage of gross domestic product that it has been in decades. Adjusted for inflation, government spending on infrastructure was lower in 2017 than it was a decade before—and as infrastructure declines, less and less of this money is devoted to the rebuilding required to solve problems, while more and more is required for stopgap patches and repairs. Some states are picking up the slack—after the accidental collapse of the I-35W bridge in 2007, Minnesota raised the gas tax to fund $2.5 billion in statewide bridge repairs. The rest of the states, especially the poor ones, remain accident-prone.

(As this book headed to press, Congress was preparing to vote on an infrastructure financing bill that would begin to repair a nation brimming with dangerous conditions—the largest dose of federal infrastructure spending in more than a decade. If the bill has passed by the time this book is in your hands, it will be a step away from the unguarded cliff, certainly, but that unguarded cliff remains a step away. And this new infrastructure financing could also create new problems. For example, despite a $435 billion repair backlog, the legislation does not require states to fix old highways or make them safer before using the funds to widen existing highways, increasing dangerous conditions, or before using the funds to build new highways, making it more likely that more people drive—a dangerous condition unto itself. And the legislation does not bar "regressive safety goals," so states can get funding to build new roads even if it is predictable that those roads will cause traffic accidents to increase.)

In 2012, researchers at Brown University analyzed fourteen years of accidental death in the United States—a massive study of 1.6 million victims. Both individual poverty and impoverished places tracked with the highest rates of accidental death every single year. Places with more poverty also had more people who died by accident. Worse, this gap, between the accident-proneness of places rich and poor, had widened with time.

Both being poor and living in a poor place are dangerous conditions—and they overlap in a way that increases the likelihood of accidents. Take road infrastructure as an example. One of every five miles of highway pavement is considered by the American Society of Civil Engineers to be "in poor condition." The U.S. Department of Transportation estimates that more than a third of people who die in traffic accidents die because the roads on which they were killed need to be repaired, redesigned, or replaced. Nationwide, pedestrian fatalities are higher for people living in poverty.

You can see where these accidents fall geographically on the so-called Car Death Belt, two horizontal stretches across the Deep South and the Great Plains that see the highest road fatality rates in the country. The Car Death Belt tracks with poverty, GDP, income, even the count of college graduates in a state. One way to pay for the infrastructure that could change the dangerous conditions along the Car Death Belt is the federal gas tax, a major source of federal funding for road infrastructure.

The gas tax has not risen since 1993. And those low gas prices, exempt from two-plus decades of inflation, encourage people to drive rather than use other, less risky modes of transportation—so as roads across the country get more dangerous by disinvestment, they're more crowded with people likely to get into an accident.

These dangerous conditions—individual poverty overlapping with institutional poverty—exist outside cars, too. Accidental deaths by falling, drowning, and poisoning are all rising fastest in the poorest places. In counties where automakers have shut down domestic car factories, the number of people who accidentally overdose on opioids is 85 percent higher than the national average.

When these people die, the story told is of one accident that happened. But it did not *just happen*. It was written in the asphalt cracks and en route to the hospital. Economic geography so strongly affects accidental death rates that people who live in poverty in rich places live longer than equally poor people who live in poor places. Wealth is a risk insulator and poverty is a risk amplifier. Rich people who live in poor areas live as long as rich people in wealthy areas. But the opposite is true for poor people who live in poor places; they live significantly less long and die by accident more often than their impoverished counterparts who live in rich places. Money is a halo in America, and just standing nearby catches some of the glow.

While having money or being money-adjacent protects, poverty in America isn't just deadly—it is a status that we shame. The fact that a person living in poverty is more likely to be Black, Latino, or Indigenous compounds this stigmatization. Data bears this out: more than two of every five Americans blame people in poverty for being poor, chalking up economic inequality to the effects of drugs, alcohol, and bad personal decisions.

And it turns out that this tendency—blaming the poor for being poor—scratches a deep itch in our brains. The fact that poor people die more often by accident may make some people feel more comfortable with economic inequality.

Bad Things Happen to Bad People

One of the reasons that we don't spend money to protect people from accidents is the same reason that many Americans blame poor people for their poverty: the human error explanation absolves us of the responsibility. But blaming human error is also a well-documented cognitive bias that helps us see an unjust world as just. This bias—known as the "just world fallacy"—helps us feel more comfortable in a cruel world by focusing on individual behavior to explain systemic failures and structural inequality. In particular, we zero in on anything that reinforces the belief that good things happen to good people and bad things happen to bad people. In short, the fallacy is believing that the world is fair.

Kevin Smith, a professor of sociology at Lamar University who studies economic manifestations of the just world fallacy, explains that people will go to great lengths to maintain this belief. When we see an accident happen, he explains, we will justify it with information we do not have—finding a way to say that whoever was killed or injured must have deserved it. It is a cognitive bias toward blaming human error.

The classic experiment to explain the just world fallacy involves two groups of subjects watching a woman taking a test and getting shocked for her wrong answers. The first group gets to compensate the test taker for her suffering, and the second just has to watch her suffer. Asked about the test taker afterward, the first group insists that she is a good person, but the second group insists that she is awful. To make themselves feel better about living in a world where the woman could suffer without recompense, the second group *needed her* to be a bad person, deserving of her fate.

By this logic, the nut behind the wheel is more than a clever marketing phrase used to disguise a dangerous car; instead, it represents a natural human impulse to comfort oneself while rubbernecking an accident. In a just world, a drug user who died of a drug overdose becomes a criminal addict who failed to control himself. In a just world, the pedestrian killed in an accident is a jaywalker, the driver impaled on a steering column is a nut behind the wheel, and the worker who loses an arm to an unguarded machine is accident-prone.

Of course, the world is not just, and none of this is true—it just makes us feel better.

Seeing just deserts in another person's pain separates us from that pain. Belief in a just world is another way to say: *It could never happen to me*. This reasoning is a way of maintaining mental equilibrium in the face of injustice or chaos. Establish the causal chain, and you preserve your mental health. Otherwise, we must accept that we live in a world of randomness where justice does not prevail. That's a very unsettling cognitive state.

Smith has conducted a series of experiments on how the just world fallacy appears to explain wealth and poverty. In a poll of random Texans, he cataloged how people felt about statements such as "These days, Blacks have the same opportunity as whites to get good jobs in America" and "If you work hard in this city, you will eventually succeed." People who believed in the just world fallacy were more likely to agree with those statements—and those people were less likely to perceive structural and social inequalities. Those people were also privileged: white people were more likely to believe in the just world fallacy, and so were the wealthy, and so were Republicans. These just world believers were also more likely to blame human error and more likely to denigrate whoever was hurt. In another study, Smith sought people's opinions as to why the rich were rich and the poor poor. Among the offered reasons, the answers that just world believers chose most often were human error responses—that "hard work and initiative" were an explanation for the wealthy and "loose morals and drunkenness" or "lack of efforts by the poor themselves" explained the impoverished. The people who agreed with those statements were overwhelmingly rich.

Knowing what we know about poverty and accidents, you can see how this would justify the status quo—and cause more accidents. If the people atop the social order believe in poverty as a form of justice, and poor people more often die by accident, then nothing could or should be done about accidents. In fact, by this logic, accidents are good—a righteous punishment for bad actions or weak character.

Researchers at UCLA and Harvard found that people who believe in the just world fallacy also tend toward authoritarianism, religiousness, conservatism, and general support of the status quo. Other research confirms this—such as that survey we cited earlier in this chapter, which found that more than 40 percent of Americans blame poor people for being poor. It also broke out the results by political stance and found that a large majority of conservatives placed the blame for poverty on bad life choices and a lack of hard work. There is some hope, however, on the horizon. At least one recent poll shows that this misconception that the world is fair has been fading over time, and across party lines. More and more people see that poverty is not an accident or an error but a systemic condition. Still, many are seeking a "just world."

"It is the same way that a couple of decades ago people blamed AIDS on the actions of the AIDS patients—it just produces cognitive consistency. It makes the world cognitively, mentally stable," Smith tells me. "Those with a very strong sense of belief in a 'just world' think the poor must have done something at some point that resulted in their poverty—that they do not work hard, that they are spendthrifts, that they are lazy, that they are promiscuous, that they abuse drugs—and in that way, they deserve the punishment of poverty."

Of course, this is not how the world works.

The poor are not bad, the rich are not good, and the victims of accidents are not accident-prone. Human error as a cause of accidents is a false construct. Blame, in accidents, reveals the psychology of the blamer and not much else.

That said, blame can still contribute to the rising number of accidents in America. In 2017, then U.S. secretary of housing and urban development Ben Carson told a reporter that poor people just have a bad attitude:

Poverty, to a large extent, is also a state of mind. You take somebody who has the right mindset, you can take everything from them and put them on the street, and I guarantee in a little while they will be right back up there. And you take somebody with the wrong mindset, you can give them everything in the world, they will work their way right back down to the bottom.

"Poverty is a state of mind" is Carson's version of the just world fallacy, and because he was powerful, his belief could translate to more accidental death, especially for poor people. In 2020, Carson endorsed a federal budget that would cut, by $8.6 billion, his ability to do his job—build and maintain housing for people in poverty. It's a fine decision if you believe poverty is merely a state of mind. But if you live in poverty, that missing $8.6 billion could result in a lot more holes in the Swiss cheese between you and an accident.

As individuals, we blame to insulate ourselves from pain and to pretend that justice prevails. The national status quo of economic inequality supports this illusion of fairness. If accidents befall the poor because they are poor, and poor people deserve their poverty, it follows that the rich deserve their riches as well. It's a belief in justice that leads us to defend and maintain the underlying structures of injustice and then blame those accidentally killed.

Chapter Eight

Blame

B lame is how we control the terror stirred up by the seeming randomness of accidental tragedy. There is nothing productive in this process. As the shame and vulnerability researcher Brené Brown describes
it, "Blame is simply the discharging of pain and discomfort." To prevent
accidents, we need to sit with the discomfort.

Kevin Smith, the sociologist who studies our pervasive search for
a just world, understands this urge as more than his area of research.
Smith's son Shelby died in a car accident on a Texas highway. And afterward, everyone wanted to know if Shelby was to blame.

Shelby Smith was on his way to work in the middle of the day in
fine weather, driving a car in fine condition, when he missed an exit,
rolled his car, and died.

"People would try to make sense of it. Why did this accident happen?
Why is it that a horrible thing happened to a good kid?" Smith tells me.
"I can remember it well. People would ask me if the police said he was
driving too fast or did he have anything in his blood system—they would
not ask me that directly, but I would hear that people wanted to know
whether he had been drinking or using drugs or whatever."

This is Smith's area of expertise. He knows the psychological comfort
that every prying person is searching for when they seek a place to lay
blame for the tragedy. But still, his voice cracks when telling me this story.

"Like everyone else, I have searched and searched and searched for my cognitively satisfying explanations for why the accident occurred," he says. "These aren't mean-spirited people trying to slap you when you are down. They are just trying to make sense of the horror of it. I do not know what happened in that particular horrific moment, and we never will, but people want to know, and they want to make sense of it."

The fact that these people were not malicious is an important point. Where the nut behind the wheel, the accident-prone worker, and the criminal addict are vehicles for blame used by powerful profiteers to avoid the cost of an accident—whether that cost is solving the problem or providing compensation—blame is something we all do for less mean-spirited reasons. Laying blame makes a terrifying, unfamiliar event less frightening and more familiar. Blame produces not just a sense of relief but also a sense of power. When we blame someone for an accident, we condense all the world's complexity, all those layers of Swiss cheese, to one kernel of cause: a single villain.

The ability to keep the uncontrollable world at bay is quite a power—which is one reason we blame victims most of all: because the dead cannot contest that power. That is what happened to Allison Liao.

How Did I Get Here?

On October 6, 2013, in Flushing, Queens, three-year-old Allison Liao told her grandmother, Chin Hua, that she wanted watermelon. Chin Hua shuttled the girl downstairs from their home and across Main Street to the store three blocks away. Watermelon procured, the pair walked back across Main Street.

In the crosswalk, an SUV driver struck Allison and Chin Hua. The child died.

As to what went wrong, reports varied: it was either the child's fault or the fault of both the child and her grandmother, the story went. Police officers told the *Daily News* that Allison darted in front of the SUV after breaking free from her grandmother. The radio station 1010 WINS reported that Allison broke free from her grandmother. A reporter from the local CBS affiliate cited several witnesses who placed blame on Chin Hua herself. Chin Hua was eating watermelon and not looking where the child was going, one told CBS. The driver insisted that the child ran in front of his car.

For months, this was the story of the death of Allison Liao—an unruly child and an irresponsible grandmother, both to blame for the child's death. It is also entirely false.

Around a year later, video footage uncovered by the police in their investigation was made public—a dashboard camera recording an unobstructed view of the killing of Allison Liao. In the video, the three-year-old girl and her grandmother cross Main Street, hand in hand, in the crosswalk, with the Walk sign shining white upon them. A driver, attempting to make a left turn behind them onto Main Street, hits them with his SUV. The driver strikes Chin Hua with the front bumper, then runs Allison over with his front and back tire. Allison Liao never leaves her grandmother's grasp. Chin Hua is right there in the street beside her. The pedestrians had the right of way. All the stories were a lie.

What happened after Allison Liao's death is worth examining because it is egregious and there is proof. The collective behavior of bystanders, reporters, and police officers is shocking. A group of eyewitnesses and professional investigators created a completely false narrative—torturing a family already in mourning. One way we can understand their behavior is in how these various parties arrived at the scene.

Reports that responsibility for the accident fell on the child and her grandmother first came from three sources—television news media, witnesses, and police officers—and how each got there may have affected how they placed blame when they arrived. All three populations are likely to have a personal association with driving a car, and likely arrived at the accident site in a vehicle. The accident occurred in Queens, which is rare among New York City boroughs in that most households own a car. Police officers spend most of their time in patrol cars. Television newscasters, requiring heavy equipment, would almost always arrive on the scene of an accident via a news van. We can hypothesize that the witnesses, police officers, and television reporters who blamed Allison Liao for the accident in some way identified with the driver who killed her via a potent fear that the same outcome might befall them: *What if I ran over a child?*

But as someone who walks almost everywhere, I immediately blamed the driver upon hearing the story of Allison Liao's death. My blame was seated in fear of being killed in the same manner as Allison.

Psychologists call this "defensive attribution"—when your blame for an accident is biased against people unlike yourself because you feel threatened by the pain and discomfort that accidents stir up. Rather than serving as an arbiter of justice, blame is just a mechanism to protect ourselves, revealing little other than what team a person is already on. Sometimes these teams are obvious—people who drive cars versus people who do not, people of your race or economic class versus others—but sometimes, it's how we tell the story of an accident that decides who is to blame and how we blame them.

Hide the Cocaine

When witnesses recounted what happened to Allison Liao, they were making a judgment about human error. Seeking to discharge the pain and discomfort of what they'd witnessed, they decided who did something wrong. But hearing their telling of the accident could affect who you felt was to blame, too.

In the early 1990s, a psychologist at Ohio University named Mark Alicke conducted an experiment to better understand the relationships that people form to an accident when they have some personal distance from it—not the person hurt or the person who made a mistake or the people who saw it happen, but the rest of us. He found that how people felt about what happened *before* an accident decided everything about how they laid blame after.

In the experiment, Alicke split his subjects into two groups and told each group different versions of the story of a car accident. In one version, a young driver was speeding so he could get home in time to hide an anniversary gift for his parents. In the other, a young driver was speeding so he could get home in time to hide a vial of cocaine from his parents. There were other dangerous conditions in both versions: an oil spill in the road, a tree branch blocking a sign. The young driver collides with another car, injuring the other driver. All of the outcomes, but only some of the intentions, were bad.

Alicke asked subjects in the study how much control the young driver had over each accident and to what degree he was to blame in either scenario. Opinion changed significantly based on which story the subjects heard. The driver who wanted to hide his coke was considered more to blame for the accident. He was also considered *more in control of its outcome* than the driver who wanted to surprise his parents. In both scenarios, the accident was unintentional. The driver made the same exact bad decision about the one condition that was within his control—he sped. But for people hearing these stories, one person was significantly more to blame for their accident, and they thought the person who was more to blame had more power over the outcome. People exaggerated the driver's control over the accident, blaming him more when they didn't like him. Alicke branded this "culpable control"—how our opinions about something unrelated to an accident can direct blame for that accident and whether we understand it as an accident at all.

The result is a tribalism of blame. Subjects judged the young driver based on his motives, hewing to opinions they would have had about drugs or speeding long before hearing this story. In other versions of the experiment, Alicke and other researchers have found that such judgments can also spring from personal experience (whether or not we ourselves ever drove too fast or hid cocaine, for instance) and personal characteristics (such as reputation, attractiveness, race, class, or gender). In this way, blame works in reverse. We blame first and then work backward to tell a story that legitimizes where we place our blame.

"The process has a big corruption component built in," Alicke tells me. "We're not born to be Solomon; we're born to make quick judgments about who's going to help us and who's going to harm us, and that can lead to some big mistakes."

The process of blame that Alicke experimented with was interpersonal, but the same corruptible blame can be institutional. A real-world example of this can be found in the different ways two driving-related limits are enforced: the speed limit and the blood-alcohol content (BAC) limit. If the speed limit is 25 mph, no one will pull you over for driving 30 mph. In Texas, you only get demerit points on your license if you are driving 10 percent over the speed limit. In New York City, automated speed enforcement cameras only trigger a ticket if you drive 10 mph over. The blood-alcohol content limit, on the other hand, makes driving *at* the limit illegal. The BAC limit in every state is 0.08. At 0.08, you go to jail. In this example, blame is not relative to the potential for harm, since both offenses kill around the same number of people every year, and just a few degrees' difference on either metric—speed or drunkenness—can affect the outcome of the accident. The difference is what is blameworthy: everyone speeds, an honest mistake, the thinking goes, but only bad people drive drunk.

Bias, fear, solidarity, and outcomes can all shape a blame judgment. In this way, how you evaluate an accident is dictated by where you ultimately want to locate blame. If two people have a fight and you prefer one of them to the other, that will define how you see the first insult, the first punch, and your assumptions about their intentions. You have a gut blame reaction first and work backward from that.

But if someone wants to, they can ensure you have one gut reaction or the other.

Body Cam POV

At the beginning of this book, a mob chased down a truck driver who accidentally killed a boy in the street. It is unlikely that the entire mob witnessed the accident, but the entire mob did agree on whom to blame.

Amid the rage and fear that drives a mob, these people likely experienced what social psychologists call blame conformity, or blame contagion—when everyone's feelings fall in line behind blame for a single villain.

Researchers have found that people have a strong urge to agree about who is to blame in any given accident—and that when some outspoken accuser presents blame in public, everyone else tends to support that view. Eyewitness statements influence other eyewitness statements so powerfully that hearing whom someone else blames can change your memory of who you thought was to blame.

In one study of this phenomenon, subjects watched a video of two men, both distracted by their phones, bumping into each other in a crosswalk. The men's actions are neutral and the two appear equally at fault. They look alike and move similarly. After watching the video, the subjects read one of three versions of an eyewitness statement. If a subject read a statement that blamed one of the men, they were more likely to blame that man. The subjects who read a blameless witness statement were unlikely to blame anyone. The results were the same whether the subjects were questioned immediately after the experiment or a week later.

The problem with blame—beyond our tendencies toward bias and tribalism—is twofold: we all fall in line behind the dominant voice, and someone with an agenda can manipulate what that voice says.

A similar experiment on blame conformity involved researchers showing one hundred people another video of a man bumping into another man. Half saw this from the perspective of a body camera, like those that many police officers are required to wear, and half from the perspective of a dashboard camera, like those installed on most police cruisers. The researchers found wide disagreement in how viewers explained this interaction—hostile or accidental—based on the perspective from which they observed it. People who viewed the incident from a dashboard camera found the bumping to be significantly less accidental and more intentional than those who viewed it from a body camera. The researchers suspect that this is because the body camera puts viewers in the physical, visual perspective of the person who bumps the other, engendering a sort of solidarity.

Researchers then applied the same test to police officers' real-life footage. In one video, a cop breaks a car window; in another, a cop shoots a person. People who watched the scene from the officer's perspective via the body camera rated the acts as being more accidental and less deserving of blame or punishment. People who saw the neutral view from the dashboard were more likely to judge the officer at fault.

Perspective can put a distorted lens on the truth, and powerful people can use these distortions to control how we blame. Police officials can control the narrative of an accidental shooting by simply selecting which video to release. Perhaps it is no coincidence that the rightful rage in response to police killings has risen with the advent of bystander videos of the events.

At best, blame is a bad way to understand accidents, and at worst, blame is an effective tool for powerful people to manipulate an accident's aftermath. Blame can stand in the way of preventing accidents and destroy the lives of the people who survive them.

Wardrobe Malfunction

Two cognitive scientists at Stanford conducted a series of experiments to understand how blame for an accident can change how a person is penalized for their mistakes.

In one experiment, they told two groups of subjects near-identical stories about a woman named Mrs. Smith who accidentally started a fire at a restaurant by dropping her napkin on a candle, toppling the candle, igniting the tablecloth, and overturning the table, thereby igniting the carpet. In one version of the telling, they phrased all the descriptions to blame Mrs. Smith: *She had ignited the napkin, she toppled the candle, she overturned the table*, and so on. In another version, all the descriptions removed the actor from the sentence instead of using explicit blame language: *The napkin had ignited, the table overturned, the carpet ignited.* The researchers asked each group of subjects to what degree they blamed Mrs. Smith for the fire and how much a court should require her to pay the restaurant in damages. The group who read the story that used language blaming Mrs. Smith deemed her more responsible and assigned her a higher cost of responsibility.

In a second experiment using the same parameters, the researchers told subjects that an independent panel had already assigned a level of blame to Mrs. Smith: high, medium, or low. The higher the level of blame that subjects were told the independent panel assigned, the more they thought she should pay. That's how powerful blame is. Think about how these results could play out on a jury asked to choose a punishment for someone already accused of a crime.

In a related study, researchers asked subjects to consider the 2004 Super Bowl halftime show, when Justin Timberlake accidentally exposed Janet Jackson's breast on live national television. In the study, four groups of subjects read about the "wardrobe malfunction." Some also watched a video of the incident. Half of the subjects read an account that blamed Justin Timberlake (*he unfastened and tore*), and the other half read one that assigned no blame—*a snap unfastened, the bodice tore.* Regardless of whether or not the subjects watched a video of the incident to form their own opinions, those who read the telling that blamed Timberlake deemed him more responsible and suggested that he pay $30,000 more in fines than did subjects who read the blameless account. Blame is contagious and can bear real consequences.

Unfortunately, in the actual incident that inspired this study, blame was apportioned even more unfairly. At the time of the 2004 Super Bowl, few blamed the white man who committed the act. Even he testified to the fact that hardly anyone blamed him. Instead, popular opinion and major corporations blamed the Black woman who had her clothing ripped off.

Officials at the next Grammy Awards banned Janet Jackson from attending, while Justin Timberlake performed at the ceremony. Les Moonves, then president of Viacom, ordered VH1, MTV, and all affiliated radio stations to stop playing Jackson's music, and as a result, her first album following the Super Bowl sold far worse than expected. Despite Jackson being significantly more famous and well regarded at the time of the incident, her career declined afterward while Timberlake's ascended. In 2018, he would return to the Super Bowl halftime show. Jackson has never appeared there again.

Blame is enough to wreck the career of a global celebrity whom the world watched stand on stage while another celebrity ripped off her clothes. For the rest of us, lacking the defensive powers of clout, money, and millions of witnesses, the potential consequences are all the more potent: legal, moral, financial. These consequences, however, are personal and individual. But blaming one person for an accident can also have more far-reaching consequences, affecting how and if dangerous conditions change.

Walking Vehicular Homicide

An especially egregious example of the structural consequences of blame comes from Georgia. In the spring of 2010, Raquel Nelson, with her three children, got off a bus and stood at the intersection of Austell Road and Austell Circle in Marietta, waiting to cross the street directly across from her home. Nelson, a single mom, moved her family around by bus, like most people in her apartment complex, because she could not afford a car. Though the bus stop was right across the street from Nelson's home, the nearest crosswalk across the four-lane highway was a twenty-minute walk up and back down the other side of the street. Like most people in her complex, Nelson walked her kids across the busy street instead of going out of her way. This time, on April 10, 2010, it was dark because the family had missed a prior bus, and her four-year-old was carrying a goldfish in a plastic bag—a lot of reasons to not go out of their way. When they crossed the street, a man named Jerry Guy ran over one of Nelson's children with his van. Guy fled the scene. The four-year-old child, A.J., died from his injuries. Nelson and the other two children survived.

Guy was partially blind, admitted to drinking and taking pain medication early that day, and had been previously convicted of two hit-and-run accidents on the same day in 1997, one on the same road where he struck Nelson's son. Police charged him with the hit-and-run, cruelty to children, and vehicular homicide. In time, a judge dropped all charges but the hit-and-run. Guy was sentenced to two years in prison and ended up serving six months.

A judge also charged Nelson in her son's death: with reckless conduct, with crossing the street somewhere other than the crosswalk, and shockingly, somehow, with vehicular homicide. There's no homicide-level crime for being a pedestrian, but the urge to blame Nelson was powerful enough that the charge for killing someone with your car was applied. An all-white jury convicted Nelson, a Black woman, on the last charge. She faced up to three years in prison until her case attracted national media attention, and a judge offered her a retrial. She ended up with a year's probation and forty hours of community service for the crime of someone else killing her child. She would likely need to run across the four-lane highway where her son died to reach the bus to attend that community service.

Bringing criminal charges against Jerry Guy, a partially blind intoxicated repeat-offender hit-and-run driver who killed a child, is a reasonable manifestation of blame. Perhaps this punishment will be enough to keep him off the road. Bringing criminal charges against Raquel Nelson, a single mother with only two hands who needed to cross a highway with three children, is a grotesque manifestation of blame. But blaming either of them does little to prevent the accident from happening again, because blame fails to address the dangerous conditions that produced this accident, namely the absence of a crosswalk at an intersection pedestrians need to navigate.

Raquel Nelson lived in a suburb built for people with cars; she and a growing population couldn't afford one. There was a bus stop but no crosswalk. There was an apartment complex and an intersection but no traffic light. There was a four-lane highway but no easy way across. In Atlanta and the surrounding metropolitan area, drivers killed more than 1,100 pedestrians between 2010 and 2019, many in the exact same way that Nelson's son was killed. As many as one in every four times a pedestrian is hit by a driver in the Atlanta metro area, the accident occurs within 100 feet of a bus stop. Expand the radius to within 300 feet of a bus stop, and you have accounted for nearly half of pedestrian accidents. Both Georgia and the Atlanta metro area are included in the state and city lists of the top twenty most dangerous places in the United States for pedestrians year after year.

Scott Higley, director of strategic communications for the Georgia Department of Transportation, explained in an email that in the aftermath of the accident, a team from metro Atlanta Traffic Operations went to the site to investigate. That investigation consisted of counting the number of pedestrians, such as Nelson and her neighbors, who needed to run across the street. Higley did not respond to questions about how many people would have needed to run across the street that day for the agency to take action, saying only that "there were not enough" to justify installing a crosswalk and traffic signal.

If the Georgia DOT was following one of those rule books that Eric Dumbaugh introduced us to, "enough" would be 100 people risking their lives running across the street every hour for four hours, or five people, such as Nelson's child, being hit by cars in a year—that's the rule defining when it is warranted to install a traffic signal at an intersection or mid-block crossing. If only 99 people were counted running across the street, and if one of those 99 got hit, the engineer, following the rules, would not be who was blamed.

In an interview with National Public Radio, David Goldberg, a spokesperson for Transportation for America, had a more pointed way to explain metro Atlanta Traffic Operations' decision not to install a crosswalk for Nelson and her neighbors. The agency did not address the safety issue, because addressing it would be tantamount to admitting that there was a problem that the traffic engineers who designed the road and the state and local officials who enabled them needed to solve. Blaming Guy or Nelson made all that disappear.

"If they were to go out and fix the problem," he explained, "it would be a tacit acknowledgment that the problem existed."

Fixing the problem means there is a problem. Blaming someone means there is no problem at all.

Blame the Egg for Cracking Against the Pan

The chief consequence of blame is the prevention of prevention. In finding fault with a person, the case of any given accident appears closed.

Studies show that this simple act—finding someone to blame—makes people less likely to see systemic problems or seek systemic changes. One prompted subjects with news stories about a wide variety of accidents: financial mistakes, plane crashes, industrial disasters. When the story blamed human error, the reader was more intent on punishment and less likely to question the built environment or seek investigation of organizations behind the accident. No matter the accident, blame took the place of prevention.

You can find a prime example of this in your bicycle helmet: a basic, low-cost shock absorber. Upon contact with a hard surface, the helmet absorbs some of the impact, reducing the risk of a concussion. When the helmet is absent, blame steps in.

Helmets help, to a point. If you are cycling on a rural road, hit a pothole, and fly off your bicycle, a helmet would act as a significant injury preventer, cushioning the impact. But if you are cycling on an urban road and a 4,000-pound car or a 13,000-pound truck runs you over, you and your helmet would be crushed.

Despite these facts, in the aftermath of a bicycle accident, the helmet-wearing or helmetless status of the person on the bicycle is almost always mentioned; it appears regularly in news coverage and accident reports.

When a drunk driver killed Eric, the *New York Times* pointed out that he was not wearing a helmet. He was also struck head-on by a 2000 BMW 528i, weighing 3,495 pounds and traveling around 60 miles per hour. Mentioning whether or not Eric wore a helmet is akin to blaming an egg for cracking against a pan.

A large body of evidence shows that the best way to prevent cycling accidents is to create separation in the road between bikes and cars. The human error of not wearing a helmet is irrelevant if you can change the dangerous conditions of mixed traffic. This reduces the number of drivers who exceed the speed limit, and the number of accidents, injuries, and deaths for cyclists, drivers, and pedestrians.

There is also evidence that drivers are more reckless when driving near cyclists wearing helmets, that laws requiring helmets make people less likely to ride a bike, that repealing those laws makes people more likely to ride a bike, and evidence that this effect—fewer people riding bikes—actually increases the number of per capita bike accidents. While a higher number of people who ride bikes in an area is linked to fewer bicyclists showing up injured at local hospitals, there is no such correlation for areas that require bicycle helmets by law. Among countries with high rates of bicycling, the ones where people wear helmets *the least* also have the lowest cyclist fatality rates. In the United States, which has the highest rate of helmet use of all those countries, the rate of cyclist fatalities is also highest. Even Giro, one of the largest helmet manufacturers in North America, says that the company does not design their helmets to protect you from cars.

None of this is to say helmets are bad or unhelpful—just a distraction from the actual problem. Like a seat belt, a bicycle helmet can reduce the likelihood and degree of injury in the case of some accidents. But the blame—such as noting whether a person killed riding a bike was or was not wearing a helmet—can actually increase the likelihood of further accidents by causing a disregard for dangerous conditions.

And across the country, helmet laws are enforced in a way that indicates that even police do not believe the purpose of the laws is safety.

In Seattle, police write as many as 60 percent of helmet citations to unhoused people. A study of helmet tickets in that city found that Black people on bikes were summonsed four times as often and Indigenous people twice as often as white people on bikes. In Tampa, as many as 80 percent of cyclists stopped were Black, even though Tampa is only around a quarter Black—the problem was so bad there that the U.S. Department of Justice investigated. The *Dallas Morning News* found that no citations were issued for bike helmets in wealthy white neighborhoods, despite plenty of cyclists without helmets in those neighborhoods. In fact, excluding those summonses issued in the central business district, 96 percent were issued in majority-minority neighborhoods and 86 percent in majority-poverty neighborhoods. The *Los Angeles Times* found eleven incidents over a fifteen-year period where a bicycle stop escalated to police killing the person on a bike—all the victims were Black or Latino. Similar results are found in cities across the country, from Oakland to New Orleans to Washington, DC.

The bicycle helmet is such a predominant manifestation of blame in cycling accidents in the United States that a researcher at Heidelberg University in Germany was inspired to track it. He analyzed the bicycle safety advice of twenty-five U.S. cities; the overhyping of helmets was so common that he declared it "a fixation." Blame was central to the fixation, with helmet-oriented safety advice more likely to be both moralizing and given special attention—exclamations, italics, graphic depictions—where other safety advice was stated plainly. The helmet, he concluded, is a way to see the death of a cyclist as an accident, to lay blame as a handy distraction from the central and systemic dangerous condition: cars can kill people.

Noting the lack of a bicycle helmet is a dog whistle for human error, like invoking the jaywalker, or the nut behind the wheel, or the criminal addict. And researchers have found that when we read about an accident and hear mention of human error, such as not wearing a helmet, it draws us like moths to a flame. This is true to such a degree that reading about an accident where someone was found to blame triggers an increased desire for punishment and a disregard for changing institutional or dangerous systemic conditions, such as an unsafe street.

Say we swap a bike accident for an accident involving a person on foot and "wearing a helmet" for "wearing dark clothing." One study did precisely this and found that for people reading the story of the accident, blame followed the mention of human error. Researchers gave subjects one of three versions of a story about a fatal pedestrian traffic crash: one called the event an accident and focused on what the pedestrian did, including what color clothing they wore; one focused on what the driver did; and one focused on what the driver did in the context of the built environment, including the nature of the street and the number of others killed in traffic accidents that year. Subjects who read the version focused on the pedestrian's behavior—including dog whistles to human error, such as clothing color—believed that the pedestrian was more to blame. The same was true of the driver-focused version; those readers blamed the driver. But the researchers in this study uncovered something else: an antidote to this blame tribalism. Subjects who read the version of the story that did not mention clothing color but contextualized the accident in the built environment were as much as 250 percent more likely not to blame either person. This last group was also more likely than the others to support preventative changes to the built environment, such as lower speed limits, wide sidewalks, and marked crosswalks, and less likely to support what the researchers called a "Walk Smart! Campaign" to "train pedestrians to cross the street more carefully." Looking, even briefly, at the layers of safety failures that led to an accident helped people eschew blame in support of changing dangerous conditions. Putting aside blame is the first step to changing the environments that put us at risk.

A similar relationship can be found in how money is spent, and who dies by accident. One study of budgets, accidental death, and U.S. cities with a population of 100,000 or more found that while higher income inequality was associated with higher accidental death rates across the board, two factors made those rates rise or sink. Those cities that spent more money on police—blaming people, and trying to perfect their behavior—had a 23 percent higher rate of accidental death than the ones that spent less. And cities that spent more on roads—correcting dangerous conditions—had a 14 percent lower rate of accidental death than the others.

Other research corroborates the inverse relationship of punishment and prevention. One study cataloging twelve years of police traffic stops in thirty-three states could find no correlation between the number of traffic stops and the number of people killed in traffic crashes in the state. We can find the corollary of this relationship in almost every accident, where the people with the power to change dangerous conditions disregard them as soon as a human error is found. In fact, it's a pattern so pronounced that the U.S. Air Force discovered it seven decades ago.

How to Prevent an Accident

After World War II, an Air Force captain named Richard Jones and an Air Force psychologist named Paul Fitts made a groundbreaking connection between human error and dangerous conditions. Wanting to understand how deadly mistakes occurred among trained pilots, Fitts and Jones collected 460 accounts in which pilots described their own mistakes in the cockpit during the war. Among the accounts, Fitts and Jones immediately found patterns. Mistakes repeated across pilots, scenarios, and cockpit models. In the accounts, they identified six types of errors, repeated again and again. And remarkably, each of these error types could be chalked up to the airplanes' design. The two men published their findings in 1947—"Analysis of Factors Contributing to 460 'Pilot Error' Experiences in Operating Aircraft Controls."

Fitts and Jones put "pilot error" in scare quotes with good reason. They found that most accidents that were blamed on pilot error could actually be attributed to the design of airplane controls. The plane itself was a dangerous condition. Airplane manufacturers had designed instruments for very different functions that were identical in appearance, and had located crucial buttons and levers in different places on different models of planes. To name one common example, pilots kept confusing the flaps and gear levers—and they did this because the flaps and gear levers looked the same, felt the same, and were not located in a standard place or order: sometimes flaps on the left, sometimes flaps on the right. One of these devices changed the aircraft's lift and drag, and it was the same size and shape as, and right next to, one that released the landing gear. It was under these conditions that pilots flying through war zones sometimes dropped the landing gear when they meant to increase the ascent of the plane.

In isolation, before Fitts and Jones, each of these instances looked like individual human errors, one pilot accidentally pulling one incorrect lever. But taken together, the mistakes revealed a pattern of obvious, predictable, and highly preventable outcomes caused by the planes' design. When Fitts and Jones put aside "pilot error," they could see the dangerous conditions built into the cockpit. "It should be possible," they wrote, "to eliminate a large proportion of aircraft accidents by designing instruments in accordance with human requirements."

This was a brand-new idea. Building for human requirements would come to be known as "human factors engineering"—observing how brains and bodies work and then building environments to match.

The most groundbreaking part of Fitts and Jones's study was this: Instead of ending their investigation by blaming the pilot, they used blame as the notification to *begin* their investigation. They concluded that pilot error is almost always a consequence of some flaw in the built environment.

Even so, blaming human error remains the industry norm today. It is as tempting to the experts as it is to all of us—even among plane accident investigators. To prove the pervasiveness of blame for human error even among these professionals, a human factors engineer and cognitive psychologist cataloged every major accident investigation conducted of the National Transportation Safety Board (NTSB) between 1999 and 2006. In seven years, all but one NTSB investigation blamed people—inexperience, bad judgment, bad planning, and pressing the wrong buttons. And even in their investigation of that one exception, where the cause of the accident was clearly mechanical, NTSB implicated an inspector in charge of manufacturing quality assurance.

Formal accident investigations *start* with the assumption that someone failed, usually the person closest to the disaster, and work backward. Starting anywhere else—such as the assumption that the built environment surrounding the accident was unsafe—would threaten the status quo.

From Fitts and Jones, Sidney Dekker has carried these ideas into the twenty-first century and built a career of applying them in industrial workplaces around the world. He studies how we fail, how systems can make us safe, and especially how we react to human error. In his book *The Field Guide to Understanding "Human Error,"* Dekker explains that this tendency to blame is understandable. There is pressure to preserve reputations, and identifying a low-level bad guy can save face. But the result is that the same accidents happen again and again. Blaming human error is a win-win for those in power who do the blaming. It sends a message that the accident was not a systemic problem but "just a local glitch in an otherwise smooth operation"—and it makes the blamers look like intelligent go-getters taking action to address the problem.

"Every time that we are confronted by the deep complexity of where these systems failures come from, we seem to revert back to the wish to explain suffering in fifteen seconds, and say, *but ah-ah-ah, we found the culprit, we found the one engineer who signed this off when he shouldn't have,*" Dekker tells me. We forget that the pilot or the worker or the pedestrian or the driver or the drug user is a product of their environment, just like us.

Blame and the punishment that follows may satisfy the thirst for vengeance. But we cannot punish and learn at the same time. Punishment keeps in place the belief that the system is safe and the human error was the aberration. Learning requires recognizing the failures built into the system and changing the system. Punishment has nothing to do with prevention.

Research backs this up, at least in the workplace. Studies have found that the more retribution workers faced when they made a mistake, the less likely their coworkers were to disclose dangerous conditions. Other studies have identified that fear of punitive workplace policies inhibited workers' interest in coming forward to report problems. And still others found that workplaces that blamed workers themselves for getting hurt meant that injuries were less likely to be reported, which meant, of course, that the dangerous conditions remained.

"Punishment focuses the attention on only one contributing factor or component. In a complex system, you can never explain, let alone improve, its functioning by reference to the performance or nonperformance of a single component. That is literally nonsensical," Dekker explains. "Complex systems fail and succeed because of the interaction between a whole host of factors."

Instead of blame and punishment, Dekker advocates analyzing the layered systems that lead to an accident. I agree, but I want to be real. To do this would require thought and consideration, self-assessment and self-knowledge, empathy for the person who would normally be blamed, and the will, usually political and financial, to move change through often intractable systems—be those local governments or large corporations.

Consider the killing of Raquel Nelson's little boy again. If you wanted to blame human error, you could say that what caused the accident was (a) Nelson crossing the street outside of a crosswalk or (b) Guy driving on pain medication after drinking with a medical condition. But if you actually wanted to solve the problem, you would need to ask why (a) and (b) were allowed to occur. Nelson crossed the street outside the crosswalk because there was no crosswalk provided, and she had three kids to manage, but she also crossed the street outside the crosswalk because she could not afford a car. Guy drove with a medical condition because the state of Georgia gave him a driver's license despite that condition and likely because he needed to drive, and he drove into a child because the Georgia Department of Transportation declined to install a crosswalk and traffic signal where people needed to cross the street. Those are just the holes in a few layers of Swiss cheese. You can go deeper, uncovering condition after condition. Taken together, the accidents are inevitable.

To see the deeper story, as Dekker advocates, we would need first to reject blame for Nelson and Guy, and accept the disquieting truth that it could happen to us, too. The land use committees that allowed an apartment complex to be built on the far side of a bus stop would need to reconsider their approval process, the public transit operator who decides where to put the bus stops would need to rethink their planning process, and the Georgia Department of Transportation would need to rewrite their road design policies to prioritize safety over traffic efficiency. And all the leaders behind those systems would have to resist the temptation to blame one another, as well as the urge to blame the dead and the accident-prone. Even in the barest-bones version of the story, the one that ignores the racial, economic, geographic, and infrastructural inequities that made Nelson need the bus and Guy keep driving, prevention is a challenge. But the alternative is worse.

When we put aside blame, we can see how accidents happen when dangerous conditions converge, when the holes in the Swiss cheese line up—and how blaming someone leaves these conditions in place for the same accident to happen again and again. But what if a person wanted to line up the holes? What if someone, seeing a system full of weak points, conditions primed for an accident, decided to take advantage?

How Not to Prevent a Terrorist Attack

The man who killed my best friend was a prime candidate for blame. He checked a lot of the boxes that we know prompt finger-pointing—he was: (1) a man who appeared non-white (2) with a non-Anglo name (3) who was driving a fancy car (4) drunk (5) leaving a party and (6) speeding (7) on the sidewalk (8) to avoid a traffic jam.

Worse still for him, the consequences of his errors were severe, and his victim was relatable. Eric was not a stigmatized person but a young, healthy, handsome public school teacher. The newspapers told a story of a bad guy killing a good guy, and of justice triumphing in the end. The man who killed Eric went to prison. Eric was still dead. The story was over.

But if you listened above the din of blame and criminal prosecution, you could hear another story from people who walked and jogged and rode bicycles on the same sidewalk where Eric died.

Eric was killed on a recreation path dividing the Hudson River from the West Side Highway, an eight-lane thruway that runs along the west side of Manhattan. From above, if you are looking north, it goes like this: river/path/highway/the rest of Manhattan. But in some places, between the river and the path, there are facilities built out onto piers—a tow pound, an athletic center, parking lots, and public docks—and to travel between those facilities and the highway, a driver has to cross the path. It is the most heavily used biking and walking path in the United States. It was also designed with a double yellow line down the middle, identical to every two-way road in America.

The man who killed Eric was at an office holiday party at one of those facilities built out onto the piers, on the far side of the walking and biking path and the highway, the night he made a wrong turn—and his actions were written off as a drunken aberration. But in the comment section of every story of Eric's death, people who used the path pointed out that this, *exactly this*, happened all the time. People in cars appeared on the path every day—some cops, some parks department workers, people taking shortcuts, people who were lost.

The evidence of the problem was more than anecdotal. Six months before Eric died, and forty blocks north on the same path, a police tow truck driver ran over and killed a doctor named Carl Henry Nacht in front of his wife. Nine years after Eric died and ten blocks south on the same path, a drunk driver ran over and killed a woman named Olga Cook. A year after Eric died, some local activists surveyed people using the path— more than a third of passersby had seen cars driving there. That survey was part of an effort by activists, after Eric's death, to push government officials to install permanent barriers on the path, ones that would prevent drivers from entering the many places that appeared to welcome them onto the path. The activists called for officials to close as many car access points as possible and to protect the others with steel barricades. They also monitored the path and identified seven locations where conditions were most clearly dangerous, spots where drivers regularly entered the path or appeared to be invited in, and published them in a list with solutions: narrow the driveways that cross the path, install barriers to prevent cars from taking the path that Eric's killer drove, paint the path to not look like a road, and add signs and lights that reiterate the message.

Government officials even provided evidence that these were not unreasonable requests. Around the time that Olga Cook was killed on the path, and nearby, Goldman Sachs opened a giant office space on the river side of the path. Outside the building, at the company's request, government officials installed stout metal bollards. You could still plow your car down the path, but not into the front door of Goldman Sachs—admission of the risk in one location while continuing to disregard it everywhere else.

The activists noted that the recommendation chief among their proposed solutions—a barrier between cars and people—could help with more than just accidents. This solution could help prevent crimes, too. In fact, they wrote that government officials had already done this elsewhere, placing big metal blockades outside many government buildings after the September 11 attacks. This suggestion would prove prophetic.

On October 31, 2017—almost eleven years after a man killed Eric—another man, Sayfullo Saipov, rented a truck and steered it right through the holes in the Swiss cheese. Unlike the man who killed Eric, Saipov was not drunk but murderous. But like the man who killed Eric, Saipov drove onto the path and headed downtown. And like the man who killed Eric, Saipov drove full speed down the center of the path. Right around where the man killed Eric, Saipov drove over twenty people. It was a sunny morning on a holiday, and the crowds were thick. Saipov injured twelve people. He killed eight.

Saipov had entered the path at West Houston Street, one of the seven locations that the activists had identified ten years earlier as prime spots where drivers regularly entered the path.

This was a crime of opportunity. It was not an accident. But for a person with murderous intentions, the known danger of the place made the likelihood of success there predictable. The accident that killed Eric was a road map for a murderer.

No one protected the tens of thousands of people who every day fill America's most crowded biking and walking path—no matter how many people were killed there by accident—until someone killed there on purpose.

Chapter Nine

Prevention

I n the 1850s, a cholera epidemic swept through London, until a British
doctor named John Snow figured out how to prevent the spread of the
disease. This is where epidemiology, as a profession, begins.

At the time, people thought cholera was spread through the air by
"vapors," but Snow suspected the illness was waterborne. He mapped
cholera outbreaks and found that they clustered around one water
source. Knowing that the water source was tainted, Dr. Snow didn't
teach people how to boil water, draw a map to a safer source, or blame
people who got cholera for not listening to him. Instead, he instructed
officials to take the pump handle off the dirty well. He changed the
environment that produced infections, and they subsided. This is one
way to tackle prevention.

The other way—convincing people to change—is exceedingly difficult, according to the epidemiologist Susan P. Baker, whom we met in
the introduction. Like Crystal Eastman and Hugh DeHaven before her,
it was at the morgue that she discovered the critical lessons of her career.
Baker spent four decades doing pioneering research on the injuries of
the dead, which she used to fight for widespread adoption of the first
child car seat, to develop the Injury Severity Score system that emergency
rooms still use to triage patients, and to lobby for a wealth of injury-
preventative technologies from airbags to home sprinkler systems. In

that time, she found little evidence that you could stop people from making mistakes. And besides, she tells me, changing their environment is easier—it just costs money. This is one reason the United States leads wealthy nations in accidental death—we don't spend money to change the built environment to make people safe.

Epidemiologists such as Baker often compare people's differing approaches to disease and accidents to show why it is more effective to change conditions than to try to change people. If we focused on human error during the polio era, for example, the only method of preventing the disease would have been discouraging the use of swimming pools. To prevent AIDS, we would only encourage abstinence. If we treated disease like we do accidents, there would be no polio vaccine and no medications to treat HIV. But we don't treat disease the way we do accidents—except when disease intersects with accidents. There is medicine to treat HIV, for example, but the tools and resources that reduce accidental HIV transmission, such as access to clean syringes, are often made illegal in favor of just telling people not to do drugs and punishing them when they do.

And while we have no conventional medicine that can prevent accidents or reduce their spread, we can prevent them—if we choose to do so. Looking at the breadth and depth of the conditions that stack up ahead of any given accident, there is no shortage of things to fix. It is a question of what we are willing to give up to save a life—depending on the accident, money, time, convenience, and the social order of our lives could all be on the table.

How to Prevent a Terrorist Attack

In 2009—three years after Eric died—an urban planner with the City of New York testified in a deposition hearing about Eric's death and the path where someone killed him. The planner oversaw construction projects for the Department of Transportation, including those along the path where Eric died.

In the deposition, a lawyer shows the planner a photo. It is the spot where the man who killed Eric saw a traffic jam ahead on the highway, and turned onto the pedestrian path. The lawyer points to a yellow thing in the photo; he calls it a pylon. The planner corrects him: It is usually called a flexible bollard. The lawyer asks: What is the purpose of this?

"It is to delineate the bikeway for cyclists so that they know where it is and where the center track is to encourage bifurcated use of it, and also as a warning to motorists, to some extent, I guess," he said.

He is saying that the primary purpose of the flexible bollard is to make cyclists keep to the right. It also has a possible lesser purpose: to alert, but not stop, people in cars.

"These yellow flexible bollards, if a motor vehicle was to come into contact with them," the lawyer asks the planner, "would they collapse, or go down, or do something else?"

"They would collapse," the planner answers, "and then they would probably spring back up after the vehicle had passed."

Bollards can be flexible and plastic, such as those that government officials used to protect the bike path, and they can be concrete and steel, such as those officials used to protect the waterfront offices of Goldman Sachs. Traffic engineers chose bollards for the bike path that would collapse, just in case a driver needed to drive through.

Little changed after the accident that killed Eric. The next day, government workers reinstalled the same flexible bollard his killer had driven over.

But a few days after Sayfullo Saipov drove over the same bollards again, the City of New York and the New York State Department of Transportation installed concrete and steel barricades at every entrance to the path. At thirty-one driveways where drivers were permitted to cross the path, new barricades blocked them from turning onto the path, and at twenty-six pedestrian intersections where drivers were not normally permitted but could still potentially fit through, new barricades made the space too small for a car to fit past. It was airtight—government officials simply worked together to prevent what had happened from happening ever again. Murder merited a preventive response in a way that multiple identical accidents did not.

A few hours after Saipov injured twelve and killed eight people in Manhattan, right where another man killed my best friend, I wrote an article about the overlap between the two crashes—an accident and a terrorist attack, vehicular manslaughter and vehicular homicide. I talked about the bollards that both drove over and around, each flexible, each placed with room to pass, a warning sign of potential human error instead of a blockade to protect people from getting hurt. But I also took a broad look at the systemically dangerous conditions that paired the events. The connection, I wrote, was cars, mixed with streets full of people. Same place, same time of year, same weapon—the only distinction was that we call one an accident. This had happened before, I wrote, it will happen again, and we could prevent it. It was days after the attack, before officials decided to install those concrete and steel barricades. I proposed a broader solution: limiting drivers' access to places in cities that are full of people walking and biking.

A few hours after the article published, my inbox filled up. People called me a fucking moron and a crazy bitch and a variety of anti-Semitic epithets. Conservative luminaries picked up the article and batted it around on social media, with similar insults stated more politely for a public audience. (Like the just world believers Kevin Smith identified, the people I infuriated most, the most inveterate blamers, were conservatives.)

An editorial in the *Washington Examiner*, responding to what I wrote, said that, should society follow the preventative measures I had proposed, it would be akin to letting the terrorists know that they had won. "We can't keep adjusting our lifestyles to complement the evil intentions and acts committed by terrorists," it read. "We shouldn't stand for that. You have to defeat evil."

In general, all the opposition added up to this: Talking about prevention is an act of surrender. Talking about anything but blame and punishment lets the bad guys win.

The vitriol of those reactions told me I was onto something. It turns out that "prevention" is a word easily used, with wildly different meanings. Some people, like those at the *Washington Examiner*, pretend that punishment is preventative. And others, like William Haddon, pay attention to what happens when people make mistakes, and prioritize preventing people from getting hurt. With that priority in place, Haddon found a million ways to prevent any given accident.

Taming Tigers

In 1970, William Haddon—a man with a thick resume in accident prevention: first administrator of the National Highway Traffic Safety Administration, head of the Insurance Institute for Highway Safety, president of the Highway Loss Data Institute—wrote a small editorial in the *American Journal of Public Health* that would change how we understand accidents. It was titled "On the Escape of Tigers: An Ecologic Note."

In it, he argues that all injury in this world, intentional and unintentional, comes from the interaction between a fragile human body and some form of energy—energy released, energy consumed, energy caught in the back of the head. He reduced the energy to types: kinetic (crashes, falls), thermal (fires, freezing), chemical (drugs, poisons), electrical (shocks), and ionizing radiation (nuclear meltdowns). You can trace every dangerous condition back to these energies loosed upon the world. And prevention, he had realized, is about controlling those energies.

As with those tigers in his title, we can control the harm of a tiger attack by controlling the release of a tiger. Haddon was being clever but not facetious. He was asking his reader to reconsider how they responded to accidents. A tiger got out! Is it more useful to punish the zookeeper or design a better tiger cage? The correct answer starts with separating the *cause* of the accident from the *harm* of the accident. The latter is important and the former is not. Control the dangerous conditions and you take human error off the table. "One can eliminate losses in broken teacups by packaging them properly," Haddon wrote, "even though they be placed in motion in the hands of the postal service, vibrated, dropped, piled on, or otherwise abused." In short, you cannot prevent human error, but you can control the built environment to prevent death and injury.

We can control the ferocious energy of an escaped tiger by preventing the release of said tiger, right? And how do you prevent the release of the tiger? By the logic of the *Washington Examiner*, you could train the zookeeper to hold tighter onto the tiger's leash, or fire the zookeeper, or bomb the country where the tiger came from or where the zookeeper went to zookeeper school, or tell the tiger it is a bad tiger, or beat the tiger.

Personally, I would rather have a tiger cage. (Or, if the tiger is no longer metaphorical, a plan to safely relocate the tiger back to its natural habitat.) Haddon's example is extreme and therefore beneficial. Few would argue that you can change the nature of a tiger or that a zookeeper could learn to be stronger than a tiger, so you need to build an environment that can control a tiger.

Or, try the same approach to Eric's death. "Separate, in space or time, the energy being released from the susceptible structure, whether living or inanimate," Haddon wrote, and provided precisely my example: "the use of sidewalks and the phasing of pedestrian and vehicular traffic, the elimination of vehicles and their pathways from community areas commonly used by children and adults." Or, to say it plainly: ban cars.

Of course, banning cars is not simple, and prevention, by Haddon's account, is not singular—in the above example, he suggests building sidewalks, phasing traffic, banning cars, and eliminating roads to control the kinetic energy of a car accident. Prevention is a multitude of harm reductions thrown at the problems of the world: buckshot, not a bullet. Haddon calls these "countermeasures." One countermeasure is "prevent the creation of the hazard"—for example, shut down production of the SIG Sauer P320. Another two countermeasures are "prevent the release of hazards that already exist" and "reduce the amount of the hazard"— child-resistant pill containers would prevent the release, in this case, and blister packaging for opioids would reduce the amount. Haddon wrote ten countermeasures in all, but you get the gist.

Haddon's countermeasures respond to energy as *a source of harm.* This introduces a slight shift in how we talk about accidents. By controlling energy, we can *entirely prevent* some accidents, such as by placing a steel bollard on a biking and walking path, so it is impossible to drive down and so that the initial mistake never occurs. We can also *prevent the harm* of others, such as by installing a speed governor on a car, so that even when a mistake occurs (for instance, hitting the gas too hard), the energy is controlled, thus reducing the likelihood of death and injury. But controlling energy can be bigger than tangible barriers and limits; it can also occur by providing tools and resources. You can prevent drunk driving accidents by offering transportation options that allow people to get drunk without driving; you can prevent accidental overdoses by making naloxone as ubiquitous as aspirin; you can prevent accidental fires by installing an automatic sprinkler system in every home in America; you can prevent accidental death caused by overheating or freezing by nationalizing the utility industry and making safe home temperatures a right, not a privilege—this is all just energy controlled.

Before Haddon, "it was an accident" was the shortest story you could tell about what happened when something went wrong. Haddon made the story long and detailed and made it far less likely that we would keep telling the same story again and again.

We can see a Haddon approach in Portugal in 2001, when the country responded to a rise in accidental drug overdoses and needle-borne disease transmission. At the time, an estimated 1 percent of the population was addicted to heroin and the country had the highest HIV infection rates in the E.U. Then, after decades of just incarcerating people for drug use, officials took a different tack. Portugal decided to instead control the problem by changing several dangerous conditions. It decriminalized the use of all drugs. This reduced the power of the black market, and helped keep superpotent synthetic additives such as fentanyl from the drug supply—"to reduce the amount of energy marshalled," in Haddon's countermeasures. It provided access to safer drug use by offering sterile tools and injection sites monitored by doctors. This lowered the likelihood for disease transmission—"to modify appropriately the contact surface, subsurface, or basic structure." And, should overdose occur, this made quick treatment possible—"to move rapidly in detection and evaluation of damage that has occurred or is occurring, and to counter its continuation and extension," according to Haddon. And Portugal also expanded medical treatments for substance use disorders. This provided a way for people to overcome addiction—"strengthen the structure, living or nonliving, that might otherwise be damaged by the entry transfer," in Haddon's words. (William Haddon was long dead at this point; the applicability of his countermeasures to modern-day drug accidents in Portugal is testament to their genius.)

Haddon's countermeasures work together, providing people with a wealth of resources to support their survival. These sorts of countermeasures work so well for drug-related accidents that, according to researchers in the U.S., for every dollar spent on treatment, municipalities can save more than a dollar by no longer needing to fight as many drug-related crimes, and $1 spent on syringe exchange saves at least $6 on the societal cost of HIV.

The results reinforce each other, too. In Portugal, accidental opioid overdose declined in tandem with accidental transmission of HIV. The number of people in drug treatment rose more than 62 percent. Also from Portugal comes a lesson that Haddon does not offer. Prevention may require patience—a hard decision. Murders rose for seven years after drugs were decriminalized, as any change to the drug market would increase violent crime. But by 2008, the murder rate began to fall. By 2014, it was the lowest it had been in at least two decades. It has remained that way.

We don't need to look as far off as Portugal to find proof of Haddon's concept of interlocking forces that prevent death and injury. Harm prevention devices are so thoroughly woven into our lives that we rarely think about them: airbags, seat belts, traffic lights, fire sprinklers, safety scissors, trigger locks, sharps containers, bagel guillotines, bannisters, fire escapes, buoyed ropes that mark the deep end of the pool. These are all ways to modify the world around us to reduce the chance and degree of accidental harm. This form of prevention accepts that accidents happen.

Make the World Safe for Drunks

Susan P. Baker, who worked alongside Haddon for decades, tells me that one way to understand his ideas is to focus on the lowest-common-denominator user—the worst driver, the most tired employee, the most distracted pedestrian. If you want to minimize damage, don't fixate on fixing that person. Instead, build an environment that controls the energy that person may come into contact with. She calls this her most controversial stance—that we should make the world safe for drunks.

"The bottom line is if you make this world safe for drunks, you make it safe for everybody," Baker tells me. "If you focus on making the world safe for the average, reasonably smart, sober person, then the drunks, the sleepyheads, the guy who is worried about his child's operation and trying to get home in time for it, it is not going to be safe for them."

Today, we do the opposite. We build roads exclusively for perfect people. Expecting perfection to prevent accidents can be seen in the U.S. government's response to the current rise in pedestrian fatalities. Between 2009 and 2019, the U.S. Department of Transportation (DOT) reported a massive 51 percent rise in the number of pedestrians killed in the United States, from a little over 4,000 a year to more than 6,000. Notably, deadly accidents for people walking and biking rose in inverse to fatal accidents for drivers and passengers; as more people were killed outside of cars, more people in cars survived.

For every year of this rising tide, the federal government analyzed the data, and then responded in a way that insults Haddon's legacy. One 2018 analysis charts what people walking and biking were doing right before they were run over—it is simply a list of human errors: "not visible (dark clothing)," "inattentive (talking, eating, etc.)," "in roadway improperly," "dart/dash." Notably, there is only analysis of victims' errors. An examination of the actions that drivers took prior to running someone over is not included.

While the body count grew, the U.S. DOT expanded on a list they published alongside each year's analyses—*Important Safety Reminders.* There is one list for drivers and one for pedestrians. The advice for people on foot includes: "Be visible at all times. Wear bright clothing during the day, and wear reflective materials or use a flashlight at night." For people in cars: "Look out for pedestrians everywhere, at all times. Very often pedestrians are not walking where they should be." Notably, on both lists, the pedestrian, who has the least power and is the most at risk, is either responsible or to blame. The list of safety reminders repeats year after year, like a record skipping at a murder mystery party where people keep disappearing.

The implication of these analyses is that the rise in pedestrian fatalities is a matter of human errors. This is not true. Pedestrian deaths are rising—and rising inverse to the deaths of people in cars—because more people are driving larger, more powerful vehicles, such as SUVs, pickup trucks, and minivans. Average weight of a vehicle involved in a fatal crash rose by more than 390 pounds between 2000 and 2018. At the same time, the share of vehicles on the road that are SUVs has risen around 60 percent. Between 2009 and 2016, there was an 81 percent rise in the number of pedestrians killed by SUVs. One researcher estimated that between 2000 and 2018, if every SUV, pickup, and minivan on the road were instead a sedan, there would be 8,131 people walking around alive today.

Not only are people more likely to be crushed by these more powerful vehicles or be pulled under them instead of landing on the hood, but the height of these vehicles also reduces drivers' ability to see pedestrians. The 2021 model of the Cadillac Escalade SUV, which weighs over 5,000 pounds, is almost six and a half feet tall. If children are sitting in front of that vehicle, they're invisible unless they are more than ten feet away. The number of children killed in accidents caused by this lack of visibility—when a driver moving forward in a parking lot or driveway runs someone over, what is now being called a "frontover" accident—has risen 89 percent in the last decade.

Backing up is not much better: The rear blind zone in a large SUV is nineteen feet long for a driver of average height. If you're short, the blind zone is thirty-one feet.

Despite the talk of pedestrians carrying flashlights and not being where they're supposed to be, none of this was news to the U.S. government. Their engineers had known for decades that larger, faster, more powerful vehicles are more likely to kill and injure. As long ago as 1975, the U.S. DOT itself figured out that three factors most determined whether or not a person was injured in a car accident: how much the vehicle weighed, how high it was off the ground, and how much higher its front end was compared to a pedestrian. By 1997, the department demonstrated that large vehicles such as SUVs and pickup trucks were significantly more likely to kill a pedestrian in a crash than smaller cars. And these vehicles have only grown—in physical size and in numbers on our roads—since. As early as 2001, researchers predicted that the popularity of SUVs would reverse the then-ongoing decline in pedestrian deaths. In 2015, as the rise in fatalities continued, DOT research again pointed to the rise in high-profile sport utility vehicles as the cause. They found that adults were two to three times more likely to be killed when struck by an SUV than by a sedan, and children four times as likely. But still, as pedestrian fatalities rose, the DOT urged pedestrians to "walk with care." Notably, the only government agency with the power to regulate how vehicles are built in the United States is the National Highway Traffic Safety Administration, a wing of the U.S. DOT.

In general, traffic fatalities primarily involve the most vulnerable, and the SUV-pedestrian crisis is not an exception. In New York City, pedestrians under seventeen and over sixty-five are significantly more likely to be killed by an SUV driver than are individuals in any other age group. Women are less likely to buy big cars such as SUVs and are more likely to be killed in traffic accidents. Low-income people are more likely to drive older cars with worse crash test ratings and are more likely to be killed in traffic accidents. The owners of big cars such as SUVs are disproportionately white. And, as we know, the pedestrians most likely to be killed in any traffic accident are Black, Latino, and Indigenous.

Haddon's countermeasures provide a wealth of ways to change this equation. But it's important to note that Haddon's model does not take into account that an accidental trigger pull is more likely if the person on the wrong side of the gun is Black, and that a car accident is more likely if you live in the swath of America where no one is paying to fix the roads. And racism and economic inequality are not energy, in Haddon's parlance. But if we apply his countermeasures with knowledge of the racism and class disparities already built into our environment, we can target prevention, fixing the places where change is most needed first.

The SUVs that automakers push into the American car market are not just known by the government to be deadly to pedestrians but are deadly in ways that require their being taken off the road, or at the very least restricted, elsewhere. In the United States, thanks to Ralph Nader and William Haddon, all motor vehicles are tested and rated on how safe they are for the people inside. But since 1997 in Europe and 2003 in Japan, vehicles have also been tested and rated for how safe they are for pedestrians, too, should the driver hit someone. European and Japanese automakers regulate the safety of vehicles for the safety of people inside *and* out—and make drivers aware of the safety of the vehicle they are buying.

When these regulations were first published internationally on the advice of the United Nations, and adopted elsewhere, the United States declined to follow suit. While the National Highway Traffic Safety Administration did recommend creating a system of mandatory pedestrian safety ratings for all vehicles, General Motors objected, and the U.S. DOT has let the process stall since 2015. As a result, the number of pedestrians killed in traffic accidents in the United States grew by half between 2009 and 2019, but in Europe and Japan, more people survived. Pedestrian fatalities fell by more than a third in a decade in Europe and by more than half since 2000 in Japan. In 2020, British lawmakers began debating banning the import of U.S. SUVs because the built-in risk was too great.

Instead of adopting international standards for pedestrian safety, officials blamed human error when the bodies began to pile up. They called for pedestrian perfection. As then U.S. secretary of transportation Elaine Chao put it in 2020, after declaring October to be the agency's annual Pedestrian Safety Month, "We are all pedestrians at some point in our day, and safety is a shared responsibility!"

You could see this as a harmless public service announcement from a government official. You could also see it as a way to let education stand in for prevention. The methods of prevention are known and disregarded in favor of the toothless message that perfection will save your life.

The number of pedestrian deaths is rising because U.S. officials fail to act. But in another area of rising accidental death—those resulting from slip-and-fall injuries—the government is taking action. Except the action that government officials have taken to prevent falls is to punish medical professionals when falls happen on their watch. The official response to the rising number of deaths due to falls is to couple those toothless PSAs with enforcement, and that is causing more accidents.

Warning: Ice Is Slippery

Falls are the most common cause of accidental death for older Americans—more deadly for that population than traffic accidents, poisoning, or any other form of injury. The number of Americans killed in falls has grown steadily in the decades since the 1980s, rising to the number two or three cause of accidental death, depending on the year. Between 1999 and 2019, the number of accidental fall deaths grew by more than 199 percent. This is in part because of the country's aging population. But it is an epidemic not helped by a focus, among those officials tasked with fall prevention, on perfecting human behavior and punishing mistakes—instead of helping people learn to control the energy of a downward fall.

Falling is an accident that most of us don't consider often. Even among the largely ignored epidemic of accidental death, falling is perhaps the least discussed of all. But in 2019, people died in accidental falls at a rate more than sixty-five times greater than that of accidental shootings. That year, some 39,443 Americans died in falls. Yet one is a topic for the nightly news, and the other remains invisible on our radar—except in one place: government.

In 2005, the National Council on Aging launched its Falls Free Initiative, and every September hosts Falls Prevention Awareness Week. The Centers for Disease Control and Prevention created STEADI: Stopping Elderly Accidents, Deaths, and Injuries—an education program. The version of this program developed by the National Institute on Aging lists how to prevent falls and fractures, including: "Be very careful when walking on wet or icy surfaces. They can be very slippery!" Other tips include wearing good shoes, not drinking alcohol, and getting enough sleep. It is all so broad as to be obtuse. And all the advice wraps up under a tagline repeated again and again in brochures and images to share on social media (*Falling is not a normal part of aging!*) and punning prompts to avoid error (*Take these steps to prevent a fall!*).

"Prevent a fall" is, of course, a remarkably useless piece of advice. Falling is an inevitable part of being human. I don't know about you, but I trip, slip, and stumble all the time—and I fall even though I am well aware that ice is slippery.

These public service announcements, while unhelpful, are also relatively innocuous. But in an effort to control the epidemic of fall-related fatalities, and save some money, the U.S. government has coupled these education programs with a far less innocuous system of financial penalties for hospitals. In 2008, the Centers for Medicare and Medicaid Services issued a directive: if a patient fell at the hospital, and the U.S.

government was paying for their care, they would punish the hospital. (Almost all older Americans, those most at risk for a fall, are enrolled in Medicare.) Falling became what the U.S. government called a "never event" for hospitals—meaning an accident so bad it should never occur. After the policy took effect, if a person fell in the hospital, Medicare or Medicaid would not cover treatment of any conditions that resulted from the fall. The hospital would have to cover those costs. When the Affordable Care Act passed, the government increased the penalties. At the same time, the Centers for Medicare and Medicaid Services reduced general payments to hospitals with the highest fall rates.

The result of all this enforcement is an epidemic of older people being cyclically readmitted to the hospital to treat the consequences of overzealous restrictions on falling. Declaring falls a "never event" with financial consequences meant that hospitals started to prevent falls on their premises in ways that made them *more likely* when patients went home. Nationwide, able-bodied older patients scheduled for brief hospital visits found themselves confined to bed by side rails, instructed not to move, and bound by motion-sensor alarms that rang when they tried to walk themselves—despite research that shows those alarms do not work. Because the muscles of an older person can deteriorate after just a few days of physical confinement, a hospital visit meant that some older people were leaving the hospital in worse shape than when they arrived.

One study of this phenomenon used data on more than 2,200 older patients admitted to two hospitals in Ohio, looking at what is known as Activities of Daily Living function—such as the ability to wash, eat, and get dressed on your own. Researchers found that, while in the hospital, these patients' diseases or injuries got better, but the patients' functionality got worse—because their movement was restricted. Between admission and discharge, more than a third of all patients studied, and more than half of patients eighty-five and older, were significantly less able to wash, eat, and get dressed on their own—much less walk without falling.

Researchers studying nurses and nursing assistants in hospitals found that the "never event" enforcement program—which included daily announcements at shift change, weekly and daily emails, signage, and monthly discussion groups about preventing falls—created such a culture of fear of falls that nurses restricted patients from moving in an effort to protect themselves and their coworkers. The result, those researchers concluded, was that nurses adjusted how they cared for patients, restricting patients' mobility and, as a result, their healing processes.

Falling is perhaps the most uncomplicated of accidents. There are very few layers of Swiss cheese between a person and the floor, which is why the act helps to explain how prevention really works. The U.S. government has provided ample evidence of how trying to prevent failure makes everything worse. You cannot prevent mistakes, but you can cushion the blow.

Falling Is a Motor Skill

Mike Grigsby, a retired biomedical engineer and martial arts instructor in Ohio, is not immobilizing older adults or telling them to just stop falling. Instead, he's teaching people to change the conditions surrounding a fall. He is doing the opposite of the Centers for Medicare and Medicaid Services. He tells older adults that they will very likely fall and gives them the power to control that energy.

"We know that basically a fear of falling will make you more likely to fall because of the way it cramps your movements. Your movements get a lot more tentative and your balance gets worse," he tells me. All those public service announcements warning older people that ice is slippery drive him crazy. "They know that they need to get rid of the fear of it, but their idea of getting rid of the fear is to deny it, sort of like: *Just say no to gravity.*"

Like many martial arts practitioners, Grigsby was already an expert in falling when a friend had a bad fall. She came out of the fall with a broken wrist and a phobia of her kitchen floor. After her wrist healed, Grigsby offered to teach her how to fall. She was his first student.

In 2012, he created a program he calls Fearless Falling to teach people how to control the conditions under which they hit the ground. He focuses on two techniques, what he calls slapping and sitting. Slapping is what you do if you trip and are about to land on your face—students slap a triangle-shaped mat, imitating the forward motion that would allow their arm muscles to absorb the force of a forward fall. Sitting is what you do if you slip and are about to fall on your back—he teaches students to tuck their chin to their chest, and sit down as close to their feet as possible, putting the body in a safe fetal position instead of a sprawl that risks a head impact. His students learn to control their falls and absorb the energy of the impact into the more resilient places on their bodies—such as an arm muscle, rather than a fragile wristbone.

Over the years, Grigsby has taught some 460 students, primarily senior citizens, how to fall in central Ohio. Sometimes his students get back in touch to say they've had a serious fall—he counts some three dozen of these phone calls and emails—each one insisting that knowing how to fall meant their injuries were less severe. A few reported they were convinced it saved their life.

Grigsby is not alone. In the Netherlands, "falling classes" are gaining in popularity. Hundreds of these classes are taught by occupational therapists and paid for, in part, by some Dutch insurance companies. Participants walk on beams and tilt out of chairs. They navigate unstable ground with canes. But most importantly, they throw themselves down onto fluffy mats—and learn how best to hit the ground.

These classes provide simple skills to transform the kinetic energy of a downward tumble. But even for far more complicated accidents—such as accidental disease transmission from drug use—there are simple routes to prevention. For people who use drugs, a basic tool—a clean syringe—is all that is needed. However, unlike falling, using drugs is considered an egregious and unforgivable human error. As a result, that tool can be tough to get your hands on. Making the world safe for the stigmatized is a much more uphill battle.

Doing Crimes to Reduce Harm

In the 1980s, there was a heroin problem across Merseyside, U.K., including in Liverpool and surrounding cities and towns. In tandem, HIV transmission was rising. Officials developed a response to illegal drug use that was then unheard of from government sources: the Mersey Harm Reduction Model, practiced at service centers that became a welcoming and safe space for drug users, free of stigma. There, people could dispose of dirty drug-use equipment and obtain clean equipment, reducing their exposure to dangerous conditions.

The goals of the Mersey Regional Drug Training and Information Centre were hierarchical. First, officials sought to reduce needle sharing, then to reduce the injection of drugs, then to reduce the use of street drugs, and, last, to reduce drug use in general. This hierarchy was important: officials at Mersey structured it in order of the potential for harm and nothing else. Caring whether or not people used drugs was last on the list, because drug use alone causes less peril than any of the other behaviors addressed in the hierarchy.

The results of the new program were significant. People who'd been using heroin for twenty-five years showed up at a drug treatment center for the first time. Liverpool became such a methadone hub that a third of all people filling prescriptions in England were doing so there. And most importantly, the HIV epidemic then exploding in other cities around the world didn't happen there. A 1996 survey of residents found only twenty people in the whole metro area who had contracted HIV through drug injection, some of whom moved to Liverpool after becoming ill.

The ideas of Mersey have since spread and advanced. In ten countries (eight in Europe, plus one each in Australia and Canada), safe injection sites provide a clean and medically monitored environment for drug use. Everywhere this approach has been introduced has seen a reduction in drug use and overdose death. We've already seen the most dramatic example of this in Portugal. The country made harm reduction into official government policy, removing the question of human error entirely from the equation by legalizing all drug use, and putting the ability to control the conditions of drug use in the hands of drug users through widely accessible treatment clinics, needle exchanges, and safe injection sites. Portugal's HIV infection rate was 96 percent lower in 2015 than it was in 2000, when drugs and needles were illegal.

Until very recently, no safe injection sites existed in the United States, and threats from the federal government met local attempts to open one. (In the summer of 2021, Rhode Island authorized a two-year pilot program where people could consume drugs they had already obtained under the supervision of trained staff.) But other versions of harm reduction have appeared, especially with the opioid epidemic.

In Little Falls, Minnesota, a town of less than 9,000 people, the local government slowed a growing heroin problem by treating drug users as though they were not evil but in need of assistance. The town spent $1.4 million in state grants to increase access to addiction medication and set up programs where users were offered treatment instead of jail. These programs addressed all that addiction might entail—not just naloxone for an overdose and buprenorphine for withdrawal, but doctors who know how to spot addiction and are trained to offer help without judgment. The local hospital helped more than 600 people ease off opioids, and in the emergency room, requests for painkillers went from the number one reason for visits to outside the top twenty. In Huntington, West Virginia, once known as the "overdose capital of America," an old pharmacy became a counseling center that helped with jobs, housing, and addiction treatment. Accidental overdoses fell 40 percent in a year.

But not all the outcomes are positive. In another West Virginia town, Charleston, a needle exchange—the state's largest—opened in 2015. Lines were out the door, the staff helped 400 people a week, and the exchange would sometimes give out as many as 5,000 needles a day. And it worked: while there were HIV outbreaks in neighboring counties, Charleston was spared. Two years later, the exchange closed amid complaints of an abundance of discarded needles. The mayor criticized the project as a "needle mill" and a "mini-mall for junkies."

Because of places such as Charleston, harm reduction is often unofficial: not policy but protest; one person helping another.

In 2015, Jamie Favaro was at a national harm reduction conference when Tracey Helton Mitchell, author of *The Big Fix: Hope After Heroin*, got onstage for a talk about using the internet to reduce the harm of drug use. At the time, Favaro was already well versed in the field of harm reduction. She had worked in needle exchanges for well over a decade, including founding one in the Washington Heights neighborhood of New York City in 2005. But these were small, local efforts. Mitchell's presentation made her realize she could be reaching far, far more.

Mitchell spoke about meeting people on Reddit drug recovery forums who lived in rural areas where ambulances could take an hour to respond to a 911 call. By the time help arrived, the person was dead. To help these people, from her home in California, Mitchell began mailing naloxone across the country. It was accessible where she was, but not in much of the country.

Favaro had already built a syringe exchange from the ground up, but a brick-and-mortar syringe exchange could only help people within a certain radius. If she could scale up Mitchell's model, she realized she could reduce the risk of death or disease for many more drug users.

Two years later, she launched NEXT Harm Reduction, America's first online and mail-based harm reduction program. The organization set up two secure, encrypted web portals—NEXT Distro, a syringe exchange, and NEXT Naloxone, for the overdose reversal drug—and started shipping around the country in 2018.

"The three main reasons why individuals have difficulty accessing harm reduction supplies or naloxone are due to location, cost, or stigma," Favaro tells me. "Both programs are specifically designed for such people that cannot access resources in person."

The need for this enterprise comes from a lack of access to supplies and medicines that can prevent overdose and disease transmission.

Favaro posits that the accidental deaths and illnesses that might result from making preventative solutions inaccessible may be what some people think those who use drugs deserve.

"The government doesn't want to give naloxone to people who use drugs, because they want drug overdose to have some type of consequence," she notes. A lack of access is another, more roundabout way to respond to accidents with punishment in place of prevention. She points out that accidental overdoses are the highest in states where naloxone is the hardest to access, making the overdose reversal drug a tool of power and control. If you give police naloxone, then drug users are forced to choose between the risk of death and the risk of incarceration, she says, but if you provide naloxone to people, communities can choose to use drugs or not, without having to wager their life or freedom in the negotiation.

Soon after NEXT Harm Reduction launched, Favaro began getting requests from all over the country. They were especially pressing: from people who were sharing syringes, reusing syringes twenty times or more, unsure about their HIV status. Some had overdosed multiple times but could not access naloxone because of complicated state restrictions or cost or both. NEXT operates legally in New York, Favaro explains, but soon after opening, it was also operating in another 56 percent of U.S. counties in thirty-eight states. At this point, I realize that the whole scope of the work of NEXT might not be entirely legal, but Favaro declines to go off the record.

"First and foremost, we are harm reductionists, and we believe in direct action, and that direct action and activism is necessary to support people who use drugs," she says. "The main concern is the security and the privacy of the people we support. As harm reductionists, we are not as concerned about our own legal standing or well-being as we are for the people who we serve."

Favaro and other harm reductionists have leaped forward from the ideas of William Haddon. They're not just trying to understand how people die by accident and how to stop it. They are paying attention to the unequal way that accidental death and injury falls across America, and they are responding accordingly. They are refusing to accept one preventable death and putting their own money, comfort, and well-being on the line to prevent the accidental harm of others.

What If Instead No One Dies

Claes Tingvall, a traffic safety specialist in Sweden, is far from the world of drugs and West Virginia, but for him, the same idea applies. We must pay whatever price we can to protect human life, he tells me.

In January 1995, a few weeks after Tingvall became director of traffic safety in Sweden, the Swedish minister of transport asked him a question: *What kind of target should we set for how few people are killed in traffic?*

What happened next would save an untold number of lives. As a government bureaucrat, Tingvall did something he wasn't supposed to do, and the minister of transport did something, as a politician, that she wasn't supposed to do: they both hoped for the best possible outcome, regardless of what it would cost.

No one should die in traffic accidents, he said to the minister of transport. He compared what the Swedish call "the road transport system" to the workplace. Already the country believed that no one should die in work accidents, and many worked on the roads—why was transportation any different? "That suddenly clicked in her head immediately and she smiled at me and said that's a very good idea," Tingvall recalls to me. "The rest of the room, they almost fainted because you're not allowed to say something like that, because nothing is supposed to be more important than anything else in the planning of the road transport system."

In Sweden, the old way to design roads was to balance safety, efficiency, and cost—it was important that no one die, but it was equally important that no one was late to work and that none of it cost too much. This is still the expectation of U.S. transportation systems. What Claes Tingvall and the Swedish transport minister began that day would come to be called Vision Zero—they threw out the old desire to balance safety, cost, and efficiency in favor of a single goal: zero deaths.

This was a shift in responsibility. No more would the government blame jaywalkers and nuts behind the wheel for their deaths. Instead, when someone died on the road, government officials and traffic engineers were responsible; *they* had to explain how *they* had let it happen. And instead of designing for a perfect human, those officials began designing roads from the starting point: What might go wrong? Blame, in the form of traffic enforcement, was deprioritized. Instead, the road was built to reduce the harm of inevitable mistakes.

Sweden is manifesting Haddon's ideas, but also, like Favaro, taking them a step further. Vision Zero puts people's safety first, sacrificing convenience and cost wherever necessary.

In two decades, as traffic volume grew, Sweden cut the number killed on the roads by half. Today the per capita rate of fatal traffic accidents in Sweden is less than a third of that in the U.S. The people who made the roads were accountable to the people who used them. And this simple act—assigning accountability to the people with the most power—meant that the people with the ability to prevent accidents finally did just that.

Chapter Ten

Accountability

Accountability is the act of taking responsibility. In accidents, this is often confused with punishment—after an accident, finding fault with human error, and punishing the person who erred. A traffic ticket looks like accountability for an accident. A jail sentence looks like accountability. But these punishments do nothing to prevent death or injury.

Punishment is just a way to force someone to take responsibility for *making* a mistake—but in this process, no one is responsible *for the mistake itself.* We are so focused on the person that the predictable, preventable path that led to the accident remains unchanged. In this hunt for an individual to be held accountable for their errors, we lose the ability to be accountable for dangerous conditions—and a wealth of information about prevention.

The workplace safety expert Sidney Dekker explains that effective accountability means putting ourselves in the shoes of the person who erred. Put ourselves in their shoes, and we can understand how the accident occurred and where the power to prevent death or injury lies. From this perspective, we can make recommendations. Dekker notes that these recommendations can be what he calls low-end or high-end, and warns against the former.

"The ease of implementation and the effectiveness of an implemented recommendation generally work in opposite directions. In other words: the easier the recommendation can be sold and implemented, the less effective it will be," he writes. "Alternatively, recommendations can aim high, at structural decisions regarding resources, technologies, and pressures that people in the workplace deal with."

High-end recommendations, he writes, "are substantial, structural, or wholesale." They are more expensive and involve people far outside the accident, typically people with power. That, Dekker says, is where the real work to control accidents is done.

In making recommendations after an accident, two goals are central: that we are guided by empathy and that we aim to repair harm. These intentions are inextricable from the process of being accountable. We empathize, and as a result, we learn—seeing why people made the decisions they made at the time. If we can do this, we can see how a syringe exchange can prevent an accident, as can a blister pack, or a traffic signal and a crosswalk, or teaching a medical student to recognize ingrained racism.

Like the nail to a person with a hammer, if the only tool in our toolbox is punishment, we will only ever see human error. But because real accountability is about repairing harm, it can break the cycle of accidents that happen again and again. Accountability can patch the holes in the Swiss cheese.

As the prison abolition leader Mariame Kaba puts it, "You cannot have safety without strong, empathic relationships with others." This is exactly the point of Jamie Favaro's work—ensuring the safety of people who use drugs requires seeing them with empathy and providing the tools and resources they need to survive using drugs. And this is the point of Claes Tingvall's work—ensuring the safety of people who use the roads requires placing their safety above all other considerations, as you might do for yourself.

In terms of structured and wholesale accountability, what we have in the United States is less empathic and less concerned with repair. We have a patchy network of systems that charge corporations and governments money for failing to prevent accidents, in hopes that cost is enough to inspire prevention: inspections, regulations, tort law. Starting in 1911, for example, workers' compensation laws made companies accountable for work accidents by giving those accidents a cost.

Ralph Nader sees this structured, systemic accountability as critical to preventing accidents, and the word "accident" as an obstacle to prevention.

"Accident," he tells me, "is an anti-cognitive and anti-intellectual and anti-values word, and it is used to exculpate corporate crime."

I ask him what we should say instead. He has suggestions.

"You've got a nonnormative choice: You can just call it a crash, bloodshed, poisoned water. Or you could basically say a corporate homicide," Nader says.

In the past two hundred years of corporate homicide, to use Nader's term, there's been no shortage of powerful people refusing to be accountable for accidents. There have been small inroads made, however, to systematize accountability.

Nader is responsible for many of these inroads. He turned the idea that corporations should be formally accountable for accidents into U.S. law. His work led to the creation of wholesale accountability systems in U.S. government: the National Highway Traffic Safety Administration, the Occupational Safety and Health Administration, the Environmental Protection Agency, and the Consumer Product Safety Commission— each a system of worker and consumer safety regulation to prevent a certain type of accident.

Government regulations issued and enforced by these agencies encourage corporations to take responsibility for patching the holes in the Swiss cheese by imposing financial penalties for letting people die by accident. When those regulations fail to prevent an accident, the use of tort law can fill in the gaps, providing financial recourse via legal action for the injured or the families of the dead, and a systemic incentive for corporations to prevent future accidents.

These accountability systems were only ever financial—a way to force responsibility on those who care only about money—but even this relatively narrow idea of accountability is actively subverted and weakening every year. Roughly every other president for the past forty years has run on a platform of anti-regulatory ideology, and even those who haven't have done little to protect regulations. The number of people who've filed a tort lawsuit has been in steady decline for more than two decades, closely following the decline of the average amount awarded to accident survivors and their families. Even the limited systems of accountability we have are being dismantled, subverted, and overtaken by the corporations they are supposed to hold to account.

The Unregulated Automated Death of Samya Stumo

Federal regulation is the most powerful system we have to prevent accidents, but for four decades, corporate influence has been picking apart corporate accountability. This is deceptive because federal regulations are not dismantled but "captured"—a government agency subtly controlled by the very powers it is charged to regulate. Regulatory capture is when a regulator appears to be functioning as a check on an industry but in reality has been overtaken by that industry—such as the 2017 appointment of a corporate mining executive to run the agency that is supposed to protect miners from dangerous conditions in mines.

On June 27, 2011, in Raleigh County, West Virginia, a coal mine crew leader named Joseph Cassell was killed when a portion of the mine where he worked, Eagle No. 1 Mine, owned by Rhino Resource Partners, accidentally collapsed. The Mine Safety and Health Administration (MSHA) investigated and found that the only machine available for miners to use to install wood and bolts to hold up the mine walls was not powerful enough, forcing the miners to install this safety infrastructure in the weakest parts of the wall. This was not news—the agency had warned the company about a rising number of safety violations such as this a few months before. It was a known dangerous condition that led to a predictable accidental death, one for which the company paid $44,500 in fines.

David Zatezalo was a chief executive of Rhino Resource at the time of the accident, and this was not the first accidental death on his watch—mine workers had been killed in accidents at mines owned by companies where he was an executive in Ohio and Kentucky in 2001, 2003, and 2007. President Trump appointed him to run the Mine Safety and Health Administration in 2017. His first act was to revoke a regulation that required safety inspectors to inspect mines while miners were working. The new rule also said that if a company fixed a safety hazard quickly, MSHA would be forced to erase the violation from the record. The goal here, the regulatory agency said, was to "reduce the regulatory burden" and "reduce and control regulatory costs." The result is that inspectors are less likely to spot dangerous conditions and it is harder to trace dangers, including the one that caused this accident, over time.

The appearance of accountability remains because the agency and its regulations still stand, and we are lulled into thinking that there is an effective check on corporate power in place when there is none. According to Ralph Nader, this leaves us fooled into believing that we're protected—and this was how Nader's grandniece, Samya Stumo, was killed in 2018, when Ethiopian Airlines Flight 302 crashed. It was the second fatal crash of a Boeing 737 Max, a plane that Boeing and the Federal Aviation Administration (FAA) knew was unsafe.

"Regulatory capture is worse than having no regulation because it gives a facade to regulation and deceives the people," Nader tells me. "They think the FAA is really protecting them. They have no idea of the delegation and abdication of safety to Boeing."

Captain Chesley B. "Sully" Sullenberger, a man famous for manually overriding a broken plane to make a safe landing in the Hudson River, explained what went wrong at Boeing in testimony before Congress after the second 737 Max accident. The plane, he said, was plagued by designed-in aerodynamic and automation failures that made the accidents inevitable. But Boeing told a human error story—blaming the accidents on the pilots and how they failed in interacting with the automated systems.

The 737 Max was a redesign of the old 737. During production and testing, engineers and test pilots discovered that the new design, now more fuel efficient, also made the craft less aerodynamic. Instead of stopping work to remake the plane, Boeing added software, a system known as MCAS. To cover for the plane's poor maneuverability, the software would sometimes push down the plane's nose without input from the pilot. If this software failed, Boeing expected the pilot to fix it. To review: Boeing built a plane that was difficult to fly, then added software that autocorrects these difficulties, but decided that if that software fails, the pilot should save the day by figuring out how to fly the difficult-to-fly plane.

"It has been suggested that even if the MCAS software had flaws, the pilots on these flights should have performed better and been able to solve the sudden unanticipated crises they faced," Sullenberger told the committee. "Boeing has even said that in designing MCAS they did not categorize a failure of MCAS as critical because they assumed that pilot action would be the ultimate safeguard."

Boeing's assumption contradicts everything that experts know about human interaction with automation—namely, that people are bad at monitoring machines. Even the most talented pilots tend to zone out when autopilot functions are engaged. Sullenberger told the committee that we must do better than building flawed airplanes and expecting pilots to compensate for their flaws. Pilots can handle an emergency like he did when a bird strike paralyzed his plane over the Hudson, but the crisis should not be an aircraft designed with built-in traps.

And, it turned out, the Boeing 737 Max was full of traps.

MCAS—that is, Maneuvering Characteristics Augmentation System—operated by automatically lifting the tail of a plane and moving the nose down, based on data from a sensor on the front of the aircraft. If the aircraft was approaching a stall—and the 737 Max was prone to stalling—this action would prevent it. The sensor at the front of the plane recorded the angle of oncoming airflow. If the angle was too high, it told the software that a stall was coming, automatically activating it.

But it only took a single sensor to trigger this whole process—just one incorrect reading could do it. That's what happened in *both* 737 Max accidents. The sensors took bad readings that said the plane was stalling when it was not, and the automated software lowered the nose of the aircraft as far as it would go. Even if a pilot realized that the software had bad data, the software would resist their attempts to control the plane. The machine steered the plane into the ground. Boeing didn't even tell pilots that MCAS existed or how it worked.

This accident was allowed to happen—and happen twice—because the organization with the power to ground the planes, the Federal Aviation Administration, is captured by Boeing, more or less. Government regulation should have patched many of these holes to prevent the approval of an unstable airplane constructed in haste, except that at the FAA, the safety monitors were in Boeing's control.

Regulatory capture invades every corner of airplane design. For example, airplane safety used to be monitored by engineers who were hired by and reported to the FAA. At Boeing's encouragement, and as part of a deregulatory agenda of his second term as president, George W. Bush turned this regulation over to the airplane manufacturers. Boeing would now hire safety monitors, and they would report to Boeing, and these monitors would fight the FAA when the FAA sought changes before certifying an airplane to fly. The results of this power transfer are evident in the Boeing Max case on multiple levels.

First, the head of aviation safety at the FAA at the time of these accidents, Ali Bahrami, was a former lobbyist for Boeing. And before the accidents, Bahrami successfully lobbied from inside the FAA to give Boeing more control, and the FAA less control, of approving the design of new airplanes. Moreover, when Boeing tested MCAS using flight simulators, pilots reported back to their employer that the system was buggy. Boeing didn't report that to FAA regulators. The company also removed all mentions of MCAS from pilot manuals, a decision that the FAA supported.

"It's fundamentally embedded in the handling qualities of the airplane. So when you train on the airplane, you are being trained on MCAS," CEO Dennis Muilenburg told reporters when news of the omission came out. "It's not a separate system to be trained on." So it went unmentioned. Boeing defended this decision by explaining that the purpose of MCAS was to make the plane *feel like* it flew the same as the earlier generation of 737s. Boeing kept pilots in the dark because, to make sense as a design decision, MCAS, which corrected a known aerodynamic inefficiency in the plane, had to be considered like any other integral machinery in the plane.

The *New York Times* reported that before the first 737 Max crashed, the pilot handed control over to the co-pilot. He then spent his final minutes, before he began to pray for his life, paging through the pilot manual, trying to determine what was going wrong. This was futile; any mention of MCAS had been removed.

It was a predictable accident and a massive one, followed five months later by the exact same. The pair drew enough attention to ground 737 Max flights nationwide and launch congressional hearings into Boeing's role in the regulatory process.

But as Crystal Eastman taught us, these large accidents draw our attention by their magnitude, while most people die by accident in ones and twos. These accidents killed 346 people in 2018 and 2019, the vast majority of people killed in plane crashes either year. In those same years, 36,560 and 36,096 were killed, respectively, on America's roads. These little accidents catch far less attention but are subject to an even more insidious regulatory failure than Boeing's capture of the FAA. With some car accidents, the regulator doesn't pretend to regulate; it declines to regulate at all—and with a new generation of driverless cars being field-tested on America's roads, this failure to regulate threatens us all.

The Unregulated Automated Death of Elaine Herzberg

Uber came to Arizona to field-test their driverless cars because the governor promised that he would not regulate how Uber tested their vehicles on state roads. After California ejected the company's vehicles for failing to comply with regulation and running their driverless cars through several red lights (a failure which Uber blamed on human error), Arizona extolled the lack of accountability it could offer.

"Arizona welcomes Uber self-driving cars with open arms and wide open roads," the governor wrote in a 2016 statement announcing the arrival of Uber's driverless test vehicles. "While California puts the brakes on innovation and change with more bureaucracy and more regulation, Arizona is paving the way for new technology and new businesses."

Two years later, in March 2018, an Uber driverless car detected Elaine Herzberg crossing mid-block on an Arizona street and ran her over. Despite the car's having detected something in its path, it did not stop, because Uber did not program the car to recognize people walking outside of crosswalks. After the fact, the logs showed that the system appeared to recognize Herzberg as an unknown object, a vehicle, then a bicycle in quick succession. Of course, a driverless car *could* be programmed to hit the brakes every time a bug comes at the windshield or to disengage whenever anyone walks within twenty feet of the car. But this one wasn't. Instead, Uber had actually disabled the emergency braking system on the vehicle—turning off what should be the last-gasp fail-safe.

Uber says this was done "to reduce potential for erratic vehicle behavior." One way to understand this is via a metric that automakers use to demonstrate the success of their automation—known as "disengagements," or the number of times driverless car automation turns off or requests human assistance. The fewer disengagements, the more advanced and safer a company's automation appears. Uber may have switched off the built-in emergency brake—which could have stopped the car for Herzberg—because the emergency brake being switched on would have made disengagements more likely; a safety device doing its job would have made the vehicle *appear* less safe.

Uber could make these decisions at will—and not just because the car that killed Elaine Herzberg was driving in Arizona. While state regulations vary to a massive degree, prior to 2021, at the federal level, the National Highway Traffic Safety Administration (NHTSA) had issued zero regulations for autonomous vehicles. That changed when, in response to recommendations from the National Transportation Safety Board's investigation into Herzberg's killing, NHTSA required companies, for the first time, to report safety data, including accidents and injuries, to the federal government. Otherwise, there are no safety standards outside the ones that apply to normal cars—though makers of driverless cars are actively lobbying to be exempt even from those. As of 2019, more than 1,400 driverless cars were being tested, and around half of states allow field tests on public roads. In 2019, the U.S. Department of Transportation set aside $21 million—not to regulate the industry but the opposite: "to facilitate the development of autonomous vehicles by reducing regulatory barriers."

Joan Claybrook was the chief lobbyist for Ralph Nader before she came to work for William Haddon at NHTSA. In 1977, President Carter appointed her to run the organization. There, in the late 1970s, she proved that the Ford Pinto had a defective gas tank that caused the vehicle to burst into flames in an accident. She also confirmed that Ford knew this; the company had conducted a cost-benefit analysis of how much it would need to spend to make the gas tanks stronger. It was cheaper, Ford found, to pay settlements from tort lawsuits of burn victims. In response, Claybrook led the creation of new regulations that required automakers to build safe fuel systems. It was one of the twenty-odd motor vehicle safety standards she passed into law during her tenure, including requirements for seat belts, roof crush resistance, and child car seats. Today, she tells me, new regulations are far less common. The U.S. Department of Transportation should be issuing regulations for autonomous vehicles, for example, but the agency has said that the automakers can make their own rules.

As a result, she says, autonomous vehicles are not ready for field-testing, especially in cities dense with people walking and biking. As an example, Claybrook points out that while human drivers need a vision test, there is no such requirement for driverless cars. NHTSA has required no proof that the vehicles' sensors can see in daylight or in darkness, or can identify small objects, children, animals, or markings on the highway. She says that NHTSA has wholly abandoned its mandate as a regulator. "Philosophically, they do not believe in regulation," she tells me. "It has nothing to do with public health and safety. It has nothing to do with whether people are going to die in these crashes. It has to do with the political, philosophical perspective that they shouldn't regulate anything. And it is really criminal."

Instead of regulation, NHTSA has issued what it calls "voluntary guidance" for autonomous vehicles. NHTSA is the only federal regulatory agency that could restrict the ability of Uber, or any other car company, to let robots accidentally kill people. But the agency defines its role in the process differently—"identifying and supporting the development of automation-related voluntary standards." And of course voluntary standards hardly encourage accountability. The regulator has volunteered not to regulate.

The Death of Federal Regulation

The federal government should be our most widespread system of accident prevention. Federal safety regulation is why cars all come with seat belts and airbags, why workplaces are free of asbestos and untended explosives, and why pork sausages contain only pork. But today, the federal regulatory system is drastically weakened—a large hole in the Swiss cheese—and people who profit from accidents know this. Instead, accidents happen because corporations control and manipulate the regulatory processes that could prevent them. For example, Purdue Pharma did not market OxyContin equally across the United States; the company focused on states with the fewest and weakest prescription regulations. This led to more prescriptions in these states and more accidental overdoses there, too.

Amit Narang, an expert in regulatory policy at Public Citizen, the nonprofit consumer advocacy organization founded by Ralph Nader in

1971, explains the purpose of federal regulatory agencies as protective. "Generally speaking, these agencies were given authority by Congress specifically to implement laws that are designed to protect certain parts of the public," he tells me—namely workers and consumers.

Between the 1950s and the 1970s, activists in the environmental movement, the anti-nuclear and anti-war movements, and the labor movement led a wave of demand for government protection from corporations. These protest movements led to the passage of the Clean Air Act and the Clean Water Act, the banning of the pesticide DDT, and the creation of the Environmental Protection Agency, the Consumer Product Safety Commission, the National Highway Traffic Safety Administration, the Nuclear Regulatory Commission, and the Occupational Safety and Health Administration.

In 1980, Americans elected Ronald Reagan on a platform of defanging those very agencies. He would issue an executive order requiring that every regulation be subject to a cost-benefit analysis—truly saying the quiet part out loud: it is not worth saving lives if it costs money. For the next forty years, corporate lobbyists fought hard and successfully not only to dismantle safety regulations but to shift the public mindset about government protection.

There is a lot of evidence that regulations save lives and a lot of propaganda that regulations stifle the economy, Narang explains—but there is little or no evidence to support the propaganda. Still today, it is common for regulatory agencies to work toward the goals of corporations and for those agencies to think like the corporations they regulate.

Take the decision for the National Highway Traffic Safety Administration to compel an automaker to recall a car. Car recalls are prompted by accidents that happen repeatedly due to a defect such as failing brakes on Toyotas or Jeeps that catch fire. But these recalls differ in the United States and abroad, even for the same cars and parts. Between 2004 and 2014, at least forty-two different vehicle defects prompted the recall of vehicles abroad. In every case, those exact same vehicles were allowed to remain on American roads. In every case, NHTSA failed to use its regulatory power to force a recall. As of 2017, NHTSA investigations into vehicle defects were at an all-time low—down more than 93 percent since 1989.

At the same time that corporations capture their regulator, they also lobby to weaken the agencies in other ways—by reducing budgets and staff. The budget of the Environmental Protection Agency, adjusted for inflation, is less than half what it was in 1979. While our economy and population have grown, and Congress has increased the responsibilities of the EPA, the agency tasked with protecting us from environmental injury has shrunk. The staff of the Occupational Safety and Health Administration has shrunk, too—in 2019, the number of workplace inspectors on staff was lower than at any time in OSHA history. In just two years, between 2016 and 2018, the agency reduced inspections related to protecting workers from accidental overheating by nearly half, conducted 20 percent fewer inspections related to accidental chemical exposure, and reduced by 25 percent inspections that could prevent accidental explosions. But before 2016, the situation was already bad.

In 2013, the West Chemical and Fertilizer Company in West, Texas, caught fire and exploded. The blast flattened buildings for a five-block radius leaving a ninety-three-foot-wide, ten-foot-deep crater, killing at least fifteen people, including ten firefighters, and injuring another two hundred. OSHA had last inspected the plant in 1985—twenty-eight years earlier. The EPA permitted the plant to self-report, which it did, reporting no risk of fire or explosion, even though the plant held 270 tons of ammonium nitrate, the main ingredient in the 1995 Oklahoma City bombing, and 54,000 pounds of anhydrous ammonia—a toxic volatile fertilizer known for its ability to blind, burn, and suffocate. Those self-reports are how the EPA prioritizes inspections.

Regulations are preventative, and when regulation fails, people die. These were all called accidents—the West, Texas, explosion; the Uber driverless car killing; the Boeing 737 Max crashes; the Rhino Resource mine collapse—but Narang tells me that they are choices born of greed.

"Corporations do not want to sacrifice any profits, and compliance with regulations means that they are spending money that would otherwise be profits," Narang says. It's not just the cost of complying with a regulation that corporations want to avoid but the legal liability for a broken rule. "If they are able to fundamentally undermine the power of these regulatory agencies, then they are going to be subject to not only less compliance costs, but less legal liability. They will have more control over their employees because their employees will not be able to enforce their rights."

Early in this book, we learned how corporate executives would point to employee safety handbooks in the aftermath of an accident. By pointing to these rules—even if they were impossible to follow—executives could make the case that accidents were caused by employees breaking rules, distracting from whatever dangerous conditions led to the accident. For themselves, however, corporate executives seek the opposite—a world without rules and regulations, where everything that goes wrong is an accident. Regulatory capture and the dismantling of regulations return us all to the early days of the Industrial Revolution, when disaster was blamed on the least powerful—the accident-prone worker, the jaywalker, the criminal addict, the nut behind the wheel.

Deregulation has a societal cost. Taxpayers pay for the ambulances, health care, and reconstruction of public infrastructure destroyed in the accidents that follow unwatched industries. The Office of Management and Budget measures these costs, and what would be lost if there were no regulations at all. It estimated the societal benefit of 137 regulations issued between 2006 and 2016 to be as high as $911 billion. The estimated annual benefit of regulatory protection is somewhere between $103 and $393 billion. That's a cost that we, not corporations, will pay more and more as deregulation continues.

Fortunately, as federal regulators grow more and more beholden to the companies they regulate, the civil court system offers another system of accountability. It is how the family of Elaine Herzberg reached a financial settlement with Uber, and how the families of those killed on Lion Air Flight 610 and Ethiopian Airlines Flight 302 brought a lawsuit against Boeing. Tort law provides accountability after an accident, but, more importantly, it gives an incentive to prevent similar accidents in the future. It is a rare form of punishment that reduces accidents, since it holds accountable the powerful people who actually control whether or not accidents happen. But corporate influence has weakened this system as much as it has weakened government regulation.

The Death of Civil Justice

Tort law is the law of accidents. It allows people to sue corporations or governments after the worst occurs. These lawsuits can create accountability in a few ways. Tort lawsuits help people or their families get compensated after a corporation or government accidentally injures or kills someone. And the prospect of a suit should encourage corporations and governments to fix dangerous conditions before an accident happens. And tort lawsuits, because they typically occur as public trials, can also alert citizens and the government about serious problems they might not have otherwise known about.

But today, people file fewer and fewer tort lawsuits, and more courts seal documents in the cases that do make their way through. In 1993, around ten in 1,000 people filed a tort suit; in 2015, fewer than two in 1,000 did—a difference of 1.7 million cases. The reason for this decline is laws that restrict your right to go to court, particularly if you are in an accident caused by a corporation. These restrictions are known as "tort reform."

Tort reform is a nefarious bit of wordplay—it sounds like a good thing, doesn't it?

It is not. Tort reform is a euphemism for an infringement on your right to sue in civil court. The wordplay and the reforms are both crafted by the people who profit from that infringement.

In 1986, a few hundred of the largest corporations in the United States, together with the insurance industry, formed the American Tort Reform Association. Twelve years later, the U.S. Chamber of Commerce created its own "tort reform" branch, the Institute for Legal Reform, which is now one of the largest lobbying groups in the country. Around that time, small and seemingly grassroots tort reform groups cropped up, too. But these, too, were funded by corporations—in the guise of tax-exempt advocacy groups that appeared to be organized by average Joes who wanted to limit their own right to sue: Citizens Against Lawsuit Abuse, Stop Lawsuit Abuse, Lawsuit Abuse Watch, People for a FAIR Legal System. All of these were actually founded and funded by corporations seeking to protect themselves from accountability for accidents. Together these organizations have pushed a raft of laws across the United States that limit people's ability to hold corporations accountable.

The Michigan Product Liability Act, for example, provides pharmaceutical companies with widespread immunity from being sued by people hurt by their products. It says that you cannot sue a drug manufacturer for unintentional harm caused by a drug if federal regulators approved the drug. That was enough to stop even a $20 million lawsuit filed by the state attorney general against the drug manufacturer Merck for selling an arthritis pill that caused heart attacks and strokes. And it's why countless victims of the opioid epidemic in Michigan are struggling to sue Purdue Pharma today.

Michigan's Product Liability Act is unique to that state, but the Ten-Year Statute of Repose Act is on the books in nineteen states. The Statute of Repose Act limits product liability to ten years after purchase—even if the product kills you. While that might sound reasonable (if stingy) for, say, your washing machine, tort reform legislation is intentionally broad, vague, and wide-reaching—and thus can be applied to products that affect far more people and should last far longer. So when a carnival ride in Ohio, the Fire Ball, accidentally broke apart mid-ride in 2017, throwing bodies across the fairgrounds, killing one eighteen-year-old, shattering the legs of another rider, and injuring at least seven others, it was impossible to sue the people who made the ride. That tort suit was impeded even though a metal support beam in the ride was completely corroded—a flaw so common and dangerous that the manufacturer sent out multiple warnings over a number of years alerting ride owners that this may occur. But the Fire Ball was more than ten years old when the accident happened, so the dead and injured were out of luck in more ways than one.

The Product Liability Act and the Ten-Year Statute of Repose Act are just two examples of what the American Legislative Exchange Council (ALEC) calls "model legislation"—namely, laws it writes or promotes Mad Libs–style for any lawmaker to drop into their state, many of them aimed at limiting your ability to sue corporations in case of accidental harm. One—the Comparative Fault Act—frees a corporation from liability for an accident and prevents people from suing if the corporation is 49 percent responsible or less. Others—such as the Noneconomic Damage Awards Act and the Full and Fair Noneconomic Damages Act, notably deceptive names—limit the amounts that juries can award and the amounts that a corporation can be made to pay for pain, hardship, and diminished quality of life after an accident. ALEC has a wealth of these laws waiting for the right lawmaker. The bills are introduced regularly in statehouses across the country, often verbatim as ALEC wrote them, and, what's worse, they pass at a higher rate than does most legislation.

With these restrictions, tort law cases have been decreasing for twenty years. But one area of tort has been exempt from this decline: contract disputes—people being sued for having debt, being foreclosed on, or not being able to pay rent. Between 1993 and 2015, these cases jumped from 18 percent of civil filings to more than half. It's an area of tort law that Joanne Doroshow, the lawyer behind the Center for Justice & Democracy, the nation's first and only consumer organization dedicated to fighting tort reform, refers to as "going after the little guy."

"Very, very few people who are hurt accidentally ever go to court," Doroshow tells me. "If you look at the statistics, tort lawsuits have been dropping like a rock for a long time. The only real increases you see are debt collections by banks and big companies."

The decline in tort lawsuits against corporations has been aided by effective rhetoric around tort lawsuits—such as the phrase "litigious society." Doroshow explains that the litigious society is a myth invented by corporations to protect corporations. Much of the support for tort reform is a response to this rhetoric—clever marketing by the most often sued corporations. The rhetoric has trickled into our discourse in the form of a wealth of mocking euphemisms for enacting your right to justice: "free money," "frivolous lawsuit," "ambulance chaser."

And all of this is a victory for the corporations. Perhaps the classic case of this rhetorical victory involves the temperature of McDonald's coffee.

In 1992, a woman sued the company after she accidentally spilled coffee on her lap. My earliest memory of it was a satire in the pages of *MAD Magazine*. Mockery abounded in pop culture of the era. On *Seinfeld*, Kramer sued Java World. Jay Leno and David Letterman monologued hot coffee jokes. Toby Keith included "Spill a cup of coffee, make a million dollars" in a sarcastic country song about the tainted American dream. The McDonald's coffee case became known by the rhetoric: a woman in a litigious society looking for free money in a frivolous lawsuit aided by an ambulance-chasing lawyer. This story is wrong.

Here's what really happened: McDonald's policy required that their franchisees keep coffee at a temperature of 180 to 190 degrees. The industry standard temperature for safe, drinkable coffee at the time was 30 to 40 degrees lower. Human skin feels pain beginning at 111 degrees, first-degree burns begin at 118, and second-degree burns at 131. McDonald's had 700 reports of severe accidental burns from their coffee.

In February 1992, a seventy-nine-year-old grandmother named Stella sat in a parked car in a McDonald's parking lot next to her son, who had just purchased some food there. She spilled the coffee in her lap. They rushed her to the hospital. Second- and third-degree burns covered 16 percent of her body. The coffee so thoroughly burned the skin off her inner thighs and genitals that it exposed muscle and fatty tissue. She required multiple skin grafts. She spent eight days in the hospital and required two years of medical care.

Stella's family contacted McDonald's and asked them to cover her medical costs, which totaled around $10,000. McDonald's offered $800. So the family sued McDonald's. During discovery, it came out that the coffee was being heated well above industry standards, and that the company had hundreds of reports of earlier accidental burns. In the trial, the jury ordered McDonald's to pay Stella nearly $3 million covering her medical costs, her legal costs, and compensation for her pain and suffering.

Stella's family did not get $3 million. McDonald's appealed the ruling and they ultimately settled for a confidential amount we can presume to be a lot less.

"Tort reform associations around the country got ahold of this case, as they often do when they see a case they can manipulate and make fun of. They started to do that with this case, and got it elevated to the level of popular culture," Doroshow says. "So a lot of people started to hear about it, and all they knew about it was: I spill coffee on myself and I get $3 million. It perpetuated a very incorrect and negative view of people that go to court, of juries as being out of control, of why we need to have tort reform or caps on damages, of crazy people winning crazy amounts of money—that they are the problem and they need to be stopped."

While this rhetoric persists, the arguments for tort reform have been largely disproven. One of these arguments is that we need it because doctors, afraid of medical malpractice lawsuits, will order vast numbers of unnecessary tests to cover their asses. But a study in the *New England Journal of Medicine* found that the passage of tort reform in three states did not affect the number of medical tests ordered or hospital admissions in those states. In Missouri, the opposite of tort reformers' predictions proved true. An increase in medical accidents—misdiagnoses, mis-dosed medication, injuries sustained under doctors' care—followed a tort reform cap on financial damages in medical malpractice. The Missouri Foundation for Health reported on the real result of the laws in 2012: "The only clear impact has been a drop in the number of claims and lawsuits made, and a more profitable malpractice insurance industry."

The success of tort reform is especially hazardous to society because it curtails a tort system that, in creating accountability, has proven highly effective at preventing deadly accidents. In the 1980s, accidental deaths caused by poor anesthesiology practices led to a handful of major tort lawsuits. These prompted reform: better machines, monitoring, and training, and quotas for how much time off anesthesiologists needed between shifts. Within a decade, the number of people accidentally killed by anesthesia fell from one in 6,000 patients per year to one in 200,000.

There's also good reason to believe that tort reforms cause accidents by reducing the threat of lawsuits of the kind that so profoundly reformed anesthesiology. Of the nine U.S. states that currently cap non-economic damages—the amount of money that can be recovered for pain and suffering, impairment, and disfigurement—in tort cases related to products or personal injuries, six have a higher than average rate of accidental death compared to the rest of the country. Three are in the top ten states with the highest accident rates in the country.

The result of all this is that the cost of accidents is manageable for corporations. When tort reforms cap the amount of money that an accident will cost a corporation, accidents can be built into the cost of business. Then there is no need to fireproof a factory, recall a car, safely bottle a pill, or stop selling an addictive drug—because the accidents that result are expected, and affordable.

Restoring Justice

While regulations are captured and tort lawsuits dwindle, there is a different vision of accountability growing in response to accidents around the country. It is a formal and sometimes court-sanctioned version of repair-based accountability called restorative justice.

Ken Jaray was a trial lawyer for people injured in accidents when he first heard about the process. At the time, he was representing accident victims in tort lawsuits, and also acting as mediator to resolve accident disputes—brought in when people on both sides wanted to settle out of court. That work made very clear to him that there was no clear path to accountability after accidents. His work was transactional—money was changing hands—but from his perspective, neither party ended up feeling any better about what had happened, and nothing was done to prevent it from happening again.

"The court system doesn't provide an adequate forum for the resolution of accident disputes," Jaray explains. The courts dealt with money and punishment, but his clients wanted the person who harmed them to explain what happened, to make amends, and to attempt to repair the damage. "What it left out was the human element," he says.

In search of an answer, he found the practice of restorative justice and began incorporating it into his court cases. Restorative justice lets people who have been harmed in an accident decide what needs to be said or done to make it right. Where criminal justice laws are intended to punish an offender, restorative justice laws are intended to repair the harm caused. And that can look a lot of different ways—that's the point: restoration can be an apology, an explanation, a pledge to do or not do something. Restorative justice laws—which allow judges and juries to offer people the option to participate in the process as part of their sentence—are on the books in thirty-two states. The idea is that, in addition to paying to fix a car or covering a worker's medical bills, the people involved in an accident may need to address the emotional harm caused by the accident, on both sides.

Jaray uses the example of a medical accident. Sure, you could file a malpractice claim, but what's missing is the connection between doctor and patient—an explanation, an apology, an understanding of how this accident is going to be avoided and not happen again—the sort of stuff that would make a person hurt in a medical accident feel safe going to the doctor again. None of that happens in litigation. Restorative justice fills in the gaps.

"My clients were still suffering. Although we would resolve their claims, they were still asking the questions: How did this happen? How is it that this isn't going to happen again? They wanted an understanding of why it happened, and in many cases, they wanted an acknowledgment by the person who caused the injury, in the form of an apology. It was important to their healing," Jaray tells me.

And he could see the difference in his injured clients. Those who had accepted the situation and forgiven the person who caused the harm fared better, physically and mentally, than those who didn't.

One particular accident, and the restorative justice process that followed, stuck with him. A young man named Dylan Salazar was driving drunk with his best friend, David Conard. Salazar crashed and flipped the car six or seven times. He survived, and Conard died.

Salazar is known as "the responsible party" in a restorative justice process—he went to prison. For Conard's surviving family and for Salazar, that court process was traumatic. The two parties, who had not seen each other since before the accident, were not permitted to speak in court. A terrified young man and an angry, grieving family were shuffled in and out of the courtroom without contact.

Jaray's partner was representing Salazar. They both knew that restorative justice could help here, but, Jaray says, the outcome surprised even him. It took a lot of prodding, but his partner convinced the Department of Corrections to allow a restorative justice process.

Both sides prepared. Ground rules were set. That was enough to bring the two parties together in a room.

In a video of the process, you can see Salazar, crying, apologize. He tells Conard's family that he has wanted to apologize since that night, that he is so sorry for what he took from them. The victim's brother hands a tissue across the table. At the end of the process, the mother of the dead young man and the man who accidentally killed her son thank each other. They embrace.

"She was obviously just stricken with grief until she had an opportunity to sit down with this young man face-to-face and recognize his pain, and have him recognize her pain," Jaray recounts. Conard's mother said she was reborn that day. Later, the family talked about how, at that moment, they didn't only stop hating the man who killed their son and brother but started to love him.

Jaray talks about the restorative justice process as an antidote to the blame and shame that so often follow an accident. Typically, that process goes like this: A restorative justice practitioner brings a victim together with the responsible party, and in recognition of the way that an accident can ripple outward to affect a large group, members of the community can be there, too. The victim, or in the case of a fatal accident, their surviving friends or family, can ask questions: Why did you do that? Why did you hurt my child? Why did you not look where you were going? And in hearing answers from the responsible party, the victim or their loved ones can explain how what happened impacted them. Then, prevention is sought by asking: How are we going to repair the harm? How are we going to fix this?

We can't guarantee that this will prevent a future accident, but becoming aware and accountable can only help.

This is the typical process, but restorative justice can take many forms—such as what the parents of Allison Liao sought. Even after that dashboard camera video was released, showing a driver killing their three-year-old daughter while she crossed the street holding her grandmother's hand, there was no criminal prosecution for the driver, so the Liaos initiated a tort case. They wanted proof that the driver had taken responsibilities for his actions—and that started with knowing if the driver had seen the same video they had. In pretrial discovery for their civil suit, their lawyer asked the man if he had watched the video. He had not, and, he said, he would not. This mattered to the Liaos, so in an unconventional out-of-court settlement, their lawyer stipulated the terms: the driver would watch the video, the driver would take responsibility in a public letter for the crash for which the little girl and her grandmother had been blamed, and the driver would voluntarily not drive for five years.

It is not justice. It is not prevention. Instead, it is a way to transform the pain of an accident—not a problem solved, but people, at least somewhat, repaired.

To prevent an accident takes something more.

Love and Rage

Late in the Trump administration, the federal government acquiesced to railroad corporations and adopted a rule that would allow highly flammable liquid natural gas to be transported by train across the country. The industry insisted that the potential for accidents was minimal. Or, as Ian Jefferies, of the Association of American Railroads, put it, "99.99 percent of all hazmat moved by rail reaches its destination without any incident whatsoever."

Of course, if you live on the wrong side of the tracks, you're much more likely to find yourself in the other 0.01 percent.

Vanessa Keegan, who lives along the planned liquid natural gas rail route, understood this. She testified in opposition to the decision: "If an accident happens, we don't get to show up the next day and say: Look, I told you so."

For those of us left behind after an accident, there is so much lost, but one strange ability gained: we can show up. I realized it the day after Eric died, when a *Daily News* reporter knocked on my door, looking for a quote and a story about my dead best friend. *Oh*, I remember thinking, *this is on me now*. And in the intervening years, I've found that what we say and do matters immensely. One of the most effective responses to accidents and the systems that allow them can be found in what those left behind do with their pain.

In New York City, I work with a group called Families for Safe Streets. Its members have either survived a traffic accident or have lost someone to a traffic accident—though they would never, ever use the A-word. In fact, I helped them start a campaign called Crash, Not Accident to get newscasters and public officials to swear off the word "accident" in reference to traffic crashes. The people in this group take care of each other. They also put their pain to good use.

Amy Cohen helped found Families for Safe Streets—her son, Sammy, was killed at age twelve by a van driver in Brooklyn who accelerated around a car that had stopped to let the boy cross. The speed limit in

New York City was 30 mph then. Amy organized protests that convinced state officials to lower it. Two years after a driver killed Amy's son, another child was hit on the same street, now with a lower speed limit. That child lived.

Judith Kottick is another founder of the group—her daughter, Ella, was killed at age twenty-three by a bus driver. When Judith looked into it, she found that a woman named Hui Wu had been killed by a bus driver in the exact same spot a few years before. Then, a year after a bus driver killed Judith's daughter, a man named Edgar Torres was killed by a bus driver there, too. Three dead in five years, at the same intersection, each in a crosswalk with the Walk sign shining white on them—a right-of-way that meant little to their fate, repetition like some perverse Groundhog Day. Judith organized protests and memorials. It took two years, but in 2016 city officials agreed to redesign the intersection, shutting down a street to limit vehicle access. No one has been killed there since.

These are stories of people who spoke for the dead, who took responsibility and demanded accountability.

I call these acts of love and rage. Jamie Favaro shipping naloxone across state lines is an act of love and rage, and so was Crystal Eastman's trip to Pittsburgh, and so were all those people lying down on the road to a PCB landfill in North Carolina so the dump trucks full of poison could not pass. It is an act of love to demand accountability for the dead. And it takes rage to prevent the same accidents from happening again. When I talk to those left behind, such as Cohen and Kottick, they can recognize the good that has been done—the lowered speed limit, the safer intersection—but they rage at the cost they have paid. Accidents are predictable and preventable. It should not require so much loss and so much rage to stop something so wholly in our power to stop. But this is the work left to those of us left behind. Our love and rage are all we have.

Conclusion

~~Accident~~

Eric James Ng was born on February 8, 1984, to Tony and Wendy Ng, the only brother to an older sister, Alison. Eric was killed on December 1, 2006.

There was not enough life in between those days—and I would give everything I have for just one day more.

But, between those days, there was also so much life.

Eric taught math at a Brooklyn middle school. Eric rode a bike. Eric wrote poetry. Eric organized protests. Eric ran our high school's literary magazine and got a scholarship to college. Eric could listen to a song on the radio just once and then play it on his guitar. When I met him, he could play the violin, and the bass, and the guitar. Then one year Eric just taught himself the keyboard. Then the next year he taught himself the drums.

Once, Eric snuck into the audience of MTV's *Total Request Live* and then rushed on camera to reveal a homemade NO WAR IN IRAQ shirt, interrupting the broadcast days before Congress would vote to proceed with the illegal war. Once, he got arrested in the street with a few hundred others, leading a party uptown to disrupt a meeting of the Republican National Convention. We locked arms then until the cops pulled us apart.

When something was wrong, Eric always said so. When Eric was angry, he always took action. Eric brimmed with love and felt no doubt in his rage. That was how he signed his emails—*love and rage, Eric*.

Eric would have been so jealous that I talked to Ralph Nader.

Eric had great hair and big muscles and could dance better than anyone I knew. Eric would do one-handed cartwheels in the pit at the basement punk shows where we would spend our weekends, and everyone would step back, like, *wow*. Eric was kind. Eric was loved. Eric was very funny. Eric drew his own tattoos. Eric was impossibly cool.

Eric was sixteen when I met him working at a summer camp. I taught sports. He worked maintenance. He liked to say that I found him picking up trash.

Eric was magnetic, and I fell in love, right away. I still feel proud to say he loved me, too.

Eric was killed at age twenty-two.

It is difficult to not be angry about all the time that Eric lost to premature death. It is difficult to reconcile the absences: the phone calls I will never receive, the letters I will never write, the number of times that I won't smile because he's just walked in and lit up the room.

It is difficult to understand how very much is lost when we lose someone at twenty-two.*

Long before I started writing this book, when Eric was still alive, I rode a bike everywhere I went, and so did he, and so did everyone we knew. Eric and I and all these people in New York City who got around on bikes—we always said the same thing whenever we parted: *Ride safe*. This was before the City of New York began installing protected bike lanes on its streets, so people died all the time. Even before we lost Eric, everyone knew someone who had been killed and we had each had too

---

* One of the most difficult parts of loss is the feeling of frustration at being unable to explain what is gone. I rewrote these few paragraphs more times than anything in these pages, always feeling that I failed to meet the breadth of his worth.

many close calls to count. We said *ride safe* because we were well aware that threats were everywhere, inescapable.

I wrote much of this book during the coronavirus pandemic. Writing a book entails a lot of emailing and calling strangers, and in that time, I caught myself picking up a new version of my old goodbye: *Stay safe*, I would say, to supermarket clerks and delivery workers, and the many experts cited in these pages. Yet I know better than most that staying safe is not up to us. Riding safe doesn't matter if you get hit by a truck, and if you have to go to work in a pandemic it's no accident if you get sick. These are not accidents but the inevitable outcomes of a society built on inequality, where the powerful are allowed to profit alongside pain and suffering. But *stay safe* is not an instruction. Rather, it is hopeful prayer. In long form it looks like this: *May you stay safe. May the forces that control who lives and dies in America act toward your protection. May you stay safe, and should you not, may you get a better story than "it was an accident."*

But Was It *Really* Not an Accident?

I heard one question repeated again and again throughout the process of writing this book. There were variations, but it all came down to this:

But what if *this* really was an accident?

I heard this from intelligent, well-intentioned people I respect—accident prevention professionals, engineers, and academics. They would lean in for the *really*, in a sort of desperate plea.

When I pressed, I found that each was thinking something else:

What if *I hurt someone* in an accident? What if *I was to blame*? What if something bad happened *but I didn't mean it*?

They were afraid of making a mistake, and being blamed. This is what happens when a country prizes punishment above all else. The fear of being blamed is so powerful that it made them disregard their potential to prevent harm. Which is why I'd always say this next:

Why does it matter if anything is an accident or not?

When we call something an accident, we feel better at once, and at once, we fail to prevent it from happening again. Only by overcoming this tendency can we prevent accidents. It's critical to remember that the police officer who hauled off Joseph Weitz at the beginning of this book did nothing to prevent the next child from being run over, but also that the mob that chased down Joseph Weitz was just as wrong and just as useless.

I understand why we do what we do with accidents, why we pass them over, hurry to move on. The world is already overflowing with terror. It is a lot to ask to add accidents to all that, to stop passing over these tragedies and instead ponder and scrutinize them like we do all the other pain in the world. It is even harder to do the work of getting people the tools, support, and resources they need to survive.

Accidents are not a design problem—we know how to design the built environment to prevent death and injury in accidents. And accidents are not a regulatory problem—we know the regulations that will reduce the accidental death toll. Rather, accidents are a political and social problem. To prevent them, we only need the will to redesign our systems, the courage to confront our worst inclinations, and the strength to rein in the powerful who allow accidents to happen.

What Comes Next

Around 170,000 people will die by accident next year. I can tell you this because around 170,000 people died by accident last year, and not much is going to change.

These numbers are a predictable minimum, but going forward, without action, we can expect that number to rise because 170,000 does not account for the accidental deaths to come as our planet becomes more fragile, our regulatory agencies less effective, and our built environment more automated. As the gig economy expands, fewer people will be protected from the danger of their jobs, and more people will die in work accidents. As the delivery economy expands, more Americans' workplaces will be the open road, and more people will die in traffic accidents. As the corporate anti-regulatory agenda advances, the regulations that make accidents expensive for corporations will be rolled back, one by one, and accidents, from oil spills to post-hospital slip-and-falls, will rise.

As global warming escalates, accidents will rise in surprising ways. We will accidentally freeze to death in unheated homes in places that never used to have snow—such as the 210 who died, most of hypothermia, when a snowstorm struck Texas in 2021. We will accidentally overheat in our apartments when the power goes out, which has been happening at an increasing rate as the world gets warmer—the number of power failures has risen 60 percent since 2015, and already, an estimated 12,000 a year die premature, heat-related deaths. We will accidentally drown when the remnants of larger-than-ever storms strike as hard as the storms themselves—such as the forty-three who died in and around New York City in 2021, many killed in flooded basement apartments when the lingering aftermath of a hurricane that made landfall as far away as Louisiana broke rainfall records all the way over on the East Coast. And climate emergencies will drive us to desperate migration, which too will lead to accidents, such as those killed crossing the U.S.-Mexico border in 2021—in April, thirteen dead of the twenty-five people crammed inside an SUV crossing into California, and in August, at least ten killed of the thirty crammed inside a van crossing into Texas.

In all cases, blame will distract us in ways that sound new but hark back to the age-old patterns that this book traces through history. The food app company will blame the delivery courier killed in a bike accident for breaking traffic laws, even though their job is impossible to do without breaking traffic laws. The developer will blame the construction worker killed in a fall for breaking work rules about fall-arrest harnesses, even though they would be fired if they took the time to suit up. The drug company will blame the drug user killed by an overdose, even though naloxone could have saved them, if only it were accessible in their state.

And a new era of accidents will dawn as more automakers test driverless cars on public roads, more retailers replace employees with machines, and plane manufacturers build new automated systems into the act of flying. We'll soon see deaths born not of human mistakes but of the inhuman nature of machines programmed to ignore human life.

We've already gotten a taste of what this will look like in Amazon warehouses, where automation arrived in the form of robots moving merchandise to fulfill orders. With these robots came a rising accidental injury rate—as high as 50 percent more than warehouses without automation—in part because Amazon used the robots as an excuse to speed up production. The company aimed to lower the accident rate in 2018 by 20 percent; instead, the accident rate rose. In 2019, the company aimed for 5 percent; the accident rate rose again. Amazon failed to meet its goals because while it kept aiming for accident rate reductions, it also kept raising the production quota for workers. Of course, these are just the injuries that we know of. A first aid manager at a DuPont, Washington, Amazon warehouse—where the rate of accidental injury was higher in 2019 than at any Amazon warehouse in the country, and five times higher than the industry average—reported that his bosses offered workers under his care pizza parties if a shift was completed with no accidents reported, so workers didn't report injuries, since they didn't want to deprive their colleagues of a free meal.

While climate change and automation cause more accidents, I predict we will hear less and less about the systems of accountability that Crystal Eastman and Ralph Nader fought for—the laws and rules that create a cost for accidents. And if I am right, accidents will continue to rise.

As we die more by accident, I predict that we will also hear more about how protecting us from accidents is actually an infringement on our liberty. The trigger lock that protects a child from being accidentally shot is an infringement on Second Amendment rights. The regulatory agency is an oppression of the rights of the free market. The independent contractor may not have access to workers' compensation, but they are free to work wherever they please. You are free to buy the largest SUV you wish, even when the hood blocks your view of the child playing in your driveway.

Without seismic change, this is our future.

Accidents happen in America, and happen here at outsize rates compared to our peer countries around the globe, because everything in America is built with a mind toward profit and thrift, and on a foundation of white supremacy, a culture of punishment, and a myth of self-reliance. The solution is simple: Stop punishing mistakes and pretending that people are perfectible. Trade in the bootstraps parable for an acceptance that people need tools and resources to survive, and an insistence that society should provide them. Apply a harm reduction model to every corner of the built environment. Construct workplaces, roads, and homes, but also laws and policies, with a focus on reducing accident-related damage, cushioning the blow of everything, and protecting life, health, and dignity at any and all cost. Remember that the people who die most often by accident are often the most vulnerable—the youngest and the oldest, the most discriminated against and least wealthy—and start there. Start by concerning yourself with vulnerability.

There are large and specific steps that we can take to end the accident epidemic in America. We can repeal every tort reform law and every rule requiring cost-benefit analyses of regulations. We can begin to rein in corporate influence in government policy by rewriting campaign finance laws. We can reclaim the integrity of the federal regulatory system by placing more restrictions on corporate lobbyists' ability to take government jobs. We can immediately and fully fund regulatory agencies, and give them two mandates: to increase safety inspections and investigations, especially of the largest corporations, and to start issuing new safety regulations and not stop. We can increase the tax burden on the wealthiest Americans and the largest corporations to finance the infrastructure spending that is necessary to protect the rest of us from accidents. We can pass laws that require sprinklers in every new home and fences around every swimming pool and regulations that mandate the installation of all currently available autonomous safety technology—automatic emergency braking, blind spot detection, alcohol detection sensors, and speed governors—in every car. We can mandate that all SUVs are sized to minimize damage, that traffic lights are timed for pedestrians instead of drivers, and that homes are designed so the sink and stove are right next to each other—so no one ever has to carry a pot of boiling water across a room. We can require every teenager to be trained to use naloxone, and to do the Heimlich maneuver and CPR as a condition of their graduation. We can give accidents an extraordinary cost and charge that cost to those with the power to control dangerous conditions. We can create systems of reparation for historical and current dangerous conditions that cause accidents unequally along racial and geographic lines. We can focus our energy on reducing harm while eschewing blame for human mistakes. We can challenge the culture of white supremacy, classism, and stigmatization that allows accidents to continue. We can shift the perspective from which we see accidents, from a seat of power to the shoes of those killed and injured, and we can rein in American capitalism and restrict the free market until corporate leaders prize accountability over profit.

Since we cannot do any of that alone, let's start here:

Let's build our own environments with the assumption that the people around us will make mistakes. Then, we can recognize the power and energy in our control, however limited, and, where we can, control it. For example, we can drive smaller, less powerful cars, and whenever possible, choose a less risky alternative to driving—walk, ride a bike, and take the bus. We can get trained to use naloxone and carry it with us in case we ever witness an accidental overdose. As we age, and with older people in our lives, we can seek out martial arts practitioners to practice the skill of falling. If we see a person who is drunk, we can make sure they have a safe way home. In our homes and offices, we can install the ramps and grab bars that make the environments more accessible to the least able. We can lock our guns and our pills away. We can unionize our workplaces. We can demand all of this from the most powerful people we have access to—our bosses, our landlords, the local government officials who control our built environment—seeking tools and resources that make safety accessible for the most vulnerable. And we can do all of this with awareness of our own stack of Swiss cheese—where we are protected from accidents that others may be exposed to by way of stigma, racism, and economic inequality—and commit to reducing the danger of accidents for the most needful first. And when the official response to an accident is education or enforcement, we can question what that effort will actually prevent.

Start with empathy. Watch for the stigmatization and bias built into the system. Listen for the cry of human error when it is thrown adjacent to accidents like a distracting flare. When blame seems like the only answer, put yourself in the shoes of the injured party and listen to their side of the story.

Blame is a food chain. Always look to the top. Who has the most power? Who can have the greatest effect? The answer is very rarely the person closest to the accident—the reckless driver, or the pilot who pulled up when he should have pulled down, or the power plant operator who fell asleep on the job. People who blame individuals for accidents and crimes are almost always drawing attention away from the systems that allowed the death and injury, and the vast potential for prevention. Where you can, point back to what can actually change the trajectory of any given accident.

Listen, too, for the word "accident" when it is spread over death and destruction like a dampening blanket. Find the nuance in every accident. Reject the accident described without a systemic explanation. Demand a longer, more detailed story. Ask why the Swiss cheese is stacked the way it is. Every accident is born of overlaid failures. Find the systems that led to an accident—the big and the small, the personal and the systemic, the design of the road and the racism of vehicular homicide prosecution as well. This is the only way to prevent accidents.

I do not use the word "accident." I felt discomfort at every instance of the word in this book. I am embarrassed when it slips off my tongue. Knowing all that I now do, it sounds like a slur, because it can stand in for one, because *it was an accident* is as much a dog whistle as "inner city" or "entitlement spending" in a world where racism and economic inequality are so intertwined with accidental death.

You can, and should, stop saying "accident," too. But far more important than not saying the word is hearing all the blame and distraction that comes with it—when you say it to others and when others say it to you. Sure, don't say "accident," but also, let *it was an accident* be an alarm bell, a jumping-off point which makes you ask: How? And why? And has it happened before? And will it happen again? If you hear the word "accident" and in response you ask these questions, we will have taken a leap forward.

Today, hundreds of thousands of lives, an uncountable number of life-altering injuries, and the threat of immeasurable environmental destruction rest on our acceptance that blaming the individual is best, that bad things happen to bad people, and that somehow personal responsibility will save us all. But seeing accidents for what they are means refusing to accept anything as an accident anymore. Because nothing is an accident. Nothing ever was.

Acknowledgments

This book was written in Crown Heights and Bay Ridge, Brooklyn, and in the Frederick Lewis Allen Room at the main branch of the New York Public Library in Manhattan. It was exactingly fact-checked by Katherine Barner, to whom I am grateful for all the ways she made me appear less fallible. Any mistakes or omissions that made it through the fact-checking process to the book in your hands are mine and mine alone.

First and foremost, I want to thank Wendy and Tony Ng, for bringing Eric into the world, and his sister, Alison, who shaped him immensely. Eric changed my life. Thank you for sharing him with me for his brief time in this dangerous place, and permitting me to write about his death.

At Writers House, my agent, Stephen Barr, carried the spirit of my love and rage into finding a home for this book—so much so that he included a photo of me being arrested, protesting, in his pitches. At Simon & Schuster, I was lucky to have the clear-eyed Tzipora Baitch as a reader and rigorous editor, as well as Janet Byrne, Andrea Gordon, Jordan Koluch, Jamie Selzer, Kyle Kabel, Sara Kitchen, Richard Ljoenes, and Jackie Seow making me look good.

But most especially, at Simon & Schuster, I need to acknowledge Eamon Dolan. His has become a household name in my apartment over the past few years, so exalted and so often repeated was his guidance.

To say he edited this book feels like a stark understatement; Eamon nurtured this project as much as he chiseled it out of rock. He did not just make this book into much more than anything I could have accomplished alone, he also taught me how to write a book in the process. I am in his debt.

My gratitude also goes to the many, many reporters, researchers, and experts whose work is quoted and cited in these pages. The argument I put forth in this book floats on the back of a massive body of research and reporting that I had little hand in creating but benefited from immensely. While many are named in these pages, I want to call out Sidney Dekker, whose work I turned to again and again, and in whose ideas I found answers at every dead end.

This book would not have been possible without a number of people who knew and loved Eric. I owe them thanks: to Scott Schwartz, for sneaking me in the back door of academia; to Lauren Spencer, the sister of my heart, for always walking with me; to Sarah Paule and Maura Roosevelt, for the unending solidarity; to my parents, Gloria and John Singer, for teaching me to question everything; to my most longtime friends, for waiting patiently for my attention and often talking me through the maze of arguments on these pages.

There are others, too, who did not have the pleasure to know Eric, but who aided me immensely nonetheless. Elena Santogade saw that this was a book before it was a book, and steered me through the dark waters of publishing. My colleagues at Transportation Alternatives, past and present, and their indefatigable energy for the fight, kept me motivated. And the members of Families for Safe Streets reminded me of the worth of this project and inspired me at every turn. I especially want to thank the survivors and people left behind after "accidents" who were gracious and brave enough to talk to me about their lives and their pain: Amanda Leigh Allen, Dulcie Canton, Amy Cohen, Adam and MaryBeth Gillan, Debbie and Harold Kahn, Judith Kottick, Hsi-Pei Liao and Amy Tam-Liao, James Linder, Dana Lerner, and Kevin Smith.

The biggest acknowledgment of all goes to my spouse, Andrew

Hinderaker, who read my drafts, calmed my fears, interrogated my arguments, reminded me of my course when I got lost in the words, patiently relayed my ideas back to me in plain language, picked me up when this all felt too sad, and carried greater than his share of our collective life to make time and space for me to write this book. None of this would be possible without you, love. Thank you.

To everyone else, stay safe.

Notes

Introduction: Not an Accident

Unless otherwise noted, the accidental death data referenced in this chapter and through-out this book is sourced from the National Center for Health Statistics of the Centers for Disease Control and Prevention (CDC) using the Wide-ranging Online Data for Epidemiologic Research (WONDER) or Web-based Injury Statistics Query and Report-ing System (WISQARS) databases. These databases contain different levels of detail and up-to-dateness, and were chosen based on the information sought. For these searches, I used alternatively the most recent data available (for WISQARS, 2019, and for WONDER, 2016) or the entire time period available (for WISQARS, 1981–2019, and for WONDER, 1999–2016) based on the nature of the search—using the entire time period available wherever possible to avoid the outlier data of one year skewing my search. For accuracy, I always used age-adjusted rates. When I write "white people," I am referring to what the CDC calls non-Latino Caucasians. By "Latino people," I mean Latinos of all races. By "Indigenous people," I mean Native American and Alaska Natives of all ethnicities, and the same all-ethnicity inclusiveness is used when I refer to "Asian people" or "Black people." Any time that I use other terms in the text ("people of color," for example), it is because the research I am referencing uses them. (All this data is obtained from death certificates and is far from perfect. In the *New Yorker*, see "Final Forms" by Kathryn Schulz for an explanation as to why.) In writing this introduction, I especially benefited from interviews with Ken Kolosh, statistics manager at the National Safety Council; Dr. Martin Makary; Susan P. Baker, co-author of *The Injury Fact Book*; Arwen Mohun, author of *Risk: Nego-tiating Safety in American Society*; and Mark Aldrich, author of *Safety First: Technology, Labor, and Business in the Building of American Work Safety, 1870–1939* and *Death Rode the Rails: American Railroad Accidents and Safety, 1828–1965*. I benefited as well from a few important articles: "Accidents and Acts of God: A History of the Terms," by Hermann Loimer and Michael Guarnieri in *Public Health Then and Now*; "Landmarks in the History of Safety," by Michael Guarnieri in the *Journal of Safety Research*; and "Reflections on a Half Century of Injury Control" by J. A. Waller in the *American Journal of Public Health*. I am grateful to Marco Conner DiAquoi, Sarah Paule, and Greg Shill for their legal advice.

1 *More people die by accident*: National Safety Council, "Accidental Deaths Hit Highest Number in Recorded U.S. History," November 29, 2018.

1 *The accidental death toll in the United States*: There are 374 seats, for example, on a United Airlines Boeing 747-400 (See united.com/web/en-us/content/travel/inflight /aircraft/747) and there are more than 462 accidental deaths a day (See "All Unintentional Injury Deaths," National Center for Health Statistics, "Accidents or Unintentional Injuries," cdc.gov/nchs/fastats/accidental-injury.htm), so the accidental death toll is equivalent to at least 1.3 fully loaded 747 airplanes falling out of the sky every day.

1 *Americans die by accident more than*: Melonie Heron, "Deaths: Leading Causes for 2017," *National Vital Statistics System Statistics Reports* 68, no. 6 (2019).

1 *Why are accidents killing us more than ever*: The rate and number of annual accidental deaths in the United States has been rising since 1992. At that time, 33 of every 100,000 people died by accident, a little less than 84,000 a year. In 2019, around 50 of every 100,000 people died by accident, more than 173,000 people a year. See CDC WISQARS Fatal Injury Reports, webappa.cdc.gov/sasweb/ncipc /mortrate.html.

2 *One person dies by accident*: Ibid.

2 *Black people die in accidental fires*: Ibid.

2 *Indigenous people are nearly three times as likely*: Ibid.

2 *People in West Virginia die by accident at twice the rate*: Grant Suneson, "Wealth in America: Where Are the Richest and Poorest States Based on Household Income?," *USA Today*, October 8, 2018; CDC WONDER Compressed Mortality File, wonder .cdc.gov/cmf-icd10.html.

2 *The Bulletin of the Atomic Scientists has set their doomsday clock*: John Mecklin, "Closer Than Ever: It Is 100 Seconds to Midnight," *Bulletin of the Atomic Scientists*, January 23, 2020.

3 *In The Injury Fact Book, Second Edition, there is a list*: Susan P. Baker et al., *The Injury Fact Book*, 2nd ed. (New York: Oxford University Press, 1991), 298–99.

4 *The book was a first-of-its-kind compendium*: Ibid., v–vii.

4 *Inside, the three times Baker uses*: Ibid., 17, 21, 36.

5 *"The word 'accident' erroneously implies"*: Ibid., 36.

5 *The National Highway Traffic Safety Administration banned*: Nancy Knechel, "When a Crash Is Really an Accident: A Concept Analysis," *Journal of Trauma Nursing* 22, no. 6 (2015): 321–29.

5 *the British Medical Journal banned*: Ronald M. Davis and Barry Pless, "*BMJ* Bans 'Accidents': Accidents Are Not Unpredictable," *British Medical Journal* 322, no. 7298 (2001): 1320–21.

5 *The New York City Police Department said*: Sarah Goodyear, "It's No 'Accident': NYPD Changes the Way It Talks About Traffic Deaths," *Bloomberg CityLab*, March 11, 2013.

5 *At a meeting of the American Copy Editors Society*: Angie Schmitt, "Associated Press Cautions Journalists That Crashes Aren't Always 'Accidents,'" *Streetsblog USA*, April 4, 2016.

5 *In 1961, the American psychologist J. J. Gibson*: Michael Guarnieri, "Landmarks in the History of Safety," *Journal of Safety Research* 23, no. 3 (1992): 151–58.

5 *"Two of its meanings are incompatible"*: Ibid.

6 *The physician William Haddon, the first*: Loimer and Guarnieri, "Accidents and Acts of God: A History of the Terms."

6 *In the archives of the* New York Times: Historical frequency measured via ProQuest Historical Newspapers: *New York Times* with Index; modern frequency via Google Trends.

6 *One in twenty-four people in the United States*: National Safety Council, "Lifetime Odds of Dying for Selected Causes, United States, 2015–2019," Injury Facts, injury facts.nsc.org/all-injuries/preventable-death-overview/odds-of-dying/data-details/.

6 *And . . . problem is distinctly American*: Steven H. Woolf and Laudan Aron, eds., *U.S. Health in International Perspective: Shorter Lives, Poorer Health* (Washington, DC: The National Academies Press, 2013), 28–31; at the time of this study, the accidental death rate of Finland alone was similar to that of the U.S., but while U.S. rate rose, the Finnish rate has since declined precipitously (Official Statistics of Finland, "Accidents caused the death of 2,400 persons in 2018," Helsinki: Statistics Finland, stat.fi/til/ksyyt/2018/ksyyt_2018_2019-12-16_kat_005_en.html).

7 *Yet the U.S. government offers more money for research into*: Leslie A. Gillum et al., "NIH Disease Funding Levels and Burden of Disease," *PLoS One* 6, no. 2 (2011): e16837.

7 *This began to shift in 2016*: "Physical Injury—Accidents and Adverse Effects," *Estimates of Funding for Various Research, Condition, and Disease Categories*, National Institutes of Health: Research Portfolio Online Reporting Tools (2021), report.nih.gov /funding/categorical-spending; Comprehensive Addiction and Recovery Act (CARA), Public Law 114–98, Sec. 108.

7 *Still, in 2019, injury research*: Jeromie M. Ballreich et al., "Allocation of National Institutes of Health Funding by Disease Category in 2008 and 2019," *JAMA Network Open* 4, no. 1 (2021).

7 *Accidental fatalities and injuries cost us*: National Safety Council, "Societal Costs," Injury Facts, injuryfacts.nsc.org/all-injuries/costs/societal-costs/data-details.

7 *Accidents add up to $2,800*: "Distracted Driving, Falls, Opioids Cause Spike in Unintentional Death Rate," *Environmental Health and Safety Today*, May 10, 2017.

8 *In 1986, Baker counted 95,277*: Centers for Disease Control and Prevention National Vital Statistics System, "Leading Causes of Death, 1900–1998," Table 288: Deaths and death rates for 15 leading causes of death in specified age groups, by race and sex: United States, 1986, cdc.gov/nchs/data/dvs/lead1900_98.pdf.

8 *Thirty years later, in 2016*: CDC WISQARS Fatal Injury Reports, webappa.cdc.gov /sasweb/ncipc/mortrate.html.

8 *Accidental death had become the third most likely*: "Accidental Injury Rises to Third Leading Cause of Death in the U.S.," CBS News, January 17, 2018.

8 *From 1992 to 2019, the number*: Prior to 1992, the rate and number of accidental deaths had been falling since the late 1960s and early 1970s (see: injuryfacts.nsc .org/all-injuries/historical-preventable-fatality-trends/deaths-by-cause/). The rise in accidental deaths is significant in *number* because it is rising so much faster than the population; however, the rise in the *rate* of accidental death is also significant: since 1992 the rate of accidental death has risen by 55 percent (see: injuryfacts.nsc .org/all-injuries/costs/societal-costs/data-details for this). See CDC WISQARS Fatal

Injury Reports (webappa.cdc.gov/sasweb/ncipc/mortrate.html) for all following, rounded to the nearest decimal point: From 1999 to 2019, the number of accidental deaths rose significantly in accidents involving cutting or piercing (99 percent rise); falls (200 percent); drug poisoning (457 percent); non-drug poisoning (249 percent); suffocation (29 percent); motorcycles struck by vehicles (103 percent); bicyclists struck by vehicles and other non-specified causes (36 percent); pedestrians struck by vehicles and other non-specified causes (27 percent); and pedestrians struck by vehicles alone (47 percent). Since 1999, the rate of accidental deaths has more than doubled in falls, drug poisoning, and non-drug poisoning. The number of accidental deaths between 1992 (83,952) and 2019 (173,040) rose by 106 percent (CDC WISQARS Fatal Injury Reports, webappa.cdc.gov/sasweb/ncipc/mortrate.html), and the U.S. population between 1992 (253,620,000) and 2019 (328,239,523) rose 29 percent. See "No. 4. Components of Population Change, 1980 to 1999, and Projections, 2000 to 2050" in United States Census Bureau, "Statistical Abstract of the United States: 2000," 8, and "2019 U.S. Population Estimates Continue to Show the Nation's Growth Is Slowing," United States Census Bureau Press Release No. CB19-198, December 30, 2019.

8 *The rate of accidental death*: National Safety Council, "Overview," Injury Facts, injuryfacts.nsc.org/all-injuries/overview.

8 *For people age one to age forty-four*: Centers for Disease Control and Prevention, "Top Ten Leading Causes of Death in the U.S. for Ages 1–44 from 1981–2019," Injury Prevention and Control, cdc.gov/injury/wisqars/animated-leading-causes.html.

8 *An accident injures ninety-two people*: National Safety Council, "Preventable Deaths: Minute by Minute," Injury Facts, injuryfacts.nsc.org/all-injuries/preventable-death-overview /minute-by-minute.

8 *Doctors, medical examiners, and coroners produce*: Department of Health and Human Services, ed., *Medical Examiners' and Coroners' Handbook on Death Registration and Fetal Death Reporting* (Hyattsville, MD: Department of Health and Human Services, Centers for Disease Control and Prevention, National Center for Health Statistics, 2003), 11–14.

9 *For instance, medical examiners disagree*: Catherine Barber and David Hemenway, "Too Many or Too Few Unintentional Firearm Deaths in Official U.S. Mortality Data?," *Accident Analysis & Prevention* 43, no. 3 (2011): 724–31; Judy Schaechter et al., "Are 'Accidental' Gun Deaths as Rare as They Seem? A Comparison of Medical Examiner Manner of Death Coding with an Intent-Based Classification Approach," *Pediatrics* 111, no. 4 pt. 1 (2003): 741–44; Maggie Koerth, "What Counts as an Accident?," FiveThirtyEight, July 13, 2016.

9 *That is a small gap*: CDC WISQARS Fatal Injury Reports, webappa.cdc.gov/sasweb /ncipc/mortrate.html.

9 *In 2016, medical researchers at Johns Hopkins University*: Martin A. Makary and Michael Daniel, "Medical Error—The Third Leading Cause of Death in the US," *British Medical Journal* 353 (2016): i2139.

9 *Medical examiners use a document*: Interview with Dr. Martin Makary.

9 *"We have an under-reporting and an under-appreciation"*: Ibid.

10 *In the paper, Makary offers this*: Makary and Daniel, "Medical Error—The Third Leading Cause of Death in the US."

10 *Accidents as we know them began*: Arwen Mohun, *Risk: Negotiating Safety in American Society* (Baltimore, MD: Johns Hopkins University Press, 2013): 1–7.

10 *Then so many died*: Peter D. Norton, *Fighting Traffic: The Dawn of the Motor Age in the American City* (Cambridge, MA: MIT Press, 2011): 38–46.

10 *The rate of accidental death*: National Safety Council, "Percent Change of Age-Adjusted Death Rates from 1900 to 2019 (Indexed to 1900), United States," Injury Facts, injuryfacts.nsc.org/all-injuries/historical-preventable-fatality-trends/where-weve-been.

10 *Since then, the rate of accidental death*: National Safety Council, "Overview."

11 *the government approved the sale of naloxone*: Narcan/Naloxone Hydrochloride, U.S. Food and Drug Administration New Drug Application #016636.

11 *The U.S. government first required carmakers*: "Drivers Disconnecting Seat Belt Locks," *New York Times*, August 18, 1974.

11 *In 1995, the U.S. Occupational Safety and Health Administration*: OSHA, Final Rule on Fall Protection in the Construction Industry—Docket No. S206-2006-0699 (formerly Docket No. S-206).

11 *Airbag regulations began in 1998*: Lauren Pacelli, "Asleep at the Wheel of Auto Safety? Recent Air Bag Regulations by the National Highway Traffic Safety Administration," *Journal of Contemporary Health Law & Policy* 15, no. 2 (1999): 739–77.

11 *Yet traffic fatalities skyrocketed in*: National Highway Traffic Safety Administration, "Traffic Safety Facts Annual Report Tables," cdan.nhtsa.gov/tsftables/tsfar.htm; Camila Domonoske, "'Tragic': Driving Was Down in 2020, but Traffic Fatality Rates Surged," National Public Radio, March 5, 2021; Elizabeth Garza, "Construction Fall Fatalities Still Highest Among All Industries: What More Can We Do?," *National Institute for Occupational Safety and Health Science* (blog), April 10, 2019; Centers for Disease Control and Prevention, "The Drug Overdose Epidemic: Behind the Numbers," cdc.gov/opioids/data/index.html.

11 *Newspapers would later report*: "Manhattan: Man Sentenced for Fatal Crash," *New York Times*, January 4, 2008.

11 *I learned that the driver said that he was going 25 miles per hour*: New York State Department of Motor Vehicles Police Accident Report MV-104A, Department of Transportation investigation memorandum, and deposition from driver all obtained via Freedom of Information Law requests to relevant agencies of the City of New York.

Chapter One: Error

To understand the early history of accidental death in the United States and the use of error as a pawn in accidents, as outlined in this chapter, I relied on Crystal Eastman's *Work-Accidents and the Law: Volume 2 of the Pittsburgh Survey*; Bryant Simon's *The Hamlet Fire: A Tragic Story of Cheap Food, Cheap Government, and Cheap Lives*; Christopher Leonard's *Kochland: The Secret History of Koch Industries and Corporate Power in America*; Peter D. Norton's *Fighting Traffic*; Mark Aldrich's *Death Rode the Rails* and *Safety First*; Arwen P. Mohun's *Risk*; the second edition of Ralph Nader's *Unsafe at Any Speed: The Designed-In Dangers of the American Automobile*; as well as interviews with

National Safety Council chief statistician Ken Kolosh, and interviews with all the authors, excepting Eastman, listed above.

15 *A human error is a mistake*: Erik Hollnagel, *Barriers and Accident Prevention* (London: Routledge, 2004), "A Little Etymology," in chapter 1, "Accidents and Causes."

16 *Accidents happen when errors occur under dangerous conditions*: Hollnagel, *Barriers and Accident Prevention*, "Latent Conditions," in chapter 2, "Thinking about Accidents."

16 *Sidney Dekker, airplane pilot*: Sidney Dekker, *The Field Guide to Understanding 'Human Error'* (Burlington, VT: Ashgate, 2006), 1–20.

16 *Applied to work accidents*: Ibid., 1–14.

17 *The New View says that*: Ibid., 15–20.

17 *For subscribers to the Bad Apple Theory*: Ibid., 1–20.

18 *In 1908, the year that Ford introduced*: "Motor Vehicle Traffic Fatalities, 1900–2007: National Summary," U.S. Department of Transportation Federal Highway Administration, fhwa.dot.gov/policyinformation/statistics/2007/pdf/fi200.pdf.

18 *By 1935, fatal traffic accidents had grown*: H. W. Magee, "Why Gamble with Death," *Popular Mechanics* 66, no. 5 (November 1936): 714–719.

18 *But when these accidents killed pedestrians*: In his book-length examination of the changing conception of streets in the early days of the automobile, historian Peter Norton describes anger driving the murder accusation: "To frightened parents and pedestrians the problem was far simpler: they blamed automobiles and their drivers, regardless of the circumstances. City people were angry. Their anger is shown in mob attacks on reckless motorists." See: Norton, *Fighting Traffic*, 25–27.

18 *On a Thursday in the spring of 1931*: Norton first identified the trend that Ouser's story illustrates in *Fighting Traffic* (21–36), both that bystanders might call drivers who killed pedestrians "murderers," and that those bystanders might turn into a mob. For the story of the death of Irwin Ouser, I relied on the 1930 U.S. Census and took some liberties in assuming what the incident would have looked like based on two contemporary newspaper accounts: "Truck Kills Boy, Driver Saved by Cop from Mob," in the *New York Daily News*, and "Driver Is Menaced After Killing Child," in the *New York Times*, both from May 29, 1931, and both without bylines.

18 *The first air-conditioned passenger train*: John Geist and Allison Seyler, "Passenger Car Air Conditioning: The Quest to Be First," *From the B&O Railroad Museum . . .* (blog), July 26, 2018.

18 *Earlier that month, President Herbert Hoover*: Andrew Glass, "President Hoover Dedicates Empire State Building, May 1, 1931," *Politico*, May 1, 2018.

18 *Ten years earlier, there had been less than half*: Federal Highway Administration Office of Highway Information Management, "State Motor Vehicle Registrations, by Years, 1900–1995," in *Highway Statistics Summary to 1995*, Section II/Table MV200: fhwa.dot.gov/ohim/summary95/mv200.pdf.

19 *The first-ever reported fatal traffic accident in America*: "Fatally Hurt by Automobile: Vehicle Carrying the Son of Ex-Mayor Edson Ran Over H. H. Bliss, Who Was Alighting from a Trolley Car," *New York Times*, September 14, 1899; David G. Allan, "Surprising Details About First American Killed by a Car: On this day in history we are offered a cautionary tale," BBC, September 13, 2013.

19 *The headlines of those 1920s news stories describe*: Norton first documented this in *Fighting Traffic* (26–37). These headlines are all from the *New York Times*, from May 12, 1921; June 26, 1923; and September 21, 1924.

20 *Stories like these, which are all from*: Norton first documented this in *Fighting Traffic* (21–36). I also traced the beginning and end of this trend through a ProQuest Historical Newspapers search of the archives of the *New York Times* under the search terms "driver," "auto," and "mob."

20 *They called the project*: Norton, *Fighting Traffic*, 29. See also: "Playground Appeal Cites 'Murder Map'; City Club Shows Mishaps to Children Fewer in Areas with Play Facilities," *New York Times*, July 21, 1930.

20 *"Each black dot on the map marks a spot"*: "City Club Maps Auto Death Areas in 1926," *New York Times*, June 27, 1927.

21 *In the beginning, the story*: Norton, *Fighting Traffic*, 29.

21 *the walking people of America*: Interview with Norton, author of *Fighting Traffic*. See also his paper "Street Rivals" (abstract): "Before the American city could be physically reconstructed to accommodate automobiles, its streets had to be socially reconstructed as places where cars belong" ("Street Rivals: Jaywalking and the Invention of the Motor Age Street," *Technology and Culture* 48, no. 2 [2007]: 331–59).

21 *William Bunge relocated the map to Detroit*: William Bunge, "Map 2.16: Children's Automobile 'Accidents' in Detroit," in *Nuclear War Atlas* (Oxford: Basil Blackwell, 1989), digital.library.cornell.edu/catalog/ss:19343514. Hat tip to photographer Dmitry Gudkov for introducing me to Bunge.

21 *"Going to school forces children to cross dangerous streets"*: Collector's Notes on William Bunge, Map 2.16, *Nuclear War Atlas*.

22 *But . . . William Bunge was not*: Ibid.

22 *To overcome this, automakers*: Norton, "Street Rivals."

22 *Automakers and sellers, car parts manufacturers*: Norton interview. See also: Peter Norton, "Four Paradigms: Traffic Safety in the Twentieth-Century United States," *Technology and Culture* 56, no. 2 (2015): 326 and Norton, *Fighting Traffic*, 74–75, 212–20.

22 *He spent years searching the early records*: At the time, these interest groups called themselves "Motordom." Norton, *Fighting Traffic*, 4.

23 *Before the 1920s, the term "jaywalker" was*: Norton, *Fighting Traffic*, 65–101.

23 *Each accused the other of*: Tom Vanderbilt, "In Defense of Jaywalking," *Slate*, November 2, 2009.

23 *When a New York City police commissioner*: Norton, *Fighting Traffic*, 65–101.

23 *The automobile lobby marketed, pushed, and popularized*: Ibid.

23 *It was part of an intensive campaign*: Norton interview and *Fighting Traffic*, 95–101.

23 *That transformation began in Cincinnati*: Norton, *Fighting Traffic*, 95–101.

23 *In 1923, the people of Cincinnati*: Ibid.

24 *Struck by a car going 23 mph*: Brian Tefft, "Impact Speed and a Pedestrian's Risk of Severe Injury or Death," AAA Foundation for Traffic Safety, September 2011, 1.

24 *An immeasurable number of people*: Had the speed governor proposal passed, it undoubtedly would have proven effective in reducing traffic fatalities in Cincinnati and thus normalized mandated in-vehicle speed control as an effective safety tool. This evidence could have, in time, led to its widespread requirement. Instead,

exceeding the speed limit was a factor in more than one in every four U.S. traffic fatalities in 2019.

24 *today cars' speedometers go as high*: Chris Weller, "Why Speedometers Go to 140 or 160 MPH, Even if Cars Can't Drive That Fast," *Business Insider,* November 22, 2017.

24 *The Cincinnati Automobile Dealers Association raised $10,000*: Norton, *Fighting Traffic,* 95–101.

24 *In the Cincinnati speed-governor fight*: Norton interview.

24 *The gun lobby would copy*: Peter Norton in Daniel Kolitz, "What Technology Has Accidentally Killed the Most People?," *Gizmodo,* June 15, 2020.

24 *But in short order, the automobile lobby*: Norton, *Fighting Traffic,* 29–46.

25 *St. Louis, Baltimore, and Pittsburgh*: Norton, *Fighting Traffic,* 34–38.

25 *The protest movement made conspicuous*: Norton, *Fighting Traffic,* 30, 42–43.

25 *The auto lobby devised*: Norton, *Fighting Traffic,* 71–87, 175–206.

25 *The goal was to teach*: Norton interview.

25 *Norton found that local driving clubs, like*: Norton, "Street Rivals."

25 *In Los Angeles*: Norton, "Street Rivals," 351.

25 *In New York City, the Automobile Club*: Norton, *Fighting Traffic,* 370.

26 *In early 1924, the National*: Norton, "Street Rivals."

26 *A few months after the news service began*: Norton, "Street Rivals," 357.

26 *In 1927, the president of the Chrysler Motor Car Company*: Walter Chrysler, "The Only Cure for Auto Accidents," *The Outlook,* April 27, 1927.

26 *Chrysler's "only cure" was education*: Ibid.

27 *In time, automakers would invent*: Norton, "Four Paradigms," 319–34.

27 *Traffic accidents kill about as many people*: The apex of traffic fatalities in that era was 1937, when more than 37,000 were killed ("Motor Vehicle Traffic Fatalities, 1900–2007"). Traffic fatalities reached their current peak in 2020, when an estimated more than 42,000 were killed (National Safety Council, "Motor Vehicle Deaths in 2020 Estimated to Be Highest in 13 Years, Despite Dramatic Drops in Miles Driven," nsc.org/newsroom/motor-vehicle-deaths-2020-estimated-to-be-highest).

27 *During a recent rise in the number of pedestrians killed*: Data was preliminary at the time of this writing, but it appears the rise in pedestrian deaths continued into 2020. For a prime example of how blame was handed out, see Leah Asmelash, "Smartphones, Warm Weather and SUVs Are All to Blame for the Highest Number of Pedestrian Deaths in More Than 30 Years, Report Says," CNN, February 27, 2020.

27 *When the fatality rate began to climb*: Ford Corporate, "One Step Ahead of Pedestrians: Ford's Pre-Collision Assist Helps Predict Distracted 'Petextrians' Movement," ophelia.sdsu.edu:8080/ford/03-30-2018/innovation/petextrian.html.

27 *That one didn't catch on, but*: Kelcie Ralph and Ian Girardeau, "Distracted by 'Distracted Pedestrians'?," *Transportation Research Interdisciplinary Perspectives* 5 (2020): 1–14.

27 *(In reality, it is estimated to be)*: Judith Mwakalonge, Saidi Siuhi, and Jamario White, "Distracted Walking: Examining the Extent to Pedestrian Safety Problems," *Journal of Traffic and Transportation Engineering* 2, no. 5 (2015): 327–37.

27 *drove legislators in New York City*: Gersh Kuntzman, "City to State: 'Distracted Pedestrians' Is Not a Thing," *Streetsblog NYC,* September 2, 2019.

28 *Automakers first learned it from a campaign*: In an interview, Norton explained that

it was in industry in the nineteenth century that use of the word "accident" rose as a way to protect employers from liability: "Early automobile safety campaigns were modelled on industrial safety campaigns where the word accident was used, with clearly some intention of excusing the employer and trying to shift the blame onto the worker." See also: Norton, *Fighting Traffic*, 19–20, 29–39.

28 *The so-called careless worker appeared*: John C. Burnham, *Accident Prone: A History of Technology, Psychology, and Misfits of the Machine Age* (Chicago: University of Chicago Press, 2009), 33–34. Burnham's book is a long take on the origins of the accident-prone worker and other historical "bad apple" theories of why work accidents happen. However, Burnham is a "bad apple" believer, so read with caution. For a short, less blameful version of this story, see Paul Swuste, Coen van Gulijk, and Walter Zwaard, "Safety Metaphors and Theories: A Review of the Occupational Safety Literature of the U.S., U.K. and The Netherlands, Till the First Part of the 20th Century," *Safety Science* 48, no. 8 (2010): 1000–1018.

28 *As a wide range of new industrial technologies*: Record-keeping at the time was not what it is today, so this is likely a significant undercount. Either way, the accidental death of workers was always an economic calculus for corporations. As Mark Aldrich puts it in *Safety First*, "The new machines and processes and their dangers were not the product of 'disembodied historical forces.' Instead, the new technology reflected the efforts of individuals and businesses to increase production and cut costs under conditions in which work injuries were of little economic consequence. For during these years judges crafted a common law of employers' liability that encouraged economic development by placing most of the burden of work injuries on the injured employee." See also: John Fabian Witt, *The Accidental Republic: Crippled Workingmen, Destitute Widows, and the Remaking of American Law* (Cambridge, MA: Harvard University Press, 2006), 2.

28 *The idea that certain workers were more likely*: Burnham, *Accident Prone*: 33–34.

28 *These laws brought about a massive shift in financial liability*: Interviews with Mark Aldrich.

29 *Workers' compensation laws changed that arrangement*: Aldrich interview.

29 *This cost inspired the owners of America's largest corporations*: Aldrich, *Safety First*, 104.

29 *Wisconsin was the first state*: While New York State passed a workers' compensation law prior to Wisconsin, it was immediately overturned. Patrick J. Kiger, "How the Horrific Tragedy of the Triangle Shirtwaist Fire Led to Workplace Safety Laws," History.com, March 27, 2019.

29 *The following year, industrialists from all over the Midwest*: Frank A. Epps, "National Cooperation in Safety," in *Transactions: National Safety Congress, Part I: 1925 Proceedings of the National Safety Council* (Cleveland, OH: National Safety Council, 1925), 778–79.

29 *As more states followed Wisconsin's lead*: Emily Holbrook, "A Century of Safety," *Risk Management* 60, no. 5 (2013): 16–17.

29 *Suddenly safety education was everywhere*: Norton covers this briefly in *Fighting Traffic*, 33–39, and Aldrich details it extensively in *Safety First* (see chapter 4, "A Management Responsibility").

29 *One common place to find*: Aldrich, *Safety First*: 12–67.

29 *The posters offered obvious, often infantilizing advice*: The National Council for
    Industrial Safety would change its name to the National Safety Council in 1914. If
    you are interested in design from the first half of the twentieth century, look these
    up. The catalogs were published at least through the 1960s, and each is a beautiful,
    if blameful, chronicle of the iconic design trends of each era. Example taken from
    National Safety Council Posters Catalog: 1930 Safety Posters (Chicago: National Safety
    Council, 1930); Aldrich cites others in *Safety First*, 133, 138.

29 *By 1930, the posters were so popular*: *National Safety Council Posters Catalog*, 89.

30 *On these posters, "Otto Nobetter" appeared*: Norton, "Street Rivals," 341–42; Aldrich,
    Safety First, 137–38.

30 *Around this time, corporate interests also seized*: Lee Vinsel, "Safe Driving Depends
    on the Man at the Wheel: Psychologists and the Subject of Auto Safety, 1920–55,"
    Osiris 33, no. 1 (2018): 191–209.

30 *Attempts to define and measure accident-proneness*: Frank A. Haight, "Accident-
    Proneness: The History of an Idea," in *Traffic and Transport Psychology: Proceedings
    of the ICTTP 2000*, eds. Talib Rothengatter and Raphael D. Huguenin (Amsterdam:
    Elsevier, 2004), 421–32.

30 *One study correlated a low accident rate among pilots*: W. A. Tillman, "Accident
    Proneness," *Canadian Journal of Occupational Therapy* 25, no. 4 (1958): 135–39.

30 *Another proposed that professional drivers*: Burnham, *Accident Prone*: 79–81.

30 *Among coal miners who had more accidents*: J. Cotter Hirschberg et al., "A Study of
    Miners in Relation to the Accident Problem: Psychiatric Evaluation," Divisions of
    Mental Hygiene and Industrial Medicine, University of Colorado Medical Center:
    553–55.

30 *A staff psychologist at the Process Engineering Corporation*: Anthony Davids and
    James T. Mahoney, "Personality Dynamics and Accident Proneness in an Industrial
    Setting," *Journal of Applied Psychology* 41, no. 5 (1957): 303–6.

30 *Another psychologist spent a few months*: Tillman, "Accident Proneness."

30 *Notably, for all these attempts to psychologize mistakes*: There are many sources
    debunking accident-proneness, but I most enjoyed A. M. Adelstein, "Accident Prone-
    ness: A Criticism of the Concept Based upon an Analysis of Shunters' Accidents,"
    Journal of the Royal Statistical Society 115, no. 3 (1952): 354–410; Mark D. Rodgers
    and Robert E. Blanchard, "Accident Proneness: A Research Review," Office of Avi-
    ation Medicine of the FAA Civil Aeromedical Institute, May 1993, 1–4; and most
    especially, the only amusing technical study I ever read, Frank A. Haight's "Accident
    Proneness: The History of an Idea."

31 *It was not until the 1940s that researchers at last began*: Haight, "Accident Proneness."

31 *As one research review put it, the body of work attempting to prove*: Rodgers and
    Blanchard, "Accident Proneness: A Research Review," 2–3.

31 *In industrial work across the country*: Ideas about the role of the safety manual,
    and how work accidents relate to the pace of work, come from an interview with
    Christopher Leonard, author of *Kochland: The Secret History of Koch Industries and
    Corporate Power in America* (New York: Simon & Schuster, 2019) and *The Meat
    Racket: The Secret Takeover of America's Food Business* (New York: Simon & Schuster,
    2014), and his reporting, where cited.

32 *Leonard tells me a story from his book*: Christopher Leonard, "Rising Profits, Rising

Injuries: The Safety Crisis at Koch Industries' Georgia-Pacific," ProPublica, August 8, 2019.

32 *Koch Industries paid $21 billion*: Ibid.

32 *When Leonard was reporting . . . many higher-ups*: Ibid.

32 *Again and again, Leonard found stories*: Ibid.

33 *At Georgia-Pacific, starting in 2012*: Christopher Leonard, *Kochland*, 525.

33 *If the only job of executives is to*: Leonard interview.

33 *This tension between safety and production defines*: Ibid.

34 *Leonard describes sitting in the office*: Ibid.

35 *On September 3, 1991, the Imperial Food Products factory*: Ideas about the role of the racist stereotype in fatal work accidents and the story of the fire at the Imperial Foods chicken processing plant in Hamlet, North Carolina, come from an interview with Bryant Simon, author of *The Hamlet Fire: A Tragic Story of Cheap Food, Cheap Government, and Cheap Lives* (New York: New Press, 2017), and from that text where cited. His book is an extraordinary, moving, and intricate deep dive into a single accident, and one that I strongly recommend.

35 *It is a photo of a door inside the factory that bore a sign*: Mark A. Friend and James P. Kohn, *Fundamentals of Occupational Safety and Health*, 4th ed. (Lanham, MD: Government Institutes/The Scarecrow Press, 2010), 160.

36 *Simon calls this process a social autopsy*: Simon interview.

36 *The journalists Simon met*: Ibid.

36 *The story was that the owners of Imperial Foods*: Paul Nowell, "Witnesses: Trapped Workers Screamed, Pounded Locked Doors; 25 Dead," Associated Press, September 4, 1991.

36 *It is almost the same story as the one told*: For a long version of the Triangle fire and its implications, see: David Von Drehle, *Triangle: The Fire That Changed America* (New York: Atlantic Monthly Press, 2003). For a short version, see: Arthur F. McEvoy, "The Triangle Shirtwaist Factory Fire of 1911: Social Change, Industrial Accidents, and the Evolution of Common-Sense Causality," *Law & Social Inquiry* 20, no. 2 (1995): 621–51.

37 *In Hamlet, Simon heard the rumor*: Simon interview; Nowell, "Witnesses."

37 *the aftermath of the Hamlet fire differs*: Ibid. See also: Marlena Scott, "Many Women Who Died in the Triangle Shirtwaist Factory Fire of 1911 Were Young Immigrants," *Teen Vogue*, March 25, 2019.

37 *That big ideological switch did not happen*: Ibid.

37 *The lawyer who represented the owners of Imperial Foods*: Ibid. See also: Simon, *The Hamlet Fire*, 208–21.

38 *On the fire's first anniversary*: Ibid. See also: Simon, *The Hamlet Fire*, 191–221.

38 *In the Black church*: Ibid.

39 *This poem was published in the* Plain Dealer: "Philosopher of Folly's Column," *Plain Dealer*, November 17, 1930, 10.

39 *As a cartoon driver in a fedora put it*: Burnham, *Accident Prone*, 115.

39 *In the 1950s, this trope drove Ralph Nader*: Academy of Achievement, "Ralph Nader on Perseverance," *Keys to Success: In Their Own Words*, achievement.org/video /ralph-nader-28.

40 *"For decades the conventional explanation preferred by the traffic safety establishment"*:

Ralph Nader, *Unsafe at Any Speed: The Designed-In Dangers of the American Automobile* (New York, Bantam, 1973), xiii.

40 *He tells this story in an updated edition of his book*: The story of McNamara's time at Ford comes from the 1973 reissue of Nader's *Unsafe at Any Speed*. The reissue is important because it is there that Nader debunks a myth oft repeated to this day— that safety did not sell. It did.

40 *In 1955, Robert McNamara, then an executive*: Nader, *Unsafe at Any Speed*, ix–lxxii.

41 *"At GM, cars were promoted as dreamboats"*: Ibid., ix.

41 *This was a real threat to GM*: Ibid., ix–lxxii.

43 *Then, in 1966, Congress invited Nader to testify*: 89th Congress, 1st Session, "Federal Role in Traffic Safety: Hearings Before the Subcommittee on Executive Reorganization" (Washington, DC: U.S. Government Printing Office, 1965), 1296.

43 *When federal officials proposed new safety standards*: John D. Morris, "Ford Safety Data Sought by Haddon; End to Sales Drop Seen," *New York Times*, December 16, 1966.

44 *While driverless cars are a ways off*: Liisa Ecola et al., "The Road to Zero: A Vision for Achieving Zero Roadway Deaths by 2050," RAND Corporation, 2018, rand.org /pubs/research_reports/RR2333.html.

Chapter Two: Conditions

To understand the early history of accidents in the U.S. and how control over conditions in the built environment affected the likelihood of death and injury, I relied on Crystal Eastman's *Work-Accidents and the Law*; Ralph Nader's scholarship on Hugh DeHaven in *Unsafe at Any Speed*; Mark Aldrich's *Death Rode the Rails* and *Safety First*; Arwen Mohun's *Risk*; the article "Safety in Accidents: Hugh DeHaven and the Development of Crash Injury Studies" by Amy Gangloff in *Technology and Culture*; and two works by David Fairris: his book *Shopfloor Matters: Labor-Management Relations in 20th Century American Manufacturing* and the article "Institutional Change in Shopfloor Governance and the Trajectory of Postwar Injury Rates in US Manufacturing, 1946–1970" in the *Industrial Labor Relations Review*; as well as interviews with Gangloff, Fairris, Mohun, and Aldrich, and also Carl Nash, an engineer and physicist formerly with the Public Interest Research Group and the National Highway Traffic Safety Administration; Peg Seminario, longtime director of occupation health and safety for the American Federation of Labor and Congress of Industrial Organizations; Celeste Monforton, co-author of *On the Job: The Untold Story of Worker Centers and the New Fight for Wages, Dignity, and Health*; and Christopher Leonard, author of *Kochland: The Secret History of Koch Industries and Corporate Power in America* and *The Meat Racket: The Secret Takeover of America's Food Business*.

46 *Psychologists call your desire to ask*: John D. DeLamater, Daniel J. Myers, and Jessica L. Collett, *Social Psychology*, 8th ed. (Boulder, CO: Westview Press, 2015), 227–31.

46 *There is significant evidence that*: The tendency is so common that the *Onion* once lampooned it with the headline "Investigators Blame Stupidity in Area Death" (May 25, 2005). A short explanation can be found at DeLamater, Myers, and Collett, *Social*

Psychology, 233–34. See also: Richard J. Holden, "People or Systems? To Blame Is Human. The Fix Is to Engineer," *Professional Safety* 54, no. 12 (2009): 34–41.

47 *It may be poor judgment:* Norway and Finland are prime examples—lots of cycling, lots of ice and snow, and a low rate of death. You can find their low fatality rates here: Alberto Castro, Sonja Kahlmeier, Thomas Gotschi, "Exposure-Adjusted Road Fatality Rates for Cycling and Walking in European Countries" (discussion paper, International Transport Forum: 168 Roundtable, Paris, 2018). And a good explanation of how Finland changes conditions on the street here: Peter Walker, "Why Finland Leads the Field When It Comes to Winter Cycling," *Guardian,* February 8, 2020.

47 *Railroads were the site of one of the first:* Aldrich interview; Mark Aldrich, "History of Workplace Safety in the United States, 1880–1970," *Economic History Encyclopedia,* August 14, 2001.

48 *For a decade in the late 1870s and early 1880s:* Supreme Court Justice Clarence Thomas, "Norfolk and Western Railway Company, Petitioner, v. William J. Hiles, 516 U.S. 400," Supreme Court of the United States, February 27, 1996.

48 *Early statisticians counted 11,000 workers:* "Statement of George G. Crocker," *Automatic Couplers and Power Brakes: Hearing Before the Committee on Interstate and Foreign Commerce of the House of Representatives* (Washington, DC: Government Printing Office, 1892), 16.

48 *As a point of comparison:* Bureau of Labor Statistics, "National Census of Fatal Occupational Injuries in 2019," U.S. Department of Labor news release, December 16, 2020, bls.gov/news.release/pdf/cfoi.pdf.

48 *These numbers were some of the first statistics:* Aldrich interview.

48 *Considering the power of railroads:* Ibid.

48 *Or, as an editor at* Harper's: 89th Congress, 1st Session, "Federal Role in Traffic Safety: Hearings Before the Subcommittee on Executive Reorganization" (Washington, DC: U.S. Government Printing Office, 1965), 294.

48 *Instead, this was a rare instance:* Aldrich interview.

49 *Railroad companies endorsed the legal:* Aldrich interview.

49 *Between 1890 and 1909, coupling accidents:* Mark Aldrich, *Death Rode the Rails: American Railroad Accidents and Safety, 1828–1965* (Baltimore, MD: Johns Hopkins University Press, 2006), 114.

49 *By 1902, just 2,000 died:* Tony Long, "April 29, 1873: Railroads Lock and Load," *WIRED,* April 29, 2009.

49 *When work accidents in America first began to rise:* Aldrich interview. See also: Dino Drudi, "The Evolution of Occupational Fatality Statistics in the United States," *Fatal Workplace Injuries in 1993: A Collection of Data and Analysis* (Washington, DC: Bureau of Labor Statistics, 1993), 2.

49 *These were stories of catastrophe:* Crystal Eastman, *Work-Accidents and the Law: Volume 2 of the Pittsburgh Survey* (New York: Charities Publication Committee, 1910), 34–36.

49 *Mine explosions and fifty-car train derailments:* Ibid.

50 *Between the summer of 1906 and the summer of 1907:* Ibid., 3–15.

50 *It was the first-ever:* "Miss Eastman presents the findings of the first systemic investigation of all cases occurring during a representative period in a representative American district. No body of facts has hitherto been available, and the investigation

could scarcely have been better timed in relation to constructive efforts toward the establishment of industrial justice." (Paul U. Kellogg, director of the Pittsburgh Survey, in a foreword to *Work-Accidents and the Law*, v–vi.)

50 *Their discussion—or the part of it that she could hear*: Ibid., 34.

50 *From the coroner, Eastman obtained the reports*: Ibid., 11–15.

50 *Eastman hired . . . an Italian investigator*: Ibid., 3–7.

51 *Allegheny County, which included*: Ibid., 3–15.

51 *"There is no bright side to this situation"*: Ibid., 14–15.

52 *In December 1907, a few months after*: Mark Aldrich, "Preventing 'The Needless Peril of the Coal Mine': The Bureau of Mines and the Campaign Against Coal Mine Explosions, 1910–1940," *Technology and Culture* 36, no. 3 (1995): 483–518.

52 *For weeks the nation spoke of the accident*: Eastman, *Work-Accidents and the Law*, 34.

52 *"Such catastrophes rouse the attention"*: Ibid.

52 *"Most of the men in the community"*: Ibid., 84–86.

53 *Eastman's investigation proved*: Ibid., 84–103.

53 *Of all the accidents Eastman tracked*: Ibid., 103–7.

53 *She explained the economic disaster left behind*: Ibid., 120–26.

54 *She drew attention to the mothers*: Ibid., 132–43.

54 *Eastman was a New Yorker*: Gregory P. Guyton, "A Brief History of Workers' Compensation," *The Iowa Orthopaedic Journal* 19 (1999), 106–10.

54 *The commission came back with much data*: "Compulsory Workmen's Compensation Act Unconstitutional," *New York Labor Bulletin* 13, no. 1 (1911): 60.

54 *In 1910, the reforms took effect*: Michael Duff, "How the U.S. Supreme Court Deemed the Workers' Compensation Grand Bargain 'Adequate' Without Defining Adequacy," *Tulsa Law Review* 54, no. 3 (2019): 375–405.

55 *Two months later, in Wisconsin*: Patrick J. Kiger, "How the Horrific Tragedy of the Triangle Shirtwaist Fire Led to Workplace Safety Laws," History.com, March 27, 2019.

55 *The decline in work accidents*: Witt, *The Accidental Republic*, 187–88.

56 *In the fall of 1917, while thousands*: Unless otherwise noted, the details of Hugh DeHaven's life come from Nader, *Unsafe at Any Speed*, 69–125; a February 17, 1985, profile by Ronald Kotulak in the *Chicago Tribune* titled "Seat Belts Save, Research Shows"; Amy Gangloff, "Safety in Accidents: Hugh DeHaven and the Development of Crash Injury Studies," *Technology and Culture* 54, no. 1 (2013): 40–61; interviews with Amy Gangloff; and Hugh DeHaven, "Mechanical Analysis of Survival in Falls from Heights of Fifty to One Hundred and Fifty Feet," *War Medicine* 2 (1942): 586–96.

57 *Among those miracles was Louis Zito*: Ralph Nader, "Head Knocker/Hugh DeHaven and Collision Safety," *In the Public Interest*, March 21, 1980, nader.org/1980/03/21/head-knockerhugh-dehaven-and-collision-safety.

57 *Walter Cronkite interviewed Zito*: Louis Zito, interview by Walter Cronkite, *The Search*, "Automobile Safety Research," CBS, 1954, youtu.be/qAh-ScgRMOc.

59 *Scientists making their most conservative estimates*: C. J. Kahane, "Lives Saved by Vehicle Safety Technologies and Associated Federal Motor Vehicle Safety Standards, 1960 to 2012—Passenger Cars and LTVs—with Reviews of 26 FMVSS and the Effectiveness of Their Associated Safety Technologies in Reducing Fatalities, Injuries, and Crashes," National Highway Traffic Safety Administration, Report No. DOT HS 812 069, January 2015.

60 *Rather, worker injuries fell from World War II*: Unless otherwise noted, information about shifts in work accidents after World War II comes from David Fairris, "Institutional Change in Shopfloor Governance and the Trajectory of Postwar Injury Rates in U.S. Manufacturing, 1946–1970," *Industrial and Labor Relations Review* 15, no. 2 (1998): 187–203, and interviews with Fairris.

60 *It wasn't workers' compensation laws alone*: Thomas C. Frohlich and John Harrington, "Mine, Steel, Auto Workers Were Involved in Some of the Biggest Strikes in American History," *USA Today*, April 8, 2020.

60 *The number of unionized workers rose*: Gerald Mayer, "Union Membership Trends in the United States," Congressional Research Service Report for Congress, August 31, 2004; National Safety Council, "Preventable Injury-Related Deaths by Principle Sector, United States, 1903–2018," Injury Facts, injuryfacts.nsc.org/all-injuries/historical-preventable-fatality-trends/class-of-injury.

62 *On June 12, 1972, the cargo door blew off*: To tell the story of the crash of Flight 981 and the Applegate memo, I relied on Moira Johnston, *The Last Nine Minutes: The Story of Flight 981* (New York: William Morrow, 1978), and Richard Witkin, "Engineer's Warning on DC-10 Reportedly Never Sent," *New York Times*, March 12, 1975. I am grateful to Peter Norton for turning me on to this so-predictable-it-was-predicted accident.

62 *"'Murphy's Law' being what it is"*: Vicki L. Golich, "Appendix 5: The Applegate Memo," in *The Political Economy of International Air Safety: Design For Disaster?* (London: Palgrave Macmillan, 1989), 115–18.

62 *"This corrective action becomes more expensive"*: House Committee on Interstate and Foreign Commerce, Special Subcommittee on Investigations, "Air Safety: Selected Review of FAA Performance," United States Congress (1974): 17.

Chapter Three: Scale

For this chapter, I relied heavily on interviews with safety expert Sidney Dekker, author of *Foundations of Safety Science: A Century of Understanding Accidents and Disasters, Safety Differently: Human Factors for a New Era, Just Culture: Balancing Safety and Accountability*, and *The Field Guide to Understanding 'Human Error'*; former nuclear industry spokesperson Maggie Gundersen and former nuclear engineer Arnie Gundersen, founders of Fairewinds Energy Education; Nick Pidgeon, a professor of environmental psychology and risk, and director of the Understanding Risk research group at Cardiff University in the U.K.; Alex Wellerstein, author of *Restricted Data: The History of Nuclear Secrecy in the United States*; Lee Clarke, author of *Mission Improbable: Using Fantasy Documents to Tame Disaster*; social psychologist David DeSteno; Alan Diehl, author of *Silent Knights: Blowing the Whistle on Military Accidents and Their Cover-Ups*; Elizabeth Loftus, a professor of psychology, criminology, and cognitive science at Stanford; Kim Arcand and Megan Watzke, NASA scientists and authors of *Magnitude: The Scale of the Universe*; and ichthyologist Prosanta Chakrabarty. For further reading in detail on how accidents of scale happen, I recommend the second editions of both Charles Perrow's *Normal Accidents* and Barry Turner's *Man-Made Disasters* (which Nick Pidgeon coauthored), both of which are approachable, especially considering the complexity of the content, as well as any work by Sidney Dekker that you can get your hands on.

65 *The range of radioactive contamination includes*: Alexey V. Yablokov and Vassily B. Nesterenko, "Chernobyl Contamination Through Time and Space," *Annals of the New York Academy of Science* 1181 (2009): 5–30.

65 *Researchers estimate that 41,000*: Elisabeth Cardis et al., "Estimates of the Cancer Burden in Europe from Radioactive Fallout from the Chernobyl Accident," *International Journal of Cancer* 119, no. 6 (2006): 1224–35.

65 *That all changed in 1990*: Julie Miller, "Paying the Price for Blowing the Whistle," *New York Times*, February 12, 1995.

66 *Still, few were news outside the occasional drunk celebrity*: Amanda Rosa, "M.T.A. Bus Plunges 50 Feet and Dangles from Overpass After Crash," *New York Times*, January 15, 2021; Thomas Tracy et al., " 'Extremely Troubling': Driver of MTA Bus That Plunged onto Cross Bronx Expressway Refused to Take Drug Tests After Wreck," *New York Daily News*, January 15, 2021.

66 *Those two crashes combined killed only*: The two Boeing Max crashes killed a total of 346 people. Approximately 42,000 were killed in traffic crashes in 2020, according to National Safety Council estimates.

67 *Two factors increase the risk of a nuclear accident today*: Unless otherwise noted, the story of the accident at Three Mile Island and other nuclear accidents comes from an interview with Arnie and Maggie Gundersen.

68 *Shutting down stopped more atoms from splitting*: Union of Concerned Scientists, "How Nuclear Power Works," ucsusa.org, July 27, 2010, updated January 29, 2014.

70 *Imagine a stack of Swiss cheese*: My education in systemic accidents comes from interviews with Nick Pidgeon, who co-authored the second edition of Barry Turner's *Man-Made Disasters* (Oxford, U.K.: Butterworth-Heinemann, 1997), and from Charles Perrow's *Normal Accidents: Living with High-Risk Technologies* (Princeton, NJ: Princeton University Press, 1999) and James Reason's *Managing the Risks of Organizational Accidents* (Aldershot, Hampshire, U.K.: Ashgate, 1997).

70 *But the holes are unique to each slice*: James Reason, "Human Error: Models and Management," *British Medical Journal* 320, no. 7237 (2000): 768–70.

71 *Reason called this alignment*: Ibid.

71 *The role of human error in all this, Reason wrote*: James Reason, *Human Error* (Cambridge:, U.K.: Cambridge University Press, 1990), 173.

72 *The sinking of the* Titanic *and what happened afterward*: Arnie Gundersen told me this story, but you can also read it in Susan Q. Stranahan, "The Eastland Disaster Killed More Passengers Than the *Titanic* and the *Lusitania*. Why Has It Been Forgotten?," *Smithsonian Magazine*, October 27, 2014.

73 *While the commission formed by*: Charles Perrow, "The President's Commission and the Normal Accident," in *Accident at Three Mile Island: The Human Dimensions*, ed. David L. Sills, C. P. Wolf, and Vivien B. Shelanski (New York: Routledge, 1982): 173–84.

73 *More major oil spills occurred*: "Oil Tanker Spill Statistics 2019," ITOPF, 8–9: itopf .org/fileadmin/data/Documents/Company_Lit/Oil_Spill_Stats_publication_2020.pdf.

73 *In 1972, fatal airline accidents hit a twenty-year high*: Casey Tolan, Thom Patterson, and Alicia Johnson, "Is 2014 the Deadliest Year for Flights? Not Even Close," CNN, July 28, 2014.

73 *in 1977, two 747s crashed into each other*: Patrick Smith, "The True Story Behind the Deadliest Air Disaster of All Time," *Telegraph*, March 27, 2017.

73 *Each was tracked back to the last person involved*: Nick Pidgeon, "In Retrospect: Normal Accidents," *Nature* 477, no. 7365 (2011): 404–5.

73 *In analyzing Three Mile Island*: Perrow, *Normal Accidents*, 15–31.

73 *Perrow defined complexity in terms of coupling*: Ibid., 72–100.

75 *In the six years after the meltdown*: Steve Wing et al., "A Reevaluation of Cancer Incidence Near the Three Mile Island Nuclear Plant: The Collision of Evidence and Assumptions," *Environmental Health Perspectives* 105, no. 1 (1997): 52–57.

75 *Cleaning up Three Mile Island*: "14-Year Cleanup at Three Mile Island Concludes," Associated Press, August 15, 1993.

75 *Property damages cost an estimated*: Benjamin K. Sovacool, "The Costs of Failure: A Preliminary Assessment of Major Energy Accidents, 1907–2007," *Energy Policy* 36, no. 5 (2008): 1802–20.

75 *He points me to the work of the late Dr. Steve Wing*: Wing et al., "A Reevaluation of Cancer Incidence Near the Three Mile Island Nuclear Plant."

75 *Another study two decades later*: David Goldenberg et al., "Altered Molecular Profile in Thyroid Cancers from Patients Affected by the Three Mile Island Nuclear Accident," *Laryngoscope* 127, supplement 3 (2017): S1–S9.

75 *"Not to say that there weren't any radioactive releases"*: Brett Sholtis, "Thyroid Cancer Study Re-ignites Debate over Three Mile Island Accident's Health Effects," *York Daily Record*, March 18, 2019.

76 *The* Exxon Valdez *dumped 11 million gallons of crude oil*: Susan Lyon and Daniel J. Weiss, "Oil Spills by the Numbers: The Devastating Consequences of Exxon Valdez and BP Gulf," Center for American Progress, April 30, 2010.

77 *It took until 2014 . . . a full quarter century*: John R. Platt, "25 Years After Exxon Valdez Spill, Sea Otters Recovered in Alaska's Prince William Sound," *Scientific American*, March 5, 2014.

77 *Researchers estimate the death toll at between 300,000 and 2 million birds*: Jennifer Balmer, "Seabird Losses from Deepwater Horizon Oil Spill Estimated at Hundreds of Thousands," *Science*, October 31, 2014; Center for Biological Diversity, "A Deadly Toll: The Devastating Wildlife Effects of Deepwater Horizon—and the Next Catastrophic Oil Spill," biologicaldiversity.org/programs/public_lands/energy /dirty_energy_development/oil_and_gas/gulf_oil_spill/a_deadly_toll.html.

77 *An estimated more than 320,000 sea turtles*: Nathan F. Putman et al., "Deepwater Horizon Oil Spill Impacts on Sea Turtles Could Span the Atlantic," *Biology Letters* 11, no. 12 (2015): 20150596.

77 *People reported finding oiled birds*: Christine Dell'Amore, "Gulf Oil Spill 'Not Over': Dolphins, Turtles Dying in Record Numbers: Report Warns That 14 Species Are Still Struggling from the 2010 Disaster," *National Geographic*, April 9, 2014.

77 *In 2019, nine years after*: "Hundreds of Dolphins Have Died Along Gulf Coast Since February, Scientists Say," Associated Press, June 15, 2019.

78 *Even if we understood scale and likelihood*: I learned about how we misunderstand the scale and scope of large disasters, and why that leaves us open to persuasion, from interviews with NASA data visualization scientists Kimberly Arcand and Megan

Watzke, and psychologist David DeSteno, author of *How God Works: The Science Behind the Benefits of Religion* (New York: Simon & Schuster, 2021).

78 *Studies of how predicting likelihood can go wrong*: Eric J. Johnson and Amos Tversky, "Affect, Generalization, and the Perception of Risk," *Journal of Personality and Social Psychology* 45, no. 1 (1983): 20–31.

79 *Manipulating our feelings about a nuclear accident*: Gundersen interview.

79 *In the days following the Three Mile Island meltdown*: Ivey DeJesus, "40 Years After Three Mile Island Accident, Debate over Safety of Nuclear Energy Still Goes Back and Forth," *PennLive Patriot News*, March 26, 2019.

79 *You can track this narrative-setting*: Andrew Nikiforuk, "Why We Pretend to Clean Up Oil Spills," *Hakai Magazine*, July 12, 2016.

79 *Less than a month after the Deepwater Horizon exploded*: "BP Oil Storage Tank Washes Ashore on Florida Beach," *Reuters*, June 13, 2010.

80 *David Rainey, a vice president at BP*: Clifford Krauss, "In BP Indictments, U.S. Shifts to Hold Individuals Accountable," *New York Times*, November 16, 2012.

80 *following the spill, Mississippi governor Haley Barbour*: "Transcript: Desperate Attempt to Plug Oil Leak," CNN, May 6, 2010; "Transcript: Gov. Haley Barbour on 'FNS,'" Fox News, June 7, 2010.

80 *Except that diffusing our panic can also diminish*: DeSteno interview.

80 *For all the news coverage of oil recovery efforts*: Douglas Wolfe et al., "The Fate of the Oil Spilled from the Exxon Valdez," *Environmental Science and Technology* 28, no. 13 (1994): 560A–568A.

81 *BP said they recovered 25 percent*: Nikiforuk, "Why We Pretend to Clean Up Oil Spills."

81 *In general, after an oil spill*: Ibid.

81 *After an oil spill, all the attention goes to*: Unless otherwise cited, the ichthyologic effects of the Deepwater oil spill are all from interviews with Prosanta Chakrabarty.

82 *The pancake batfish was on the front page of CNN*: Kelly Lynch, "Little-Known Pancake Batfish Could Be One of Oil Spill's Early Victims," CNN, June 16, 2010.

82 *Thanks to GPS data*: Prosanta Chakrabarty, Calvin Lam, Jori Hardman, Jacob Aaronson, Parker House, and Daniel Janies, "SPECIESMAP: A Web-Based Application for Visualizing the Overlap of Distributions and Pollution Events, with a List of Fishes Put at Risk by the 2010 Gulf of Mexico Oil Spill," *Biodiversity and Conservation* 21, no. 7 (2012): 1865–76.

83 *In 2020, researchers uncovered the fact that the spill*: Darryl Fears, "The Toxic Reach of Deepwater Horizon's Oil Spill Was Much Larger—and Deadlier—Than Previous Estimates, a New Study Says," *Washington Post*, February 12, 2020.

83 *While the oil slick, as seen in satellite images*: Igal Berenshtein et al., "Invisible Oil Beyond the Deepwater Horizon Satellite Footprint," *Science Advances* 6, no. 7 (2020).

84 *Before you accuse me*: Trevor Hawes, "Permian Has More Than Half of US Oil Rigs," *Midland Reporter-Telegram*, May 14, 2018; Jude Clemente, "The Great American Oil and Natural Gas Pipeline Boom," *Forbes*, August 6, 2019.

84 *the accidental fatality rate for workers in the oil and gas industry*: Centers for Disease Control and Prevention, "Fatal Injuries in Offshore Oil and Gas Operations—United States, 2003–2010," *Morbidity and Mortality Weekly Report* 62, no. 16 (2013): 301–4.

84 *In one Permian Basin county*: Kiah Collier, "As Oil and Gas Exports Surge, West Texas Becomes the World's 'Extraction Colony,'" *Texas Tribune*, October 11, 2018.
84 *The rise in oil production directly correlated*: Laurel Harduar Morano, Andrea L. Steege, and Sara E. Luckhaupt, Centers for Disease Control and Prevention, "Occupational Patterns in Unintentional and Undetermined Drug-Involved and Opioid-Involved Overdose Deaths—United States, 2007–2012," *Morbidity and Mortality Weekly Report* 67, no. 33 (2018): 925–30, Collin Eaton and John D. Harden, "Oil and Drugs: A Toxic Mix," *Houston Chronicle*, May 30, 2018.

Chapter Four: Risk

This chapter is based on interviews with Paul Slovic and Baruch Fischhoff of Decision Research, and their many studies cited below, as well as interviews with a number of traffic engineers, including Eric Dumbaugh, Don Kostelec, Charles Marohn, Richard Retting, Bill Schultheiss, and Gary Toth; journalist Alexander Yablon, who formerly wrote about guns in America for the *Trace*; Patrick Blanchfield, author of *Gunpower: The Structure of American Violence*; lawyer Jeff Bagnell; pediatrician Milton Tenenbein; and Adam and MaryBeth Gillan, two extraordinarily brave parents and advocates for drug safety. To learn more about how the Gillan family is honoring Maisie's memory, and the legislation they are fighting to pass, see: PurpleLightProject.com.

87 *Engineers build almost all crash test dummies*: Keith Barry, "The Crash Test Bias: How Male-Focused Testing Puts Female Drivers at Risk," *Consumer Reports*, October 23, 2019.
87 *At the National Highway Traffic Safety Administration*: There is also a ninety-seven-pound, four-foot-eleven-inch crash test dummy representing such a small percentile of the female population that NHTSA does not even bother to mention it. You can see all of NHTSA's crash test dummies at nhtsa.gov/nhtsas -crash-test-dummies.
87 *No crash test dummies account*: Barry, "The Crash Test Bias."
88 *Perhaps it's no surprise, then*: Joe Young, "Vehicle Choice, Crash Differences Help Explain Greater Injury Risks for Women," Insurance Institute for Highway Safety, February 11, 2021.
88 *"People do things that are not optimal"*: Unless otherwise cited, my understanding of risk perception comes from interviews with Baruch Fischhoff and Paul Slovic. Also see Sarah Lichtenstein et al., "Judged Frequency of Lethal Events," *Journal of Experimental Psychology: Human Learning and Memory* 4, no. 6 (1978): 551–78, and Baruch Fischhoff et al., "How Safe Is Safe Enough? A Psychometric Study of Attitudes Toward Technological Risks and Benefits," *Policy Sciences* 9, no. 2 (1978): 127–52.
89 *We tend to underestimate the risk of a car accident*: Fischhoff interview. See also: Lichtenstein et al., "Judged Frequency of Lethal Events," and Fischhoff et al., "How Safe Is Safe Enough?"
89 *Consider our strong and opposing reactions*: Slovic interview. See also: Fischhoff et al., "How Safe Is Safe Enough?"; Lichtenstein et al., "Judged Frequency of Lethal Events"; Ali S. Alhakami and Paul Slovic, "A Psychological Study of the Inverse

Relationship Between Perceived Risk and Perceived Benefit," *Risk Analysis* 14, no. 6 (1994): 1085–96.

90 *Arguably, in terms of our individual survival*: Ricky L. Langley and Sandra Amiss Mort, "Human Exposures to Pesticides in the United States," *Journal of Agromedicine* 17, no. 3 (2012): 300–315; Centers for Disease Control and Prevention, "Prescription Opioid Overdose Death Maps," cdc.gov/drugoverdose/data/prescribing/overdose -death-maps.html.

90 *But because we have bad feelings about pesticides*: Slovic interview.

90 *We feel a thing is riskier if we dread it*: David Ropeik, "Understanding Factors of Risk Perception," Nieman Reports, December 15, 2002.

91 *When a traffic engineer changes the design of a street*: Richard A. Retting, Susan A. Ferguson, and Anne T. McCartt, "A Review of Evidence-Based Traffic Engineering Measures Designed to Reduce Pedestrian–Motor Vehicle Crashes," *American Journal of Public Health* 93, no. 9 (2003): 1456–63; Eric Dumbaugh and Wenhao Li, "Designing for the Safety of Pedestrians, Cyclists, and Motorists in Urban Environments," *Journal of the American Planning Association* 77, no. 1 (2010): 69–88; and Reid Ewing and Eric Dumbaugh, "The Built Environment and Traffic Safety: A Review of Empirical Evidence," *Journal of Planning Literature* 23, no. 4 (2009): 347–67, to name a few.

91 *Eric Dumbaugh, a civil engineer*: Interview with Eric Dumbaugh, professor of urban and regional planning at Florida Atlantic University, associate director of the Collaborative Sciences Center for Road Safety, and associate editor of the *Journal of the American Planning Association*. Unless otherwise cited, this section relies on his expertise.

91 *The other tactic was to insist*: Dumbaugh put this to me succinctly: "What happened was in the 1950s and '60s, we got as a nation very concerned with traffic crashes, and what we wanted to do, in part on behest of the automobile manufacturers, was figure out how do we address the dangers that are designed into the system rather than looking at the inherent dangers of the automobiles themselves." In *Unsafe at Any Speed*, Nader lambasted this practice: "Concentrating on highway design rather than vehicle design serves two important purposes of General Motors management. First, it is extraordinarily cheap. The work keeps three or four engineers busy at the proving ground [a crash testing site] crashing a few cars against some guard rails and bridge parapets for the benefit of visiting delegations and provides the company with the material for endlessly repetitive papers at technical meetings. Second, there are no tooling costs implicit in highway design suggestions. Safer highways, obviously, are paid for by the public, not by General Motors" (151–52).

92 *At the time, no federal agency*: Dumbaugh interview. See also: Eric Dumbaugh and J. L. Gattis, "Safe Streets, Livable Streets," *Journal of the American Planning Association* 71, no. 3 (2005): 283–300.

92 *But early traffic engineers did know*: Dumbaugh and Gattis, "Safe Streets, Livable Streets," 283–300.

92 *From these two factors*: Ibid.

92 *Without much data, this soon became the rule*: Note the forgiving roadside was not a bad idea, but a deeply ethical premise over-applied without nuance. "If a mother turns to look at her baby and she goes off the road and hits a pole that shouldn't have

been there, that turns a mishap into a fatal event. I think that's too high a penalty for being human," is how William Haddon, then head of the Insurance Institute for Highway Safety, described it in a 1977 article in the *Atlanta Journal-Constitution*. "We've all been miseducated that the way to solve this problem is to have more squads of police chasing Americans so that they wouldn't drive 120 miles per hour rather than arranging cars so they can't go that fast." (Mike Feinsilber, "His Concept of 'Epidemic': Death in Cars," *Atlanta Journal-Constitution*, November 6, 1977, 11-B) See also: Daniel S. Turner, "A Primer on the Clear Zone," *Transportation Research Record* 1122 (1987): 86–95.

93 *Engineers today still learn*: Dumbaugh interview; Dumbaugh and Gattis, "Safe Streets, Livable Streets."

93 *Investigating the disparity between the rules and reality*: Ibid.

93 *Dumbaugh found that most accidents*: Eric Dumbaugh, "Design of Safe Urban Road-sides: An Empirical Analysis," *Transportation Research Record* 1961, no. 1 (2006): 74–82.

93 *In 2020, he took a similar approach*: Eric Dumbaugh, Dibakar Saha, and Louis Merlin, "Toward Safe Systems: Traffic Safety, Cognition, and the Built Environment," *Journal of Planning Education and Research* (2020): 1–13.

94 *Most of the time, when a traffic engineer*: Dumbaugh interview.

94 *Once engineers design that fast road*: Ibid.

94 *As one engineering rule book puts it*: American Association of State Highway and Transportation Officials, *A Policy on Geometric Design of Highways and Streets*, 6th ed. (Washington, DC: AASHTO, 2011), 54.

94 *As development arrives on a new road*: Dumbaugh interview.

95 *For example, in 2018, the National Highway Traffic Safety Administration attributed*: National Highway Traffic Safety Administration, "Speeding," *Traffic Safety Facts, 2018 Data*, April 2020, crashstats.nhtsa.dot.gov/Api/Public/ViewPublication/812932.

95 *When designing roads based on drivers' faulty perceptions of risk*: Dumbaugh interview.

96 *According to those rules*: The *Manual on Uniform Traffic Control Devices* also offers the option of installing a crosswalk and signal if 190 people cross in one hour, or five accidents happen in one year at the same location where people get hurt and/or wreck their cars. That's "Section 4C.05 Warrant 4, Pedestrian Volume" and "Section 4C.08 Warrant 7, Crash Experience" of the 2009 edition of the *Manual on Uniform Traffic Control Devices*, published by the U.S. Department of Transportation.

96 *Ninety-nine people running across*: Bill Schultheiss, the director of design at the traffic engineering firm Toole Design and a member of the Bicycle Technical Committee and the Pedestrian Task Force of the National Committee on Uniform Traffic Control Devices, has been leading an effort to change the *Manual on Uniform Traffic Control Devices* and confirmed my understanding of the document. In an interview, he pointed out that items in the manual, like pedestrian warrants (a "warrant" being the threshold that needs to be met to make intervention warranted), are not at all neutral, but traffic engineers tend to pretend that they are. "It's all about minimizing drivers' delay, not maximizing the safety or comfort of the person crossing the street. Values are implied in guidance like this," he tells me. "Our profession has an ethical mandate to provide for the safety of the public, and yet we pretend that

these warrants don't have an ethical or moral value to them, and that is not true. It is all designed around motorists having priority in our system."

96 *Engineering schools across the country*: Dumbaugh interview; interview with Charles L. Marohn Jr., author of *Confessions of a Recovering Engineer: Transportation for a Strong Town*.

96 *One study surveyed 117 transportation engineering programs*: Frank Gross and Paul P. Jovanis, "Current State of Highway Safety Education: Safety Course Offerings in Engineering and Public Health," *Journal of Professional Issues in Engineering Education and Practice* 134, no. 1 (2008).

97 *The men wear camouflage*: To see videos of the SIG Sauer P320 in (unintentional) action, search YouTube for "Sig Sauer P320 Drop Test." Videos from prior to 2018 feature the weapon before SIG Sauer launched its Voluntary Upgrade Program. Hat tip to journalist Alexander Yablon for turning me on to this story.

97 *After SIG Sauer signed a half-billion-dollar contract*: Jose Pagliery, "Trigger Warning," CNN, June 6, 2018.

97 *The army called out the defect*: Ibid.

98 *In Stamford, Connecticut, a police officer dropped*: Ibid.

98 *In Orlando, a cop let his holstered P320 slip*: Shannon Butler, "Mina Tells Officers to Have Gun Checked After Police Sergeant Shot in Knee," WFTV.com, April 6, 2018.

98 *A sheriff's deputy in Virginia*: Pagliery, "Trigger Warning."

98 *On their website, the FAQ began*: See the "Frequently Asked Questions" section of the Sig Sauer P320 Voluntary Upgrade Program at sigsauer.com/support/p320 -voluntary-upgrade-program.

98 *SIG Sauer trotted out the human error story*: This section, unless otherwise noted, comes from my interview with lawyer Jeff Bagnell.

98 *SIG Sauer settled with Deputy Vadnais*: Todd Bookman, "SIG Sauer Settles Lawsuit Alleging Gun Discharged Without Trigger Pull," New Hampshire Public Radio, June, 3, 2019.

99 *Semiautomatic pistols*: While I've fired a gun or two in my day, this explanation comes from Jeff Bagnell.

99 *Yet guns never are recalled, because they have a unique privilege*: Jeff Brazil and Steve Berry, "Federal Safety Law Targets 15,000 Items, but Not Guns," *Los Angeles Times*, February 1, 1998.

99 *This completely upends a gun owner's perception*: Bagnell interview.

100 *In fact, most gun owners cite protection*: Sara Kehaulani Goo, "Why Own a Gun? Protection Is Now Top Reason: Perspectives of Gun Owners, Non-owners," Pew Research Center, May 9, 2013; Ruth Igielnik and Anna Brown, "Key Takeaways on Americans' Views of Guns and Gun Ownership," Pew Research Center, June 22, 2017; Federal Bureau of Investigation Uniform Crime Reporting Program, "Crime in the United States: Table by Volume and Rate per 100,000 Inhabitants, 1998–2017," ucr.fbi.gov/crime-in-the-u.s/2017/crime-in-the-u.s.-2017/topic-pages/tables /table-1.

100 *Psychologists researching why people buy guns*: Wolfgang Stroebe, N. Pontus Leander, and Arie W. Kruglanski, "Is It a Dangerous World Out There? The Motivational Bases of American Gun Ownership," *Personality and Social Psychology Bulletin* 43, no. 8 (2017): 1071–85.

100 *These are not actual risks but perceptions*: Lisa Marie Pane, "Background Checks, a Metric for Gun Sales, Hit All-Time High," Associated Press, July 1, 2020.

100 *Two researchers in Massachusetts tracked a spike*: Meredith Wadman, "Accidental Gun Killings Surged After Sandy Hook School Shooting," *Science*, December 7, 2017.

100 *People might feel less in control in states*: Lisa Hepburn et al., "The Effect of Child Access Prevention Laws on Unintentional Child Firearm Fatalities, 1979–2000," *Journal of Trauma* 61, no. 2 (2006): 423–28.

101 *Adam and MaryBeth Gillan took no risks*: Adam and MaryBeth Gillan were kind and brave enough to tell me about Maisie in a telephone interview and email correspondence. I am grateful to Matt Kenny for introducing us.

102 *In this case, and for the more than sixty thousand children*: Safe Kids Worldwide, "Safe Storage, Safe Dosing, Safe Kids: A Report to the Nation on Safe Medication," safekids.org/sites/default/files/documents/ResearchReports/medicine-safety-study-2012.pdf.

103 *Dr. Milton Tenenbein is a pediatrician focused on emergency pediatric toxicology*: Interview with Milton Tenenbein, a professor of pharmacology and therapeutics in the department of pediatrics and child health at the University of Manitoba.

103 *Before this, when a child died*: Tenenbein interview.

103 *This legislation was a huge success*: W. W. Walton, "An Evaluation of the Poison Prevention Packaging Act," *Pediatrics* 69, no. 3 (1982): 363–70.

103 *But from the 1980s to today*: Tenenbein interview.

104 *More than six hundred children under the age of five*: Office of United States Senator Chuck Schumer, "Following This Year's Heart-Breaking Opioid Poisoning Death of Rochester Infant, Schumer Stands with Maisie Gillan's Parents and Calls on FDA to Use New Powers Granted in Schumer-Backed Law, Requiring All Drug Companies to Use Safer Blister Packaging for Opioids ASAP," press release, November 18, 2019.

104 *The evidence shows a direct risk reduction*: Milton Tenenbein, "Unit-Dose Packaging of Iron Supplements and Reduction of Iron Poisoning in Young Children," *Archives of Pediatric and Adolescent Medicine* 159, no. 6 (2005): 557–60.

104 *In the aftermath of Maisie's death*: Victoria E. Freile, "Death of Baby Maisie to Overdose Prompts Calls for Safer Packaging of Opioids," *Democrat and Chronicle*, November 18, 2019.

105 *Within a year of Maisie's death*: Wendy Wright, "Senator Schumer and Brighton Family Call on FDA to Make Changes," Spectrum News 1, November 18, 2019.

105 *The U.S. government only declared*: Mark R. Jones et al., "A Brief History of the Opioid Epidemic and Strategies for Pain Medicine," *Pain and Therapy* 7, no. 1 (2018): 13–21.

105 *Congress passed the very first piece of national legislation*: The Comprehensive Addiction and Recovery Act was signed into law on July 22, 2016. More than 493,000 people died of an accidental drug poisoning (ICD-10 Codes: X40–X44) between 1999 and 2016—and with each year that passed, more died than the last. See: The Comprehensive Addiction and Recovery Act (CARA), Public Law 114-198; CDC WISQARS Fatal Injury Reports, webappa.cdc.gov/sasweb/ncipc/mortrate.html.

Chapter Five: Stigma

My understanding of stigma benefited greatly from interviews and correspondence with Amanda Leigh Allen, who is incarcerated for involuntary manslaughter and drug sales in North Carolina; David Herzberg, author of *White Market Drugs: Big Pharma and the Hidden History of Addiction in America* and *Happy Pills in America: From Miltown to Prozac*; Sheila Vakharia, deputy director of the Department of Research and Academic Engagement for the Drug Policy Alliance; therapist Judith Kottick, whose child was killed in a traffic crash, and who spoke to me about her own experience of stigma and how it both related to and differed from the experiences of parents she met who lost children in a drug overdose; photojournalist Hilary Swift; Nancy Campbell, author of *OD: Naloxone and the Politics of Overdose*; Jamie Favaro, founder and executive director of NEXT Harm Reduction; and Dr. Kim Sue, medical director at Harm Reduction Coalition and author of *Getting Wrecked: Women, Incarceration, and the American Opioid Crisis*. I learned of Amanda Allen's story from reporting in the *Charlotte Observer* by Ames Alexander.

107 *Since Maisie's death, Adam and MaryBeth Gillan*: Gillan interview, follow-up via email; David Andreatta, "Monroe County Passes 'Maisie's Law' to Combat Opioid Overdoses," WXXI News, February 9, 2021.

107 *But lawmakers revised*: Gillan interview, follow-up via email.

107 *The legislators said they revised*: "The legislation was modified from its original version, which would have required pharmacies to provide a naloxone dose upon filling a customer's first prescription for opioids. Legislators said the mandate was impractical for pharmacies and could lead to unused naloxone doses circulating in public." (Andreatta, "Monroe County Passes 'Maisie's Law' to Combat Opioid Overdoses.")

108 *Instead, government officials argue*: "I don't agree with giving an opioid antidote to non–medical professionals," the deputy director of the White House Office on National Drug Control Policy told National Public Radio in 2008. "Sometimes having an overdose, being in an emergency room, having that contact with a health care professional is enough to make a person snap into the reality of the situation and snap into having someone give them services" (Richard Knox, "Overdose Rescue Kits Save Lives," National Public Radio, January 2, 2008). In 2018, two economists went so far as to suggest that the overdose reversal drug was "a moral hazard" (Jennifer L. Doleac and Anita Mukherjee, "The Moral Hazard of Lifesaving Innovations: Naloxone Access, Opioid Abuse, and Crime," Discussion Paper Series, IZA Institute of Labor Economics, April 2018, ftp.iza.org/dp11489.pdf). See also: Alexander R. Bazazi et al., "Preventing Opiate Overdose Deaths: Examining Objections to Take-Home Naloxone," *Journal of Health Care for the Poor and Underserved* 21, no. 4 (2010): 1108–13.

108 *At least when it comes to drugs*: Jordan O. Smith, Scott S. Malinowski, and Jordan M. Ballou, "Public Perceptions of Naloxone Use in the Outpatient Setting," *Mental Health Clinician* 9, no. 4 (2019): 275–79.

108 *Unspoken in this belief*: Colleen L. Barry et al., "Stigma, Discrimination, Treatment Effectiveness, and Policy: Public Views About Drug Addiction and Mental Illness," *Psychiatric Services* 65, no. 10 (2014): 1269–72.

108 *We view them differently because of stigma*: Erving Goffman, *Stigma: Notes on the Management of Spoiled Identity* (Englewood Cliffs, NJ: Prentice Hall, 1963), 3.

109 *Stigma is what doctors call*: Alexander C. Tsai et al., "Stigma as a Fundamental

Hindrance to the United States Opioid Overdose Crisis Response," *PLOS Medicine* 16, no. 11 (2019): e1002969.

109 *There is also "accidental addiction"*: My understanding of so-called accidental addiction and how it relates to drug-use stigma comes from interviews with Sheila Vakharia of the Drug Policy Alliance, Jamie Favaro of NEXT Harm Reduction, Dr. Kim Sue, medical director of the Harm Reduction Coalition, and drug historian David Herzberg.

109 *Erving Goffman is the psychologist*: The term first originates with the Greeks, who used it to mean a more literal tattoo or brand marking enslaved people or people who committed a crime. See also: Goffman, *Stigma*, 3.

109 *Goffman also defined two types of people*: Rachel A. Smith, "Segmenting an Audience into the Own, the Wise, and Normals: A Latent Class Analysis of Stigma-Related Categories," *Communication Research Reports* 29, no. 4 (2012): 257–65.

110 *A study by cognitive neuroscientists*: Stephanie C. Echols, Joshua Correll, and Jean Decety. "The Blame Game: The Effect of Responsibility and Social Stigma on Empathy for Pain," *Journal of Cognitive Neuroscience* 22, no. 5 (2010): 985–97.

110 *Even twenty years into the opioid epidemic*: "Americans Recognize the Growing Problem of Opioid Addiction," Associated Press, April 2018.

110 *One in three people say*: Barry et al., "Stigma, Discrimination, Treatment Effectiveness, and Policy."

111 *Amanda Leigh Allen's story is inseparable*: I learned of Allen's story from reporting by Ames Alexander in the *Charlotte Observer* ("Dealer Tried to Warn Buyer That the Drugs Were Dangerously Strong but It Was Too Late,") and I have also relied here on my own correspondence with Allen in prison.

112 *When a rising number of OxyContin overdoses*: Sara Randazzo and Jared S. Hopkins, "OxyContin-Maker Owner Maligned Opioid Addicts, Suit Says," *Wall Street Journal*, March 29, 2019; Patrick Radden Keefe, "The Family That Built an Empire of Pain," *New Yorker*, October 23, 2017.

112 *By 2001, there was clear evidence*: Barry Meier and Melody Petersen, "Sales of Painkiller Grew Rapidly, but Success Brought a High Cost," *New York Times*, March 5, 2001.

113 *Richard Sackler, then president of Purdue Pharma*: Danny Hakim, Roni Caryn Rabin, and William K. Rashbaum, "Lawsuits Lay Bare Sackler Family's Role in Opioid Crisis," *New York Times*, April 1, 2019.

113 *"They are the culprits"*: Barry Meier, "Sacklers Directed Efforts to Mislead Public About OxyContin, Court Filing Claims," *New York Times*, January 15, 2019.

113 *The company would continue to advertise the drug*: Art Van Zee, "The Promotion and Marketing of OxyContin: Commercial Triumph, Public Health Tragedy," *American Journal of Public Health* 99, no. 2 (2009): 221–27; Rebecca L. Haffajee and Michelle M. Mello, "Drug Companies' Liability for the Opioid Epidemic," *New England Journal of Medicine* 377, no. 24 (2017): 2301–5.

113 *Known addictive drugs such as OxyContin*: Van Zee, "The Promotion and Marketing of OxyContin."

113 *Illegal substitutes for those drugs*: Allison Bond, "Why Fentanyl Is Deadlier Than Heroin, in a Single Photo," *STAT*, September 29, 2016.

113　*Tools needed to use drugs safely*: Alyssa M. Peckham and Erika H. Young, "Opportunities to Offer Harm Reduction to People Who Inject Drugs During Infectious Disease Encounters: Narrative Review," *Open Forum Infectious Diseases* 7, no. 11 (2020): ofaa503; German Lopez, "Needle Exchanges Have Been Proved to Work Against Opioid Addiction. They're Banned in 15 States," *Vox*, June 22, 2018; National Harm Reduction Coalition, "Training Guide: Syringe Access Landscape," harmreduction.org/issues/syringe-access/landscape-report/state-by-state.

113　*Medication to stop an overdose*: Annie Correal, "Overdose Antidote Is Supposed to Be Easy to Get. It's Not," *New York Times*, April 12, 2018; Jake Harper, "Reversing an Overdose Isn't Complicated, but Getting the Antidote Can Be," *Kaiser Health News*, May 16, 2018; Lisa Rapaport, "Many U.S. Drugstores Fail to Provide Naloxone for Opioid Overdoses," *Reuters*, November 13, 2018; Christina A. Spivey et al., "Evaluation of Naloxone Access, Pricing, and Barriers to Dispensing in Tennessee Retail Community Pharmacies," *Journal of the American Pharmacists Association* 60, no. 5 (2020): 694–701.

113　*Drug illegality makes people feel unsafe*: Melissa Tracy et al., "Circumstances of Witnessed Drug Overdose in New York City: Implications for Intervention," *Drug and Alcohol Dependence* 79, no. 2 (2005): 181–90; Stephen Koester et al., "Why Are Some People Who Have Received Overdose Education and Naloxone Reticent to Call Emergency Medical Services in the Event of Overdose?," *International Journal of Drug Policy* 48 (2017): 115–24.

113　*And medication that helps control addiction*: Alaina McBournie et al., "Methadone Barriers Persist, Despite Decades of Evidence," *Health Affairs*, September, 23, 2019; Richard A. Rettig and Adam Yarmolinsky, eds., *Federal Regulation of Methadone Treatment* (Washington, DC: National Academies Press, 1995), chapter 1, "Introduction."

113　*Researchers estimate that, at most, 4 percent*: Mark Olfson et al., "Trends in Intentional and Unintentional Opioid Overdose Deaths in the United States, 2000–2017," *Journal of the American Medical Association* 322, no. 23 (2019): 2340–2342.

113　*And researchers have also found*: William Feigelman, John R. Jordan, and Bernard S. Gorman, "Parental Grief After a Child's Drug Death Compared to Other Death Causes: Investigating a Greatly Neglected Bereavement Population," *Omega* 63, no. 4 (2011): 291-316.

115　*David Herzberg has the second-best job title*: Interview with David Herzberg, author of *White Market Drugs: Big Pharma and the Hidden History of Addiction in America* and *Happy Pills in America: From Miltown to Prozac*.

115　*He notes that one of the reasons*: Herzberg interview. See also: Steven H. Woolf and Heidi Schoomaker, "Life Expectancy and Mortality Rates in the United States, 1959–2017," *Journal of the American Medical Association* 322, no. 20 (2019): 1996–2016. See also: Van Zee, "The Promotion and Marketing of OxyContin."

115　*Between 1995 and 2001*: Van Zee, "The Promotion and Marketing of OxyContin."

115　*The Drug Enforcement Administration did not begin*: Scott Higham, Sari Horwitz, and Steven Rich, "76 Billion Opioid Pills: Newly Released Federal Data Unmasks the Epidemic," *Washington Post*, July 16, 2019.

116　*Between 1999 and 2020, well over 840,000 people*: Centers for Disease Control and

Prevention, "The Drug Overdose Epidemic: Behind the Numbers," cdc.gov/opioids /data/index.html.

116 *As the death toll rose too precipitously*: Herzberg interview.

116 *The drug companies endorsed this message*: One of these websites, RxSafetyMatters .org, was built by Purdue to "combat prescription drug diversion and abuse" of Oxy-Contin, "frequently a target of drug abusers" (Alaric DeArment, "Purdue Launches RxSafetyMatters.org," *Drug Store News*, July 2, 2011). Amid the tort lawsuits aimed at the company's knowing and masking the addictive nature of the drug, Purdue quietly took down the website, but the Wayback Machine has it, and it is a study in blaming human error (visit web.archive.org/web/*/rxsafetymatters.org and choose any snapshot 2016 or prior). I learned of the site from "How Big Pharma Hooked America on Legal Heroin" by Kelly Bourdet for *Vice*, September 18, 2012. You can read about Purdue's think tanks and article placements here: David Armstrong, "Inside Purdue Pharma's Media Playbook," ProPublica, November 19, 2019.

116 *As one essay in the* New York Times: Sally Satel, "Doctors Behind Bars: Treating Pain Is Now Risky Business," *New York Times*, October 19, 2004.

116 *A doctor who worked for a think tank*: Armstrong, "Inside Purdue Pharma's Media Playbook."

117 *But over time the epidemic*: Herzberg interview.

117 *America's first opioid epidemic arrived*: Ibid.

118 *Some overdoses were accidents*: Ibid.

118 *One group of people using addictive drugs*: Ibid.

118 *The other crisis belonged to the people*: Ibid.

118 *Less than forty years after that issue*: Ibid.

119 *The first drug law, the Pure Food and Drug Act of 1906, protected the doctor-visiting class*: Ibid.

119 *By these laws, a person who could visit a doctor*: Ibid.

119 *The "war on drugs" may have been invented*: Ibid.

119 *Even as the drug war*: David Herzberg, "Entitled to Addiction? Pharmaceuticals, Race, and America's First Drug War," *Bulletin of the History of Medicine* 91, no. 3 (2017): 586–623.

120 *When drug use is stigmatized*: Interview with Dr. Kim Sue, physician, medical director of the Harm Reduction Coalition, and author of *Getting Wrecked: Women, Incarceration, and the American Opioid Crisis*.

120 *Take a person who is in treatment*: Sue interview. For a breakdown of types of stigma, see Tsai et al., "Stigma as a Fundamental Hindrance to the United States Opioid Overdose Crisis Response."

120 *But even if people are using together*: Sue interview.

120 *It's also much easier for a doctor*: Ibid.

121 *Without addiction-mitigating drugs*: Ibid.

121 *Methadone, the other safe substitute for people addicted*: McBournie et al., "Methadone Barriers Persist, Despite Decades of Evidence"; Rettig and Yarmolinsky, *Federal Regulation of Methadone Treatment*.

121 *Overdosing may not only be*: Sue interview.

121 *For example, naloxone, the drug that*: Correal, "Overdose Antidote Is Supposed to

Be Easy to Get. It's Not"; Harper, "Reversing an Overdose Isn't Complicated, but Getting the Antidote Can Be"; Rapaport, "Many U.S. Drugstores Fail to Provide Naloxone for Opioid Overdoses."

121 *One study of Tennessee pharmacies*: Spivey et al., "Evaluation of Naloxone Access, Pricing, and Barriers to Dispensing in Tennessee Retail Community Pharmacies."

121 *In a study of California pharmacies*: Talia Puzantian and James J. Gasper, "Provision of Naloxone Without a Prescription by California Pharmacists 2 Years After Legislation Implementation," *JAMA* 320, no. 18 (2018): 1933–34.

121 *In a Texas study, 31*: Kirk E. Evoy et al., "Naloxone Accessibility Without a Prescriber Encounter Under Standing Orders at Community Pharmacy Chains in Texas," *JAMA* 320, no. 18 (2018): 1934–37.

121 *Three years after New York State*: Ibid.

121 *And, because these structural stigmas overlap*: Bianca DiJulio et al., "Kaiser Health Tracking Poll: November 2015," Kaiser Family Foundation, kff.org/health-reform /poll-finding/kaiser-health-tracking-poll-november-2015.

121 *Government officials can also stigmatize drug use*: Sue interview.

122 *At first, Sue explains, the response*: Ibid.

122 *Even this limited dose of assistance*: Mitch Legan, "Indiana Needle Exchange That Helped Contain a Historic HIV Outbreak to Be Shut Down," National Public Radio, June 3, 2021.

122 *West Virginia passed a law*: Lauren Peace, "Judge Rules Law Restricting West Virginia Needle Exchange Programs Can Stand," *Mountain State Spotlight*, July 15, 2021.

122 *New Jersey evicted its largest syringe exchange*: Tracey Tully, "As Overdoses Soar, This State's Largest Needle Exchange Is Being Evicted," *New York Times*, August 10, 2021.

122 *This practice of offering forgiveness to the addicted*: Ibid.

122 *We also find stigmas baked into the federal budget*: Drug Policy Alliance, "The Federal Drug Control Budget: New Rhetoric, Same Failed Drug War," January 2015, drugpolicy.org/sites/default/files/DPA_Fact_sheet_Drug_War_Budget_Feb2015.pdf; Drug Policy Alliance, "Trump Budget Doubles Down on Drug War," press release, February 12, 2018, drugpolicy.org/press-release/2018/02/trump-budget-doubles -down-drug-war.

122 *Researchers have found that*: Edward Shepard and Paul R. Blackley, "U.S. Drug Control Policies: Federal Spending on Law Enforcement Versus Treatment in Public Health Outcomes," *Journal of Drug Issues* 34, no. 4 (2004): 771–85.

123 *Other studies have found*: Tsai et al., "Stigma as a Fundamental Hindrance to the United States Opioid Overdose Crisis Response."

123 *People who use drugs cite the stigmatization*: Brandon Muncan et al., "They Look at Us like Junkies: Influences of Drug Use Stigma on the Healthcare Engagement of People Who Inject Drugs in New York City," *Harm Reduction Journal* 17, no. 1 (2020).

123 *Say you become addicted to opioids*: Herzberg walked me through this thought exercise in how doctor access and drug criminalization can compound the stigmas a person carries.

123 *If you don't have a prescription*: Ibid.

124 *Drug laws did not develop*: Herzberg, "Entitled to Addiction? Pharmaceuticals, Race, and America's First Drug War."

124 *In the 1970s, 1980s, and 1990s*: Drug Policy Alliance, "A History of the Drug War," drugpolicy.org/issues/brief-history-drug-war.

124 *Over the past forty years, the United States has overall increased*: The Sentencing Project, "Criminal Justice Facts," sentencingproject.org/criminal-justice-facts.

124 *Significantly more federal prisoners*: Federal Bureau of Prisons, "Offenses," accessed July 17, 2021, bop.gov/about/statistics/statistics_inmate_offenses.jsp.

124 *In 1980, fewer than 41,000 people*: The Sentencing Project, "Criminal Justice Facts."

124 *Judges and prosecutors increased*: Pew Charitable Trusts, "Issue Brief: Federal Drug Sentencing Laws Bring High Cost, Low Return," pewtrusts.org/en/research-and -analysis/issue-briefs/2015/08/federal-drug-sentencing-laws-bring-high-cost-low -return.

125 *And considerably more Black people*: Drug Policy Alliance, "The Drug War, Mass Incarceration and Race," January 2018, drugpolicy.org/sites/default/files/drug-war -mass-incarceration-and-race_01_18_0.pdf.

125 *More than one in every four people*: Ibid.

125 *Doctors are significantly more likely*: Hillary Kunins et al., "The Effect of Race on Provider Decisions to Test for Illicit Drug Use in the Peripartum Setting," *Journal of Women's Health* 16, no. 2 (2007): 245–55.

125 *Drug use is generally equally prevalent*: Substance Abuse and Mental Health Services Administration, "Results from the 2018 National Survey on Drug Use and Health: Detailed Tables" (Rockville, MD: Center for Behavioral Health Statistics and Quality, Substance Abuse and Mental Health Services Administration), 72–74.

125 *But for decades . . . accidental drug overdose*: Monica J. Alexander, Mathew V. Kiang, and Magali Barbieri, "Trends in Black and White Opioid Mortality in the United States, 1979–2015," *Epidemiology* 29, no. 5 (2018): 707–15.

125 *Proof of this arrived when the most popular opioids*: Austin Frakt and Toni Monkovic, "A 'Rare Case Where Racial Biases' Protected African-Americans," *New York Times*, November 25, 2019.

125 *For at least twenty years, from 1979 to 2000*: Alexander, Kiang, and Barbieri, "Trends in Black and White Opioid Mortality in the United States."

126 *When Purdue Pharma released OxyContin*: Van Zee, "The Promotion and Marketing of OxyContin."

126 *Black people were protected in part*: Frakt and Monkovic, "A 'Rare Case Where Racial Biases' Protected African-Americans."

126 *Other stigmas stacked up to protect*: Astha Singhal, Yu-Yu Tien, and Renee Y. Hsia, "Racial-Ethnic Disparities in Opioid Prescriptions at Emergency Department Visits for Conditions Commonly Associated with Prescription Drug Abuse," *PLOS One* 11, no. 8 (2016): e0159224; Mark J. Pletcher et al., "Trends in Opioid Prescribing by Race/Ethnicity for Patients Seeking Care in US Emergency Departments," *Journal of the American Medical Association* 299, no. 1 (2008): 70–78.

126 *Researchers have found that some doctors and medical students*: Kelly M. Hoffman et al., "Racial Bias in Pain Assessment and Treatment Recommendations, and False Beliefs about Biological Differences Between Blacks and Whites," *Proceedings of the National Academy of Sciences* 113, no. 16 (2016): 4296–301.

126 *Had white and Black prescription opioid rates*: Frakt and Monkovic, "A 'Rare Case Where Racial Biases' Protected African-Americans."

126 *In 2010, white people were dying*: Ibid.

126 *The epidemic was significant enough*: Black people (1978–2002) and "non-white" people (1900–1977, which includes all other races but not Latino people) died by accident (all accidental death totaled) at a higher rate than white people every year since as far back as 1900, which were the earliest comprehensive records I could find, through 2002, when opioid drug overdoses shifted the dominant paradigm. All unintentional injury deaths, broken out by year and race, for 1981 to 1998 and for 1999 to 2019 can be searched via CDC WISQARS Fatal Injury Reports (webappa .cdc.gov/sasweb/ncipc/mortrate.html); years 1961 to 1980 can be found in the "Vital Statistics of the United States" publication for each year, with accidental death broken out by race in "Volume 2: Mortality, Part A," typically on pages 1–20 or 1–22 (1961–1964: cdc.gov/nchs/products/vsus/vsus_1939_1964.htm, and 1965–1979: cdc .gov/nchs/products/vsus/vsus_1965_1979.htm); "Vital Statistics in the United States, 1940–1960," by Robert D. Grove and Alice M. Hetzel for the National Center for Health Statistics, covers those years, and accidental deaths are broken out by race on pages 372–73 (cdc.gov/nchs/data/vsus/vsrates1940_60.pdf); and "Vital Statistics in the United States, 1900–1940," by Forrest E. Linder and Robert D. Grove for the National Office of Vital Statistics, covers those years, and accidental deaths are broken out by race on pages 366–67 (data.nber.org/vital-stats-books/vsrates1900_40 .CV.pdf). Note that for all years 1978 and prior, race is not broken out further than "white" or "non-white" and "white" or "all other."

126 *Today, that gap is shrinking*: Keturah James and Ayana Jordan, "The Opioid Crisis in Black Communities," *Journal of Law, Medicine, and Ethics* 46, no. 2 (2018): 404–21.

126 *White opioid overdoses are leveling off*: Kaiser Family Foundation, "State Health Facts: Opioid Overdose Deaths by Race/Ethnicity," kff.org/other/state-indicator /opioid-overdose-deaths-by-raceethnicity.

126 *In 2019, accidental drug overdoses returned*: CDC WISQARS Fatal Injury Reports, Centers for Disease Control and Prevention, "Opioid Overdose Data Analysis and Resources: Overdose Death Rates Involving Opioids by Type, United States, 1999–2019," webappa.cdc.gov/sasweb/ncipc/mortrate.html; "Overdose Death Rates Involving Opioids by Type, United States, 1999-2019," Centers for Disease Control and Prevention Opioid Overdose Data Analysis and Resources, cdc.gov/drugoverdose /data/analysis.html.

127 *Doctors prescribe buprenorphine*: Pooja A. Lagisetty et al., "Buprenorphine Treatment Divide by Race/Ethnicity and Payment," *JAMA Psychiatry* 76, no. 9 (2019): 979–81.

Chapter Six: Racism

This chapter is based on interviews with epidemiologists Chukwudi Onwuachi-Saunders and Dana Loomis; forensic pathologist Brad Randall; Dan Bouk, author of *How Our Days Became Numbered: Risk and the Rise of the Statistical Individual*; Tara Goddard, a professor of urban planning at Texas A&M University who studies the intersection of transportation and social psychology; Joseph F. C. DiMento, author of *Changing Lanes: Visions and Histories of Urban Freeways*; and Kevin Kruse, author of *White Flight: Atlanta and the Making of Modern Conservatism*; as well as the books *How to Be an Antiracist* by Ibram X. Kendi and *Racecraft: The Soul of Inequality in American Life* by Karen E.

Fields and Barbara J. Fields. While his story did not make it onto these pages, I learned a great deal from correspondence with James Linder, a Black man who was sentenced to twenty-eight years in prison on drug-induced homicide charges in Illinois, and from an interview with his lawyer, Henry H. Sugden III. Linder was charged with the accidental overdose death of the white girlfriend of a white man he sold drugs to, and tried for that crime not in the county where those drugs were sold or where the victim died but in the adjacent, 93 percent–white county where the victim happened to live. Linder's sentence of twenty-eight years came from an all-white jury that deliberated for less than three hours and was more than double the longest sentence the county had assigned to the crime in five years. The white boyfriend, who actually gave the victim the drugs and who lied to medical professionals about her drug use, precluding intervention with naloxone, was given probation. (See also: drugpolicy.org/james-linders-story.)

129 *In his book* The Field Guide to Understanding 'Human Error': Dekker, *The Field Guide to Understanding 'Human Error*,' 21–63.
129 *Picture a tunnel as seen from the outside*: Ibid.
130 *For one, we could assume*: Ibid., 24–28.
130 *Or we could detail all the ways*: Ibid., 21–28, 39–44.
130 *"The problem about taking the position"*: Ibid., 46.
130 *Dekker encourages us instead*: Ibid., 36–38.
131 *Just as accident-proneness is not*: Ibram X. Kendi, *How to Be an Antiracist* (New York: One World, 2019), 44–55.
132 *This cycle creates stigma and an illusion*: Karen E. Fields and Barbara J. Fields, *Racecraft: The Soul of Inequality in American Life* (New York: Verso, 2012), 16–24.
132 *Nationwide, Latino people are more likely*: CDC WISQARS Fatal Injury Reports, webappa.cdc.gov/sasweb/ncipc/mortrate.html.
132 *In New York City, Latino people are also more likely*: Michael Andersen, "NYC Bike-on-Sidewalk Tickets Most Common in Black and Latino Communities," *Streetsblog USA*, October 21, 2014; Julianne Cuba, "NYPD Targets Black and Brown Cyclists for Biking on the Sidewalk," *Streetsblog NYC*, June 22, 2020.
132 *Knowing these facts*: Echols, Correll, and Decety, "The Blame Game: The Effect of Responsibility and Social Stigma on Empathy for Pain"; Jennifer N. Gutsell and Michael Inzlicht, "Intergroup Differences in the Sharing of Emotive States: Neural Evidence of an Empathy Gap," *Social Cognitive and Affective Neuroscience* 7, no. 5 (2012): 596–603.
132 *A racist New York City community board member*: Katie Honan, "Only 'Illegals' Use Bike Lanes in Corona, Trump-Backing Board Member Says," *DNAinfo*, March 1, 2017.
133 *In the late 1980s*: United Church of Christ Commission for Racial Justice, "Toxic Wastes and Race in the United States: A National Report on the Racial and Socioeconomic Characteristics of Communities with Hazardous Waste Sites," 1987, nrc.gov/docs/ML1310/ML13109A339.pdf.
133 *That study inspired Paul Slovic*: James Flynn, Paul Slovic, and C. K. Mertz, "Gender, Race, and Perception of Environmental Health Risks," *Risk Analysis* 14, no. 6 (1994): 1101–8.
133 *In a nationwide survey, Slovic asked*: Ibid.

133 *Non-white people felt at risk more often*: Ibid.

133 *To determine the "why" behind all this data*: Ibid.

134 *In 2000, Slovic reran the study*: Melissa Finucane et al., "Gender, Race, and Perceived Risk: The 'White Male' Effect," *Health, Risk & Society* 2, no. 2 (2000): 159–72.

134 *In 2004, another researcher published a similar study*: K. Brent, "Gender, Race, and Perceived Environmental Risk: The 'White Male' Effect in Cancer Alley, LA," *Sociological Spectrum* 24, no. 4 (2004): 453–78.

134 *The people exposed to these*: Wesley James, Chunrong Jia, and Satish Kedia, "Uneven Magnitude of Disparities in Cancer Risks from Air Toxics," *International Journal of Environmental Research and Public Health* 9, no. 12 (2012): 4365–85.

134 *The 2004 study found the same*: Brent, "Gender, Race, and Perceived Environmental Risk."

134 *Risk perception researchers have found*: Dan M. Kahan et al., "Culture and Identity-Protective Cognition: Explaining the White-Male Effect in Risk Perception," *Journal of Empirical Legal Studies* (2007): 465–505.

134 *Slovic, writing in 1997*: Paul Slovic, "Trust, Emotion, Sex, Politics, and Science: Surveying the Risk-Assessment Battlefield," in *Environment, Ethics, and Behavior*, ed. M. H. Bazerman et al. (San Francisco: New Lexington, 1997), 277–313.

135 *Doctors generally diagnose two ways*: This section come from Brad Randall, Paul Thompson, and Anne Wilson, "Racial Differences Within Subsets of Sudden Unexpected Infant Death (SUID) with an Emphasis on Asphyxia," *Journal of Forensic and Legal Medicine* 62 (February 2019): 52–55, and from an interview with Randall.

135 *The rate of the latter, accidental suffocation*: CDC WISQARS Fatal Injury Reports, webappa.cdc.gov/sasweb/ncipc/mortrate.html.

135 *In 2019, researchers at Sanford School of Medicine*: Randall, Thompson, and Wilson, "Racial Differences Within Subsets of Sudden Unexpected Infant Death (SUID) with an Emphasis on Asphyxia."

136 *In Jacksonville, Florida*: Topher Sanders, Kate Rabinowitz, and Benjamin Conarck, "Walking While Black: Jacksonville's Enforcement of Pedestrian Violations Raises Concerns That It's Another Example of Racial Profiling," ProPublica, November 16, 2017; Smart Growth America, "Dangerous by Design: 2021," smartgrowthamerica .org/wp-content/uploads/2021/03/Dangerous-By-Design-2021.pdf.

136 *Similar studies have found evidence*: Gersh Kuntzman, " 'Jaywalking While Black': Final 2019 Numbers Show Race-Based NYPD Crackdown Continues," *Streetsblog NYC*, January 27, 2020; Gersh Kuntzman, "NYPD's Racial Bias in 'Jaywalking' Tickets Continues into 2020," *Streetsblog NYC*, May 7, 2020.

137 *Racism is prevalent, too, in sentencing*: Edward L. Glaeser and Bruce Sacerdote, "The Determinants of Punishment: Deterrence, Incapacitation, and Vengeance," Harvard Institute of Economic Research: Discussion Paper #1894, April 2000.

137 *In 2000, researchers at Dartmouth*: Ibid.

137 *In 2019, on average, U.S. drivers killed twenty-one pedestrians*: CDC WISQARS Fatal Injury Reports, webappa.cdc.gov/sasweb/ncipc/mortrate.html.

138 *Even the moment after stepping into the crosswalk*: This section comes from Tara Goddard, Kimberly Barsamian Kahn, and Arlie Adkins, "Racial Bias in Driver Yielding Behavior at Crosswalks," *Transportation Research Part F: Traffic Psychology and Behaviour* 33 (2015), 1–6, as well as an interview with Goddard.

138 *Goddard wanted to know if racism*: Goddard, Kahn, and Adkins, "Racial Bias in Driver Yielding Behavior at Crosswalks."

139 *In any case, one result is*: CDC WISQARS Fatal Injury Reports, webappa.cdc.gov /sasweb/ncipc/mortrate.html.

140 *Compared to traffic accidents*: Ibid.

140 *The rate of accidental shooting deaths is relatively low*: Ibid.

140 *In 2003, researchers at the University of Washington*: Anthony Greenwald, Mark Oakes, and Hunter Hoffman, "Targets of Discrimination: Effects of Race on Responses to Weapons Holders," *Journal of Experimental Social Psychology* 39 (2003): 399–405.

141 *It didn't matter if the researchers*: Ibid.

141 *Two social psychologists did a meta-analysis*: Yara Mekawi and Konrad Bresin, "Is the Evidence from Racial Bias Shooting Task Studies a Smoking Gun? Results from a Meta-Analysis," *Journal of Experimental Social Psychology* 61 (2015): 120–30.

141 *Black people . . . are more likely than white people to be killed by police*: Frank Edwards, Hedwig Lee, and Michael Esposito, "Risk of Being Killed by Police Use of Force in the United States by Age, Race–Ethnicity, and Sex," *Proceedings of the National Academy of Sciences* 116, no. 34 (2019): 16793–16798.

141 *While these shootings*: Sarah DeGue, Katherine A. Fowler, and Cynthia Calkins, "Deaths Due to Use of Lethal Force by Law Enforcement: Findings from the National Violent Death Reporting System, 17 U.S. States, 2009–2012," *American Journal of Preventive Medicine* 51 (2016): S173–S187.

141 *In these, too, the people shot*: Scott Glover et al., "A Key Miscalculation by Officers Contributed to the Tragic Death of Breonna Taylor," CNN, July 23, 2020.

141 *Or Daunte Wright*: Becky Sullivan and Vanessa Romo, "Officer Who Fatally Shot Daunte Wright with 'Accidental Discharge' Is Identified," National Public Radio, April 12, 2021.

141 *Or Eurie Stamps*: Kevin Sack, "Door-Busting Drug Raids Leave a Trail of Blood," *New York Times*, March 18, 2017.

141 *Or Aiyana Mo'Nay Stanley Jones*: Rose Hackman, "'She Was Only a Baby': Last Charge Dropped in Police Raid That Killed Sleeping Detroit Child," *Guardian*, January 31, 2015.

141 *Or Iyanna Davis*: Ibid.

141 *Or Alberta Spruill*: Robert F. Worth, "Commissioner Reassigns Captain Involved in Ill-Fated Harlem Raid," *New York Times*, May 24, 2003.

142 *Black people died by accident*: For a detailed list of sources, see chapter 5 endnotes: *The epidemic was significant enough.*

142 *Black and Latino people are killed by accident on bicycles at a higher rate*: CDC WISQARS Fatal Injury Reports, webappa.cdc.gov/sasweb/ncipc/mortrate.html.

142 *In fact, Black and Indigenous people are disproportionately killed*: Matt McFarland, "Traffic Deaths Jump for Black Americans Who Couldn't Afford to Stay Home During Covid," CNN Business, June 20, 2021; CDC WISQARS Fatal Injury Reports, webappa.cdc.gov/sasweb/ncipc/mortrate.html.

142 *Black people are more likely to die by any accident*: CDC WISQARS Fatal Injury Reports webappa.cdc.gov/sasweb/ncipc/mortrate.html. Cheryl Cherpitel, Yu Ye, and William Kerr, "Shifting Patterns of Disparities in Unintentional Injury Mortality Rates in the United States, 1999–2016," *Pan-American Journal of Public Health* 45 (2021): 1–11.

142 *Black babies die by accident*: CDC WISQARS Fatal Injury Reports, webappa.cdc .gov/sasweb/ncipc/mortrate.html.

142 *Black and Indigenous people are more than twice as likely as white people to freeze to death*: CDC WONDER Compressed Mortality File, ICD-10 Codes: Exposure to Excessive Natural Heat (X30); Exposure to Excessive Natural Cold (X31); Unintentional Natural/Environmental Deaths (W42, W43, W53–W64, W92–W99, X20–X39, X51–X57), wonder.cdc.gov/cmf-icd10.html.

142 *No one in America is more likely to die*: CDC WISQARS Fatal Injury Reports, webappa.cdc.gov/sasweb/ncipc/mortrate.html.

143 *The way that racism produces unequal death*: Yin Paradies et al., "Racism as a Determinant of Health: A Systematic Review and Meta-Analysis," *PLOS One* 10, no. 9 (2015): e0138511.

143 *For example, people accidentally choke*: CDC WONDER Compressed Mortality File, ICD-10 Codes: Inhalation and Ingestion of Food Causing Obstruction of Respiratory Tract (W79); Accidental Drowning and Submersion (W65–W74), wonder.cdc.gov /cmf-icd10.html.

143 *And people are also more likely to drown*: J. Gilchrist, K. Gotsch, and G. Ryan, "Nonfatal and Fatal Drownings in Recreational Water Settings: United States, 2001–2002," Centers for Disease Control and Prevention, *Morbidity and Mortality Weekly Report* 53, no. 21 (2004): 447–52.

143 *Black people are more than twice as likely*: CDC WISQARS Fatal Injury Reports, webappa.cdc.gov/sasweb/ncipc/mortrate.html.

143 *But when we talk about the racialized outcome*: Stephen Kerber, "Analysis of Changing Residential Fire Dynamics and Its Implications on Firefighter Operational Timeframes," *Fire Technology* 48 (2011): 865–91; United States Fire Administration National Fire Data Center, Federal Emergency Management Agency, "Socioeconomic Factors and the Incidence of Fire," June 1997, usfa.fema.gov/downloads/pdf/statistics/socio .pdf; Marty Ahrens and Radhika Maheshwari, "Home Structure Fires," National Fire Protection Association, November 2020, nfpa.org/News-and-Research/Data -research-and-tools/Building-and-Life-Safety/Home-Structure-Fires.

144 *A hundred years ago*: This section is from Dana P. Loomis et al., "Fatal Occupational Injuries in a Southern State," *American Journal of Epidemiology* 145, no. 12 (1997): 1089–199; Dana Loomis and David Richardson, "Race and the Risk of Fatal Injury at Work," *American Journal of Public Health* 88, no. 1 (1998): 40–44; Dana Loomis et al., "Political Economy of US States and Rates of Fatal Occupational Injury," *American Journal of Public Health* 99, no. 8 (2009): 1400–1408; and David B. Richardson et al., "Fatal Occupational Injury Rates in Southern and Non-Southern States, by Race and Hispanic Ethnicity," *American Journal of Public Health* 94, no. 10 (2004): 1756–61, and interviews with Loomis.

144 *In the past decade*: AFL-CIO, "Death on the Job: The Toll of Neglect, 2021," May 4, 2021, aflcio.org/reports/death-job-toll-neglect-2021.

144 *In the 1980s and early '90s, before Latino people*: Loomis and Richardson, "Race and the Risk of Fatal Injury at Work."

144 *(And these differences were even greater)*: Loomis et al., "Fatal Occupational Injuries in a Southern State."

146 *The United States has about 13,500*: "Exploded Trust," *Scientific American* 309, no. 1 (2013): 10–11.

146 *All in all, these sites create*: U.S. Environmental Protection Agency, "TRI National Analysis: Releases of Chemicals," January 2021, epa.gov/trinationalanalysis/releases-chemicals.

146 *One study by the NAACP found*: Lesley Fleischman and Marcus Franklin, "Fumes Across the Fence-Line: The Health Impacts of Air Pollution from Oil & Gas Facilities on African American Communities," National Association for the Advancement of Colored People, naacp.org/resources/fumes-across-fence-line-health-impacts-air -pollution-oil-gas-facilities-african-american.

146 *Researchers have also found that*: M. R. Elliott et al., "Environmental Justice: Frequency and Severity of U.S. Chemical Industry Accidents and the Socioeconomic Status of Surrounding Communities," *Journal of Epidemiology & Community Health* 58 (2004): 24–30.

146 *People of color are almost twice as likely*: Amanda Starbuck and Ronald White, "Living in the Shadow of Danger: Poverty, Race, and Unequal Chemical Facility Hazards," Center for Effective Government, January 2016, foreffectivegov.org/sites/default /files/shadow-of-danger-highrespdf.pdf.

146 *The first finding of this kind*: United Church of Christ Commission for Racial Justice, "Toxic Wastes and Race in the United States."

146 *some 550 people sat down to be arrested over plans*: Brian King, *States of Disease: Political Environments and Human Health* (Berkeley: University of California Press, 2017), 36.

146 *It would be the inception of what*: Robert D. Bullard et al., "Toxic Wastes and Race at Twenty: 1987–2007," United Church of Christ Justice and Witness Ministries, nrdc .org/sites/default/files/toxic-wastes-and-race-at-twenty-1987-2007.pdf.

147 *In maps, the Church's findings appear*: United Church of Christ Commission for Racial Justice, "Toxic Wastes and Race in the United States."

147 *No source of environmental danger is fairly distributed*: Lesley Fleischman and Marcus Franklin, "Fumes Across the Fence-Line: The Health Impacts of Air Pollution from Oil & Gas Facilities on African American Communities"; Oliver Milman, "Revealed: 1.6m Americans Live Near the Most Polluting Incinerators in the US," *Guardian*, May 21, 2019; Starbuck and White, "Living in the Shadow of Danger: Poverty, Race, and Unequal Chemical Facility Hazards"; Maninder P. S. Thind et al., "Fine Particulate Air Pollution from Electricity Generation in the US: Health Impacts by Race, Income, and Geography," *Environmental Science and Technology* 53, no. 23 (2019): 14010–19; Zoë Schlanger, "Race Is the Biggest Indicator in the US of Whether You Live Near Toxic Waste," Quartz, March 22, 2017.

147 *In 2007, that first study*: Bullard et al., "Toxic Wastes and Race at Twenty."

147 *One study of nearly 1,700 Superfund sites*: Amin Raid, Arlene Nelson, and Shannon McDougall, "A Spatial Study of the Location of Superfund Sites and Associated Cancer Risk," *Statistics and Public Policy* 5, no. 1 (2018): 1–9.

148 *Another study of over 1,800 Superfund sites*: "Population Surrounding 1,857 Superfund Remedial Sites," United States Environmental Protection Agency, Office of Land and Emergency Management, September 2020, epa.gov/sites/production/files/2015-09 /documents/webpopulationrsuperfundsites9.28.15.pdf.

148 *The results are the same if you look at Superfund sites*: Raid, Nelson, and McDougall, "A Spatial Study of the Location of Superfund Sites and Associated Cancer Risk"; Tom Boer et al., "Is There Environmental Racism? The Demographics of Hazardous Waste in Los Angeles County," *Social Science Quarterly* 78, no. 4 (1997): 793–810; Paul Stretesky and Michael J. Hogan, "Environmental Justice: An Analysis of Superfund Sites in Florida," *Social Problems* 45, no. 2 (1998): 268–87.

148 *Rates of accidental death in house fires*: CDC WISQARS Fatal Injury Reports, webappa.cdc.gov/sasweb/ncipc/mortrate.html.

148 *Redlining in the 1930s and 1940s*: Interviews with Joseph F. C. DiMento, author of *Changing Lanes: Visions and Histories of Urban Freeways*, and Kevin Kruse, author of *White Flight: Atlanta and the Making of Modern Conservatism*. See also: Candice Norwood, "How Infrastructure Has Historically Promoted Inequality," *PBS News-Hour*, April 23, 2021; Deborah N. Archer, "White Men's Roads Through Black Men's Homes: Advancing Racial Equity Through Highway Reconstruction," *Vanderbilt Law Review* 73, no. 5 (2020): 1259–330.

148 *Today, Black people are still less likely*: Michele Lerner, "One Home, a Lifetime of Impact," *Washington Post*, July 23, 2020; Tegan K. Boehmer et al., "Residential Proximity to Major Highways—United States, 2010," Centers for Disease Control and Prevention, *Morbidity and Mortality Weekly Report* 62, no. 3 (2013): 46–50.

149 *People who don't own their homes*: United States Fire Administration National Fire Data Center, "Socioeconomic Factors and the Incidence of Fire."

149 *Extreme heat is worse in redlined neighborhoods*: Brad Plumer and Nadja Popovich, "How Decades of Racist Housing Policy Left Neighborhoods Sweltering," *New York Times*, August 24, 2020.

149 *Living near highways delivers more drivers*: Luis F. Miranda-Moreno, Patrick Morency, and Ahmed M. El-Geneidy, "The Link Between Built Environment, Pedestrian Activity and Pedestrian–Vehicle Collision Occurrence at Signalized Intersections," *Accident Analysis & Prevention* 43, no. 5 (2011): 1624–34; Tefft, "Impact Speed and a Pedestrian's Risk of Severe Injury or Death."

149 *Researchers have even found that*: Kate Lowe, Sarah Reckhow, and Andrea Benjamin, "Pete Buttigieg May Not Know This Yet: Rail Transportation Funding Is a Racial Equity Issue," *Washington Post*, February 1, 2021.

149 *And the per-mile accident risk of rail travel*: Todd Litman, "A New Transit Safety Narrative," *Journal of Public Transportation* 17, no. 4 (2014): 114–35.

149 *When James Reason developed the Swiss cheese model*: James Reason, "Human Error: Models and Management," *British Medical Journal* 320, no. 7237 (2000): 768–70; Thomas V. Perneger, "The Swiss Cheese Model of Safety Incidents: Are There Holes in the Metaphor?," *BMC Health Services Research* 5, no. 71 (2005).

Chapter Seven: Money

This chapter is based on interviews with epidemiologist Chukwudi Onwuachi-Saunders; Ken Kolosh, statistics manager for the National Safety Council; Billie Jo Kipp, director of research and evaluation at the Aspen Institute Center for Native American Youth; Ozawa Bineshi Albert, movement building coordinator at Indigenous Environmental

Network; epidemiologist Deborah Girasek; Anne Case, Princeton University professor of economics and public affairs; Beth Osborne, director of Transportation for America; emergency room physician Dr. Kyle Hurst; Kevin Smith, a professor of sociology at Lamar University who studies economic manifestation of the just world fallacy; Melissa Tracy, a professor of epidemiology and biostatistics at State University of New York and co-author of an excellent article, "Estimated Deaths Attributable to Social Factors in the United States," in the *American Journal of Public Health*; and former U.S. senator and representative from North Dakota Byron Dorgan, who served as chairman of the Committee on Indian Affairs and is the author of *Reckless: How Debt, Deregulation, and Dark Money Nearly Bankrupted America* and *Take This Job and Ship It: How Corporate Greed and Brain-Dead Politics Are Selling Out America*.

151 *In 1999, Dr. Deborah Girasek, an epidemiologist*: D. C. Girasek, "How Members of the Public Interpret the Word 'Accident,'" *Injury Prevention* 5 (1999): 19–25.
151 *Girasek has a theory*: Interview with Girasek via email.
152 *When Girasek broke down her survey respondents*: Girasek, "How Members of the Public Interpret the Word 'Accident.'"
152 *These figures mirror accidental death rates*: CDC WISQARS Fatal Injury Reports, webappa.cdc.gov/sasweb/ncipc/mortrate.html; Rebecca A. Karb, S. V. Subramanian, and Eric W. Fleegler, "County Poverty Concentration and Disparities in Unintentional Injury Deaths: A Fourteen-Year Analysis of 1.6 Million U.S. Fatalities," *PLOS One* 11 (2016): 1–12.
153 *Dr. Chukwudi Onwuachi-Saunders was an agent*: Unless otherwise noted, this section is based on Chukwudi Onwuachi-Saunders and Darnell F. Hawkins, "Black-White Differences in Injury: Race or Social Class?," *Annals of Epidemiology* 3, no. 2 (1993): 150–53, as well as an interview with Onwuachi-Saunders.
153 *To Onwuachi-Saunders, it was obvious*: Onwuachi-Saunders interview.
154 *"What we found is that race is a proxy"*: Ibid.
154 *Today, Black people and people living in poverty*: Karb, Subramanian, and Fleegler, "County Poverty Concentration and Disparities in Unintentional Injury Deaths."
154 *The Great Depression and the Great Recession*: Lynne Peeples, "How the Next Recession Could Save Lives," *Nature*, January 23, 2019.
155 *when the economy was booming*: Comparison of National Safety Council, "Preventable Injury-Related Deaths by Cause, United States, 1903–2019," Injury Facts, injuryfacts .nsc.org/all-injuries/historical-preventable-fatality-trends/deaths-by-cause; "Wealth Concentration Has Been Rising Toward Early 20th Century Levels," Center on Budget and Policy Priorities, cbpp.org/wealth-concentration-has-been-rising-toward -early-20th-century-levels-2. See also: Eve Darian-Smith, "Dying for the Economy: Disposable People and Economies of Death in the Global North," *State Crime Journal* 10, no. 1 (2021): 61–79.
155 *Researchers have found that, traditionally, for every 1 percent*: Monica M. He, "Driving Through the Great Recession: Why Does Motor Vehicle Fatality Decrease When the Economy Slows Down?," *Social Science & Medicine* 155 (2016): 1–11.
155 *(The coronavirus pandemic complicated)*: Alissa Walker, "This Spring, We All Drove Much Less. Yet Traffic Deaths Went Up. Why?," *Curbed*, October 15, 2020.
155 *The fatality rate rose 8 percent*: National Safety Council, "Motor Vehicle Deaths in

2020 Estimated to Be Highest in 13 Years, Despite Dramatic Drops in Miles Driven," March 4, 2021, nsc.org/newsroom/motor-vehicle-deaths-2020-estimated-to-be -highest.

155 *Notably, this increase was racially uneven*: McFarland, "Traffic Deaths Jump for Black Americans Who Couldn't Afford to Stay Home During Covid"; National Highway Traffic Safety Administration, "Early Estimates of Motor Vehicle Traffic Fatalities and Fatality Rate by Sub-categories in 2020," *Traffic Safety Facts: Crash Stats*, June 2021, crashstats.nhtsa.dot.gov/Api/Public/ViewPublication/813118.

156 *The National Highway Traffic Safety Administration estimates*: Joan Lowy, "Traffic Accidents in the U.S. Cost $871 Billion a Year, Federal Study Finds," *PBS NewsHour*, May 29, 2014.

156 *And these costs are baked into*: Interview with Ken Kolosh, statistics manager for the National Safety Council.

156 *Medical expenses, for example*: Ibid.

156 *Increasingly, hospitals are closing*: Clary Estes, "1 in 4 Rural Hospitals Are at Risk of Closure and the Problem Is Getting Worse," *Forbes*, February 24, 2020.

156 *When the profit margin disappears*: Sean McCarthy et al., "Impact of Rural Hospital Closures on Health-Care Access," *Journal of Surgical Research* 258 (2021): 170–78.

157 *In 2019, Dr. Kyle Hurst . . . became*: Emergency Medicine News, "Congratulations to Kyle Hurst," West Virginia University School of Medicine, October 11, 2019.

157 *Bridgeport is not a big city*: Interview with Dr. Kyle Hurst.

157 *Every year, West Virginia hospitals discharge*: American Hospital Directory, "Hospital Statistics by State," ahd.com/state_statistics.html.

157 *The problem in West Virginia*: Andrew Lisa, "States with the Biggest Rural Populations," *Stacker*, April 8, 2019; Suneson, "Wealth in America."

157 *In West Virginia, about half*: Ayla Ellison, "State-By-State Breakdown of 897 Hospitals at Risk of Closing," *Becker's Hospital CFO Report*, January 22, 2021.

157 *Of the hospitals at risk*: David Mosley and Daniel DeBehnke, "Rural Hospital Sustainability: New Analysis Shows Worsening Situation for Rural Hospitals, Residents," Navigant Consulting, guidehouse.com/-/media/www/site/insights/healthcare/2019 /navigant-rural-hospital-analysis-22019.pdf.

157 *In Bridgeport, United sees more*: Hurst interview. See also: American Hospital Directory: United Hospital Center, ahd.com/free_profile/510006/United_Hospital_Center /Bridgeport/West_Virginia.

158 *But the accidents Hurst most often sees*: Hurst interview.

158 *Transit times might mean the difference*: Ibid.

159 *Often the accidents Dr. Hurst treats*: Ibid.

159 *Fires are the sixth most common cause*: CDC WONDER Compressed Mortality File, wonder.cdc.gov/cmf-icd10.html.

159 *People living in poverty might*: Hurst interview.

159 *Since 2005, 180 rural hospitals*: Ellison, "Why Rural Hospital Closures Hit a Record High in 2020."

159 *Nationwide, half of rural hospitals*: Laura Santhanam, "These 3 Charts Show How Rural Health Care Was Weakened Even Before COVID-19," *PBS NewsHour*, May 14, 2020.

159 *One in four rural hospitals are at risk*: Estes, "1 in 4 Rural Hospitals Are at Risk of Closure and the Problem Is Getting Worse."

159 *And the volunteer emergency medical services*: Ali Watkins, "Rural Ambulance Crews Have Run Out of Money and Volunteers," *New York Times*, April 25, 2021.

160 *A third of rural EMS providers*: Lucy Kafanov, "Rural Ambulance Crews Are Running Out of Money and Volunteers. In Some Places, the Fallout Could Be Nobody Responding to a 911 Call," CNN, May 22, 2021.

160 *When a local hospital closes*: George M. Holmes et al., "The Effect of Rural Hospital Closures on Community Economic Health," *Health Services Research* 41, no. 2 (2006): 467–85.

160 *The Affordable Care Act (ACA) offered funding for states*: Rachel Garfield, Kendal Orgera, and Anthony Damico, "The Coverage Gap: Uninsured Poor Adults in States That Do Not Expand Medicaid," Kaiser Family Foundation, January 21, 2021, kff.org /medicaid/issue-brief/the-coverage-gap-uninsured-poor-adults-in-states-that-do -not-expand-medicaid.

160 *Researchers tracked rural hospitals in the decade after*: The Chartis Center for Rural Health, "The Rural Health Safety Net Under Pressure: Rural Hospital Vulnerability," chartis.com/forum/insight/the-rural-health-safety-net-under-pressure-rural-hospital -vulnerability.

160 *Texas and Tennessee top the list of rural hospital closures*: The Chartis Center for Rural Health, "Crises Collide: The COVID-19 Pandemic and the Stability of the Rural Health Safety Net," chartis.com/resources/files/Crises-Collide-Rural-Health -Safety-Net-Report-Feb-2021.pdf.

160 *But even with that boon*: Ibid.

161 *In 2019, the only hospital in Mingo County*: Jenny Jarvie, "In a Time of Pandemic, Another Rural Hospital Shuts Its Doors," *Los Angeles Times*, May 16, 2020.

161 *That year, Ohio Valley Medical Center*: Sarah Kliff, Jessica Silver-Greenberg, and Nicholas Kulish, "Closed Hospitals Leave Rural Patients 'Stranded' as Coronavirus Spreads," *New York Times*, April 26, 2020.

161 *One of these would reopen as a temporary*: Tyler Barker, "Shuttered West Virginia Hospital Reopens as Temporary ER," ABC 4 WOAY, July 1, 2020.

161 *The rate of accidental death in West Virginia*: CDC WONDER Compressed Mortality File, wonder.cdc.gov/cmf-icd10.html.

161 *Looking at the state-by-state rate of accidental death*: Ibid.

161 *These states are also in the top fifteen highest*: Michael B. Sauter, "Per Capita Government Spending: How Much Does Your State Spend on You?," *USA Today*, June 29, 2018.

161 *These statistics are a result of*: Neil Irwin, "One County Thrives. The Next One Over Struggles. Economists Take Note," *New York Times*, June 29, 2018.

162 *For example, the life expectancy gap between wealthy places*: Laura Dwyer-Lindgren et al., "Inequalities in Life Expectancy Among US Counties, 1980 to 2014: Temporal Trends and Key Drivers," *JAMA Internal Medicine* 177, no. 7 (2017): 1003–11.

162 *Researchers have found a correlation*: Interview with Dana Loomis about his paper "Political Economy of US States and Rates of Fatal Occupational Injury," *American Journal of Public Health* 99 (2009): 1400–8.

162 *Other research, which correlated greater income inequality*: C. R. Ronzio, E. Pamuk, and G. D. Squire, "The Politics of Preventable Death: Local Spending, Income Inequality, and Premature Mortality in US Cities," *Journal of Epidemiology and Community Health* 58, no. 3 (2004): 161.

162 *One study that investigated the sixty U.S. roads*: Robert J. Schneider et al., "United States Fatal Pedestrian Crash Hot Spot Locations and Characteristics," *Journal of Transport and Land Use* 14, no. 1 (2021).

162 *nowhere is the decline of American infrastructure*: Binyamin Appelbaum, "Public Works Funding Falls as Infrastructure Deteriorates," *New York Times*, August 8, 2017.

162 *In the state's 2020 budget*: Jim Justice, "Executive Budget: Volume I Budget Report Fiscal Year 2022," State of West Virginia, February 10, 2021, 53.

163 *One study found that the per capita cost to states of a fatal opioid overdose*: Feijun Luo, Mengyao Li, and Curtis Florence, "State-Level Economic Costs of Opioid Use Disorder and Fatal Opioid Overdose—United States, 2017," *Morbidity and Mortality Weekly Report* 70, no. 15 (2021): 541–46.

164 *Nationwide, the census area whose residents*: CDC WONDER Compressed Mortality File, wonder.cdc.gov/cmf-icd10.html.

164 *Oglala Lakota County, with a population*: "About the Pine Ridge Reservation," Re-Member, re-member.org/pine-ridge-reservation; Patrick Strickland, "Life on the Pine Ridge Native American Reservation," *Al Jazeera*, November 2, 2016; Gabi Serrato Marks, "How Oglala Lakota People Are Standing Up to Extreme Weather," *Scientific American*, December 11, 2019.

164 *In Oglala Lakota County, dangerous conditions stack up*: Ibid.

164 *For example, to maintain tribal roads*: "Tribal Infrastructure: Roads, Bridges, and Buildings": Written Testimony of Julian Bear Runner, President of the Oglala Sioux Tribe, to the House Committee on Natural Resources, Subcommittee for Indigenous Peoples of the United States, July 11, 2019.

164 *Of the U.S. counties with the highest*: CDC WONDER Compressed Mortality File, wonder.cdc.gov/cmf-icd10.html; U.S. Census Bureau QuickFacts (V2019) for Lake and Peninsula Borough, AK; Thomas County, NE; Oglala Lakota County, SD; Corson County, SD; Todd County, SD; Yukon-Koyukuk Census Area, AK; Mellette County, SD; Sioux County, ND; Rio Arriba County, NM (the non-Indigenous-majority outlier); and Apache County, AZ.

164 *Per capita income in these areas*: Strickland, "Life on the Pine Ridge Native American Reservation."

165 *In 2015, the Bureau of Indian Education*: "Indian Affairs: Key Actions Needed to Ensure Safety and Health at Indian School Facilities," U.S. Government Accountability Office, March 10, 2016.

165 *In 2018, the Indian Health Service*: Testimony of the National Indian Health Board— Stacy A. Bohlen, CEO, to the House Appropriations Subcommittee on Interior, Environment, and Related Agencies, June 11, 2020.

165 *In the Indian Reservation Roads program*: John R. Baxter, "Hearing on Tribal Transportation: Paving the Way for Jobs, Infrastructure and Safety in Native Communities," Federal Highway Administration, U.S. Department of Transportation, September 15, 2011.

165 *Compared to the rest of the country*: Christopher Flavelle and Kalen Goodluck,

"Dispossessed, Again: Climate Change Hits Native Americans Especially Hard," *New York Times*, June 27, 2021.

165 *It is under these dangerous conditions*: CDC WISQARS Fatal Injury Reports, webappa .cdc.gov/sasweb/ncipc/mortrate.html.

165 *Infrastructure spending has been falling*: Appelbaum, "Public Works Funding Falls as Infrastructure Deteriorates."

165 *In 2018, public construction spending*: As a percent of gross domestic product, see U.S. Census Bureau, "Total Public Construction Spending: Total Construction in the United States," FRED, fred.stlouisfed.org/graph/?g=heS.

165 *Two of every five U.S. bridges are*: American Association of Civil Engineers, "2021 Report Card for America's Infrastructure," infrastructurereportcard.org/wp-content /uploads/2020/12/National_IRC_2021-report.pdf, 19–20, 27, 35, 73, 153.

166 *Local officials have shut down*: American Association of Civil Engineers, "2020 Report Card for Mississippi Infrastructure," infrastructurereportcard.org/wp-content /uploads/2016/10/FullReport-MS_2020-1.pdf, 15.

166 *In the accident-prone locales of West Virginia and South Dakota*: American Road and Transportation Builders Association, "2021 Bridge Conditions Report," artbabridge report.org/reports/2021-ARTBA-Bridge-Report.pdf.

166 *Rural roads are in such bad condition*: Insurance Institute for Highway Safety, "Fatality Facts 2019: Urban/Rural Comparison," iihs.org/topics/fatality-statistics/detail /urban-rural-comparison.

166 *Half the oil and gas pipelines*: James Conca, "The Colonial Pipeline Explosion: Do We Need Fewer Pipelines—Or More?," *Forbes*, November 3, 2016.

166 *Federal government spending*: Congressional Budget Office, "Public Spending on Transportation and Water Infrastructure, 1956 to 2017," October 2018, cbo.gov /system/files/2018-10/54539-Infrastructure.pdf.

166 *Some states are picking up the slack*: David Schaper, "10 Years After Bridge Collapse, America Is Still Crumbling," National Public Radio, August 1, 2017.

166 *(As this book headed to press)*: Emily Cochrane, "Senate Passes $1 Trillion Infrastructure Bill, Handing Biden a Bipartisan Win," *New York Times*, August 10, 2021; Aatish Bhatia and Quoctrung Bui, "The Infrastructure Plan: What's In and What's Out," *New York Times*, August 10, 2021; National Association of City Transportation Officials, "Infrastructure Investment and Jobs Act: Overview for Cities," August 2021, nacto.org/wp-content/uploads/2021/08/NACTO-IIJA-City-Overview.pdf.

167 *In 2012, researchers at Brown University*: Karb, Subramanian, and Fleegler, "County Poverty Concentration and Disparities in Unintentional Injury Deaths."

167 *One of every five miles*: "Our Nation's Crumbling Infrastructure and the Need for Immediate Action," Gregory E. DiLoreto to the Committee on Ways and Means, U.S. House of Representatives, March 6, 2019.

167 *The U.S. Department of Transportation estimates*: Ron Nixon, "Human Cost Rises as Old Bridges, Dams and Roads Go Unrepaired," *New York Times*, November 5, 2015.

167 *Nationwide, pedestrian fatalities are higher*: "America's Poor Neighborhoods Plagued by Pedestrian Deaths," *Governing*, August 5, 2014.

167 *You can see where these accidents fall*: Richard Florida, "The Geography of Car Deaths in America: The U.S. Is a Nation Divided Not Just by How People Get Around, but by How Fast They Drive," *Bloomberg CityLab*, October 15, 2015.

168　*Accidental deaths by falling, drowning, and poisoning*: Karb, Subramanian, and Flee-gler, "County Poverty Concentration and Disparities in Unintentional Injury Deaths."

168　*In counties where automakers have shut down*: Atheendar S. Venkataramani et al., "Association Between Automotive Assembly Plant Closures and Opioid Overdose Mortality in the United States: A Difference-in-Differences Analysis," *JAMA Internal Medicine* 180, no. 2 (2020): 254–62.

168　*Economic geography so strongly affects*: Neil Irwin and Quoctrung Bui, "The Rich Live Longer Everywhere. For the Poor, Geography Matters," *New York Times*, April 11, 2016.

168　*Data bears this out*: Emily Ekins, "What Americans Think about Poverty, Wealth, and Work," Cato Institute, September 24, 2019, cato.org/publications/survey-reports /what-americans-think-about-poverty-wealth-work.

169　*But blaming human error is also*: This section comes from writings by Kevin Smith, "Seeing Justice in Poverty: The Belief in a Just World and Ideas About Inequalities," *Sociological Spectrum* 5, nos. 1–2 (1985): 17–29; "I Made It Because of Me: Beliefs About the Causes of Wealth and Poverty," *Sociological Spectrum* 5 (1985): 255–67; David N. Green, "Individual Correlates of the Belief in a Just World," *Psychological Reports* 54 (1984): 435–38; as well as an interview with Smith.

169　*Kevin Smith, a professor of sociology*: Smith interview.

169　*The classic experiment to explain*: Melvin J. Lerner and Carolyn H. Simmons, "Observer's Reaction to the 'Innocent Victim': Compassion or Rejection?," *Journal of Personality and Social Psychology* 4, no. 2 (1966): 203–10.

170　*Seeing just deserts in another person's pain*: Smith interview.

170　*In a poll of random Texans*: Smith and Green, "Individual Correlates of the Belief in a Just World."

170　*In another study, Smith sought*: Smith, "I Made It Because of Me: Beliefs About the Causes of Wealth and Poverty."

171　*Researchers at UCLA and Harvard*: Zack Rubin and Letitia Anne Pelau, "Who Believes in a Just World?," *Journal of Social Issues* 31, no. 3 (1975): 65–89.

171　*Other research confirms this*: Ekins, "What Americans Think about Poverty, Wealth, and Work."

171　*There is some hope*: Pew Research Center, "Most Americans Point to Circumstances, Not Work Ethic, for Why People Are Rich or Poor," March 2, 2020, pewresearch .org/politics/2020/03/02/most-americans-point-to-circumstances-not-work-ethic-as -reasons-people-are-rich-or-poor.

171　*The poor are not bad*: Smith interview.

171　*In 2017, then U.S. secretary*: Jose A. Del Real, "Ben Carson Calls Poverty 'a State of Mind' During Interview," *Washington Post*, May 24, 2017.

172　*In 2020, Carson endorsed a federal budget*: J. Edward Moreno, "Democratic Law-makers Rip Carson over Cuts to Housing Budget, Policies," *The Hill*, March 4, 2020.

Chapter Eight: Blame

Early in the process of writing this book, it became clear that understanding blame, both why we do it and what it does to us, would be essential to truly understanding accidents in America. The writings of Sidney Dekker—especially *The Field Guide to Understanding 'Human Error'*—and interviews with Dekker were critical here, as was the work of Dianne

Vaughan on the accidental explosions during NASA's *Challenger* and *Columbia* launches. Research by Mark Alicke, Kelly Shaver, Elaine Walster, and Lera Boroditsky guided my understanding, as did the 1947 work of Paul Fitts and Richard Jones, which Dekker turned me on to. Engineer Bill Schultheiss was kind enough to help me understand how "pedestrian warrants" fit into the blame paradigm. I am grateful to Amy Tam-Liao and Hsi-Pei Liao for allowing me to tell the story of the awful blame ascribed to Allison, and for their ongoing advocacy for safe streets in New York City, as well as to their lawyer Steve Vaccaro.

173 *As the shame and vulnerability researcher Brené Brown*: Brené Brown, *Daring Greatly* (New York: Penguin Random House, 2012), 195–97.

173 *Kevin Smith, the sociologist*: Smith interview.

174 *Laying blame makes a terrifying*: In *Twilight of the Idols and the Anti-Christ*, Friedrich Nietzsche puts it like this: "To trace something unknown back to something known is alleviating, soothing, gratifying and gives moreover a feeling of power. Danger, disquiet, anxiety attend the unknown—the first instinct is to eliminate these distressing states. First principle: any explanation is better than none" (trans. R. J. Hollingdale [New York: Penguin, 1990], 62).

174 *When we blame someone for an accident*: Dekker, *The Field Guide to Understanding 'Human Error,'* 10–12.

174 *On October 6, 2013, in Flushing, Queens*: Allison Liao's story is told from the following sources: "S.U.V. Fatally Hits Girl, 3, in Queens," *New York Times*, October 6, 2013; Brad Aaron, "NYPD and Media Declare 'Accident' as Another Child Killed by NYC Motorist," *Streetsblog NYC*, October 7, 2013; Jim O'Grady, "Girl Gone: Anatomy of a New York City Pedestrian Death," *WNYC National Public Radio*, March 18, 2014; and Rebecca Fishbein, "Driver Kills 3-Year-Old in Queens, DMV Voids His Tickets," *Gothamist*, November 7, 2014, unless otherwise noted. The original CBS story blaming Liao, "Girl, 3, Struck and Killed by SUV in Flushing, Queens," October 6, 2013, is still online: newyork.cbslocal.com/2013/10/06/girl-3-struck-and-killed-by-suv-in-flushing-queens. The original *Daily News* article, "SUV Kills 3-Year-Old Girl in Queens After She Breaks Free from Grandmother," October 7, 2013, has been changed. Two years after Liao's killing, the *Daily News* quietly edited out their blame for Liao without a stated correction, and made a significant headline change. The original is cached in Chris Polansky, "Families of People Killed by Drivers Say NYPD Victim-Blaming Compounds Grief," *Gothamist*, March 13, 2019, gothamist .com/news/families-of-people-killed-by-drivers-say-nypd-victim-blaming-com pounds-grief.

175 *The driver insisted*: Fishbein, "Driver Kills 3-Year-Old in Queens, DMV Voids His Tickets."

175 *The accident occurred in Queens*: "New Yorkers and Their Cars," New York City Economic Development Corporation, April 5, 2018.

175 *Police officers spend most of their time*: Nationwide, the majority of police officers' time is spent on motorized patrol and the majority of problems that police respond to are vehicle-related (Barry Friedman, "Disaggregating the Police Function," NYU Law and Economics Research Paper No. 20-03, March 2020: 950–52).

176 *Psychologists call this "defensive attribution"*: Kelly Shaver, "Defensive Attribution:

Effects of Severity and Relevance on the Responsibility Assigned for an Accident," *Journal of Personality and Social Psychology* 14, no. 2 (1970): 101–13.

176 *Rather than serving as an arbiter*: Less than a year after my interview with Mark Alicke, he was killed in an accident in his home. May his memory be a blessing. Unless otherwise noted, the following section comes from that interview, and his study "Culpable Causation," *Journal of Personality and Social Psychology* 63, no. 3 (1992): 368–78.

177 *In other versions of the experiment*: Alicke interview. See also: Mark Alicke, "Culpable Control and the Psychology of Blame," *Psychological Bulletin* 126, no. 4 (2000): 556–74; Mark Alicke, "Blaming Badly," *Journal of Cognition and Culture* 8, nos. 1–12 (2000): 179–86; Mark Alicke and Ethan Zell, "Social Attractiveness and Blame," *Journal of Applied Social Psychology* 39 (2009): 2089–105; Shaver, "Defensive Attribution"; and Elaine Walster, "Assignment of Responsibility for an Accident," *Journal of Personality and Social Psychology* 3, no. 1 (1966): 73–79.

178 *In this example, blame is not*: There were 10,142 people killed in drunk driving accidents and 9,478 in speeding accidents in 2019. There is, of course, likely some overlap between the two. Hat tip to my colleague Philip Miatkowski for sharing this idea with me.

178 *If two people have a fight*: Alicke interview.

179 *Amid the rage and fear that drives a mob*: Craig Thorley and Jayne Rushton-Woods, "Blame Conformity: Leading Eyewitness Statements Can Influence Attributions of Blame for an Accident," *Applied Cognitive Psychology* 27 (2013): 291–96; Nathanael J. Fast and Larissa Z. Tiedens, "Blame Contagion: The Automatic Transmission of Self-Serving Attributions," *Journal of Experimental Social Psychology* 46 (2010): 97–106.

179 *Researchers have found that people*: Thorley and Rushton-Woods, "Blame Conformity."

179 *In one study of this phenomenon*: Ibid.

179 *A similar experiment on blame conformity*: Broderick L. Turner et al., "Body Camera Footage Leads to Lower Judgments of Intent Than Dash Camera Footage," *Proceedings of the National Academy of Sciences* 116, no. 4 (2019): 1201-6.

180 *Researchers then applied the same test*: Ibid.

180 *Perspective can put a distorted lens on the truth*: Kristyn A. Jones, William E. Crozier, and Deryn Strange, "Believing Is Seeing: Biased Viewing of Body-Worn Camera Footage," *Journal of Applied Research in Memory and Cognition* 6, no. 4 (2017): 460–74.

180 *Two cognitive scientists at Stanford conducted*: Caitlin M. Fausey and Lera Boroditsky, "Subtle Linguistic Cues Influence Perceived Blame and Financial Liability," *Psychonomic Bulletin & Review* 17, no. 5 (2010): 644–50.

180 *In one experiment, they told two groups of subjects*: Ibid.

181 *In a second experiment using the same parameters*: Ibid.

181 *In a related study, researchers asked subjects*: Ibid.

181 *Even he testified to the fact*: Two years after the fact, Timberlake put the unequal division of responsibility and blame this way: "If you consider it 50–50, I probably got 10 percent of the blame, and that says something about society. I think that America's harsher on women. And I think that America is, you know, unfairly harsh on ethnic

people" (Cady Lang, "A Comprehensive Guide to Justin Timberlake's Rocky History with the Super Bowl Halftime Show," *Time*, February 2, 2018).

181 *Officials at the next Grammy Awards banned*: Yashar Ali, "Exclusive: Les Moonves Was Obsessed with Ruining Janet Jackson's Career, Sources Say," *Huffington Post*, September 6, 2018; Alex Abad-Santosalex, "The Backlash over Justin Timberlake's Super Bowl Halftime Show, Explained," *Vox*, February 1, 2018.

182 *In the spring of 2010, Raquel Nelson*: Tanya Snyder, "The Streets and the Courts Failed Raquel Nelson. Can Advocacy Save Her?," *Streetsblog USA*, July 22, 2011.

182 *Nelson, a single mom*: "Child's Death Casts Light on Pedestrian Traffic Woes," National Public Radio, July 30, 2011.

182 *Though the bus stop was right across*: The *Atlanta Journal-Constitution* places the nearest crosswalk at three tenths of a mile from the bus stop, and the average adult walking speed is a bit over three miles per hour, or twenty minutes a mile, or six minutes for three-tenths of a mile. Nelson would have needed to walk that three-tenths of a mile twice (there and back) and cross the street, and it's fair to assume that an adult with three small children walks considerably slower than an adult alone, who at their fastest could have done the walk in thirteen minutes, assuming one minute to cross the five-lane highway with no wait. (Ralph Ellis, "Jaywalkers Take Deadly Risks," *Atlanta Journal-Constitution*, June 13, 2013.)

182 *This time, on April 10, 2010*: Ellis, "Jaywalkers Take Deadly Risks."

183 *Guy was partially blind*: Lisa Stark, "Mom Avoids Jail but Gets Probation After Son Killed by Driver: Raquel Nelson's 4-Year-Old Was Killed on a Georgia Road by a Hit and Run Driver," ABC News, July 26, 2011; Ralph Ellis, "Hit-Run Suspect Faced Similar Charges in 1997," *Atlanta Journal-Constitution*, August 11, 2012.

183 *She faced up to three years in prison*: Angie Schmitt, "Georgia Prosecutor Continues Case Against Raquel Nelson," *Streetsblog USA*, September 11, 2012.

183 *Raquel Nelson lived in a suburb*: "Child's Death Casts Light on Pedestrian Traffic Woes," National Public Radio, July 30, 2011.

184 *There was a four-lane highway*: David Goldberg, "Protect, Don't Prosecute, Pedestrians," *Washington Post*, August 4, 2011.

184 *In Atlanta and the surrounding*: Smart Growth America, "Dangerous by Design: 2021."

184 *As many as one in every four times*: Ellis, "Jaywalkers Take Deadly Risks."

184 *Both Georgia and the Atlanta metro area*: Smart Growth America, "Dangerous by Design: 2021."

184 *Scott Higley, director of Strategic Communications*: Via email, Higley said in full, "Back in 2010–2011 when this incident occurred, our metro Atlanta Traffic Operations staff went out into the field to conduct a traffic engineering investigation and take counts to determine if the area warranted a mid-block traffic signal based on the current pedestrian counts at that approximate location. Based on the counts, it was determined that there were not enough pedestrians at this location to meet requirements." He did not respond when I requested that he elaborate on "enough."

184 *If the Georgia DOT was following one of those rule books*: U.S. Department of Transportation, "Section 4C.05 Warrant 4, Pedestrian Volume," in *Manual on Uniform Traffic Control Devices*, 2009. Bill Schultheiss (see: chapter 4 endnotes: *Ninety-nine people running across*) explained to me that, in this case, the Georgia DOT might

have also considered an alternative to a signalized intersection: a pedestrian hybrid beacon (a non-intersection crosswalk with a traffic signal activated by request that permits drivers to proceed at their discretion). The pedestrian "warrant"—as in the threshold required to be met to make intervention warranted—is lower to install one of these: twenty people an hour. If nineteen people cross, the official answer is to let the risk remain. "That," Schultheiss explains, "tells you exactly where these priorities lie. The warrant is twenty people, but the only warrant that should matter should be a dangerous road, a bus stop, a population that's car-free and that's transit dependent."

184 *In an interview with National Public Radio*: "Child's Death Casts Light on Pedestrian Traffic Woes," National Public Radio, July 30, 2011.

185 *The chief consequence of blame*: Dekker, *The Field Guide to Understanding 'Human Error,'* 1–14.

185 *In finding fault with a person*: "With human error attributions, participants were in greater agreement with the statement that an individual deserved to be punished for the accident and in less agreement that an organization or company was responsible for the accident," Nees, Sharma, and Shore concluded. "Our findings suggested that when an accident is attributed to human error in media, the public may be less likely to expect examination or mitigation of systemic shortcomings (e.g., in design, organizational practices, etc.) that precipitate accidents." See: Michael A. Nees, Nithya Sharma, and Ava Shore, "Attributions of Accidents to 'Human Error' in News Stories: Effects on Perceived Culpability, Perceived Preventability, and Perceived Need for Punishment," *Accident Analysis & Prevention* 148, no. 6 (2021): 105792.

185 *Studies show that this simple act*: Richard J. Holden, "People or Systems? To Blame Is Human. The Fix Is to Engineer," *Professional Safety* 54, no. 12 (2009): 34–41; Tara Goddard et al., "Does News Coverage of Traffic Crashes Affect Perceived Blame and Preferred Solutions? Evidence from an Experiment," *Transportation Research Interdisciplinary Perspectives* 3 (2019); Nees, Sharma, and Shore, "Attributions of Accidents to 'Human Error' in News Stories."

185 *But if you are cycling on an urban road*: A 4,000-pound vehicle traveling at 30 mph, the speed limit in New York City, for example, would have an impact of 5,470 pounds of force. A study by Tobias A. Mattei et al., "Performance Analysis of the Protective Effects of Bicycle Helmets," *Journal of Neurosurgical Pediatrics* 10, no. 6 (2012), found that only nine of thirteen bicycle helmets tested remained viable in crash tests at 470 pounds of force. A study by Alyssa L. DeMarco et al., "The Impact Response of Traditional and BMX-Style Bicycle Helmets at Different Impact Severities," *Accident Analysis & Prevention* 92 (2016), found that children's bicycle helmets could handle an impact speed of 6 meters per second or around 13 miles per hour. A study of autopsy reports from a variety of bikes crashes in the Czech Republic—some involving motor vehicles, others not—found that only 37 percent of the fatalities reviewed could have been survivable with a helmet, and that helmets would not have helped in most high-energy cases, and especially when cars or trains were involved (Michal Bíl et al., "Cycling Fatalities: When a Helmet Is Useless and When It Might Save Your Life," *Safety Science* 105 [2018], 71–76).

186 *When a drunk driver killed Eric*: Nicholas Confessore and Kate Hammer, "Drunken Driver Kills Rider on Bicycle Path, Police Say," *New York Times*, December 3, 2006.

186 *He was also struck head-on*: The vehicle make and model come from the MV-104A

Police Accident Report, obtained via Freedom of Information Act request. The vehicle weight was obtained from CarFax.com.

186 *A large body of evidence shows*: To name a few: Jessica B. Cicchino et al., "Not All Protected Bike Lanes Are the Same: Infrastructure and Risk of Cyclist Collisions and Falls Leading to Emergency Department Visits in Three U.S. Cities," *Accident Analysis & Prevention* 6, no. 141 (2020); Wesley E. Marshall and Nicholas N. Ferenchak, "Why Cities with High Bicycling Rates Are Safer for All Road Users," *Journal of Transportation & Health* 13 (2019); and Meghan Winters et al., "Impacts of Bicycle Infrastructure in Mid-Sized Cities (IBIMS): Protocol for a Natural Experiment Study in Three Canadian Cities," *BMJ Open* 8, no. 1 (2018); Jonathan Nolan, James Sinclair, and Jim Savage, "Are Bicycle Lanes Effective? The Relationship Between Passing Distance and Road Characteristics," *Accident Analysis & Prevention* 159 (2021).

186 *This reduces the number of drivers*: Eric Jaffe, "When Adding Bike Lanes Actually Reduces Traffic Delays," *Bloomberg CityLab*, September 5, 2014; Kate Hinds, "NYC DOT Says Brooklyn Bike Lane Dramatically Reduces Speeding, Sidewalk Bicycling," WNYC National Public Radio, October 21, 2010; Marshall and Ferenchak, "Why Cities with High Bicycling Rates Are Safer for All Road Users."

186 *There is also evidence that*: Ian Walker and Dorothy Robinson, "Bicycle Helmet Wearing Is Associated with Closer Overtaking by Drivers: A Response to Olivier and Walter, 2013," *Accident Analysis & Prevention* 123 (2019): 107–13; Colin F. Clarke, "Evaluation of New Zealand's Bicycle Helmet Law," *Journal of the New Zealand Medical Association* 125, no. 1349 (2012): 1–10; Chris Rissel and Li Ming Wen, "The Possible Effect on Frequency of Cycling if Mandatory Bicycle Helmet Legislation Was Repealed in Sydney, Australia: A Cross Sectional Survey," *Health Promotion Journal of Australia* 22, no. 3 (2011): 178–83; Peter L. Jacobsen, "Safety in Numbers: More Walkers and Bicyclists, Safer Walking and Bicycling," *Injury Prevention* 9 (2003): 205–9.

186 *While a higher number of people who ride bikes*: Kay Teschke et al., "Bicycling Injury Hospitalisation Rates in Canadian Jurisdictions: Analyses Examining Associations with Helmet Legislation and Mode Share," *BMJ Open* 5, no. 11 (2015).

186 *Among countries with high rates of bicycling*: Angie Schmitt, "Why Helmets Aren't the Answer to Bike Safety—In One Chart," *Streetsblog USA*, June 2, 2016.

186 *Even Giro, one of the largest*: "There are many misconceptions about helmets, unfortunately," Giro's Eric Richter told Mark Sutton at *Cycling Industry News*. "We do not design helmets specifically to reduce chances or severity of injury when impacts involve a car." ("Discussion: Are Helmet Standards Overdue a Revision?," July 6, 2020, cyclingindustry.news/discussion-are-helmet-standards-overdue-a-revision.) See also: Carlton Reid, "Bicycle Helmets Not Designed for Impacts from Cars, Stresses Leading Maker Giro," *Forbes*, July 10, 2020.

186 *But the blame*: Holden, "People or Systems? To Blame Is Human. The Fix Is to Engineer"; Nees, Sharma, and Shore, "Attributions of Accidents to 'Human Error' in News Stories"; Goddard et al., "Does News Coverage Affect Perceived Blame and Preferred Solutions?"

187 *In Seattle, police write as many as*: David Kroman, "Nearly Half of Seattle's Helmet Citations Go to Homeless People," Crosscut, Cascade Public Media, December 16, 2020.

187 *In Tampa, as many as 80 percent of cyclists*: Kameel Stanley, "How Riding Your Bike Can Land You in Trouble with the Cops—If You're Black," *Tampa Bay News*, April 20, 2015; Greg Ridgeway et al., "An Examination of Racial Disparities in Bicycle Stops and Citations Made by the Tampa Police Department: A Technical Assistance Report," Washington, DC, Office of Community Oriented Policing Services, 2016.

187 *The* Dallas Morning News *found that*: "With Dallas Bike Helmet Law, Rules of the Ride Enforced Unevenly," *Dallas Morning News*, June 3, 2014.

187 *The* Los Angeles Times *found*: Nicole Santa Cruz and Alene Tchekmedyian, "Deputies Killed Dijon Kizzee After a Bike Stop," *Los Angeles Times*, October, 16, 2020.

187 *Similar results are found in cities*: Dan Roe, "Black Cyclists Are Stopped More Often Than Whites, Police Data Shows," *Bicycling Magazine*, July 27, 2020.

187 *The bicycle helmet is such a predominant manifestation*: Gregg Culver, "Bike Helmets—A Dangerous Fixation? On the Bike Helmet's Place in the Cycling Safety Discourse in the United States," *Applied Mobilities* 5, no. 2 (2020): 138–54.

187 *And researchers have found that when we read*: Goddard et al., "Does News Coverage of Traffic Crashes Affect Perceived Blame and Preferred Solutions?"; Nees, Sharma, and Shore, "Attributions of Accidents to 'Human Error' in News Stories."

188 *One study did precisely this*: Goddard et al., "Does News Coverage Affect Perceived Blame and Preferred Solutions?"

188 *One study of budgets, accidental death, and U.S. cities*: C. R. Ronzio, E. Pamuk, and G. D. Squire, "The Politics of Preventable Death: Local Spending, Income Inequality, and Premature Mortality in US Cities," *Journal of Epidemiology and Community Health* 58, no. 3 (2004): 161.

189 *One study cataloging twelve years*: Anuja L. Sarode et al., "Traffic Stops Do Not Prevent Traffic Deaths," *Journal of Trauma and Acute Care Surgery* 91, no. 1 (2021).

189 *After World War II*: Sidney Dekker does a wonderful job summarizing the work of Fitts and Jones in "Disinheriting Fitts and Jones '47," *International Journal of Aviation Research and Development* 1, no. 1 (2001): 7–18. See also the original: Paul M. Fitts and Richard E. Jones, "Analysis of Factors Contributing to 460 'Pilot Error' Experiences in Operating Aircraft Controls," Memorandum Report TSEAA-694-12, Aero Medical Laboratory, Air Material Command, Wright-Patterson Air Force Base, Dayton, Ohio, July 1, 1947.

189 *They found that most accidents*: Ibid.

190 *They concluded that pilot error*: Dekker, *The Field Guide to Understanding 'Human Error*,' 15–20.

190 *It is as tempting to the experts*: Holden, "People or Systems? To Blame Is Human. The Fix Is to Engineer."

191 *Formal accident investigations* start with: Perrow, *Normal Accidents*, 146.

191 *In his book* The Field Guide to Understanding 'Human Error': Dekker, *The Field Guide to Understanding 'Human Error*,' 1–14.

191 *It sends a message that*: Ibid., 10–12.

191 *"Every time that we are confronted by"*: Dekker interview.

191 *But we cannot punish and learn*: Dekker, *The Field Guide to Understanding 'Human Error*,' 183–94.

192 *Research backs this up*: Sidney Dekker and Hugh Breakey, "'Just Culture': Improving

Safety by Achieving Substantive, Procedural and Restorative Justice," *Safety Science* 85 (2016); Sidney Dekker, "The Criminalization of Human Error in Aviation and Healthcare: A Review," *Safety Science* 49 (2011).

192 *Studies have found that the more retribution workers faced*: Hester J. Lipscomb et al., "Safety, Incentives, and the Reporting of Work-Related Injuries Among Union Carpenters: 'You're Pretty Much Screwed if You Get Hurt at Work,' " *American Journal of Industrial Medicine* 56, no. 4 (2013): 389–99.

192 *Other studies have identified that fear of punitive workplace policies*: Jeffery Taylor Moore et al., "Construction Workers' Reasons for Not Reporting Work-Related Injuries: An Exploratory Study," *International Journal of Occupational Safety and Ergonomics* 19, no. 1 (2013): 97–105.

192 *And still others found that workplaces that blamed workers*: Jeanne Geiger Brown et al., "Nurses' Inclination to Report Work-Related Injuries: Organizational, Work-Group, and Individual Factors Associated with Reporting," *American Association of Occupational Health Nursing Journal* 53, no. 5 (2005): 213–17.

192 *"Punishment focuses the attention on only one"*: Email correspondence with Dekker.

194 *The newspapers told a story of*: Charles Komanoff, "January 3rd: The Wrongdoer Is Brought to Justice," *Streetsblog NYC*, December 21, 2007.

194 *It was also designed with a double yellow line*: William Neuman, "State Considering Car Barriers After 2nd Death on Bike Path," *New York Times*, December 9, 2006.

194 *People in cars appeared on the path*: The *New York Times* cited these claims while calling Eric's death an accident: "Though Mr. Cidron's wrong turn appeared to be accidental, some cyclists who frequent the path—one of the quickest routes for cyclists to travel in Manhattan—say they have been dismayed at what they described as a recent increase in vehicles traveling along it" (Confessore and Hammer, "Drunken Driver Kills Rider on Bicycle Path, Police Say"). You can find some of these comments cached in Jen Chung, "Drunk Driver Kills Cyclist on West Side Bike Path," *Gothamist*, December 2, 2006, and referenced in Joe Schumacher, "Bike Path Barriers Being Considered," *Gothamist*, December 9, 2006. The problem remained newsworthy in 2010, as seen in a May 27 story on *Gothamist* by John Del Signore, "Sharing the Bike Path with Cars on Hudson River Greenway."

194 *Six months before Eric died*: Jen Chung, "West Side Bicyclist Doctor Dies from Injuries," *Gothamist*, June 27, 2006.

194 *Nine years after Eric died*: Maya Rajamani, "Cyclist Death Caused by Bad Design at Hudson River Greenway Crossing: Suit," *DNAinfo*, July 3, 2017.

194 *A year after Eric died*: Transportation Alternatives, "A Year After Eric Ng's Death, Greenway Hazards Remain Unfixed," *Streetsblog NYC*, January 4, 2008.

194 *That survey was part of an effort*: Those activists primarily came from Transportation Alternatives, a New York City nonprofit organization. I would join the organization as a staff writer a few years later, and remain on staff there today. On permanent barriers: Transportation Alternatives, "Rethinking Bollards: How Bollards Can Save Lives, Prevent Injuries and Relieve Traffic Congestion in New York City," July 2007, 13, transalt.org/sites/default/files/news/reports/2007/rethinking_bollards.pdf.

195 *The activists called for officials*: Sharon Otterman, "Manhattan Terror Attack Exposes Bike Path's Vulnerable Crossings," *New York Times*, November 1, 2017.

195 *They also monitored the path*: Transportation Alternatives, "Drunk Driver Sentenced,

Danger Remains: 1 Year After Biker Was Killed, No Fix to the Greenway," press release, January 3, 2007; Transportation Alternatives, "A Year After Eric Ng's Death, Greenway Hazards Remain Unfixed."

195 *Government officials even provided evidence*: Eillie Anzilotti, "If Cars Are Weapons, Then Safe Streets Are the Best Counterterrorism," *Fast Company*, November 1, 2017.

195 *The activists noted that the recommendation chief among their proposed solutions*: Transportation Alternatives, "Rethinking Bollards," 15; At some point between 2007 and 2009, the City of New York installed a small number of metal barriers (bollards) along the thirteen-mile-long path. This included the entrance where the driver who killed Eric turned onto the path—however, it was placed in such a way that you could still drive right by it. (See: Otterman, "Manhattan Terror Attack Exposes Bike Path's Vulnerable Crossings.") Of close to a hundred opportunities for car drivers to enter the path, government officials protected just a few—a tacit admission of the problem while declining to fully solve it. As the *New York Times* put it after the terror attack, "Despite calls to improve safety on the path since that time, recommended steps were not taken. In particular, bollards—metal poles that would block vehicles from accessing the path—were not installed at most of the access points where cars can turn onto the path." In that article, my brilliant former colleague Caroline Samponaro, then deputy director of Transportation Alternatives, pointed out how understanding Eric's death as an "accident" ceded the ability to prevent the crime: "We have left it up to chance despite the fact that someone has been killed there before," she told the *Times*. "While terrorism is not preventable, the ability for a driver to drive there was." (See: Otterman, "Manhattan Terror Attack Exposes Bike Path's Vulnerable Crossings.")

195 *On October 31, 2017*: Benjamin Mueller, William K. Rashbaum, and Al Baker, "Terror Attack Kills 8 and Injures 11 in Manhattan," *New York Times*, October 31, 2017.

196 *Saipov had entered the path at West Houston Street*: Sarah Almukhtar et al., "Trail of Terror in the Manhattan Truck Attack," *New York Times*, October 31, 2017.

Chapter Nine: Prevention

This chapter is indebted to a 2016 opinion article in the *New York Times* by Chase Madar, "The Real Crime Is What's Not Done," and is based on the voluminous writings of physician William Haddon and epidemiologist Susan P. Baker, as well as interviews with Baker, Vision Zero founder Claes Tingvall, founder and executive director of NEXT Harm Reduction Jamie Favaro, geriatric researcher Kenneth Covinsky, and martial artist Mike Grigsby.

197 *In the 1850s, a cholera epidemic swept through London*: Theodore H. Tulchinsky, "John Snow, Cholera, the Broad Street Pump; Waterborne Diseases Then and Now," *Case Studies in Public Health* (2018): 77–99. See also: Dumbaugh and Gattis, "Safe Streets, Livable Streets."

197 *The other way*: Interview with Susan P. Baker.

197 *Like Crystal Eastman and Hugh DeHaven*: Robert W. Stock, "Safety Lessons from the Morgue," *New York Times Magazine*, October 26, 2012.

198 *And besides, she tells me*: Baker interview.

198 *If we focused on human error*: William Haddon, "The Changing Approach to the Epidemiology, Prevention, and Amelioration of Trauma: The Transition to Approaches Etiologically Rather Than Descriptively Based," *American Journal of Public Health and the Nation's Health* 58, no. 8 (1968): 1431–38; Susan P. Baker, "Childhood Injuries: The Community Approach to Prevention," *Journal of Public Health Policy* 2 (1981): 235–46.

198 *but the tools and resources*: Sue interview.

198 *Looking at the breadth and depth*: Baker interview.

198 *In 2009—three years after Eric died*: Pretrial deposition of Conn MacAogain on January 13 and January 27, 2009, at the New York City Law Department, obtained via Freedom of Information Law request to the appropriate agencies of the City of New York.

199 *In the deposition, a lawyer*: Ibid.

199 *"It is to delineate the bikeway for cyclists"*: Ibid.

199 *Bollards can be flexible and plastic*: Transportation Alternatives, "Rethinking Bollards."

199 *The next day, government workers*: Confessore and Hammer, "Drunken Driver Kills Rider on Bicycle Path, Police Say." See also: chapter 8 endnotes: *The activists noted that the recommendation chief among their proposed solutions.*

199 *But a few days after Sayfullo Saipov drove over*: Paul Berger, "Concrete Barriers to Be Installed Along Hudson River Greenway," *Wall Street Journal*, November 2, 2017.

200 *A few hours after Saipov injured twelve*: Jessie Singer, "We Should Ban Cars from Big Cities," *BuzzFeed*, November 3, 2017.

200 *Conservative luminaries picked up*: Laura Loomer tweeted "@Buzzfeed thinks we should keep Muslim terrorists in our cities but ban all cars. I'm going to go with @realDonaldTrump's travel ban" (November 4, 2017). Erick Erickson retweeted the piece, adding, "Progressivism really is a mental health illness with a defined pathological trajectory" (November 3, 2017). See screenshots at twitter.com/jessiesingernyc /status/930952210594324483.

200 *An editorial in the* Washington Examiner: Siraj Hashmi, "Let's Not Cave to Terrorists by Banning Cars in Cities," *Washington Examiner*, November 3, 2017.

201 *In 1970, William Haddon*: Unless otherwise noted, this section comes from interviews with Baker and two essays by Haddon: "On the Escape of Tigers: An Ecologic Note," *American Journal of Public Health and the Nation's Health* 60, no. 12 (1970): 2229–34, and "Energy Damage and the Ten Countermeasure Strategies," *Journal of Trauma* 13 (1973): 321–31.

201 *He reduced the energy to types*: Part of Haddon's point was that by focusing on energy we can better understand prevention. Related to this is the fact that energy is a more accurate measure of the potential harm of an accident than, say, speed. If you double your driving speed, for example, you might assume that you've doubled your risk of injury, but doubling your speed actually quadruples your kinetic energy, and as Haddon notes, in an accident, it's the energy that will kill you.

203 *We can see a Haddon approach*: Naina Bajekal, "Want to Win the War on Drugs? Portugal Might Have the Answer," *Time*, August 1, 2018.

204 *These sorts of countermeasures work so well*: Austin Frakt, "Pointers from Portugal on Addiction and the Drug War," *New York Times*, October 5, 2020.

204 *In Portugal, accidental opioid overdose*: Bajekal, "Want to Win the War on Drugs?"

204 *The number of people in drug treatment rose*: From 23,654 in 1998 to 38,532 in 2008; Hannah Laqueur, "Uses and Abuses of Drug Decriminalization in Portugal," *Law & Social Inquiry* 40, no. 746 (2015).

204 *Murders rose for seven years*: Following the initial rise in murders, there was a small decrease from 2003 to 2005 and then another rise. UN Office on Drugs and Crime's International Homicide Statistics, "Intentional Homicides (per 100,000 People): Portugal," The World Bank, data.worldbank.org/indicator/VC.IHR.PSRC.P5?loca tions=PT.

205 *Susan P. Baker, who worked alongside Haddon*: Baker interview.

205 *Between 2009 and 2019*: National Safety Council, "Pedestrian Deaths in Traffic Crashes by Year, United States, 1994–2019," Injury Facts, injuryfacts.nsc.org/motor-vehicle /road-users/pedestrians/data-details.

205 *Notably, deadly accidents for people*: The proportion of people killed "inside the vehicle" fell from 80 percent of fatalities in 1996 to 66 percent in 2019; the proportion of people killed "outside the vehicle" rose from 20 percent in 1996 to 34 percent in 2019. See: National Highway Traffic Safety Administration, "Overview of Motor Vehicle Crashes in 2019," *Traffic Safety Facts: Research Note*, December 2020, crashstats .nhtsa.dot.gov/Api/Public/ViewPublication/813060.

205 *One 2018 analysis charts what people*: Heidi Coleman and Krista Mizenko, "Pedestrian and Bicyclist Data Analysis," in National Highway Traffic Safety Administration, *Traffic Safety Facts: Research Note*, March 2018, nhtsa.gov/sites/nhtsa .gov/files/documents/812502_pedestrian-and-bicyclist-data-analysis-tsf-research -note.pdf.

206 *While the body count grew*: National Highway Traffic Safety Administration, "Pedestrians," *Traffic Safety Facts, 2011 Data*, August 2013, crashstats.nhtsa.dot.gov/Api /Public/ViewPublication/811748.

206 *Pedestrian deaths are rising*: Eric D. Lawrence, Nathan Bomey, and Kristi Tanner, "Death on Foot: America's Love of SUVs Is Killing Pedestrians, and Federal Safety Regulators Have Known for Years," *Detroit Free Press*, June 28, 2018; Insurance Institute for Highway Safety, "On Foot, at Risk," *Status Report* 53, no. 3 (2018): 1–8.

206 *Average weight of a vehicle*: From 1,744 kg / 3,845 lbs to 1,921 / 4,235 lbs. See: Justin Tyndall, "Pedestrian Deaths and Large Vehicles," *Economics of Transportation* 26–27 (2021).

206 *Between 2009 and 2016*: Lawrence, Bomey, and Tanner, "Death on Foot."

206 *One researcher estimated that*: Tyndall, "Pedestrian Deaths and Large Vehicles."

206 *If children are sitting in front of that vehicle*: Bob Segall, "13 Investigates: Millions of Vehicles Have Unexpected, Dangerous Front Blind Zone," NBC 13: WTHR, April 25, 2019.

207 *Backing up is not much better*: "The Danger of Blind Zones: The Area Behind Your Vehicle Can Be a Killing Zone," *Consumer Reports*, April 2014, consumerreports .org/cro/2012/03/the-danger-of-blind-zones/index.htm.

207 *Their engineers had known for decades*: Lawrence, Bomey, and Tanner, "Death on Foot."

207 *As long ago as 1975*: Kea Wilson, "Why Regulators Aren't Taming the U.S. Megacar Crisis," *Streetsblog USA*, June 4, 2021.

207 *By 1997, the department demonstrated*: Charles J. Kahane, "Relationships Between

Vehicle Size and Fatality Risk in Model Year 1985–93 Passenger Cars and Light Trucks," National Highway Traffic Safety Administration Technical Report DOT HS 808 570, January 1997, crashstats.nhtsa.dot.gov/Api/Public/ViewPublication/808570; Nathan Bomey, "Why SUVs Are Getting Bigger and Bigger: GM, Toyota, Ford Enlarge Hefty Vehicles," *USA Today*, December 27, 2019; Tom Voelk, "Rise of S.U.V.s: Leaving Cars in Their Dust, with No Signs of Slowing," *New York Times*, May 21, 2020.

207 *As early as 2001*: Devon E. Lefler and Hampton C. Gabler, "The Emerging Threat of Light Truck Impacts with Pedestrians," International Technical Conference on Enhanced Safety of Vehicles, May 2001.

207 *They found that adults*: Lawrence, Bomey, and Tanner, "Death on Foot."

207 *But still, as pedestrian fatalities rose*: National Highway Traffic Safety Administration, "Consumer Advisory: Traffic Safety Agency Urges Pedestrians to Walk with Care," press release, August 6, 2012.

207 *In New York City, pedestrians under*: New York City Department of Health and Mental Hygiene, "*Epi Data Brief* no. 86, Pedestrian Fatalities in New York City," March 2017.

208 *Women are less likely to buy big cars*: John Saylor, "The Road to Transport Justice: Reframing Auto Safety in the SUV Age," *University of Pennsylvania Law Review* (forthcoming, 2021); Insurance Institute for Highway Safety, "Vehicle Choice, Crash Differences Help Explain Greater Injury Risks for Women," February 11, 2021, iihs .org/news/detail/vehicle-choice-crash-differences-help-explain-greater-injury-risks -for-women.

208 *Low-income people are more likely*: Emily Badger, "The Hidden Inequality of Who Dies in Car Crashes," *Washington Post*, October 1, 2015.

208 *The owners of big cars such as SUVs*: Saylor, "The Road to Transport Justice."

208 *And, as we know, the pedestrians most likely*: CDC WISQARS Fatal Injury Reports, webappa.cdc.gov/sasweb/ncipc/mortrate.html.

208 *But since 1997 in Europe*: United States Government Accountability Office, "NHTSA Needs to Decide Whether to Include Pedestrian Safety Tests in Its New Car Assessment Program," Report to the Ranking Member, Committee on Environment and Public Works, U.S. Senate, April 2020.

208 *When these regulations were first published internationally*: Angie Schmitt, "While Other Countries Mandate Safer Car Designs for Pedestrians, America Does Nothing," *Streetsblog USA*, December 7, 2017; Insurance Institute for Highway Safety, "On Foot, at Risk."

208 *While the National Highway Traffic Safety Administration*: Lawrence, Bomey, and Tanner, "Death on Foot."

208 *As a result, the number of pedestrians killed*: Jake Blumgart, "Why Are Pedestrian Deaths at Epidemic Levels?," *Governing*, July 23, 2021; International Transport Forum, "Road Safety Data 2020: Japan," Organisation for Economic Co-operation and Development, itf-oecd.org/sites/default/files/japan-road-safety.pdf.

209 *In 2020, British lawmakers*: Roger Harrabin, "US Cars Must Be Left Out of Post-Brexit Trade Deal," BBC News, July 18, 2020.

209 *As then U.S. secretary of transportation Elaine Chao*: On Twitter (@SecElaineChao) on October 26, 2020.

209 *The number of Americans killed in falls*: Since the opioid epidemic drove accidental poisoning deaths into the number one spot, falls and traffic fatalities take turns occupying the number two and three spots, depending on the year. Looking from 1999 to 2019, traffic fatalities dominate; however, in 2019, there were 39,107 killed in traffic accidents and 39,443 killed in accidental falls. Still, the age-adjusted death rate (controlled for the effect of differences in population-age distribution) for traffic accidents is higher. See: CDC WISQARS Fatal Injury Reports, webappa.cdc.gov /sasweb/ncipc/mortrate.html.

210 *But in 2019, people died*: CDC WISQARS Fatal Injury Reports, webappa.cdc.gov /sasweb/ncipc/mortrate.html.

210 *In 2005, the National Council on Aging*: National Council on Aging, "About the Falls Free® Initiative," January 4, 2021, ncoa.org/article/about-the-falls-free-initiative.

210 *The Centers for Disease Control and Prevention created STEADI*: Centers for Disease Control and Prevention, "STEADI: Older Adult Fall Prevention," https://www.cdc .gov/falls/index.html.

210 *The version of this program developed by*: National Institutes on Aging, "Prevent Falls and Fractures," March 15, 2017, nia.nih.gov/health/prevent-falls-and-fractures.

210 *And all the advice wraps up*: You can find this all over, but for two examples, see: National Council on Aging, "Falls Prevention Awareness Week Promotion Toolkit," August 3, 2021, ncoa.org/article/falls-prevention-awareness-week-toolkit and STEADI, "Patient and Caregiver Resources," cdc.gov/steadi/patient.html.

210 *In 2008 the Centers for Medicare and Medicaid Services*: Jared Hossack, "Medicare's 'Never-Event' Initiative," *American Medical Association Journal of Ethics* 10, no. 5 (2008): 312–16.

211 *(Almost all older Americans)*: Administration for Community Living, "2019 Profile of Older Americans," May 2020, acl.gov/aging-and-disability-in-america/data-and -research/profile-older-americans.

211 *Falling became what the U.S. government*: Melissa Bailey, "Overzealous in Preventing Falls, Hospitals Are Producing an 'Epidemic of Immobility' in Elderly Patients," *Washington Post*, October 13, 2019; Hossack, "Medicare's 'Never-Event' Initiative."

211 *The result of all this enforcement*: Ibid.

211 *Because the muscles of an older person*: Interview with Kenneth Covinsky, a clinician researcher in the University of California Division of Geriatric Medicine. See also: Kenneth E. Covinsky et al., "Loss of Independence in Activities of Daily Living in Older Adults Hospitalized with Medical Illnesses: Increased Vulnerability with Age," *Journal of the American Geriatrics Society* 51, no. 4 (2003): 451–58.

211 *One study of this phenomenon*: Covinsky et al., "Loss of Independence in Activities of Daily Living in Older Adults Hospitalized with Medical Illnesses."

211 *Researchers studying nurses and nursing assistants*: Barbara King et al., "Impact of Fall Prevention on Nurses and Care of Fall Risk Patients," *Gerontologist* 19, no. 58 (2018): 331–40.

212 *Mike Grigsby, a retired biomedical engineer*: Interview with Mike Grigsby, creator of Fearless Falling.

213 *Over the years, Grigsby has taught*: Ibid.

213 *In the Netherlands, "falling classes" are gaining*: Christopher F. Schuetze, "Afraid of Falling? For Older Adults, the Dutch Have a Cure," *New York Times*, January 2, 2018.

214 *In the 1980s, there was a heroin problem across Merseyside*: Diane Riley et al., "A Brief History of Harm Reduction," in *Harm Reduction in Substance Use and High-Risk Behaviour*, eds. Richard Pates and Diane Riley (Hoboken, NJ: Wiley, 2012): 11–12.

214 *The goals of the Mersey Regional Drug Training*: Ibid.

214 *The results of the new program*: Ibid.

214 *In ten countries*: Drug Policy Alliance, "Supervised Consumption Services," drug policy.org/issues/supervised-consumption-services.

215 *Portugal's HIV infection rate*: Bajekal, "Want to Win the War on Drugs?"

215 *no safe injection sites existed*: German Lopez, "Trump's Justice Department Is Threatening Cities That Allow Safe Injection Sites: A Showdown over Safe Injection Sites Is Brewing Between the Federal Government and Cities," *Vox*, August 30, 2018.

215 *(In the summer of 2021)*: Drug Policy Alliance, "Drug Policy Alliance Statement on Rhode Island Becoming First in the Nation to Authorize Harm Reduction Centers to Prevent Overdose Deaths," press release, July 7, 2021.

215 *In Little Falls, Minnesota*: Ibid.

215 *In Huntington, West Virginia*: Dan Vergano, "Here's How One Small Town Beat the Opioid Epidemic: Little Falls, Minnesota, Didn't Do Anything Revolutionary. They Just Made a Real Effort—and Spent Real Money—Treating Addiction as a Disease, Not a Crime," *BuzzFeed News*, February 25, 2019.

215 *In another West Virginia town*: Kara Leigh Lofton, "Diving Deep into Harm Reduction, Part 1: Why W.Va.'s Largest Needle Exchange Closed," Morehead State Public Radio, November 26, 2018.

216 *In 2015, Jamie Favaro was*: Interview with Jamie Favaro, founder of NEXT Harm Reduction.

216 *Mitchell spoke about meeting people*: Ibid.

216 *Two years later, she launched*: Ibid.

217 *Favaro posits that the accidental deaths*: Ibid.

217 *She points out that accidental overdoses*: Ibid.

217 *Soon after NEXT Harm Reduction launched*: Ibid.

218 *Claes Tingvall, a traffic safety specialist*: Interview with Claes Tingvall, founder of Sweden's Vision Zero program.

218 *This is still the expectation of U.S.*: As the 2011 edition of the traffic engineers' rule book *A Policy on Geometric Design of Highways and Streets* puts it, "In selection of design speed, every effort should be made to attain a desired combination of safety, mobility, and efficiency within the constraints of environmental quality, economics, aesthetics, and social or political impacts" (2–54). In the design of U.S. roads, whether or not you live or die is of equal importance as to whether or not you sit in traffic.

219 *No more would the government blame*: Claes Tingvall and Maria Krafft, "Defending Vision Zero," *Vision Zero Cities: International Journal of Traffic Safety Innovation*, October 23, 2018.

219 *In two decades, as traffic volume grew*: Zainab Mudallal, "Why Sweden Has the World's Safest Roads," Quartz, December 31, 2014.

219 *Today the per capita rate*: Woolf and Aron, *Health in International Perspective*, 28–31.

Chapter Ten: Accountability

To better understand what accountability for accidents currently looks like, and what it would take to restore the systems that be, I spoke with Ralph Nader, who brought into being most of the mechanisms for systemic corporate accountability that do exist today, however hobbled they are since their short heyday; Joan Claybrook, former lobbyist for Public Citizen and former head of the National Highway Traffic Safety Administration; Amit Narang, regulatory policy advocate at Public Citizen; Joanne Doroshow, executive director of the Center for Justice and Democracy; Greg Shill, a law professor who specializes in transportation; and Steven Casner, a research psychologist at the NASA Ames Research Center, who helped me understand how and why necessitating that human beings monitor automated machines will often result in accidents; as well as three experts in restorative justice practices: Colorado senator Pete Lee, and practitioners Lynn Lee and Ken Jaray.

221 *The workplace safety expert Sidney Dekker*: Dekker, *The Field Guide to Understanding 'Human Error*,' 195–203.
221 *Dekker notes that these recommendations*: Ibid., 173–81.
221 *"The ease of implementation"*: Ibid., 175.
222 *High-end recommendations, he writes*: Ibid.
222 *As the prison abolition leader*: Mariame Kaba, *We Do This 'Til We Free Us: Abolitionist Organizing and Transforming Justice* (Chicago: Haymarket Books, 2021), 97.
222 *In terms of structured and wholesale accountability*: "Prosecution and regulation are not mutually exclusive, but political energy and media attention are disproportionately expended by the lust for criminal punishment," lawyer and journalist Chase Madar wrote in the *New York Times*. "Though these sorts of charges fulfill an emotional need for retribution and are of great benefit to district attorneys on the make, they are seldom more than a mediagenic booby prize. Prosecutorial responses fill the void left when health and safety regulations succumb to corporate and political pressure." ("The Real Crime Is What's Not Done," August 24, 2016.)
223 *Ralph Nader sees this structured*: Interview with Ralph Nader. In 1975, Nader described these government protections as a matter of unknowable risk and ethical governance. "Can consumers smell carbon monoxide seeping into a car, detect that the drug they are giving their children is mutagenic, or taste the cancerous pesticides that went into the production of their food? Or can they refuse to breathe the air pollution given off by local steel mills?" he wrote. "Where the consumer stands exposed to the kind of technological violence that the marketplace alone cannot contain—sharp protrusions on a dashboard, DDT, radioactive materials, asbestos fibers dumped into our lakes—then government regulation is a humane sine qua non for the public safety." (Nader, "Deregulation Is Another Consumer Fraud," *New York Times*, June 29, 1957.)
224 *every other president for the past forty years*: Interview with Amit Narang, regulatory policy advocate at Public Citizen.
224 *The number of people who've filed a tort lawsuit*: Joe Palazzolo, "We Won't See You in Court: The Era of Tort Lawsuits Is Waning," *Wall Street Journal*, July 24, 2017;

Joanne Doroshow and Emily Gottlieb, "Briefing Book: Tort Litigation by the Numbers. Center for Justice and Democracy" (2016), https://digitalcommons.nyls.edu/fac_other_pubs/17.

224 *On June 27, 2011, in Raleigh County*: Ken Ward Jr., "Trump MSHA Nominee Could Face Questions About Safety Record," *Charleston Gazette-Mail*, October 3, 2017.

225 *His first act was to revoke*: Juliet Eilperin, "Mining Safety Agency Proposes Relaxing Inspection Rule for Hard Rock Mines," *Washington Post*, September 13, 2017.

225 *The new rule also said*: Mine Safety and Health Administration, "Examinations of Working Places in Metal and Nonmetal Mines," *Federal Register: The Daily Journal of the United States Government*, April 9, 2018, federalregister.gov/documents/2018/04/09/2018-07084/examinations-of-working-places-in-metal-and-nonmetal-mines.

225 *According to Ralph Nader*: Nader interview.

225 *It was the second fatal crash of a Boeing 737 Max*: Andy Pasztor and Andrew Tangel, "Internal FAA Review Saw High Risk of 737 MAX Crashes," *Wall Street Journal*, December 11, 2019.

225 *Captain Chesley B. "Sully" Sullenberger*: Statement of Chesley B. "Sully" Sullenberger III before the Subcommittee on Aviation of the United States House Committee on Transportation and Infrastructure, June 19, 2019.

226 *The 737 Max was a redesign*: Jack Nicas and Julie Creswell, "Boeing's 737 Max: 1960s Design, 1990s Computing Power and Paper Manuals," *New York Times*, April 8, 2019.

226 *"It has been suggested that even if "*: Sullenberger statement.

226 *Boeing's assumption contradicts everything*: Interview with NASA research psychologist Steve Casner. See also: Stephen M. Casner, "The Retention of Manual Flying Skills in the Automated Cockpit," *Human Factors* 56, no. 8 (2014): 1506-16.

226 *Sullenberger told the committee*: Sullenberger statement.

226 *MCAS—that is, Maneuvering Characteristics Augmentation System*: Excellent visual reporting in the *Seattle Times* helps explain how this worked. See: Dominic Gates, "FAA Cautions Airlines on Maintenance of Sensors That Were Key to 737 MAX Crashes," August 20, 2019. See also: Gregory Travis, "How the Boeing 737 Max Disaster Looks to a Software Developer," *IEEE Spectrum*, April 18, 2019; Sullenberger statement.

227 *Boeing didn't even tell pilots*: Michael Laris, "Changes to Flawed Boeing 737 Max Were Kept from Pilots, DeFazio Says," *Washington Post*, June 19, 2019; Sullenberger statement.

227 *Regulatory capture invades every corner*: Paul Roberts, "Delegating Aircraft Safety Assessments to Boeing Is Nothing New for the FAA," *Seattle Times*, March 18, 2019.

227 *First, the head of aviation safety*: Dominic Gates, "Former Seattle FAA Official Gets Top Aviation Safety Post, After a Stint at Industry Group," *Seattle Times*, May 25, 2017.

227 *And before the accidents*: Natalie Kitroeff and David Gelles, "Before Deadly Crashes, Boeing Pushed for Law That Undercut Oversight," *New York Times*, October 27, 2019.

227 *Moreover, when Boeing tested*: David Schaper, "Boeing Pilots Detected 737 Max Flight Control Glitch 2 Years Before Deadly Crash," National Public Radio, October 18, 2019.

227 *The company also removed all mentions*: Laris, "Changes to Flawed Boeing 737 Max Were Kept from Pilots, DeFazio Says."

228 *"It's fundamentally embedded in the handling qualities"*: Benjamin Zhang, "Boeing's CEO Explains Why the Company Didn't Tell 737 Max Pilots About the Software System That Contributed to 2 Fatal Crashes," *Business Insider*, April 29, 2019.

228 *The* New York Times *reported that*: Hannah Beech and Muktita Suhartono, "Confusion, Then Prayer, in Cockpit of Doomed Lion Air Jet," *New York Times*, March 20, 2019.

228 *Uber came to Arizona to field-test*: Mark Harris, "Exclusive: Arizona Governor and Uber Kept Self-Driving Program Secret, Emails Reveal," *Guardian*, March 28, 2018.

229 *After California ejected the company's vehicles*: Sam Levin, "Uber Cancels Self-Driving Car Trial in San Francisco After State Forces It Off Road," *Guardian*, December 21, 2016.

229 *in March 2018, an Uber driverless car*: Richard Gonzales, "Feds Say Self-Driving Uber SUV Did Not Recognize Jaywalking Pedestrian in Fatal Crash," National Public Radio, November 7, 2019.

229 *Despite the car's having detected something*: Aarian Marshall and Alex Davies, "Uber's Self-Driving Car Didn't Know Pedestrians Could Jaywalk," *Wired*, November 5, 2019.

229 *After the fact, the logs showed*: "Uber Car 'Had Six Seconds to Respond' in Fatal Crash," BBC News, May 24, 2018.

229 *Of course, a driverless car could be*: Interviews with Greg Shill, a law professor who specializes in the intersection of transportation and the law, aided my understanding of Herzberg's killing. You can read more about Uber turning off Volvo's emergency braking system in Andrew J. Hawkins, "Uber Self-Driving Car Saw Pedestrian but Didn't Brake Before Fatal Crash, Feds Say," *The Verge*, May 24, 2018, and Daisuke Wakabayashi, "Emergency Braking Was Disabled When Self-Driving Uber Killed Woman, Report Says," *New York Times*, May 24, 2018. Phillip Koopman and Beth Osyk wrote a helpful paper explaining the problems with human monitors as a safety failsafe for driverless cars and the potential desire on behalf of automakers to minimize disengagements: "Safety Argument Considerations for Public Road Testing of Autonomous Vehicles," *SAE International Journal of Advances and Current Practices in Mobility* 1, no. 2 (2019): 512–23. See also: National Transportation Safety Board, "Collision Between Vehicle Controlled by Developmental Automated Driving System and Pedestrian, Tempe, Arizona, March 18, 2018," *Highway Accident Report*: NTSB/HAR-19/03, November 19, 2019: 55.

229 *While state regulations vary*: Aarian Marshall, "Who's Regulating Self-Driving Cars? Often, No One," *Wired*, November 27, 2019; Consumer Reports, "Consumer Reports: Uber Crash Should Be 'A Wake-Up Call' for Companies Developing Self-Driving Cars, DOT, and State Governments," press release, November 19, 2019; Clifford Atiyeh, "Self-Driving Cars' Look, Feel Is Clearer through Final U.S. Safety Rules," *Car and Driver*, January 23, 2021.

230 *That changed when, in response*: Clifford Law, "The Dangers of Driverless Cars," *The National Law Review* 11, no. 125 (2021); Sebastian Blanco, "NHTSA Tells Autonomous Tech Companies They Need to Report Crashes," *Car and Driver*, July 6, 2021; Marshall, "Who's Regulating Self-Driving Cars?"

230 *Otherwise, there are no safety standards*: Congressional Research Service, "Issues in Autonomous Vehicle Testing and Deployment," April 23, 2021, fas.org/sgp/crs/misc/R45985.pdf; Andrew J. Hawkins, "Congress Resurrects Push to Allow Thousands More Autonomous Vehicles on the Road," *The Verge*, April 22, 2021.

230 *As of 2019, more than 1,400 driverless cars*: Darrell Etherington, "Over 1,400 Self-Driving Vehicles Are Now in Testing by 80+ Companies Across the US," *TechCrunch*, June 11, 2019.

230 *In 2019, the U.S. Department of Transportation*: Eliza Fawcett, "Driverless Car Makers Want Congress to Free Them from State Oversight," *Los Angeles Times*, July 11, 2018.

230 *Joan Claybrook was the chief lobbyist*: Jenny King, "For 30 Years, NHTSA Has Worked to Make Cars, Highways Safe," *Chicago Tribune*, July 27, 1997.

230 *There, in the late 1970s, she proved*: Joan Claybrook, "NCAP at 40: Time to Return to Excellence," Advocates for Highway and Auto Safety, October 17, 2019.

230 *The U.S. Department of Transportation should be*: Interviews with Joan Claybrook, former head of NHTSA, and Carl Nash, former chief of the NHTSA Crash Investigation Division.

230 *As a result, she says, autonomous vehicles are not ready*: Claybrook interview.

231 *Instead of regulation, NHTSA has issued*: "U.S. Department of Transportation Releases 'Preparing for the Future of Transportation: Automated Vehicles 3.0,'" Department of Transportation press release, October 4, 2018.

231 *Instead, accidents happen because corporations*: Narang interview.

231 *For example, Purdue Pharma did not market*: Austin Frakt, "Damage from OxyContin Continues to Be Revealed," *New York Times*, April 13, 2020.

231 *Amit Narang, an expert in regulatory policy*: Narang interview.

232 *Between the 1950s and the 1970s, activists*: Ibid.

232 *In 1980, Americans elected Ronald Reagan*: For a short history, see Frank Swoboda, "The Legacy of Deregulation," *Washington Post*, October 2, 1988. And for a long one, see Craig J. Jenkins and Craig M. Eckert, "The Right Turn in Economic Policy: Business Elites and the New Conservative Economics," *Sociological Forum* 15, no. 2 (2000): 307–38.

232 *He would issue an executive order requiring that every regulation*: Presidential Exec. Order no. 12, 291, 46 Fed. Reg. 13, 193, 3 CFR (February 17, 1981), archives.gov/federal-register/codification/executive-order/12291.html.

232 *For the next forty years, corporate lobbyists*: Narang interview.

232 *There is a lot of evidence that regulations*: Ibid. See also: David Levine, Michael Toffel, and Matthew Johnson, "Randomized Government Safety Inspections Reduce Worker Injuries with No Detectable Job Loss," *Science* 336 (2012): 907–11.

232 *Car recalls are prompted by accidents*: Danielle Ivory and Rebecca R. Ruiz, "Recalls of Cars Abroad Prompt No Urgency in U.S.," *New York Times*, December 16, 2014.

233 *As of 2017, NHTSA investigations*: Jeff Plungis, "U.S. Auto-Safety Agency's Defect Investigations at Historic Low," *Consumer Reports*, June 29, 2018.

233 *The budget of the Environmental Protection Agency*: Keith Gaby, "EPA's Budget Has Been Devastated for Decades: Here's the Math," *The Hill*, January 24, 2018.

233 *The staff of the Occupational Safety and Health Administration*: Deborah Berkowitz, "Workplace Safety Enforcement Continues to Decline in Trump Administration," National Employment Law Project, March 14, 2019.

233 *In 2013, the West Chemical and Fertilizer Company*: Theodoric Meyer, "What Went Wrong in West, Texas—and Where Were the Regulators?," ProPublica, April 25, 2013; Manny Fernandez and Steven Greenhouse, "Texas Fertilizer Plant Fell Through Regulatory Cracks," *New York Times*, April 24, 2013; Colin Lecher, "What Is Anhydrous Ammonia, the Chemical at the Site of the West, Texas, Explosion?," *Popular Science*, April 18, 2013.

233 *Regulations are preventative*: Narang interview.

234 *The Office of Management and Budget*: Celine McNicholas, Heidi Shierholz, and Marni von Wilpert, "Workers' Health, Safety, and Pay Are Among the Casualties of Trump's War on Regulations," Economic Policy Institute, January 29, 2018.

234 *It estimated the societal benefit of 137 regulations*: These numbers are from 2016 because the Trump Administration failed to publish the report for three years, 2018–2020, despite being required to do so, and when they finally did publish in 2020, they published an "amalgamated" report for those years without the required regulatory cost-benefit estimate. See: Clyde Wayne Crews Jr., "Trump White House Quietly Releases Overdue Regulatory Cost-Benefit Reports," *Forbes*, January 6, 2020.

235 *Tort law provides accountability*: Interview with Joanne Doroshow, executive director of the Center for Justice and Democracy.

235 *These lawsuits can create accountability*: Ibid.

235 *But today, people file fewer and fewer*: Palazzolo, "We Won't See You in Court: The Era of Tort Lawsuits Is Waning."

235 *Tort reform is a euphemism*: Doroshow interview.

235 *In 1986, a few hundred of the largest*: Ibid. See also: F. Patrick Hubbard, "The Nature and Impact of the 'Tort Reform' Movement," *Hofstra Law Review* 35, no. 437 (2006): 437–535; Joanne Doroshow, "The U.S. Chamber's Defective Litigation Machine," *Huffington Post*, April 11, 2016; Center for Justice and Democracy, "Fact Sheet: American Tort Reform Association," centerjd.org/content/fact-sheet-american-tort-reform-association; Center for Justice and Democracy, "Factsheet: U.S. Chamber of Commerce Liability Survey—Inaccurate, Unfair and Bad for Business," centerjd.org/content/factsheet-us-chamber-commerce-liability-survey-inaccurate-unfair-and-bad-business.

236 *Around that time, small and seemingly grassroots*: Carl Deal and Joanne Doroshow, "The CALA Files: The Secret Campaign by Big Tobacco and Other Major Industries to Take Away Your Rights," Center for Justice and Democracy and Public Citizen, 1999, digital.library.ucla.edu/websites/2004_996_011/cala.pdf.

236 *But these, too, were funded by corporations*: Center for Justice and Democracy, "Fact

Sheet: 'Citizens Against Lawsuit Abuse' Groups," centerjd.org/content/fact-sheet -citizens-against-lawsuit-abuse-groups.

236 *Together these organizations have pushed*: Doroshow interview.

236 *The Michigan Product Liability Act*: Karen Bouffard, "Michigan Law Shielding Drug Makers Draws Scrutiny amid Opioid Crisis," *Detroit News*, June 14, 2018.

236 *The Ten-Year Statute of Repose Act is on the books*: John Futty, "Ohio Law May Shield Fire Ball Manufacturer in Fatal Fair Accident," *Columbus Dispatch*, September 12, 2017.

237 *The Product Liability Act*: American Legislative Exchange Council, "Product Liability Act," January 1, 1995, alec.org/model-policy/product-liability-act. See also: Sophie Hayssen, "What Is ALEC? Learn About the Organization Writing Your State Laws," *Teen Vogue*, September 25, 2020.

237 *One—the Comparative Fault Act—frees a corporation*: Brendan Fischer, "Justice Denied: 71 ALEC Bills in 2013 Make It Harder to Hold Corporations Accountable for Causing Injury or Death," Center for Media and Democracy, July 10, 2013.

237 *The bills are introduced regularly*: Molly Jackman, "ALEC's Influence over Lawmaking in State Legislatures," Brookings Institution, December 6, 2013.

237 *With these restrictions, tort law cases*: Doroshow interview.

237 *Between 1993 and 2015, these cases jumped from 18 percent*: Palazzolo, "We Won't See You in Court."

238 *Perhaps the classic case*: My understanding of the McDonald's coffee case comes from interviews with Joanne Doroshow and Ralph Nader's Museum of Tort Law (Allison Torres Burtka, "Liebeck v. McDonald's: The Hot Coffee Case"). Other coverage of the case makes my point, like a February 2021 article in *Reader's Digest*, "Remember the Hot Coffee Lawsuit? It Changed the Way McDonald's Heats Coffee Forever," which describes Stella Liebeck—a grotesquely injured seventy-nine-year-old—as someone who "sues her way to a $2.7 million jury-awarded **jackpot**." (Emphasis mine.)

239 *While this rhetoric persists*: Doroshow interview.

239 *But a study in the* New England Journal of Medicine *found*: Daniel A. Waxman et al., "The Effect of Malpractice Reform on Emergency Department Care," *New England Journal of Medicine* 371 (2014): 1518–25.

239 *An increase in medical accidents*: Larry Bodine, "Exposing the Lie of Tort Reform," *Huffington Post*, October 18, 2012.

240 *In the 1980s, accidental deaths*: Steve Cohen, "On Tort Reform, It's Time to Declare Victory and Withdraw," *Forbes*, March 2, 2015.

240 *Of the nine U.S. states that currently cap non-economic damages*: States that cap damages from Center for Justice and Democracy, "Fact Sheet: Caps on Compensatory Damages: A State Law Summary," August 22, 2020, centerjd.org/content /fact-sheet-caps-compensatory-damages-state-law-summary. Most accident-prone states from CDC WONDER Compressed Mortality File, wonder.cdc.gov/cmf-icd 10.html.

240 *Ken Jaray was a trial lawyer*: Interview with retired restorative justice practitioner Ken Jaray.

241 *Restorative justice laws*: Shannon Sliva and Carolyn Lambert, "Restorative Justice Legislation in the American States: A Statutory Analysis of Emerging Legal Doctrine," *Journal of Policy Practice* 14 (2015): 77–95.

242 *A young man named Dylan Salazar*: The story of the restorative justice process of Dylan Salazar and the Conard family comes from my interview with Ken Jaray, and interviews with Colorado state senator Pete Lee and Lynn Lee, a restorative justice practitioner, as well as a video made about the process by the Restorative Mediation Project of Colorado, available at youtu.be/URdwldPI9gg.

243 *Typically, that process goes like this*: Colorado state senator Pete Lee walked me through this.

243 *The victim . . . can ask questions*: Jaray interview.

243 *This is the typical process*: Amy Tam-Liao and Hsi-Pei Liao, "After Tragedy, a Different Justice," *Vision Zero Cities: International Journal of Traffic Safety Innovation*, July 9, 2018.

244 *Late in the Trump administration*: Susan Phillips, "'That Terrifies Me': Trump Rule Allows Natural Gas Transport by Rail in Dense Areas," National Public Radio, December 29, 2020.

244 *Vanessa Keegan, who lives along*: Ibid.

244 *Amy Cohen helped found Families for Safe Streets*: Erin Durkin, Maria Villase, and Joseph Stepansky, "Boy, 5, Hit by Car at Brooklyn Intersection Where 12-Year-Old Was Killed in 2013, Key to Vision Zero Initiative," *New York Daily News*, April 9, 2018.

245 *Judith Kottick is another founder of the group*: Jim O'Grady, "If NYC Fixed This Intersection, Why Do People Keep Dying There?," WNYC, November 6, 2014.

245 *It took two years, but in 2016*: David Meyer, "Families for Safe Streets and DOT Cut the Ribbon on Myrtle-Wyckoff Plaza," *Streetsblog NYC*, December 2, 2016.

245 *No one has been killed*: See the intersection at Vision Zero View: vzv.nyc.

245 *I call these acts of love and rage*: With nods to Mary Shelley, Erik Petersen / Mischief Brew, and the Love and Rage Revolutionary Anarchist Federation.

Conclusion: ~~Accident~~

251 *We will accidentally freeze to death*: Christine Hauser and Edgar Sandoval, "Death Toll from Texas Winter Storm Continues to Rise," *New York Times*, July 14, 2021; Shawn Mulcahy, "At Least 111 People Died in Texas during Winter Storm, Most from Hypothermia," *Texas Tribune*, March 25, 2021.

251 *We will accidentally overheat in our apartments*: The 12,000 heat-related fatality estimate does not include Alaska. See: Christopher Flavelle, "A New, Deadly Risk for Cities in Summer: Power Failures during Heat Waves," *New York Times*, May 3, 2021; Drew Shindell et al., "The Effects of Heat Exposure on Human Mortality Throughout the United States," *Geohealth* 4, no. 4 (2020): e2019GH000234.

251 *We will accidentally drown*: Anne Barnard, et al., "Flooding from Ida Kills Dozens of People in Four States," *New York Times*, September 2, 2021.

251 *And climate emergencies will drive us*: Miriam Jordan, "A Car Crash in the California Desert: How 13 Died Riding in One S.U.V.," *New York Times*, April 4, 2021; Jesus

Jiménez and Alyssa Lukpat, "10 Killed in Crash of Packed Van in South Texas," *New York Times*, August 4, 2021.

252 *We've already gotten a taste of what this will look like*: Will Evans, "How Amazon Hid Its Safety Crisis," *Reveal*, September 29, 2020.

253 *We can pass laws that require sprinklers*: Some of these ideas come from my interview with Sue Baker. See also: Stock, "Safety Lessons from the Morgue."

Index